Military Retirement Benefits in Divorce

A Lawyer's Guide to Valuation and Distribution

Marshal S. Willick

Section of Family Law
American Bar Association

Cover design by Catherine Zaccarine.

02 01 00 99 98   5 4 3 2 1

Willick, Marshal, 1958–
    Military retirement benefits in divorce/
    Marshal Willick.
        p. cm.
    ISBN 1-57073-572-7
    1. Military pensions—Law and legislation—United States.
    2. Survivors' benefits—Law and legislation—United States.
    3. Divorce settlements—United States. 4. Military spouses— Legal
    status, laws, etc.—United States. I. Title.
    KF7275.W55   1998
    343.73′ 0112—dc21   98-19147
                                                     CIP

Discounts are available for books ordered in bulk. Special consideration is given to state bars, CLE programs, and other bar-related organizations. Inquire at Book Publishing, ABA Publishing, American Bar Association, 750 North Lake Shore Drive, Chicago, Illinois 60611.

www.abanet.org/abapubs

To those whose stories of injustice moved me to start my research in this field; and to my daughter, Sarah Shayna, with love and appreciation for the many hours she was patient while I completed this work.

CONTENTS

Appendices

FOREWORD

This publication started as a project of the undersigned back in 1989 as I was going through the Chairs for the Family Law Section. The need for such a publication has been long established in the minds of those who work for military clients, either as civilian lawyers or in the numerous Judge Advocates General offices throughout the world, providing legal assistance to both parties in family law actions. By providing a concise publication such as this that lends itself to being updated, both parties in family law litigation will be assisted, no matter where they are stationed or where they now reside. Legal assistance work in the military, while I am sure is improved substantially since I did my active duty in the early 1960s, has long been the stepchild of military law. Yet the answers to questions that the legal assistance officer provides are of significant benefit to both the members and their dependents.

Military life certainly reflects the general changes in family patterns that have permeated the civilian community. Military life may reflect even more problems with family issues than civilian life, perhaps because of the frequent dislocations and the concentration of a population in a relatively young age group. Marriage problems, with post-divorce enforcement of judgments and the rising tide of illegitimacy and multistate problems related thereto call for some all-encompassing handbook on the entitlements of each party in relation to military employment. As if problems related to differing state laws were not enough, the frequent pronouncements of Congress and the Supreme Court point to the fact that, regardless of how state laws read, obscure federal laws and regulations further complicate the process. I know when I started this book I was overwhelmed. I have to congratulate Marshal Willick and the Section of Family Law Publications Development Board of the ABA for pursuing this subject and providing a major positive argumentation to the law library of every military and civilian lawyer who deals with this group of clients. No library for such a practitioner should be without it.

Michael E. Barber
Past Chair - Family Law Section
Captain, JAGC, USNR - Ret.

ACKNOWLEDGMENTS

The following people were of great assistance to me over the many years that it took to bring this book from conception to completion, and to them all I express my sincerest thanks:

Lawyers Susan Sakio, Eileen Luttrell, and Matthew Manning and Legal Assistants Sandy Jones, Jeri Coursey, Denise Gianninoto, Brad Peterson, Janet Baker, Monique Harrell, and Seth Willick of my office; Kenneth G. Raggio, Esq., and Dawn E. Fowler, Legal Assistant, Raggio & Raggio, Inc., Dallas, Texas; M.W. McCarthy, Esq., Phoenix, Arizona; Allen B. Robinson, Esq., Hayward, California; Edwin C. Schilling III, Esq., Aurora, Colorado; Michael O. Baskin, Esq., Associate General Counsel, Military Law Division, Office of General Counsel, Defense Finance and Accounting Service, Denver Center (with formal notation that there has been no official approval, endorsement, or sanction of this publication or its contents by the Department of Defense or any component of the federal government); David R. McClure, Esq., El Paso, Texas; Kathy Coombs, tax consultant, Olympia, Washington; Mr. Carlos Dequina, law student, Georgetown University Law Center class of 1999, for citation checking and commentary.

ABOUT THE AUTHOR

Marshal S. Willick is the principal of a family law firm in Las Vegas, and practices in the field of family law exclusively. In addition to his full-time practice, he writes and lectures extensively on domestic relations and legal technology issues. Mr. Willick is a Fellow of the American Academy of Matrimonial Lawyers, and a member of the Nevada, California, and American Bar Associations, and of the Family Law Sections of each of those Bar Associations. He chaired the Nevada State Bar Family Law Section from 1995 to 1997, and has the highest peer-review rating ("A/V") in the Martindale-Hubbell Legal Directory.

Mr. Willick has chaired the Congressional Relations, Military Pension/ Benefits, Bankruptcy, and other Committees of the ABA Family Law Section. He a member of the section's Legislative Lobbying Task Force, and has represented the entire ABA in congressional hearings on military pension matters. In addition to litigating a multitude of cases at all court levels in Nevada, he has assisted in hundreds of divorce and pension cases in the trial and appellate courts of about forty other states, and has participated in the drafting of various state and federal statutes in the areas of pensions, divorce, and property division.

Mr. Willick received his B.A. from the University of Nevada at Las Vegas in 1979, and his J.D. from Georgetown University Law Center in Washington, D.C., in 1982. Before entering private practice, Mr. Willick served on the Central Legal Staff of the Nevada Supreme Court for two years.

INTRODUCTION

As of September, 1997, there were 1,644,124 retired members of the uniformed services[1] receiving retired pay.[2] In fiscal year 1997, they received benefits totaling about $28.62 billion.[3] About 1.5 million people are currently on active duty in the uniformed services, some 122,216 of whom are eligible to retire at any time.[4] These numbers have changed dramatically in the post–cold war drawdown. As recently as 1990, there were more than 2 million active-duty members, over 139,000 of whom were eligible to retire.[5]

The somewhat smaller numbers of people who serve in the reserves are also accumulating retirement credit. Almost all these people have at least the possibility of receiving retired pay in the future.[6]

Many practitioners make the mistake of failing to pay sufficient attention to these actual or potential pension and retirement plans when evaluating the community or other property available for distribution upon divorce. Retirement benefits are increasingly the most valuable asset of marriages; this is particularly true in military families, when frequent

---

1. In addition to the army, air force, navy, Marine Corps, and Coast Guard, the uniformed services include the Commissioned Corps of the Public Health Service (USPHS) and the Commissioned Corps of the National Oceanic and Atmospheric Administration (NOAA). *See* 10 U.S.C. § 101(4), 37 U.S.C. § 101(4) (armed forces); 42 U.S.C. § 213a (USPHS); 33 U.S.C. § 857-4 (NOAA).
2. OFFICE OF THE ACTUARY, DEP'T OF DEFENSE, FY 1997 DOD STATISTICAL REPORT ON THE MILITARY RETIREMENT SYSTEM 10 (1998) [hereinafter FY 1997 REPORT].
3. *Id.* at 2–3.
4. *Id.* at 183, 214–17.
5. OFFICE OF THE ACTUARY, DEP'T OF DEFENSE, FY 1990 DOD STATISTICAL REPORT ON THE MILITARY RETIREMENT SYSTEM 182 (1991).
6. A "member" of any branch of the United States Armed Forces is any person who is or was appointed or who enlisted in, or who was conscripted into, a uniformed service. 10 U.S.C. § 1408(a)(5); 32 C.F.R § 63.3(m). The term "member" includes a former member.

moves make it difficult to accrue equity in a home (the "traditional" primary marital asset).

The amount of retired pay varies by the rank of the retiree. As of 1997, a retiring master sergeant (E-8) with twenty years' active duty received $1,319 per month for life; for a retiring colonel (O-6) with thirty years' service, retired pay was $4,714 per month.[7] Additionally, retirement amounts are periodically adjusted by Congress to provide cost of living adjustments to retirees.[8] Presuming 1997 retirements, the "present value" lump-sum equivalents of the retired pay that would be paid to the hypothetical sergeant and colonel, respectively, are $346,107 and $1,047,165.[9]

In military-related divorce cases, the retirement often exceeds the value of all other assets combined, *including* the equity in the marital residence. Neglecting to provide for that asset can constitute malpractice.[10] Only by being thoroughly versed in the identification and valuation of military retirement benefits can a divorce lawyer protect a military member, or a nonmilitary spouse, from potentially enormous losses. This situation is an essentially modern one; although Congress passed its first general retirement law as far back as 1861, it took nearly a hundred additional years for a systematic and comprehensive retirement system to be developed, intended for veterans of World War II.

This book provides practical guidance to lawyers engaged in cases involving military retirement benefits. It is not intended to be a compre-

---

7. FY 1996 REPORT, *supra* note 2, at 285.
8. This is explored in greater detail in Chapter Three.
9. FY 1996 REPORT, *supra* note 2, at 286. Theoretically, such a lump-sum equivalent is the amount that would have to be paid to an individual immediately in a single lump sum to give up a right to a stream of payments paid over time but totaling a greater amount. This is discussed further in Chapter Three.
10. Awards against lawyers in these cases can be significant. From *Aloy v. Mash,* 38 Cal. 3d 413, 696 P.2d 656, 212 Cal. Rptr. 162 (1985) to *Bross v. Denny,* 791 S.W.2d 416 (Mo. Ct. App. 1990) ($108,000 malpractice award against trial lawyer for not knowing that he could seek division of military retirement after change in the law), it has been made clear that any lawyer practicing divorce law is charged with knowing about the existence, value, and methodology of division of any retirement benefits that might exist. The potential liability appears to equal at least the value of the foregone benefit to the shortchanged spouse.

hensive treatise on divorce law or military law and regulations, but rather to provide rapid access to the kind of information that will assist in the negotiation and litigation of military divorce and pension cases.

Chapter One provides a capsule overview of the military retirement system and some of the areas that will be discussed throughout the book.

Chapter Two discusses the "prehistory" of this subject area, summarizing the events leading up to the cases and legislation of 1981–1983, sketching the evolution of the statute between 1983 and 1997, and discussing the most important cases that have interpreted the key statute.

Chapter Three provides examples of how to perform valuations of military retirement benefits, explaining alternatives for "ballparking" such cases at the original interview of a client, and how to obtain a more precise valuation. The components of active-duty pay and the value of reserve credits pay are discussed.

Chapters Four and Five deal with the substantive and procedural limitations and problems that the practitioner must be ready to cope with in each case. The critical consideration of jurisdiction in military cases is surveyed, along with the distinction between alimony and property division in a military case, the concept of "disposable" pay, the much-misunderstood "ten year" limitation, the holdings of the bankruptcy courts that have dealt with military retirement, and problems relating to early-retirement options. A series of "how-to" steps for turning a court order into a stream of payments is provided, along with a discussion of the various procedural problems that tend to arise in that process. Each of the primary mechanisms for obtaining payments from the military is reviewed.

There are additional benefits at issue in military cases besides the retirement pay itself. Chapter Six identifies those additional benefits and provides a basic checklist for ensuring that adequate attention has been paid to the issues raised by those benefits.

Chapter Seven turns to the nuts and bolts of litigation of military cases, from the preliminary acquisition of necessary information to dealing with factors that do not arise until after the case is over. Questions relating to whether botched cases can be repaired, and dealing with the tax ramifications of the decisions made in litigation, are also examined.

Chapter Eight and the Appendices provide a number of practice aids. These include a state-by-state review of the general treatment of military retirement benefits, looking to both statutory and decisional law; various forms and sample language for decrees, property settlements, and paperwork being directed to the military for enforcement, to assist practitioners in actual production of documents in this subject area; a glossary of terms, abbreviations, and acronyms; and some of the statutes, regulations, and other materials too lengthy or obscure to be put in the footnotes.

Throughout the book, various examples are provided when it is thought they might be helpful to understanding or illustrating application of the matters discussed.

Chapter One

OVERVIEW OF THE MILITARY RETIREMENT SYSTEM

A retired member enjoys several types of benefits. A "spouse or former spouse" (the husband or wife, or former husband or former wife, of a member who, on or before the date of a court order, was married to that member;[1] hereafter "former spouse") of such a member may, in certain circumstances, share in certain of those benefits.

First, a member retired from one of the uniformed services may receive one of three types of retirements, according to the member's status at the time of retirement: reserve, disability, or nondisability retired pay, in which the former spouse may share.[2] Second, an eligible member may provide an annuity for a dependent child or children and/or a surviving spouse or after the member's death through the Survivor's Benefit Plan (SBP).[3] Third, the dependents of a member may receive medical and health care[4] as well as military exchange and commissary shopping privileges.[5]

"Retired pay" (sometimes also known as "retainer pay") is the gross entitlement owed to a member based upon retirement law, pay grade, years of service for basic pay, years of service for percentage multiplier (if applicable), and date of retirement, or transfer to the Fleet Reserve or Fleet Marine Corps Reserve.[6] This nondisability retired pay, sometimes referred to as "longevity" retirement, is the form of military retirement

---

1. 10 U.S.C. § 1408(a)(6); 32 C.F.R. § 63.3(k).
2. 10 U.S.C. § 1407; army: 10 U.S.C. § 3911 *et seq.;* navy and marines: 10 U.S.C. § 6321 *et seq.;* air force: 10 U.S.C. § 8911 *et seq.;* Coast Guard and Commissioned Corps of the Public Health Service: 42 U.S.C. § 212 *et seq.;* Commissioned Corps of the National Oceanic and Atmospheric Administration: 33 U.S.C. §§ 857a, 857-4.
3. 10 U.S.C. § 1447 *et seq.*
4. *Id.* § 1072 *et seq.*
5. INSTRUCTION NO. 1000.13 (June 6, 1984); U.S. DEP'T OF DEFENSE DIRECTIVE 1330.17, ARMED SERVICE COMMISSARY STORE REGULATIONS, (May 4, 1978).
6. 32 C.F.R. § 63.3(o).

1

benefits most commonly involved in divorces. Divorce courts have no power to award Social Security benefits in military-related cases, just as they cannot do so in nonmilitary cases.[7]

The military retirement system can be viewed as a funded noncontributory defined benefit plan. The secretaries of the various services approve immediately payable nondisability retired pay at any age of members with credit of at least twenty years of active-duty service. Reserve retirees, however, must be sixty years old with twenty creditable years of service before being eligible to receive retired pay.

There are three different nondisability benefit formulas within the military retirement system. The first two groups are composed of members who entered service before August 1, 1986.

First, members who entered service before September 8, 1980, have retired pay equal to terminal basic pay times a multiplier. The multiplier is equal to 2.5 percent times years of service, but is limited to 75 percent. Thus, retired pay equals 50 percent of terminal basic pay after twenty years of service.

Second, military personnel who first became members on or after September 8, 1980, must use the highest three years of basic pay rather than terminal basic pay. This has the effect of lowering retired pay for members whose pay increased at any time during their last three years of service.

For members of these first two groups, the multipliers are as follows:

YEARS OF SERVICE	PERCENT OF ACTIVE-DUTY PAY
20	50 %
21	52.5%
22	55 %
23	57.5%
24	60 %
25	62.5%
26	65 %
27	67.5%
28	70 %
29	72.5%
30 or more	75 %

7. Military members have accrued Social Security benefits for all service since 1957. *See* Pub. L. No. 84-881, 70 Stat. 870 (1956) (codified at 42 U.S.C. § 410 (l)–(m)).

The third group is made up of members who entered service on or after August 1, 1986, and who retire with fewer than thirty years of service. Such members suffer a temporary penalty until age sixty-two. The penalty reduces the multiplier by one percentage point for each full year less than thirty years of service. At age sixty-two the penalty is removed and the retired-pay multiplier is restored to 2.5 percent per year, yielding the same percentage payable under the earlier system.[8] After that "restoral," however, the penalty (consumer price index adjustment minus 1 percent) returns with each cost of living adjustment (COLA) for life.

For members of this third group (who entered active service on or after August 1, 1986), the multipliers are as follows:

YEARS OF SERVICE	FORMULA	PERCENT OF ACTIVE-DUTY PAY
20	$(2.5 \times 20) - 10$	40 %
21	$(2.5 \times 21) - 9$	43.5%
22	$(2.5 \times 22) - 8$	47 %
23	$(2.5 \times 23) - 7$	50.5%
24	$(2.5 \times 24) - 6$	54 %
25	$(2.5 \times 25) - 5$	57.5%
26	$(2.5 \times 26) - 4$	61 %
27	$(2.5 \times 27) - 3$	64.5%
28	$(2.5 \times 28) - 2$	68 %
29	$(2.5 \times 29) - 1$	71.5%
30	$(2.5 \times 30) - 0$	75 %

There are also two forms of disability benefits available to members.

Briefly,[9] a member who sustains a permanent physical or mental disability in the line of duty, or who has served at least eight years and is unfit to perform his or her duties by reason of a permanent physical or mental disability, may be retired for disability. This is a "Chapter 61" disability retirement, and may be from 30 to 100 percent.

---

8. Pub. L. No. 99-348, 100 Stat. 682 (1986). *See* OFFICE OF THE ACTUARY, DEP'T OF DEFENSE, FY 1996 DOD STATISTICAL REPORT ON THE MILITARY RETIREMENT SYSTEM 1 (1997).

9. The rules governing these benefits are much more intricate than alluded to here. These benefits, however, are not directly in issue in divorce litigation.

The amount of disability retirement is the greater of two calculated sums—the accrued nondisability retired pay, or base pay multiplied by the rated percent of disability. "Base pay" is calculated in accordance with the above formulas, depending on date of entry into service. Members retiring for disability after at least twenty years of service have an alternate formula available, which increases their total retired pay in some instances.[10] The amount of retired pay received because of the disability may be paid to the member tax free, despite the congressional elimination of the tax exemption for disability retired pay in 1976.[11]

The second type of disability retired pay is through the Veteran's Administration (VA) for service-connected disabilities, which are rated from 10 to 100 percent. The benefits are *not* simply a percentage of retired pay. Rather, both disability percentages and certain specific injuries have dollar sum values, which the member can claim.[12] The benefits change over time, generally annually, in rough accord with the rate of inflation. These are "Chapter 38" benefits, and are tax free to the member. Receipt of the

---

10. The member can multiply base pay by the percentage of disability, or subtract that sum from the amount that would otherwise be granted as regular retired pay, take the disability, and also take the difference between the sums. The latter calculation will usually provide extra money to the member if service was for more than twenty years (pre-1986 enlistment) or more than twenty-three years (post-1986 enlistment).

11. Again, this is a simplification due to limited relevance. The benefits are totally tax free only for those who entered active service before September 25, 1975, those who retired for disability before January 1, 1977, or those who suffer *combat-related* disabilities.

12. *See* 32 C.F.R. § 314. Effective December 1, 1996, monthly VA disability compensation was as follows:

10%	$ 94	60%	$ 703
20%	$179	70%	$ 887
30%	$264	80%	$1,028
40%	$391	90%	$1,157
50%	$558	100%	$1,924

Additionally, certain specific injuries are given special monthly rates rather than use of the percentage tables; for example, loss of use of both feet, or a hand and a foot allows payment of $2,393 per month. If there is a 30 percent or greater disability, certain additional monthly payments are made for dependents.

benefits, however, requires a waiver by the member of an amount of retired pay equal to the sum of the disability benefits received.

Basically, only a portion of *non*disability benefits can be paid to a former spouse;[13] the U.S. Supreme Court has indicated that only *disposable* retired pay is within the substantive jurisdiction of the state courts.[14] No portion of disability benefit payments are directly payable to a former spouse for payment of alimony, child support, or as a property division.[15] There are many exceptions and work-arounds to these limitations, which are discussed throughout this book.

---

13. But see Chapter Two's discussion of the 1986 amendments to the USFSPA.
14. *See* Mansell v. Mansell, 490 U.S. 581 (1989), *remanded,* 216 Cal. App. 3d 937, 265 Cal. Rptr. 227 (Ct. App. 1989); 10 U.S.C. § 1408(a)(4).
15. 10 U.S.C. §§ 1408(a)(4)(B)–(C); 32 C.F.R. §§ 63.6(e)(2), (2)(vi).

Chapter Two

BRIEF HISTORY OF THE DEVELOPMENT OF THIS FIELD OF LAW

There is a brief but dynamic history of legislation and litigation before 1983 that led to the current federal and state laws. That history provides some clues to the probable future development of the field. Briefly, the history of law in this area breaks down to the law before 1981, the law from the seminal Supreme Court decision in *McCarty* until passage of the congressional enactment responding to that case, and developments after passage of that legislation. This section will provide a brief historical review of the factors that led to the development of law in this field.

Today, statutes and case law throughout the country generally recognize that pension benefits are marital property. The rationales for that recognition vary, but usually include the fact of accrual during marriage, the necessary deferral during marriage of present enjoyment of income, or the possibility of alternative employment that would have paid more in current wages. The current consensus is in marked contrast to the state of affairs before 1981.

A. PRE-*McCARTY*: THE DARK AGES OF MILITARY RETIREMENT LAW

Before June, 1981, the states differed considerably in their treatment of military retirement benefits upon divorce. Many state courts in the 1960s and 1970s refused to take any notice of such benefits at all, characterizing them either as sole property of the individual in which they were titled (if being received)[1] or as "mere expectancies" if not yet in collection.[2] Though some states began recognizing pensions as property as early as the 1960s,[3] many states continued to treat the income stream

---

1. Ellis v. Ellis, 191 Colo. 317, 552 P.2d 506 (1976).
2. Light v. Light, 586 S.W.2d 292 (Ky. Ct. App. 1980).
3. *See, e.g.,* Yeazell v. Copins, 98 Ariz. 109, 402 P.2d 541 (1965).

to the retiree as a factor to be considered in fixing alimony, but not as any form of property interest to be divided.[4]

Because most divorce cases end at the trial court level, the few appellate decisions issued before 1981 reveal only a shadow of what was actually happening at trial in each state. It seems reasonably clear, however, that as a general proposition, spouses across the nation were not usually awarded an interest in military retirement benefits, as such, upon divorce. In those cases in which there *was* such an award, no federal or military procedural mechanism existed for enforcement of the interest awarded, leaving spouses to rely upon whatever mechanisms were available in their state courts (contempt, for example) for enforcement of judgments generally.

For those states in which there was no law on point, the omission of military retirement benefits from divorce settlements and judgments was typically the result of simple ignorance on the parts of both the parties and their lawyers; though at least the parties to such cases knew there was a retirement to be had at the end of twenty or more years of service, it often did not occur to those involved to think of the retirement as an "asset" at issue in the divorce.

Of course, the omission of the asset was not always so innocent. Service members[5] who knew that state courts would have divided the benefits if raised sometimes simply kept quiet; if the spouse (whether represented or not) failed to present the issue and persuade the court to divide it, the member received all interest in the benefits by default. In some states, there was no mechanism for correcting such "fraud by omission."[6]

There were notable exceptions to the seeming indifference of state courts to disposition of retirement benefits. The landmark California case recognizing the importance of military retirement benefits as a marital asset was *In re Marriage of Fithian*[7] in 1974. After that time, the California courts were fairly uniform in holding all pensions, including military

---

4. *See, e.g.,* Kabaci v. Kabaci, 373 So. 2d 1144 (Ala. Civ. App. 1979).
5. The term encompasses both active-duty personnel and former members of the armed forces. *See* 10 U.S.C. § 1408(a)(5).
6. *See* Marshal Willick, *Res Judicata in Nevada Divorce Law: An Invitation to Fraud,* 4 NEV. FAM. L. REP., Spr. 1989, at 1.
7. 10 Cal. 3d 592, 517 P.2d 449, 111 Cal. Rptr. 369 (1974).

retirement benefits, to be divisible community property.[8] Other community property states noted in later decisions the practice of dividing such benefits since the 1960s.[9]

The 1970s saw an ongoing evolution in the law of property division throughout the country, with an ever-growing number of jurisdictions abandoning "title" in favor of "equitable distribution" as the foundation of their statutory schemes.[10] As pension rights became more important aspects of employment compensation generally, they became increasingly important in divorces. On the civilian side, these trends were recognized by the congressional enactment of the Employee Retirement Income Security Act of 1974,[11] which generally prohibited alienation of retirement benefits, and (eventually) the Retirement Equity Act,[12] which formalized an exception for domestic relations orders.

The evolving consciousness in the national legal community of the importance of retirement benefits resulted in a larger number of military retirements being considered—directly or indirectly—in property settlements and divorce decrees. By 1979, the American Bar Association (ABA) had formally enacted a policy resolution recommending the enactment of legislation requiring the secretaries of the armed forces to recognize state court decrees of divorce dividing retired or retainer pay.[13]

---

8. These decisions, at first, addressed benefits that were vested at the time of divorce. Eventually, this was extended to nonvested and unmatured retirement benefits as well. *See In re* Marriage of Brown, 15 Cal. 3d 838, 544 P.2d 561, 126 Cal. Rptr. 633 (1976); *In re* Marriage of Luciano, 104 Cal. App. 3d 956, 164 Cal. Rptr. 93 (Ct. App. 1980). This subject is explored at greater length in Chapter Seven.

9. *See, e.g.,* Bankston v. Taft, 612 S.W.2d 216 (Tex. Civ. App. 1980).

10. That history is beyond the scope of this work. Those interested in reviewing it may wish to start with Matthew Bender's *Valuation and Distribution of Marital Property* (J. Borvick ed., 1984 & Supp. 1995); for a quick survey, the practitioner is directed to the annual *Family Law in the Fifty States: An Overview,* published in the Winter edition of the Family Law Quarterly (D. Freed & T. Walker eds., ABA Pub'n).

11. Commonly known as ERISA, enacted as Pub. L. No. 98-397 (1974).

12. Commonly known as the REA, and enacted as Pub. L. No. 98-397 (1984).

13. *See* 1993–1994 ABA POLICY AND PROCEDURES HANDBOOK at 202 (ABA 1993), noting 1979 and 1982 resolutions approved by the House of Delegates of the ABA. The 1982 resolution, in the wake of *McCarty,* urged

Still, there was no enforcement mechanism, and by 1980 the treatment of military retirement benefits varied widely from state to state. In retrospect, it might be said that there was some inevitability to the confrontation that erupted in 1981.

B. THE *McCARTY* DECISION AND ITS EFFECT ON EXISTING STATE LAW

On June 26, 1981, the U.S. Supreme Court issued its opinion in *McCarty v. McCarty*.[14] The case originated as a simple California divorce. The parties had married in 1957, while the husband (John) was in medical school in Oregon. During his fourth year, he commenced active duty in the U.S. Army; after graduation, he served tours of duty in several different states, ending up in California. In 1976, a month after separating from his wife (Patricia), John sued for divorce in California Superior Court.

John had requested that his military retirement benefits be "confirmed" to be his separate property upon divorce. In 1977, the California trial court found that the military retirement benefits were quasi-community property.[15] The court therefore ordered the normal "time rule"[16] division of the retirement benefits.

Congress to enact legislation making all deferred compensation derived from federal employment subject to state property and divorce laws, except where specifically exempted by explicit federal legislation. *See also* Proposed Amendments to the Uniformed Services Former Spouses Protection Act, 1990: Hearings on H.R. 3776, H.R. 2277, H.R. 2300, and H.R. 572 Before the Subcomm. on Military Personnel and Compensation of the House Comm. on Armed Services, 101st Cong., 2nd Sess. (1990) (Statement of Marshal S. Willick, Chairman of Subcommittee on Federal and Military Pension Legislation, Committee on Federal Legislation and Procedures, Section of Family Law, on behalf of the American Bar Association, April 4, 1990, at 5).

14. 453 U.S. 210 (1981).
15. Essentially, quasi-community property is a label used by some community property states to describe property acquired outside the state that *would have been* community property if acquired within the state; such states divide such property as if it were regular community property.
16. A spousal share of a retirement benefit is nearly universally calculated as

John appealed, claiming that the military retirement system preempted any state community property laws. During the pendency of the appellate process, John retired in 1978. The California intermediate appellate court affirmed the trial court ruling, and the California Supreme Court denied John's petition for hearing. The U.S. Supreme Court accepted jurisdiction on appeal.

The Supreme Court started with the recitation of its claimed deference to "the laws of the States and not to the laws of the United States" in domestic relations matters.[17] The Court determined that its inquiry was (1) whether a right asserted under state law conflicts with the express terms of federal law, and (2) whether the consequences of the assertion of that right sufficiently injure the objectives of the federal program to require nonrecognition.

The Court noted John's argument that military retired pay was not a divisible community property asset, but rather future reduced compensation for reduced current services, but the Court expressly chose not to decide that question.[18] Instead, the Court found that state community property laws conflicted with the federal military retirement scheme regardless of the character of that retired pay, and thus found an implied federal preemption of state laws dividing community property. Three justices (Rehnquist, Brennan, and Stewart) dissented.

The majority held that the apparent congressional intent was to make military retirement benefits a "personal entitlement" that was solely the property of the individual service member, so that those benefits could not be considered as community property in a California divorce.[19] The arguments noted for implied preemption were the threats posed by state community property laws to the ability of Congress to raise armies, to provide for retirees, and to manage the personnel of the military.

---

one-half multiplied by a fraction, the numerator of which is the time of marriage during service, and the denominator of which is the total service time.

17. *McCarty,* 453 U.S. at 220.
18. 453 U.S. at 221–22.
19. The Court noted in passing that although Congress provided for division of civil service and foreign service retirement plans in divorce, the last three bills that would have allowed recognition of state-court division, or automatically entitled spouses to a pro rata share, of military retired pay died in committee. *See* 453 U.S. at 231.

Though *McCarty* squarely addressed only community property, the decision put into great doubt any state jurisdiction over military retirement benefits. The Court invited Congress to change the statutory scheme if division of retired pay was desired, stating, "We recognize that the plight of an ex-spouse of a retired service member is often a serious one" and noting that

> Congress may well decide, as it has in the Civil Service and Foreign Service contexts, that more protection should be afforded a former spouse of a retired service member. This decision, however, is for Congress alone. We very recently have re-emphasized that in no area has the Court accorded Congress greater deference than in the conduct and control of military affairs.[20]

The decision received significant press coverage, resulting in attention by existing special-interest groups and the formation of new groups on both sides[21] of the benefits tug-of-war between members and their former spouses.[22]

C. THE USFSPA: CONGRESS TAKES A STAND

On September 8, 1982, Congress reacted by enacting the Uniformed Services Former Spouses Protection Act (USFSPA).[23] The USFSPA rep-

---

20. 453 U.S. at 235–36.
21. The most consistently visible of the former spouse organizations is called "EX-POSE," for Ex-Partners of Servicemen/women for Equality, P.O. Box 11191, Alexandria, VA 22312. It actually was formed in March, 1980, but underwent a huge increase in membership and activity after *McCarty.* Essentially reactive organizations subsequently formed during the debate over the Uniformed Services Former Spouses Protection Act and especially after its passage. A listing of such organizations may be found in Appendix H.
22. As noted above, the term "former spouse" is used throughout this book to refer to the spouse or former spouse for the sake of simplicity, it being understood that unless otherwise stated, the reference applies as much to a present spouse after a legal separation as to a former spouse after a divorce.
23. Also commonly known as the Federal Uniformed Services Former Spouses Protection Act, or FUSFSPA, or as the Former Spouses Act, or in some

resented the congressional decision to overrule *McCarty* (at least in part[24]) and make treatment of retired pay largely dependent on the divorce laws of the jurisdictions granting decrees.

1. Overview of the USFSPA

The primary purpose of the USFSPA was to define state court jurisdiction to consider and use military retired pay in fixing the property and support rights of the parties to a divorce, dissolution, annulment, or legal separation.[25]

The USFSPA is both jurisdictional and procedural; it both permits the state courts to distribute military retirement to former spouses, and provides a method for enforcement of these orders through the military pay

---

references simply as the act. 10 U.S.C. § 1408; Pub. L. No. 97-252, 96 Stat. 730 (1982), amended by Pub. L. No. 98-94, 97 Stat. 653 (1983), Pub. L. No. 98-525, 98 Stat. 2545 (1984), Pub. L. No. 98-525, 99 Stat. 677 (1985), Pub. L. No. 99-661, 100 Stat. 3885 (1986), Pub. L. No. 101-510, § 555, 104 Stat. 1485, 1569 (1990), Pub. L. No. 102-190, § 1061(a)(7), 105 Stat. 1472 (1991), Pub. L. No. 102-484, § 653(a), 106 Stat. 2426 (1992), Pub. L. No. 103-160, §§ 555(a), (b), § 1182(a)(2), 107 Stat. 1666, 1771 (1993), Pub. L. No. 104-106, § 1501(c)(16), 110 Stat. 499 (1996), Pub. L. No. 104-193, §§ 362(c), 363(c)(1)–(3), 110 Stat. 2246, 2249 (1996), Pub. L. No. 104-201, § 636, 110 Stat. 2579 (1996).

24. In *Mansell v. Mansell,* 490 U.S. 581 (1989), the Court found that the act did not constitute a total repudiation of the preemption found by the Court to exist in *McCarty;* Congress's failure to alter the language of the act to alter this finding, when it next amended the act in 1990, implied congressional consent that at least partial preemption was intended to remain after passage of the act.

25. Act of Sept. 8, 1982, Pub. L. No. 97-252, 1982 U.S.C.C.A.N. (96 Stat.) 718 (legislative history, Pub. L. No. 97-252). The report noted that as of June 26, 1981, case decisions in "virtually all" community property states, and in many of those employing equitable distribution principles, permitted military retired pay to be considered marital property subject to division. In only the two "title" states, Mississippi and West Virginia, were pensions considered upon divorce the exclusive property of the party in whose name the asset was titled. Since that time, both of those states have adopted equitable distribution schemes.

centers.[26] The USFSPA itself does not give former spouses an automatic entitlement to any portion of members' pay. Only state laws can provide that military retirement pay can be divided in a divorce, or provide for alimony or child support.[27] Rights granted by state law are limited by federal law, even if the state law does not so provide, and even if the courts of the states do not see any such limitations.[28]

A former spouse's right to a portion of retired pay as property terminates upon the death of the member or the former spouse, unless the court order provides for an earlier termination.[29] Any right to receive payments under the USFSPA is nontransferable; the former spouse may not sell, assign, or transfer his or her rights, or dispose of them by inheritance.[30] To obtain benefits extending beyond a member's death, the former spouse must obtain designation as the beneficiary of the Survivor's Benefit Plan, which has its own technical requirements.

Nothing in the USFSPA *required* the states to consider military retirement benefits as divisible property in divorce; it merely allowed each state to develop its own laws within certain limits. Since its passage, the USFSPA has been amended several times, as Congress has altered the contours of the substantive state court jurisdiction to treat retired pay as property divisible upon divorce, and expanded and contracted the range of other benefits available to former spouses.[31]

2. The Original Enactment

There were six sections to the original USFSPA enactment, denominated Sections 1001 through 1006. Section 1001 gave the USFSPA its title.

---

26. References to "the pay centers" are generally directed to procedures before the consolidation in Cleveland, but have been left in the text to illustrate policy variations and interpretations within the military, and because many of the references are to matters continuing to be problematic in the consolidated Defense Finance and Accounting Service.
27. S. REP. NO. 97-502, at 13 (1982).
28. *See* Mansell v. Mansell, 490 U.S. 581 (1989) (criticizing conclusions reached in Casas v. Thompson, 42 Cal. 3d 131, 720 P.2d 921, 228 Cal. Rptr. 33 (1986), *cert. denied,* 479 U.S. 1012 (1987)).
29. 10 U.S.C. § 1408(d)(4).
30. *Id.* § 1408(c)(2).
31. See Section E of this chapter.

Section 1002 gave rise to new Section 1408 to Title 10 of the United States Code. Subsection (a) of the new Section 1408 defined the terms "court," "court order," "final decree," "disposable retired or retainer pay," "member," and "spouse." Subsection (b) set out the requirements for proper service of an order. Subsection (c) was the key to the statute, and also (as later cases would show) provided wording that would be the source of litigation for a decade. Sub-subsection (1) of Subsection (c) read as follows:

> Subject to the limitations of this section, a court may treat disposable retired or retainer pay payable to a member for pay periods beginning after June 25, 1981, either as property solely of the member or as property of the member and his spouse in accordance with the law of the jurisdiction of such court.

The remainder of Subsection (c) set out the nonassignability of any award to a spouse, prohibited courts from requiring members to retire, and imposed special jurisdictional rules for cases under the USFSPA. Subsection (d) set out the time limits within which the services had to comply with state court orders and set out other administrative rules, provided that direct payments to spouses would not be made unless the marriage overlapped active duty by ten years or more, and allowed for garnishments. Subsection (e) contained payment limitations and rules concerning multiple and conflicting court orders. Subsection (f) provided for nonliability of federal officers and employees for compliance or noncompliance with any order.

Section 1003 of the original enactment amended existing terms of Section 1447 of Title 10 of the United States Code, by adding a definition for "former spouse" and permitting members to designate their former spouses as beneficiaries of the Survivor's Benefit Plan.

Sections 1004 and 1005 of the original enactment amended existing terms of Section 1072 of Title 10 of the United States Code, by adding unremarried former spouses to the individuals eligible for health benefits and commissary and exchange privileges, as long as they had been married to members during twenty years of active-duty service.

Section 1006 provided effective dates for the entire enactment. The "amendments made by this title" were made effective February 1, 1983. The section of Section 1408 requiring compliance with court orders was made to apply after that effective date, "but without regard to the date of any court order." Court orders made before June 26, 1981, however, were to be honored only in accordance with the terms of the order on that date "without regard to any subsequent modifications." Section 1003 was made effective for all Survivor's Benefit Plan participants whether before, on, or after the effective date of the act. Sections 1004 and 1005 were made effective for court orders made on or after February 1, 1983.

Virtually every section of the original enactment has been the subject of litigation, or has been amended, in the ensuing years. The bulk of this book deals with the interpretations and amendments to those provisions, which are not further addressed in this section.

D. THE *"McCARTY* GAP" WINDOW PERIOD: CHAOS IN WONDERLAND

Passage of the USFSPA gave rise to a new problem of how to treat fairly those persons who had been divorced during the twenty-month "gap" between the *McCarty* decision and the congressional enactment.

The USFSPA was expressly made retroactive to the start of the gap period, but the language used left some room for interpretation.[32] Some states, such as Washington, took the federal law as sufficient to allow their courts to address gap cases under preexisting common law and statutory procedures.[33] In those states, motions could be brought to divide the retirement benefits if they had been omitted, or to divide the benefits if they

---

32. The effective-date section of the original enactment, Section 1006, read in part as follows:

   (a) The amendments made by this title shall take effect on the first day of the first month which begins more than one hundred and twenty days after the date of the enactment of this title.

   (b) Subsection (d) of section 1408 of title 10, United States Code, as added by section 1002(a), shall apply only with respect to payments of retired or retainer pay for periods beginning on or after the effective date of this title, but without regard to the date of any court order. However, in the case of a court order that became final before June 26, 1981, payments under such subsection may only be made in accordance with such order as in effect on such date and without regard to any subsequent modifications.

33. *See, e.g., In re* Marriage of Parks, 48 Wash. App. 166, 737 P.2d 1316 (Ct. App. 1987).

had been awarded solely to the member while *McCarty* was the law of the land.

Courts in other states, such as California and Idaho, ruled that no common-law remedy existed for such persons.[34] These rulings led to passage of "window" statutes specifically permitting those divorced during the gap a limited time to relitigate the division or nondivision of the retirement benefits.[35]

Nevada passed the first such statute, which expired after only six months, in 1983. Some states took much longer to pass such legislation; the most recent window period was in Illinois, which closed in January, 1989.[36]

Some states, such as Texas, which found the USFSPA inadequate by itself to allow the reopening of gap cases, still have not passed legislation permitting those divorced during the gap to bring their decrees into conformity with those divorced before *McCarty* or after the USFSPA. Divorces during the gap that gave 100 percent of the retirement benefits to the member because of *McCarty* remain unalterable in such states for lack of a mechanism through which to litigate them.[37]

One interesting aspect of the states' experiences with gap statutes is the general disregard in such cases of the jurisdictional points that have so occupied courts in other military retirement benefits cases.[38] Most courts deciding cases under state gap statutes have apparently *presumed* continuing jurisdiction for purposes of motions brought in the original divorce action pursuant to the USFSPA.[39]

---

34. *See, e.g., In re* Marriage of Barnes, 43 Cal. 3d 1371, 743 P.2d 915, ____ Cal. Rptr. 855 (1987).

35. *See* 1983 Nev. Stats. ch. 301, § 1, at 740 (expired January 1, 1984); CAL. CIV. CODE § 5124 (expired January 1, 1986); IDAHO CODE § 32-713A (expired July 1, 1988).

36. ILL. REV. STAT. ch. 40, ¶ 403 (1987) (expired January 1, 1989).

37. *See, e.g.,* Allison v. Allison, 700 S.W.2d 915 (Tex. 1985); Himes v. Himes 12 Va. App. 966, 407 S.E.2d 694 (Ct. App. 1991).

38. See Section B, Chapter Four.

39. Some courts are more explicit. *See In re* Marriage of McDonough, 183 Cal. App. 3d 52, 227 Cal. Rptr. 872 (Ct. App. 1986) (jurisdiction over member spouse retroactively granted to California courts by federal and state law regardless of member's relocation).

As time passes, and the number of living persons with *McCarty*-gap divorces decreases, it becomes less and less likely that additional states will pass window statutes.

E. CONGRESSIONAL TINKERING: AMENDMENTS TO THE USFSPA 1983–1997

Passage of the USFSPA did not end the debate that *McCarty* had begun; rather, it served to polarize those concerned into two groups— those concerned with extending and strengthening the perceived federal blessing of state-court division of military retired pay, and those concerned with undercutting or limiting the application of the USFSPA. Originally, these were essentially organizations of former military spouses, on the one hand, and retired military members, on the other. Active-duty service members, most of whom would not be affected by the statute until late in their careers or following retirement, were slower to become active. Starting in the late 1980s, a new class of concerned persons emerged, consisting of the current spouses of those whose earlier divorces had been affected by the USFSPA.

Naturally, the primary focus of these groups and individuals was on Congress, specifically the armed forces committees, and more specifically the personnel subcommittees to which this subject was delegated. It is probably fair commentary to generalize that no group has met with uniform success to date, and each of the lobbying organizations maintains an agenda unlikely to be fully accomplished.

The primary changes in the USFSPA are noted below. For the exact language of the statute as it exists at this time, please refer to Appendix B.

1. 1983: Survivor's Benefit Plan Amendments

Almost exactly one year after the original USFSPA was enacted, Congress altered certain provisions dealing with the Survivor's Benefit Plan.[40] These changes generally expanded the class of persons entitled to share in the benefits; the changes are detailed in Section B of Chapter Six.

---

40. *See* Pub. L. No. 98-94, 97 Stat. 653 (1983).

18

2. *1984: A General Cleanup of Nettlesome Language*

The 1984 amendments, enacted a little more than one year later, further modified the survivors' benefits provisions.[41] Additionally, the USFSPA was modified to *remove* the restriction previously in place that had required alimony orders, like property division orders, to recite specifically that payments are to be made in "an amount, expressed in dollars or as a percentage of disposable retired pay, from the disposable retired pay of a member to the spouse or former spouse of that member."[42]

The wording change further pointed out the dual utility of the USFSPA as enabling and enforcement legislation, because different procedural requirements were put into place for different types of orders calling for payments by members to their former spouses. Other provisions of the 1984 amendments made certain other minor wording changes and reinforced the substantive distinction discussed above. Additionally, medical benefits were extended to former spouses whose marriages overlapped the members' military service by at least fifteen but fewer than twenty years, and provision was made for those divorced before 1983.[43]

3. *1985: More Survivor's Benefit Plan Changes*

In 1985, Congress amended the USFSPA so that voluntary elections of survivor's benefits for former spouses, when such elections were filed with the court, could be enforced.[44] Certain technical changes that lowered the premiums due for coverage of former spouses were put into place.[45] An "open period" for election of survivor's benefits for a child as beneficiary in addition to a former spouse was put into place for those who had previously chosen coverage for a former spouse.[46] Spousal consent

---

41. *See* Pub. L. No. 98-525, 98 Stat. 2545 (1984). Again, these changes are detailed in Section B, Chapter Six.
42. *See* 10 U.S.C. § 1408(a)(2)(C); Pub. L. No. 98-525, § 643(a), 98 Stat. 2545 (1984).
43. These changes are addressed in detail in Section A, Chapter Six.
44. Pub. L. No. 99-145, § 722, 99 Stat. 677 (1985). This change is set forth in greater detail in Section B, Chapter Six.
45. *Id.* § 723.
46. Pub. L. No. 99-145, § 716(b), 99 Stat. 674 (1985).

was made a requirement for a member to waive the otherwise automatic choice of electing Survivor's Benefit Plan benefits at the maximum level, for retirements after March 1, 1986.[47]

4. 1986: Courts Empowered to Award the Survivor's Benefit Plan, and Other Changes

In 1986, Congress made several changes with lasting impact. For the first time, divorce courts were enabled to *order* that a member elect a former spouse as the Survivor's Benefit Plan beneficiary.[48] Certain minor changes were made relating to survivor benefits for dependent children, and the minimum age at which a surviving spouse could remarry without losing survivor benefits was lowered from sixty to fifty-five.[49] The "open period" for election of survivor benefits for a former spouse or child was extended from 1986 to 1987. After these amendments, for the first time, the existence of a partial disability award to the member did not mean a total loss of benefits to the former spouse; instead, the nondisability portion was considered divisible.[50]

5. 1990: Redefinition of Disposable Pay, and Phaseout of Older Partition Cases

In 1990, a subcommittee of the House Armed Services Committee had before it a proposal[51] that would have led to a presumptive division of military retired pay, required payments to the former spouse to begin upon the member's eligibility for retirement, eliminated the concept of "disposable" pay as a limitation on division of retired pay, and eliminated the "ten-year rule."[52] A trio of other bills[53] also pending in the committee

---

47. Pub. L. No. 99-145, § 721(a)(3)(A)(ii), 99 Stat. 676 (1985).
48. Pub. L. No. 99-661, § 641, 100 Stat. 3885 (1986). This change is addressed in Section B, Chapter Six.
49. *Id.* §§ 642, 643.
50. See Subsection 1, Section D, Chapter Four.
51. H.R. 3776, 101 Cong. (1989) (submitted by Rep. Patricia Schroeder of Colorado on November 20, 1989).
52. Discussed in Section D, Chapter Four.
53. H.R. 572, 101 Cong. (1989) (dated January 20, 1989); H.R. 2277, 101 Cong. (1989) (dated May 9, 1989); H.R. 2300, 101 Cong. (1989) (dated May 10, 1989). All were submitted by Rep. Robert Dornan of California.

would have terminated payments of military retired pay to a spouse upon the spouse's remarriage, terminated the power of state courts to order payments of retired pay corresponding with a member's eligibility for retirement, and altered the definition of disposable retired pay to further limit the pay subject to division between spouses.

The committee rejected all these proposals. By the time the House passed them, the proposed amendments had several elements. First, they terminated the power of state courts to entertain suits for partition or division of military retirement benefits omitted from divorce decrees entered before the day before the *McCarty* decision,[54] and prevented the future enforcement of any such partition or division judgments already entered.

Next, the amendments altered the definition of "disposable pay" by eliminating certain deductions from gross pay used in calculating disposable pay. The deduction for federal, state, and local taxes was eliminated entirely. The deduction for sums owed the United States was limited to amounts owed for prior overpayments of retired pay. The 50 percent of disposable pay limitation section[55] was altered from referring to Subsection (d) (dealing with all payments for property division, alimony, child support, and so on) to Subsection (c) (dealing with the division of retired pay as property); thus, the 50 percent limitation no longer applied to orders awarding a division of retired pay (up to 50 percent) plus some *other* form of award (such as alimony).

Although these changes went to lessen the *jurisdictional* limitations on the state courts, the amendments also altered the *payment* limitations to reflect the provisions of the Social Security Act, so that little effective change might be seen in specific cases.[56] The changes to disposable pay affected only decrees entered on or after February 4, 1991.[57]

When the House bill went to conference committee, the prohibition on future enforcement of partition or division judgments already entered was altered to phase out at the end of two years; that is, payments otherwise lawfully required would still be required through November, 1992. Otherwise, the bill was enacted as passed by the House originally.[58] Some

---

54. That is, June 25, 1981.
55. 10 U.S.C. § 1408(e)(1).
56. These changes are explored in greater detail in Section D, Chapter Four.
57. H.R. 4739, 101 Cong. § 555(e)(2) (1990).
58. *See* Pub. L. No. 101-510, § 555, 104 Stat. 1485, 1569 (1990).

questions were left unanswered by this phaseout to partition; those are explored elsewhere.[59]

6. 1992: Spousal Protection against Benefit Loss from Member's Court-Martial

Without any public debate, and with virtually no legislative record, a very lengthy section was added to the act.[60] The gist of the added provision is to allow payments to an abused spouse or child (or the other parent of an abused child) even if the member loses benefits through which those dependents might otherwise make claim, by abusing those very dependents.

7. 1996: Changes to Service Rules; Restrictions on Amendments to Orders; Tracing to Civil Service Retirement

Legislation in 1996 contained a few "cleanup" provisions designed to assist the procedural handling of claims. First, the limitations on service of court orders upon the pay center by only certified or registered mail was stricken, replaced with "facsimile or electronic transmission or by mail."[61] Strangely, the new provision appears to allow service by fax, but does not do what the ABA representatives at the 1990 hearings requested—allow transmission of documents by Federal Express or other private carrier, as so much other business is transacted.

More substantively, 10 U.S.C. § 1408(d) was modified to restrict the orders that may be accepted. If an order purports to modify an existing court order upon which payments are being made, and is issued by a court of a state *other than* that of the original issuing court, then the order will be disregarded, *unless* the later court issuing the later order had jurisdiction in accordance with the USFSPA's provisions *for both the member and the former spouse.*[62]

---

59. See Section H, Chapter Seven.
60. Pub. L. No. 102-484, Div. A, Title VI, Subtitle E, § 653(a), 106 Stat. 2426 (1992).
61. Pub. L. No. 104-201, Div. A, Title VI, Subtitle D, § 636, 110 Stat. 2579 (1996).
62. Pub. L. No. 104-193, Title III, Subtitle G, §§ 362(c), 363(c)(1)–(3), 110 Stat. 2246, 2249 (1996). In other words, unless the later court had jurisdic-

The same legislation also eliminated the procedural requirement for a freshly certified copy of the applicable court order for enforcement of a child support obligation, and stated that application for payments under the Social Security Act, and not the USFSPA, must be made if what is sought is enforcement of child support for a child from a member "who has never been married to the other parent of the child."

Perhaps most significantly, the amendments created an explicit tracing mechanism for the spousal interest in military retirement benefits that are waived by the member to receive civil service retirement benefits.[63] This amendment did not alter the USFSPA itself at all. Instead, it modified the civil service statutes,[64] so that the Office of Personnel Management may credit an employee for military service only if the member authorizes payments to the former spouse that are equal to whatever the former spouse would have been receiving from the military retirement. There may be a few traps in the language used, as the new provision addresses only cases in "which there has been effective service on the Secretary concerned. . . ." In other words, to trigger the new provision, it appears that the application for direct payment must have already been made before the member tried to credit his military service.

The new provision affects Civil Service Retirement System (CSRS) and Federal Employees Retirement System (FERS) retirements equally, but in any event applies only to waivers made on or after January 1, 1997.

It is by no means certain that the USFSPA has taken its final form. Political lobbying continues by those who stand to gain from making the act more beneficial for either members or their spouses. On the other hand, it seems fairly clear from the attitude of the congressional committees with responsibility in this subject area that it is perceived as a "no-win" subject politically, because any change will be viewed as an attack by at least one side. It therefore seems likely that Congress will continue to resist pressure to change the USFSPA fundamentally, to avoid the political furor likely to surround any such proposed change.

---

tion over the member by reason of domicile, residence, or consent, as set forth in 10 U.S.C. § 1408(c)(4); this is the first time the USFSPA has expressed any concern with jurisdiction of an issuing court over the former spouse.

63. Pub. L. No. 104-201, Div. A, Title VI, Subtitle D, § 637, 110 Stat. 2579 (1996).

64. 5 U.S.C. § 8332(c).

F. IMPLEMENTING REGULATIONS: INTRODUCTION TO 32 C.F.R. § 63.6

The USFSPA provides that: "The Secretary concerned shall prescribe uniform regulations for the administration of this section."[65] Regulations were finally put into place on January 18, 1985, at 32 C.F.R. §§ 63.1–63.6.[66] They were amended once, after the 1986 amendments to the USFSPA.[67] The regulations appear in Appendix C.

The regulations restate and expand upon the statutory language of the USFSPA, as well as provide definitions that mirror other provisions of federal law.[68] Sections 63.1 and 63.2 provide short statements of purpose, applicability, and scope. Section 63.3 provides definitions of terms used in the USFSPA and in the regulations. Section 63.4 states that the policy of the uniformed services is to honor requests for direct payment if the requests comply with the regulations. Section 63.5 provides that the responsibility for establishing policy rests with the assistant secretary of defense (comptroller), and directs the secretaries of the military departments to implement the regulations.

The "meat" of the regulations is in section 63.6, which restates the statutory test for eligibility of a former spouse for payments,[69] provides a list of the information that such a spouse must submit when applying,[70] and sets forth procedures and substantive tests for reviewing court orders.[71] The section also indicates how garnishments will be treated,[72] gives a list of payment limitations,[73] and details how a member and former spouse will be notified of the actions of one another and the designated agent.[74] Finally, the section specifies the nonliability of the government

---

65. 10 U.S.C. § 1408(j).
66. *See* 50 Fed. Reg. 2,667 (1985).
67. *See* 52 Fed. Reg. 25,215 (1987).
68. For example, 32 C.F.R. § 63.3(a) incorporates the definition of alimony as used in the Social Security Act, 42 U.S.C. § 662(c).
69. 32 C.F.R. § 63.6(a).
70. *Id.* § 63.6(b).
71. *Id.* § 63.6(c).
72. *Id.* § 63.6(d).
73. *Id.* § 63.6(e).
74. *Id.* § 63.6(f).

and its agents for any payments or nonpayments,[75] provides for how much will be paid and when,[76] and provides a means for requesting reconsideration of a decision to pay or not pay benefits to a former spouse.[77]

The regulations did not match the provisions of the USFSPA as of February 4, 1991, so it is clear changes were required. It took until 1995 for revised regulations to be proposed,[78] and even longer for them to be set down as effective (although the Defense Finance and Accounting Service (DFAS) has largely followed them since they were proposed). The practitioner is cautioned to examine them closely, because they may well contain substantive or procedural limitations or mechanisms not set forth at all in the USFSPA itself.

The new version of the regulations is, however, clearly an improvement over the earlier version. Until then, it was necessary to define the sum of retired pay going to the spouse as an exact percentage or sum of dollars without reference to a formula, even if some component (for example, the total number of years of service for a member still in service) was not known at the time of divorce. The military pay center typically required the spouse to go back to court after divorce to obtain a "clarifying order" formally setting forth the percentage that resulted from simple math using figures completely available to the pay center.

The changed regulations at 32 C.F.R. § 63.6 allow lawyers to use formulas in enforceable orders. It is thus possible to enter an order when a member has not yet retired, and have the military honor the order upon retirement, when the court order specifies that the denominator in a time-rule calculation is to equal the total service time.

G. BOMBSHELL CASES: THE CHANGING FACE OF WHAT THE USFSPA MEANS

Certain cases decided in this field have had an effect ranging far beyond the participants in those cases. Sometimes it is because they were culminating or summation cases, and sometimes because new ground was broken. A few of them are worth examining more closely, as they give

---

75. *Id.* § 63.6(g).
76. *Id.* § 63.6(h).
77. *Id.* § 63.6(i).
78. 60 Fed. Reg. 17,507 (1995).

insight into the rationale underlying the bulk of similar (or even contrary) cases in the field.

1. Casas v. Thompson: *California Divides Gross, Not Net*

Casas v. Thompson[79] was the single clearest restatement of the law of military retirement benefits division as it had evolved in California before 1988, and as followed by several other states.

The parties had been married since 1949, and had five children. They separated in 1965, and were divorced in 1966. The military retirement was silently omitted from the decree, although the court recited that certain other assets (stock, furniture, and an automobile) existed, and that Mr. Thompson (Max) was awarded "all of the community property of the parties." Max obtained custody of the four remaining minor children. The former Mrs. Thompson (Virginia) paid no child support.

Max retired from the navy in 1970, and began drawing nondisability retired pay. Ten years later, Virginia brought an action seeking partition of the retired pay, both prospectively and retrospectively. At the trial in 1982, Virginia's claim was denied in its entirety from the bench on the basis of *McCarty*.[80] The USFSPA was passed before entry of judgment, however; Virginia requested rehearing and was ultimately granted partition of the omitted retirement from the date she filed her petition, but no arrears. The court of appeals affirmed with a few modifications not important here.[81]

The California Supreme Court adopted the court of appeals decision as its own, with a few changes. First, the court concluded that in 1966, Virginia did indeed have an interest in the military retirement, reasoning that California held military retirement benefits to be community property in 1974,[82] and that the decision to divide those benefits could be retroactively applied because it did not overturn any settled rule of law.[83] The

---

79. 42 Cal. 3d 131, 720 P.2d 921, 228 Cal. Rptr. 33 (1986), *cert. denied,* 479 U.S. 1012 (1987).
80. McCarty v. McCarty, 453 U.S. 210 (1981).
81. Casas v. Thompson, 171 Cal. App. 3d 458, 217 Cal. Rptr. 471 (Ct. App. 1985).
82. *See In re* Marriage of Fithian, 10 Cal. 3d, 517 P.2d 449, 111 Cal. Rptr. 369 (1974).
83. *See Casas,* 720 P.2d at 927.

court next noted that actions to partition omitted assets were explicitly permitted under California law,[84] and that *McCarty* was not to be construed as acting retroactively.[85] Thus, the court concluded that Virginia could seek to partition military retirement benefits omitted from a pre-*McCarty* decree of divorce.

Turning to the question of how *much* of the benefits were divisible, the court fairly restated Max's argument that Section (c)(1) of the USFSPA limited state courts to division of *disposable* retired pay.[86]

The court found that argument "illogical," because it necessarily permitted members to take actions altering their tax status, which would have the effect of reducing the community property share payable to former spouses. Further, the court considered the USFSPA a complete repudiation of the *McCarty* holding, and considered the limiting language of the federal act to be merely procedural limitations upon garnishment. The court focused upon that portion of the legislative history that declared Congress's intent to "restore the law to what it was," and noted that previous California law had called for division of the entirety of military retirement, as it did with all other retirement benefits.[87]

Because the court concluded that the USFSPA entirely rejected *McCarty*, it found no need to look for specific authority to divide the gross amount of military retirement benefits. The court then looked at the detail of the USFSPA to see if there was any prohibition in the federal law preventing state courts from dividing gross retired pay. It rejected Max's argument that the language of the USFSPA precluded state courts from *considering* the gross amount of retired pay.[88]

Beginning from the proposition that all assets acquired during marriage were community property, the court viewed the concept of "treating" disposable pay as a mere collection limitation, leaving former spouses to other (state law) remedies for collection of all amounts ordered paid by state courts that could not be paid directly from military pay centers.[89] It concluded that characterization was left to the states by the USFSPA, and

---

84. *See* Henn v. Henn, 26 Cal. 3d 323, 605 P.2d 10, 161 Cal. Rptr. 502 (1980).
85. *Casas*, 720 P.2d at 925–28.
86. *Id.* at 928–33.
87. *Id.* at 930 & n.10 (quoting 1982 U.S.C.C.A.N. 1599).
88. The court's term was "characterize." *See Casas*, 720 P.2d at 931.
89. *Id.* at 931–33.

that in California the gross amount of a military retirement was community property subject to equal division.

As for amounts of retired pay paid to Max before Virginia's partition suit, however, the court considered the matter one of traditional notions of equity, including waiver, estoppel, and laches. Under prior California cases, the court reasoned that equitable considerations included "general considerations" as well as specific equitable defenses, in "tailoring" the amount and form of an award of prepetition arrearages. The court found Max's sole support of the children over the years a sufficient consideration, and denied to Virginia any prepetition arrearages.[90]

Casas thus presented several different aspects of military retirement benefits cases. It noted the divisibility of such benefits, confirmed that the remedy of partition was available for such benefits regardless of the date of divorce, provided that state courts were to consider the gross sum of retired pay rather than just disposable pay, and provided that amounts of retired pay paid to a member before a partition action was filed would be divisible—or not—depending on the equities of the case. Though *Casas* has been widely cited and largely followed elsewhere, not all aspects of the decision were destined to have a long life.

2. Fern v. United States: *Division of Military Retirement Is Not a Government "Taking"*

Max Thompson did not give up when the United States Supreme Court denied certiorari. By 1987, he was involved in a consolidated action filed by several notable participants in military retirement cases,[91] in a

---

90. *Id.* at 934–35.
91. John T. Flannagan, Donald Koppenhaver, and David E. Walentowski classified themselves as "final decree plaintiffs"; that is, they had been granted all rights to the military retirement as part of their original divorce or separation decrees. *See* Flannagan v. Flannagan, 42 Wash. App. 214, 709 P.2d 1247 (Ct. App. 1985); Koppenhaver v. Koppenhaver, 101 N.M. 105, 678 P.2d 1180 (Ct. App.), *cert. denied*, 101 N.M. 11, 677 P.2d 624 (1984); Walentowski v. Walentowski, 100 N.M. 484, 672 P.2d 657 (1983). Max Thompson was in the second group, self-styled "omitted asset plaintiffs," whose decrees were silent concerning the military retirement. James Powell was the only notable member of the third group, labeled "pre-*McCarty* plaintiffs," who were the subject of decrees entered before *McCarty*, which divided retired pay between them and their former spouses.

case captioned *Fern v. United States*.[92] The case was an unusual one in this field, as the defendant was not a former spouse but the United States itself.

Essentially, the suit sought to have the USFSPA declared invalid to the extent that it entitled the government to reduce the retired pay flowing to the members themselves; in other words, the members contended that regardless of any award to any former spouse, the full sum of retired pay should be paid to the members. The members' grounds were that reducing their retired pay allowed an impermissible "taking" of property in violation of the Fifth Amendment by reclassifying current pay as community property subject to division. In the alternative, the plaintiffs argued that the USFSPA unconstitutionally permitted the impairment of their individual contracts with the United States, by which they alone were to receive the entirety of their retirement benefits, or constituted a due process violation.

This representative cross section of former service members argued that their spouses had no legitimate interest in military pensions. They each supplied sworn affidavits that "throughout their years of military service they . . . believed that their retired pay was the personal entitlement of each of them."[93]

The court took the constitutional challenges head on, and found that there was no constitutional issue in state court division of military retired pay under the USFSPA. In reaching that conclusion, the court rejected the members' "equal protection" attacks on partition of pensions omitted from the initial decrees of some of the plaintiffs,[94] recounting the retirees' "odysseys through the state and federal courts challenging state court decrees dividing their retirement pay" and noting that the retirees "were unable, as a final matter, to convince any of these courts that division of their retirement pay was unconstitutional or legally improper."

The court found that partition of military retirement benefits is precisely the sort of "economic adjustments to promote the common good" that legislatures properly perform,[95] and that any retroactive effect of the USFSPA is curative, accomplishes a rational purpose, is entitled to be

---

92. 15 Cl. Ct. 580 (1988), *aff'd*, 908 F.2d 955 (Fed. Cir. 1990).
93. *Fern*, 15 Cl. Ct. at 582.
94. *Id*. at 592.
95. *Id*. at 580, 589.

liberally construed, and is shielded from constitutional attack.[96] It further found that by enacting the USFSPA, "Congress recognized the unique contributions and significant sacrifices of a military spouse, as a partner in the service member's career and to the national defense effort."[97]

The court concluded that the USFSPA served public policy, holding that it "substantially advance[s] valid public interest sufficient to justify the results which occurred subsequent to its passage."[98]

Turning to the contract clause and due process arguments, the court was no more sympathetic to the members. The court began its analysis by finding that there is no "vested right" to *any* portion of future retirement payments. The court held as follows:

> It is settled that there is no property or contractual interest in any antic-ipated level of military retired pay. The statutory right to retired pay is within the exclusive control of Congress and is always subject to change. . . . [P]laintiffs' contention is that . . . each . . . had gone through a divorce proceeding and had retained for themselves their entire military retirement pay. The Act . . . resulted in their having to share part of their military retirement pay with their ex-spouses pursuant to state courts' decrees that resulted from reopened divorce proceedings. . . .
>
> . . . Congress recognized the unique contributions and significant sacrifices of a military spouse, as a partner in the service member's career and to the national defense effort. . . .
>
> . . . It is clear from a general public policy perspective that it was not unfair to permit an ex-spouse to share in a portion of the service member's retired pay. . . . The retrospective aspect, if such there be, of the USFSPA, was intended to aid in curing a defect in the rights afforded military spouses, and, therefore, can easily be viewed as a "curative statute." Accordingly, the case for upholding the Act against constitu-tional attack is given added weight.[99]

The decision of the Claims Court was upheld by the Court of Appeals for the Federal Circuit, which noted that as between the members and the government, the USFSPA had no effect at all because the same total pay-

---

96. *Id.* at 590–91.
97. *Id.* at 590 (citing legislative history).
98. *Id.* at 585 n.4.
99. *Id.* at 587–92 (citations omitted).

ments were made before as had been made previously.[100] The court found that there was simply no property right in continued federal preemption of state law.

3. Mansell v. Mansell: *Disposable Pay Is All the States May Address*

The decision in November, 1992, of *Mansell v. Mansell*[101] (discussed at length below[102]) let Max Thompson get the last laugh, although too late to help him. By then, Ms. Casas had already died (in 1990); she apparently received everything she was supposed to get under the orders of the California courts.

As discussed below, the *Mansell* court found that the act did not constitute a total repudiation of the preemption found by the court to exist in *McCarty,* and Congress did nothing to alter this finding when it next amended the act in 1990.

Thus, *Mansell* stands for the proposition that the subject matter jurisdiction of the state divorce courts is limited to division of the disposable retired pay of members. This may be less important than was thought at the time, however, because courts have widely expressed a willingness to consider the impact of disability or other retired pay *not* considered disposable retired pay in dividing assets between spouses.

---

100. 908 F.2d 955 (Fed. Cir. 1990).
101. 490 U.S. 581 (1989).
102. See Subsection 2, Section D, Chapter Four.

Chapter Three

VALUATION OF MILITARY RETIREMENT BENEFITS: HOW AND HOW MUCH

A. METHODOLOGY

1. Division by Present Value: A Bird in the Hand

A divorce court has two ways to divide military retirement between divorcing parties. The court can assess a value to the retirement itself, putting it on the balance sheet like other assets, or the court can allocate to each party a portion of the retired pay as it is paid.

There are legitimate reasons for wishing to "trade off" the retirement benefits for other assets. Courts preferring this approach usually cite the certainty, finality, and lack of future entanglements obtained by reaching final settlement.[1] This approach is possible, however, regardless of judicial preferences, only when there are sufficient "other assets" involved in the case that the spousal share can be paid. It appears to be a truism that enlisted members, at least, simply do not accumulate much in the way of cash or tangible property during military service.

An additional problem with the "trade off" method of disposition is the inherent problem in assigning a fixed value to any defined benefit plan. A number is reached by actuarial estimate, but it is quite possible that one of the parties to any real case will be shorted, depending on the accuracy of the prognosticator's vision.

For example, any estimation of present value takes into account the time value of money, by which a present value is always less than the amount that would otherwise be paid to an individual over a period of time. Put another way, present value is the amount of money that would have to be invested today to generate a stream of payments (of principal

---

1. *See* Seifert v. Seifert, 82 N.C. App. 329, 346 S.E.2d 504 (Ct. App. 1986), *aff'd on other grounds,* 319 N.C. 367, 354 S.E.2d 506 (1987); Dewann v. Dewann, 389 Mass. 754, 506 N.E.2d 879 (1987).

and interest) that would completely exhaust the investment amount over the lifetime of the recipient.

The number reached in such a calculation changes significantly by merely varying the presumed interest rate used in the calculation. Obviously, it would take far less of a "present value" investment today to generate $1,000 per month for twenty years if you presumed a 10 percent interest rate, than it would if you presumed that the investment would be earning only 5 percent.

Just establishing the sum that would be received over time involves assumptions, including whether Congress will grant future cost of living adjustments (COLAs) to adjust future retirement payments to match the inflation rate exactly, or provide more, or less, than inflation.

For a divorce occurring while a member is still on active duty, there are even more variables, chief among which is the uncertainty that the member will actually retire at all. When the member is only halfway to eligibility for retirement, or less, it would seem little more than guesswork to evaluate the member's odds of actually retiring. This seems especially important in an era that has seen, within the twenty years of a member's regular retirement, the massive military buildup of the Reagan era, immediately followed by the unprecedented drawdown following the collapse of the Soviet Union and the end of the Cold War.

The precise length of service for a member still on active duty cannot be known. Economic conditions, the defense budget, and world crises all could change the date of separation of a member by several years. Likewise, it is usually impossible to know the rank that such an active-duty member will achieve. For each of these factors, any present value of a spousal share would have to be reduced by the percentage chance that the retirement will never come into existence at all.

When a trade-off of the spousal retirement share is contemplated, these calculations must be performed. In a contested case, it is usually necessary for each party to hire an actuarial expert to give that testimony. Such an expert must become familiar with the military retirement system, and perhaps change certain assumptions applicable in other cases. Practitioners retaining or cross-examining any experts employed in a military case should clarify all assumptions made and be prepared to address how, if at all, those assumptions in military cases differ from other pension cases.

For example, the military has its own set of mortality tables, arranged by officers and enlisted members, and by disability and nondisability retirements.[2] It seems that (at least for nondisability retirements) there is a significant reduction in member death rates by the military's screening out from eligibility those with significant health problems. In 1997, the military retiree life expectancy for a 47-year-old nondisabled retired officer was 33.48 years.[3] A nondisabled enlisted member had 29.86 years, whereas disabled officers and enlisted members at that age were given 26.97 and 24.51 years, respectively. The general population life expectancy for males was 29.4 years.[4] Thus, life expectancy (and therefore present value) can be increased or decreased depending on which table is used.

The expert must decide which set of assumptions and calculations to use. One possibility is reliance on the values provided by the Department of Defense Actuary.[5] That set of figures is revised annually, and does provide for a presumed COLA. Because of the COLA presumption and the high reliability factor that the government will make the payments owed, the actuary assumes an interest rate of only 2 percent. This greatly increases the present value.

The actuary table also incorporates various assumptions that may or may not reflect the facts of a given case. For example, it presumes service entry age of twenty years for enlisted members, and age twenty-three for officers. For these reasons and others, the actuary puts a warning on every copy of the table that the figures are "not to be used" in property settlements. Of course, the warning is overbroad; the information in the table is quite useful for "ballparking" present values, as long as the practitioner is mindful of the presumptions underlying the numbers reached.

A lawyer wishing to estimate present values can purchase computer programs that do the math involved quite quickly.[6] Such programs often

---

2. See Exhibit 5, Appendix F.

3. *See* OFFICE OF THE ACTUARY, DEP'T OF DEFENSE, FY 1997 DOD STATISTICAL REPORT ON THE MILITARY RETIREMENT SYSTEM 288 (1998) [hereinafter FY 1997 REPORT].

4. NATIONAL CTR. FOR HEALTH STATISTICS, U.S. DEP'T OF HEALTH AND HUMAN SERVICES, 2 VITAL STATISTICS OF THE UNITED STATES, 1992, § 6 Life Tables, at 12 (1996). The tables are arranged by race and sex, and are reprinted as Exhibit 6, Appendix F.

5. FY 1997 REPORT, *supra* note 3, at 284–89. This table is reproduced as Exhibit 7 in Appendix F.

6. One such program is Legal Math-Pac, offered by Custom Legal Software Corporation, 3867 Paseo del Prado, Boulder, CO 80301; 303/443-2634.

allow the user to insert the assumptions to be used, such as life expectancy, presumed interest rate, and so on. In any event, lawyers handling these cases in states that allow or require trading the present value of the retirement benefit must become well versed in all aspects of valuation, interest rate assumptions, and other factors involved. Failure to do so invites disaster at settlement or in court.

2. Division If/As/When Received: Sauce for the Goose

A division of military retired pay "in-kind" (also called an "if, as, and when" division) may be the *preferable* form of dividing retirement benefits. Such a division has the advantages of fully and fairly dividing the actual benefit received without speculation regarding actuarial valuation, inflation, life expectancies, and so on. Regardless of preferences, it may be *necessary* to divide the benefit itself if the "present value" of the retirement is so large that no other asset of the marriage could be traded to the spouse in exchange for the member keeping all the retirement.

An if/as/when distribution, however, carries with it the necessary intertwining of the parties, including the possibility of later court struggles about enforcement or interpretation of the original order for division.[7] It gives each of the parties a stake in the other's life, and death. For example, absent survivorship rights, the funds going to the former spouse terminate if the member dies. In counterpoint, if the former spouse predeceases the member, the member's retired pay goes up by whatever sum the former spouse had been receiving. Occasionally, a member cannot resist the urge to recapture those funds by trying to hasten or instigate the demise of a former spouse.[8]

---

7. The evolving interpretation of the phrase "disposable retired pay" has given rise to many such cases. If the parties were divorced in 1985, should the phrase be interpreted to mean what the Supreme Court said it meant—four years later—in *Mansell v. Mansell,* 490 U.S. 581 (1989) or what Congress redefined it to mean in 1991? Should a court attempt to divine the intention of the parties at the time of divorce? If so, how could this be accomplished if they each had a different view of the meaning?

8. Anecdotal accounts suggest that, unfortunately, there have been a number of such cases throughout the country since passage of the Uniformed Services Former Spouses Protection Act (USFSPA). Most, presumably, are discovered and addressed without ever being reported in an appellate de-

Most states that have cases approving in-kind divisions have adopted some phrasing of the "time rule" (also called the "coverture fraction"), under which the spousal share is defined as a formula. First, a fraction is established, in which the numerator is the months or years of marriage during service, and the denominator is the months or years of total service. That number is multiplied by one-half to yield the spousal share.[9]

When a decision has been made to do an in-kind division, the lawyers for both parties must be careful that the effect of the language used will be what was intended. It is not enough merely to recite that the former spouse should receive "40 percent of the retired pay," for example. Especially for the lawyer for the former spouse (for whom a mistake is more likely to result in partial or total loss of benefits), it is necessary to consider all the things that can go wrong at the time of divorce or later.

Each of the various conditions that could prevent a direct payment order from becoming effective should be considered.[10] At the minimum, the actual amount of disposable pay that will be allocated to the spouse should be determined, the jurisdictional and procedural limitations set forth in the checklist in Section D of Chapter Eight should be addressed, and the "real world" litigation considerations discussed in Chapter Seven should be examined.

B. EXAMPLES OF MILITARY RETIREMENT BENEFITS VALUATIONS

Before proceeding with these sample valuations, a brief explanation of spousal shares is in order. Except when speaking about separation pay, all discussions of division of retired pay upon divorce presume that the military member reached eligibility for retirement. These cases also presume that the parties have been lawfully married. Finally, it is presumed

---

cision (see the discussion of the *Hazlett* case in Chapter Four), or are never discovered at all.

9. *See, e.g., In re* Marriage of Gillmore, 29 Cal. 3d 418, 174 Cal. Rptr. 493, 629 P.2d 1, (1981); *In re* Marriage of Luciano, 104 Cal. App. 3d 956, 164 Cal. Rptr. 93 (Ct. App. 1980); Fondi v. Fondi, 106 Nev. 856, 802 P.2d 1264 (1990).

10. See the discussion of jurisdiction in Section B of Chapter Four, and "The 'Ten-Year' Compromise and Its Ramifications," Section E, Chapter Four.

that there is at least some overlap between the marriage and the military service (that is, not all the military service was before or after the marriage at issue).

The number of years of creditable service performed by the member, the number of years the former spouse was married to the member, and the number of years during which the marriage overlapped the creditable service is usually expressed in shorthand as three connected numbers. For example, a 20/20/20 former spouse would be one whose military spouse completed at least twenty years of creditable service, to whom the spouse was married for at least twenty years, and whose marriage overlapped the service period by at least twenty years.

As a last thought, it should be remembered that the examples discussed below *presume* that what is being divided is the gross amount of retired pay. That presumption is an oversimplification that is only close to reality for recent cases.[11]

1. Master Sergeant with 20/20/20

Harcourt and Stella were married right out of high school in 1969. Two years later, when Harcourt turned twenty, he joined the air force. He retired after exactly twenty years of service as an E-7, and the parties commenced divorce proceedings in 1991. They had $25,000 in the bank, bought a house four years previously that had $6,000 equity by appreciation, and wished to divide their property fairly.

Harcourt happened to fit the presumptions in the Department of Defense actuary table exactly. As shown by the table, the lump-sum equivalency of the retirement benefits in 1991 was $292,096. Because the parties had been married during the entire term of military service (and presuming that the court had to or wished to divide the retirement evenly), Harcourt would have been required to give Stella $146,048 to pay off the present value of her spousal share. As their entire remaining other assets amounted to only $31,000, such a lump-sum payoff was not possible.

The spousal share for an in-kind division in this case is derived by using this formula: twenty (years of marriage during service, the numerator), divided by twenty (total number of years of service, the denominator), multiplied by one-half (the spousal share). Here, Stella would have

---

11. See Section D, Chapter Four.

received exactly 50 percent. In 1991, that was half of $974 per month, or $487.

2. *Colonel with 30/30/15*

Rhett and Scarlett married in 1961, fifteen years after Rhett entered the army at age twenty-three. In the following fifteen years, he was promoted to colonel (O-6), at which rank he left the service in 1976. Fifteen years later, in 1991, the marriage broke up, and the parties were considering their options. The parties had accrued a stock portfolio valued at $150,000, a house with equity of $75,000, and liquid assets of $75,000. At divorce, Rhett was sixty-eight.

Note that the actuary table would not be appropriately used in this case; the table assumes valuation at the moment of retirement, but in this hypothetical Rhett was fifteen years older at the time of divorce.[12] The nondisability retired life expectancy table then in effect showed Rhett to have an actuarial life expectancy of 14.73 years.[13] By the time of divorce, Rhett's original $2,350 per month had increased to $4,047.[14] Plugging in that sum and the life expectancy to estimate present value, along with the 2 percent presumed interest rate, yields a present value of the entire remaining retirement of $619,161.52.

Because the parties had been married for only half the time Rhett had been in service, the spousal share for a lump-sum payoff would be computed by this formula: $619,161.52 (present value) multiplied by fifteen (years of service during marriage) divided by thirty (total years of service) multiplied by one-half (spousal share). Here, Scarlett's share of the remaining benefit came to $154,790.38. As the parties had an asset with

---

12. Because a certain number of people fall prey to accidents and similar events, a person's life expectancy increases for each year of survival; you cannot simply reduce life expectancy by a year for each year a person survives. That is why a thirty-five-year-old person may have a life expectancy of only forty-three more years, but a seventy-eight-year-old person still has a life expectancy of more than eight years.

13. OFFICE OF THE DEP'T OF DEFENSE, FY 1990 DOD STATISTICAL REPORT ON THE MILITARY RETIREMENT SYSTEM 258 (1991). This table is updated each year; the current version is reproduced as Exhibit 5, Appendix F.

14. _____, 1991 RETIRED MILITARY ALMANAC 21 (1991).

similar value, it would have been possible to cash out Scarlett's interest in the retirement.

If, for whatever reason, the parties did not wish to pay off Scarlett's interest with a lump-sum payoff, the same formula would render a spousal share of 25 percent (that is, fifteen years of marriage during service, divided by thirty years of total service, multiplied by one-half for the spousal share, which equals 25 percent). Because Rhett's monthly retirement came to $4,047, Scarlett would receive $1,011.75 per month (presumably, plus COLAs).

3. *Staff Sergeant with 14/9/9*

This scenario is the most difficult of the three, in terms of both valuation and technical complications. Fred and Ginger were married in 1982, five years after Fred joined the marines. Fred was a staff sergeant (E-6) when the marriage broke down. The parties had assets totaling only $5,000.

No table will accurately set forth the present value of Fred's retirement, because the primary factor of likelihood of retirement is missing. It would be necessary to either force the court to make an assumption, or attempt to find some statistical likelihood that a marine at a given rank with fourteen years of service would complete at least twenty years. It should then be possible to take the present value, reduce it by the appropriate percentage for this uncertainty, and then calculate the present value.

Suppose it were known—or assumed—that Fred had only a 40 percent chance of completing twenty years of service.[15] Just to be able to use the actuary's table, this hypothetical also presumes that Fred joined the service at age twenty-six, so he happens to be the same age (forty) at the time of divorce as he would have been if he joined the service at age twenty and served for twenty years.

Because the parties had been married for only nine years, the spousal share for a lump-sum payoff *as if* Fred was eligible for retirement could be computed by making a series of presumptions. If Fred was retiring in 1991, the lump-sum value would have been $255,809 (present value for an E-6 eligible to retire in 1991). Still using the actuary's 2 percent interest rate, that present value could be reduced again for the six years remaining

---

15. This number is entirely hypothetical; it bears no relation to any set of data.

for its accrual, by treating it as if it were a lump sum to be paid at that time. That makes the value $226,904.89.[16]

The reduced hypothetical present value could then be used in the usual formula: $226,904.89 multiplied by nine (years of service during marriage), divided by twenty (total years of service required for retirement), multiplied by one-half (spousal share). Here, Ginger's share of the hypothetical benefit came to $51,053.60. Finally, that number would have to be reduced by the degree of uncertainty that a retirement would accrue at all; in this case, we chose 40 percent, making Ginger's present value drop to $20,421.44.

Note that the above figure presumed retirement at Fred's rank and grade at the time of divorce. This presumption is not necessarily the one that is made in these cases.[17] It could also be debated whether the denominator should be twenty years or fourteen, as the six years yet to be served might well be already reflected in the "uncertainty multiplier." On the other hand, it could be argued that such a reduction was already accomplished by the present value reduction from $255,000 to $226,000. These are questions best addressed to expert witness accountants and actuaries.

The lawyer for the member should not simply allow present value of the retirement benefits to be calculated as if retirement was a certainty. If counsel can persuade the court that the uncertainty rises to the level of mere speculation, the court might defer the issue until the facts are known, enter an if/as/when order, or refuse to assign any value to the benefits at all.[18]

When the court elects to assign an in-kind distribution of the retirement benefits, counsel must be sure to give the same level of attention to detail as if the distribution was immediate. Failure to do so only enhances the chances of further litigation upon the member's eligibility. The simple failure of lawyers to think about deferred retirement issues at the time of divorce is probably the principal cause of postdivorce pension litigation.

---

16. These figures were derived using the Legal Math-Pac program. (See note 6.) The small reduction in present value for a six-year delay is, again, due to the very small interest rate used.
17. See Subsection 1, Section B, Chapter Seven.
18. Indeed, this is essentially the reasoning of those few remaining states that still refuse to divide the value of unvested retirement benefits at divorce. See Section E, Chapter Seven.

Some courts are loathe to engage in the sort of uncertain and error-prone speculation set forth above, and so tend to enter "wait and see" orders, reserving jurisdiction to enter proper orders regarding the retirement benefits until after the members concerned become eligible for retirement. This resolution (or, rather, nonresolution) has its downside, in terms of the certainty of later legal expenses, jurisdictional complications if one or both parties relocate, and the emotional cost of not achieving closure on an issue of primary importance.

C. COPING WITH COLAs

1. *Background and Projection of Future Use*

For whatever reason, COLAs seem to provide great difficulty to many practitioners and judges. They are a valuation factor, however, that must be taken into account in dividing military retirement benefits. Simply put, a COLA is an increase in the sum of a retirement intended to offset, fully or partly, the effect of inflationary or other changes in the cost of living.

The need for such adjustments is obvious. In January, 1972, the government's consumer price index for all urban consumers (CPI-U) was 123.2, meaning that by comparison with the base year of 1967, it took an extra $23.20 to have the same purchasing power that $100 had commanded.[19] Put another way, dollars were worth only 81 cents. By January, 1992, the CPI-U was 413.8, meaning that it took an extra $313.80 to gain the purchasing power of the original $100, or that each dollar was now worth only 24 cents. If there were no cost of living adjustments, a $1,000 per month retirement that started in 1972 would be paying the purchasing-power equivalent of only $240 per month in 1992.

Over the years, Congress has attempted to cope with increases in the cost of living in a number of ways, causing numerous changes in the method of computation of the adjustments. This has resulted in persons with identical ranks and lengths of service being paid different sums of retired pay depending upon their dates of retirement.

Even greater differences between similarly situated individuals are in store. Congress has altered the retirement system so that only *partial*

---

19. Bureau of Labor Statistics, U.S. Department of Labor, P.O. Box 193766, San Francisco, CA 94119-3766; 415/975-4567.

COLAs will accrue to retirees who entered service on or after August 1, 1986, or their survivors. COLAs for those persons will be 1 percent less than the annual change in the CPI.[20] A "one-time restoral" will go to such recipients upon the retiree reaching age sixty-two, to bring payments to the level they would have reached if the full COLA had been awarded over the years, but thereafter, only the partial COLAs will accrue.

Presuming no further change in congressional policy, the net effect of this change is to make military retirement benefits somewhat less valuable for those who will retire after August 1, 2006. The discussion of this potential decline is included here as a caution to practitioners who will have actuarial expert witnesses projecting retirements past that date, to ensure that the reduction is considered as part of the experts' assumptions.

It should also be remembered that much of the historical changes to the military compensation system, and to many of the retirement statutes, have been politically generated. The changing balances of power in Congress, and congressional reactions to real or perceived budget pressures, could alter all this in ways that cannot be predicted at any given time. Typically, it is only as deadlines (such as the implementation line of August 1, 2006) approach that Congress "discovers" and deals with allegations of unfairness. It would be a fair bet to presume that retired pay calculations will again be debated in 2005.

2. Strategic Use in Litigation

Proper use of COLAs in orders dividing military retirement benefits is critical to ensuring that the court order has the effect intended. There is no federal rule mandating whether a former spouse should be awarded future COLAs. The military pay center attempts to recognize the intention of court orders, using various assumptions.

There are two typical ways of dividing benefits between members and former spouses—by dollars and by percentages. It must be remembered that for divisions of retired pay itself as *property* (as opposed to treating retired pay as a fund from which alimony or child support or other property awards are to be paid), the order must be for payment of an amount "expressed in dollars or as a percentage of disposable retired pay."[21]

---

20. FY 1997 REPORT, *supra* note 3, at 1, 5.
21. 10 U.S.C. §§ 1408(a)(2)(C), 1408(d)(1), 1408(d)(5).

The methods of dividing the retired pay produce different results in the absence of a provision specifically stating whether COLAs are payable to the former spouse. If a decree simply recites that the military retirement is split by percentage, the military pay centers will *presume* that future COLAs are to be divided in the same proportion as the sum originally payable. Most courts reviewing percentage-division orders have likewise concluded that inclusion of cost of living increases is automatic unless specifically stated otherwise, because any other reading would in fact alter the division of the asset over time, by reducing the spouse's share relative to that of the member.[22] If the former spouse is awarded one-third of the retired pay, for example, then one-third of the COLAs will also be paid to the former spouse.

The presumption is reversed if the decree simply awards a specific sum of dollars to the former spouse. In such a case, the dollar sum payable to the former spouse will remain constant regardless of the subsequent increase of the retirement by COLA.

There are difficulties with each approach. Although COLAs are presumed, there is some difficulty in guaranteeing the sum against which the present and future percentages will be applied. For example, suppose it was anticipated that an active-duty member would receive a retirement benefit of $1,000 per month, that the former spouse would receive $500 of that sum, and that the court had ordered temporary alimony, which terminated when the retired pay was to begin. If the member took some action after the divorce that reduced his rank upon retirement, the anticipated sum would not flow to the former spouse.

Of course, the better practice, whether ordering division of a percentage or a dollar sum certain, is to specify whether COLAs are payable to the former spouse and, if so, in what amount. This clearly shows the court's intention at the time of divorce (and thus makes any postdivorce enforcement or clarification motion easier to win), but it still does not necessarily mean the court's intentions will be carried out.

It was common in earlier years for lawyers for former spouses to wish to reflect the initial award to the former spouse as a specific dollar sum, to show the court's intention clearly and to avoid the possibility of reduc-

---

22. *See, e.g., In re* Marriage of Whiting, 179 Ill. App. 3d 187, 534 N.E.2d 468 (App. Ct. 1989); Miller v. Miller, 395 Pa. Super. 255, 577 A.2d 205 (Super. Ct. 1990).

tion of disposable pay by some action of the member. For example, if the entire retirement was $1,000, and the parties had been married for exactly half the member's twenty years of service, counsel might wish the decree to recite that the former spouse was awarded $250 per month out of the sum payable for the retirement, plus 25 percent of any future COLAs. In the hypothetical discussed above, this would remove any risk that the member's postdivorce actions could lower the spousal share upon retirement.

The problem with this approach is that it results in no COLA increases going to the former spouse, as the consolidated Defense and Finance Accounting Service (DFAS) elected to follow the navy view that such an award was for a fixed sum, rather than the air force interpretation that such a provision intended to award a percentage and merely measured the initial payment. Thus, the former spouse must return to court upon the granting of each subsequent COLA to get the dollar sum adjusted to reflect the new amount payable.[23]

✐ **Practice Tip:** The lawyer for the former spouse should try to provide for the court's continuing jurisdiction to enforce its award by means of postdivorce orders. Most things that could happen after divorce to change the expectations of the parties concerning payments will work to the relative disadvantage of the former spouse, so it is that party who must make it as simple as possible to get back into court to correct later problems. The sample language included at the back of this book is intended to provide as many "fallback" provisions as possible, so that court orders can actually be made enforceable.[24]

D. WHAT TO DO WITH RESERVE CREDITS

Since 1948, reservists have had a retirement system of their own.[25] The big difference for reservists is that both service and age elements must be satisfied; the reservist must accumulate twenty years of creditable service, *and* must reach the age of sixty.

---

23. This is discussed at greater length in Subsection 4(a) of Section C, Chapter Five.
24. See Section B, Chapter Eight.
25. *See* Pub. L. No. 80-810, 62 Stat. 1081 (1948) (codified at 10 U.S.C. §§ 1331–37).

To be entitled to a "year" of creditable service, the reservist must obtain at least fifty "retirement points." A point is awarded for each day of active service, or for full-time service while performing annual active duty for training or attending required training. A point is awarded for each drill performed adequately, or for each three hours of military correspondence or extension courses that are successfully completed. There are various other ways of acquiring points. Fifteen points are awarded for membership in the reserve components or the army or air force without component. There is an annual 60-point maximum for inactive-duty points, and a maximum of 365 points may be earned each year.

It is possible to mix and match. A member of the regular services may complete the twenty years necessary for retirement by entering the reserves; as long as the last eight years are reserve service, the member will qualify for the reserve retirement program.[26] Any year in which the 50-point minimum is not reached does not count toward retirement, although the points earned in such years eventually factor into the retired pay paid to the reservist.

Figuring reserve retirement pay is complex. The total amount of retirement points earned is divided by 360 to yield "years of service" for retired pay purposes. That figure is multiplied by 2.5 percent; the resulting percentage is multiplied by the active-duty basic pay payable to an active-duty member with the same grade and number of years creditable for retirement.

The matter is even more complicated if the reserve service preceded active-duty service. A reservist who goes into extended active duty will have to accrue twenty years of *active duty* to qualify for an active-duty retirement, so all the drill periods and other items that accrued points but did not count as *active-duty* time simply do not count. However, when the former reservist attains that twenty years of active duty, all those useless-for-eligibility-to-retire points are resurrected, and are treated as days of active duty for the purpose of figuring the *amount* of retired pay payable. This form of credit was extended from officers only to include enlisted members on October 4, 1994; for those retiring after that date, the points will be credited.

---

26. It appears that this requirement was lowered to six years in reserve service, for retirements between October 5, 1994, and September 30, 1999. 10 U.S.C. § 12731(f).

As with active-duty members, there is a future distinction between reservist retirees depending on the date they entered service. For members who first entered service before September 8, 1980, the figure for "base pay" in the above calculation is the active-duty basic pay in effect for the retiree's grade and years of service *when the retired pay begins*. For members who first served after September 8, 1980, "base pay" is the *average* basic pay for the member's grade in the last three years that the member served.[27]

Practitioners therefore must be careful in all reservist cases. Counsel should be wary—in a case involving reserve component service—of any calculations that presuppose the typical "years of marriage divided by years of service" formula. Because point accumulation might have been intermittent, significantly different spousal percentages could be obtained by the two methods of figuring.[28] Special care is required for reservists who entered service after September 8, 1980, because the formula for figuring their retirement will be altered. All the "political" considerations discussed above regarding retired pay are applicable here as well.

The new "proposed regulations"[29] mandate that any "formula orders" (that is, orders phrased—usually because the member is still on active duty—with a blank to be filled in for total service performed) be framed

---

27. FY 1997 REPORT, *supra* note 3, at 3.

28. Example: Harcourt married Stella before entering service, and both divorced her and left service after exactly ten years of active duty. The divorce court reserved jurisdiction to enter an order "if, as, and when" Harcourt received retired pay. He immediately joined the reserves. It took him another twenty years of intermittent reserve duty to accrue enough points to have twenty "qualifying years" for a reserve retirement. When he turned sixty and began receiving retired pay, Stella requested a ruling that she was entitled to 25 percent of the retired pay, as her half of the half of the creditable retirement that accrued during their marriage. Harcourt countered, stating that the two parties were married for only ten years out of the thirty years he was in service, and that therefore Stella should receive only 16.67 percent of the retirement, as Stella's half of the one-third of the total service time that was served during his marriage to her. A judge locked into thinking only about the time rule, rather than the nature of the accruing benefits, might not see the logic problem with Harcourt's position.

29. 32 C.F.R. § 63.6, issued April 6, 1995, for commentary; not formally enacted as of the date of this book, but enforced per their own terms anyway.

in terms of points rather than years. Presumably this is because of the substantial inequity reported in anecdotal cases when the standard "time rule" is used. An example illustrates the point.[30]

E. THE COMPONENTS OF ACTIVE-DUTY MILITARY PAY[31]

1. Basic Pay and Overview

Generally, basic pay increases with increased rank and with length of service. A table showing the most current pay schedule available (historically, the schedule changes at least every year) is included at the end of this book.[32] Practitioners involved with cases in which the members remain on active duty should be familiar with all components of military

---

30. My thanks for the following example to lawyer Mark E. Sullivan, 1306 Hillsborough Street, Raleigh, NC 27605; 919/832-8507:

Major Bill Smith has five years of active duty and fifteen years of service in the U.S. Army Reserve. He married when he left active duty.

To compute the marital fraction according to points he acquired during active duty, we simply multiply five times 364 to get 1820 points. During his time in the reserves, he has acquired the maximum of 60 points a year (for weekend drill, "summer camp," and membership), and this equals 900 points over fifteen years. Thus his total points at twenty years are 2720, of which 900 (or about 33 percent) are marital. This means that 33 percent of his retirement pay (assuming retirement and date of separation both occur at year twenty) is marital. If his retired pay check at age sixty were $600, then the marital share would be $200 and his wife's presumptive one-half share would be $100 per month.

If we apply the marital fraction to his retirement pay using years instead of points, however, then with fifteen years of marital pension service and twenty total years of pension service, his pension is 15/20 (or 75 percent) marital. If his check were $600, then the marital portion would be $450 and the presumptive half to his wife would be $225 per month!

31. At the time this book went to print, the military began a multiyear conversion to a new housing compensation system, eliminating the Basic Allowance for Quarters (BAQ) and the Variable Housing Allowance (VHA) in favor of a new Basic Allowance for Housing (BAH) program. Both the existing and the new program are described below, to make this reference as useful as possible for as long as possible.

32. See Exhibit 1, Appendix F.

pay, not just base pay. Knowing these other components of total pay can be essential to litigation of alimony or child support cases,[33] and to property cases involving members who remain on active duty beyond eligibility for retirement.

In addition to base pay, members may receive a Basic Allowance for Quarters, Basic Allowance for Subsistence, a Variable Housing Allowance, and other miscellaneous allowances or forms of special pay. Because some of these are nontaxable, and some benefits are provided that would otherwise be costs taken out of civilian paychecks, military pay is worth somewhat more than its absolute dollar value. Accordingly, there are adjusted civilian equivalencies, known as Basic Military Compensation and Regular Military Compensation, which are discussed below.

It is *not* possible to know actual levels of compensation for a member just by rank; much more specific information about that member's situation, including duty assignment, field, living location and situation, and dependents, is necessary to determine a member's pay.

2. Basic Allowance for Quarters

The Basic Allowance for Quarters (BAQ) is a tax-free addition to take-home military pay, intended to compensate military personnel for the cost of maintaining nonmilitary housing. The rate of compensation varies by rank, and there are separate tables for "with dependents" and "without dependents" members. The most current BAQ rates are shown at the end of the book; these also tend to change annually, as base pay rates change.[34] There is no Federal Insurance Contributions Act (FICA) withholding on BAQ.

Dependents are generally spouses and/or children, and sometimes other relatives (parents, stepchildren, handicapped older child, and so on).

---

33. *See, e.g., In re* Long 921 P.2d 67 (Colo. Ct. App. 1996) (when state child support guidelines called for including "in-kind payments" as well as cash, member's choice to exercise option to receive free housing and utilities on military base permitted court to use amount of BAQ that member could have chosen to receive instead, because the value, one way or another, was part of his income, and his choice to use the benefits effectively increased his income by about 20 percent and relieved him of the primary, necessary, expense of housing).

34. See Exhibit 8, Appendix F.

Generally, the military tracks state laws to determine whether a spouse or child is lawfully "related to" or a "dependent of" a member. Members do not receive BAQ when they and their dependents live in government housing (although they may be eligible for a partial BAQ if on sea or field duty even if they are in government quarters). The military has developed special rules for determining who is entitled to what allowance when a member is married to another member (which can be important in a case involving two members embroiled in a protracted divorce action).

BAQ is a significant component of total compensation, and should certainly be included in any calculation of income available for payment of support. It is not uncommon for members to move back into government housing during a divorce, leaving their legal dependents in nongovernment quarters. Continuing to appear are anecdotal accounts of courts that have incorrectly used the BAQ amount as the total sum payable for maintenance in such situations, apparently not realizing that the BAQ was never intended to define a "reasonable" maintenance cost for dependents, but was conceived and implemented as a partial offset for the costs of housing for a member and a member's dependents, in conjunction with basic pay.

✎ **Practice Tip:** Whether a member is or is *not* receiving BAQ during a divorce, counsel should examine whether any court orders would be significantly altered if the impending divorce, custody order, or member relocation caused the member's pay to change. If there would be any significant change, it might be preferable to do some advance planning by putting into the order an alternative level of support order to plan for such a change of circumstances. In this way, it might be possible to avoid a return to court for modification.

3. Basic Allowance for Subsistence

The Basic Allowance for Subsistence (BAS) is a tax-free addition to take-home military pay, intended to compensate military personnel when they are on leave or authorized to mess separately, when rations in kind are not available, or when they are assigned to duty under emergency conditions when no government rations are available. The rate of compensation varies by status as "enlisted" or "officer" rank; officers have a monthly allowance, while enlisted members have a daily rate that varies according to why it is being received. The most current available BAS rates are provided at the end of the book; historically, they have changed annually along with basic pay rates.[35] There is no FICA withholding on BAS.

The amounts involved in a BAS adjustment are fairly small, and will not make a significant difference to most determinations of support payable based on income. Still, the BAS should be considered in appropriate cases.

On January 1, 1998, the military began to phase in a new BAS system, intended to correct pay inequities among enlisted service members and to link future changes in BAS to an "appropriate and credible" food cost index. Generally, the changes were expected to increase the level of the subsistence allowance for enlisted personnel receiving in-kind subsistence and no BAS.

The reform terminated the linkage between the subsistence allowance growth and increases in basic pay. Interestingly, the problem here was the reverse of that in the BAQ/Variable Housing Allowance situation, because the military concluded that the BAS had increased faster than food costs, essentially overcompensating members. The new BAS program ties changes in the subsistence allowance to an independent U.S. Department of Agriculture (USDA) index reflecting "the true cost of food."

The phase-in was predicted to take four to six years, and be complete when the enlisted BAS rate was equal to the USDA food plan index. When complete, the BAS reform was intended to entitle all enlisted service members to full BAS at all times, once they finished basic training.

The military designed the reformed system to allow for a uniform payment of BAS to members when they are deployed, and to end complaints of "pay inequity" between those enlisted members receiving BAS and those receiving in-kind subsistence. Under the new system, enlisted members receiving in-kind subsistence in a government dining facility also receive a "partial BAS," based on the difference between BAS and the equivalent value of the government-provided meals.

4. Variable Housing Allowance

The Variable Housing Allowance (VHA) is intended to protect members from the variable prices for similar housing in different areas of the

---

35. See Exhibit 9, Appendix F.

country. It is a tax-free allowance that varies in amount by rank and by location. It is paid only to members who are not in government housing and who receive BAQ; there are two sets of tables, one for those with dependents and one for those without dependents. Reviews of housing costs for adjustments of the VHA are conducted semiannually. Defense department sources indicate that about a third of all military personnel in the continental United States receive some level of VHA.

The VHA is intended, essentially, to eliminate the effect of variations in housing costs, so that members enjoy the same real income whether stationed where housing is cheap or where it is expensive.

As with BAQ, the sums involved in VHA are often a significant portion of total monthly compensation. Of course, whether it is a factor at all will vary from case to case, depending upon whether the member is at a location accorded a significant VHA adjustment, and whether in the circumstances of the case the allowance is being claimed. The comments above regarding BAQ and advance planning are equally applicable here.

Over the years, there were several proposals to eliminate the VHA and replace it with some other form of pay variation according to location, but none met with sufficient support in the military, and Congress, to result in any actual change until 1998.

5. Basic Allowance for Housing

On January 1, 1998, the services began a six-year phase-in of a new housing allowance system called the Basic Allowance for Housing (BAH), a single monthly payment meant to replace separate payments of VHA and BAQ. The services had been receiving complaints for some time that the old housing allowance system was unable to keep up with housing costs, causing members to pay too much in out-of-pocket costs.

BAH is based on rental costs by pay grade, dependency status (with dependents or without dependents), and location, and is supposed to provide members with housing compensation based on comparable civilian costs of housing. Civilian comparability considers both salary and location. During the phase-in period, those who had larger benefits under the old BAQ/VHA system retain the benefit levels previously enjoyed, as long as their "status" remains unchanged (location, rank, and so on). Increases in allowances in the new system are tied to the growth of housing costs, thus protecting members from erosion of benefits.

The BAH rates for 1998 were based largely on the VHA housing census conducted in 1997, but the phase-in was designed to shift increasingly to the numbers produced by the new data and methodology. The BAH for a given pay grade and dependency status in a specific geographic location is the difference between the local average monthly cost of housing for that pay grade and dependency status and a percentage between 15 percent and 20 percent of the nationwide average monthly cost of housing for that pay grade.

The military predicts that by the end of the phase-in, the plan should produce increases in housing allowances in high-cost housing areas, decreases in housing allowances in medium to low-cost housing areas, increases in housing allowances for many enlisted grades, and decreases in housing allowances for many officer grades.

6. Miscellaneous Allowances and Special-Pay Provisions

There are many other allowances that might be involved in a given case, including allowances for uniform and civilian clothing, family separation and overseas housing and stations, dislocation, travel, and transportation. Again, the peculiar circumstances of the parties involved must be examined by counsel before a determination can be made about whether there are additional income sources to consider.

Bonuses are frequently payable for enlistment and reenlistment, or for special proficiency. There are additional bonuses for members who are trained in particularly valuable fields, making it more important to the services to retain them. Counsel should make themselves aware if during a case the member has recently received such a bonus, or is about to do so.

There are a host of special-pay classes, which generate additional income to members who perform certain duties based on rank and years of service. These include flight pay, sea pay, special-assignment pay, hazardous-duty pay, and hostile-fire/imminent-danger pay. Obviously, information specific to the member must be acquired to determine which, if any, of these special-pay classes may be involved in a particular case.

The simplest and most straightforward way to obtain information about a member's current pay is to review the Leave and Earnings Statement (LES) issued monthly to most members. (Those who have arranged direct bank deposits of their pay instead get mailed quarterly or annual statements.) The LES provides a listing of gross pay, all special pay and allowances, taxable amounts, any allotments being paid, and the net pay remaining. With an information release signed by the member, a printout of historical information showing the same information can be requested from any military installation through the relevant military pay center.

For some years, extra income has been available to members leaving the services in the form of separation pay or readjustment or severance pay. During the post–Cold War drawdown particularly, there are—and presumably will continue to be—additional special incentives of various sorts for members to leave service rather than continue until their next reenlistment date, or until retirement. These programs are being quickly proposed and altered, but counsel in all active-duty cases should consider benefits for early separation that may be payable in lieu of retirement benefits, and determine the availability of mechanisms for division of those benefits under local law.[36]

The topic of "early-out" payments and how courts have treated them is addressed in greater detail in Chapter Seven, which discusses anticipating changes in status.[37]

7. Basic Military Compensation and Regular Military Compensation

As noted above, several components of compensation to military members are nontaxable. Additionally, there are various other hidden forms of compensation, such as use of commissary and exchange stores, medical care for members and dependents, potential accrual of retirement benefits, built-in dependency and indemnity compensation, survivor benefits, life insurance, and other items. All these hidden forms of compensation would require payments of money—one way or another—if enjoyed by civilian public or private-sector employees. This makes military salaries less directly comparable to those of civilians.

---

36. This common-sense approach has been followed in many jurisdictions by unpublished trial level or appellate opinions. *See, e.g.,* Order Dismissing Appeal in Case No. 19756, Banta v. Banta, (Nev. Sup. Ct., Mar. 9, 1989) (decree requiring division of pension "when [h]usband receives it" compels immediate division when husband got severance pay after being fired). The subject is explored at length in Subsection 1(b) of Section B of Chapter Seven.

37. See Subsection 1(b), Section B, Chapter Seven.

The Department of Defense Actuary, however, devised a means of reasonable comparison by adding together basic pay, quarters allowance (cash or in-kind), a subsistence allowance (cash or in-kind), and the federal tax advantages attributable to the nontaxable allowances. This is the Basic Military Compensation (BMC), which varies by rank and years of service. A table showing most current BMC levels available (the figures are updated annually) is included at the end of the book.[38] Updated information can be obtained from the Department of Defense Actuary or in the almanacs listed at the end of the book, which reprint the official tables.

A member's BMC, plus that member's VHA, if any, gives a reasonable comparison of that member's military pay with civilian figures.[39] The BMC, when added to the *average* VHA (and the added tax advantage of that benefit) yields the Regular Military Compensation (RMC).[40] Although there does not appear to be much appellate discussion of these figures (probably because the numbers involved are not large enough to warrant the costs of appeal), anecdotal accounts indicate that very few lawyers even suggest basing child and spousal support on these adjusted figures.

    ✑ **Practice Tip:** Lawyers representing nonmember spouses should suggest using BMC or RMC as the base figures for calculating child support and spousal support under state guidelines, because those figures are determined by the military authorities to be more accurate representations of the value of military pay, and because the recipients of such awards will be in the "real world" where the financial equivalencies will be largely unavailable. Member's lawyers should note that spouses and children still receive some of those benefits, such as medical and commissary access.

The Department of Defense Actuary estimates that basic pay comprises only 77 percent of BMC, or 73 percent of RMC.[41] Because military

---

38. See Exhibit 10, Appendix F.
39. FY 1997 REPORT, *supra* note 3, at 7.
40. See Exhibit 11, Appendix F. Apparently because of some uncertainties involved in the changeover from a BAQ/VHA system to the BAH system, only BMC (not RMC) tables were available for 1998. The appendices therefore include both 1997 and 1998 information, as available.
41. FY 1997 REPORT, *supra* note 3, at 7.

retired pay is based only on basic pay, it should be noted that the relative value of retired pay as compared with active-duty pay is not as great as it seems. For a twenty-year retiree, retired pay is equal to only about 38 percent of BMC or 35 percent of RMC; for a thirty-year retiree, the figures are 60 percent of BMC or 56 percent of RMC.[42]

---

42. *Id.*

Chapter Four
SUBSTANTIVE LIMITATIONS
AND QUESTIONS

A. IMPORTANCE OF DISTINCTION BETWEEN ALIMONY AND PROPERTY DIVISION

A court order may provide that a former spouse be paid an amount as alimony or child support.[1] Alimony includes, but is not limited to, periodic payments for separate maintenance, spousal support, and maintenance.[2] Alimony does not include a division of property or child support. Child support is defined in the regulations as periodic payments for the support and maintenance of a child or children.[3] Child support includes, but is not limited to, payments to provide for health care, education, recreation, and clothing, or to meet other specific needs of such child or children.[4]

Unlike a property division (discussed below), there is no minimum requirement regarding the duration of the marriage during active-duty years for enforcement of alimony or child support by direct payment. Even if the member and the former spouse marry after the member retires, the former spouse may obtain direct payment of such awards from retired pay.

The origin of this particular oddity of the Uniformed Services Former Spouses Protection Act (USFSPA) is fairly clear, and is explained in a later section of this chapter.[5] The distinction in enforceability has, of course, not been lost on litigators in the field. It is not unusual, in cases in which a property division would be unenforceable, to find an "unmodifiable alimony" clause inserted where the property division clause

---

1. 10 U.S.C. §§ 1408(a)(2)(B)(i)–(ii).
2. 32 C.F.R. § 63.3(a).
3. *Id.* § 63.3(c).
4. *Id.* The regulations limit the definition to being "subject to and in accordance with State law under 42 U.S.C. § 662(b)."
5. See Section E, entitled "The 'Ten-Year' Compromise and Its Ramifications."

would have gone. An example of such a clause is contained in the forms section at the end of the book.[6]

For the moment, it is sufficient to note that the *title* of an award made by stipulation of counsel or court order could well be determinative of the ultimate ability of a former spouse to obtain enforcement of the award. Most changes to the USFSPA have ignored these litigation practicalities, and have focused upon the concept of dividing military retired pay as property.

Additionally, as discussed below, the law does *not* provide that an order awarding alimony or child support has to provide specifically that payments are to be made in dollars or as a percentage of retired pay "from the disposable retired pay of a member."[7] Property awards must do so to satisfy the definition of "court order." Unfortunately, anecdotal accounts suggest that the distinction is lost on the military pay center, which apparently holds spousal support and child support orders to the same restrictions as property awards. No known published opinion has ordered the pay center to honor a "dollar plus percentage" award in a support case, although in theory such an award should be entirely enforceable; presumably, when the pay center has provided a roadblock, the path of least resistance (and cost) has been to obtain a "clarifying order" rather than attempting to force the pay center to comply.

B. JURISDICTION: SPECIAL RULES

Special jurisdictional rules must be followed in military cases to get an enforceable order for division of the benefits as property (these rules do not restrict alimony or child support orders). In other public and private plans, any state court judgment valid under the laws of the state where it was entered is generally enforceable to divide retirement benefits; this is not true for military retirement benefits.

It is critically important for practitioners to understand these rules clearly—especially counsel to a former spouse filing against a member who is on active duty or who resides, even in part, outside the jurisdiction. If the court fails to achieve proper jurisdiction over the member under the terms of *both* state law and the USFSPA, the resulting decree provisions

---

6. See Section B, Chapter Eight.
7. See 10 U.S.C. § 1408(a)(2)(C).

purporting to divide military retired pay could be entirely disregarded. Given the uncertainties inherent in any form of partition or other corrective action,[8] such a mistake could be fatal to the former spouse's claim.

This is so because the USFSPA by its own terms divests state courts of power to divide retired pay as property unless the jurisdictional provisions of the act are satisfied.[9] The rules are applied in a manner similar to that familiar to practitioners in state courts for establishing *personal* jurisdiction over the member. Case law suggests, however, that in determining whether these jurisdictional requirements have been met, the court is determining whether it has *subject matter* jurisdiction to make valid orders concerning retired pay.[10]

These rules originated from congressional fear of forum shopping by former spouses eager to divide military retirement benefits, and from concern that members would have the retirement benefits disposed of in a state in which the member had no connection other than being present by reason of military orders.[11] The concerns underlying those "anti-forum-shopping" rules have largely disappeared due to the near-universal adoption of community property and equitable distribution provisions by the states. (There does not appear to be any evidence that the concerns ever had a foundation in any actual cases.) The federal jurisdictional rules have, however, created problems apparently not anticipated when they were adopted—Congress created exactly the sort of forum-shopping problem that it intended to avoid.

For example, several states have declared that their "long-arm" statutes, otherwise applicable in divorce actions, were preempted by the USFSPA regarding jurisdiction of the state courts over the retirement benefits.[12] Because those decisions frequently removed the divorce court's jurisdiction over the most valuable asset of a military marriage, the end result was disproportionate asset divisions in favor of the members.

---

8. See Section H, Chapter Seven.
9. 10 U.S.C. § 1408(c)(4).
10. *See* Steel v. United States, 813 F.2d 1545 (9th Cir. 1987); Lewis v. Lewis, 695 F. Supp. 1089 (D. Nev. 1988).
11. *See* H.R. CONF. REP. NO. 97-749, 2d Sess. (1982), *reprinted in* 1982 U.S. C.C.A.N. 1571; *see also In re* Marriage of McDonough, 183 Cal. App. 3d 52, 227 Cal. Rptr. 872 (Ct. App. 1986).
12. See the discussion of relevant cases in Subsection 4 of this section.

A former spouse alert to these rules could choose to file for divorce wherever the member claimed to be a "resident," to gain federal jurisdiction over the retirement benefits. That state, however, might very well lack jurisdiction under *its own* law to grant a divorce, as it is quite possible that neither party would actually live there at the time of filing. Even if the court had jurisdiction to grant the divorce, the other property and the children of the parties would at least be at an inconvenient location, and could even be outside the scope of the court's power, requiring the former spouse, again, to file a second action in another state.

It seems to be the general rule that the jurisdictional provisions of the USFSPA are inapplicable to cases, decided before *McCarty v. McCarty,* 453 U.S. 210 (1981), in which the military retirement benefits were divided.[13] Anecdotal accounts, however, continue to appear in which those divorced before the USFSPA report that pay centers applied the jurisdictional limitations retroactively, rendering unenforceable those divorce decrees validly obtained under state law before June, 1981, but of course, this did not comply with the *later-enacted* jurisdictional limitations. In such cases, there is no mechanism to bring those decrees into "compliance"; the former spouses can do little but file a federal suit or continue informal efforts to convince the pay centers to recognize their orders.

If nothing at all is said in a court order about division of retired pay, the silence on the matter is construed by the military pay center as an award of the entirety of the military retirement benefits to the member— there is no presumptive share for military benefits as there is for foreign service benefits.[14] The lawyer for the former spouse therefore cannot afford to ignore the jurisdictional issues, and cannot afford to make a mistake in applying them.

This is not to say that there are no strategic choices for the former spouse's lawyer, who—state law permitting—could seek bifurcation of property issues or seek a substantial alimony award.[15] If proper federal jurisdiction over the military member cannot be achieved, and the objective is to divide military retired pay as property, the cautious practitioner should probably advise the former spouse to pursue the divorce action

---

13. *See, e.g.,* Steel v. United States, 813 F.2d 1545, 1552 n.3 (9th Cir. 1987).
14. *See* Pub. L. No. 96-465, § 814, 94 Stat. 2113 (1980).
15. See Subsection 2, Section E, which addresses ways of coping with cases that do not satisfy the ten-year rule.

wherever the military member resides. Although that may be grossly inconvenient, the downside risk if jurisdiction is not established may leave no other reasonable choice.

As discussed at length in Chapter Seven,[16] it is extremely dangerous for a former spouse to take default against a member if the former spouse hopes to divide military retired pay as property. The availability of a default divorce judgment should be treated by the former spouse's lawyer as a malpractice trap.

One simple step that lawyers for former spouses should always take is to ensure that each property settlement agreement and decree recites on its face that the court *has* jurisdiction over the member under both applicable state law *and* the USFSPA.[17] When there is any chance of a challenge, this should be followed up with a specific finding of the kind of jurisdiction the court has (among the three choices set forth below). Including that one sentence can save a great deal of grief at the enforcement stage of the case.

An order dividing retired pay as the property of the member and the former spouse will be honored by the military agencies only if the issuing court exercised personal jurisdiction over the member by reason of (1) residence in the territorial jurisdiction of the court (other than by military assignment), (2) domicile in the territorial jurisdiction of the court, or (3) consent to the jurisdiction of the court.[18] These limitations override state long-arm rules, and must be satisfied in addition to any state law jurisdictional requirements.[19]

It should also be remembered that the time at which jurisdiction is tested is the present (that is, the time of filing of the current proceeding). Previous jurisdiction by the court under the USFSPA—such as when the divorce decree did not dispose of the benefits and a partition action was filed—has been found to be insufficient by the state courts that have considered the question, although there are two federal cases holding otherwise.[20]

---

16. See Section D, Chapter Seven.
17. For a basic form of such a recital, see the sample language in Section B, Chapter Eight.
18. 10 U.S.C. § 1408(c)(4).
19. *See* Kovacich v. Kovacich, 705 S.W.2d 281 (Tex. App. 1986); Tarvin v. Tarvin, 187 Cal. App. 3d 56, 232 Cal. Rptr. 13 (Ct. App. 1986).
20. *See* Messner v. District Court, 104 Nev. 759, 766 P.2d 1320 (1988); *contra*

As noted previously, an exception to the scrutiny of such jurisdictional matters appeared in many *"McCarty*-gap" cases, in which continuing jurisdiction over the persons who had divorced in a given state was simply presumed. In the absence of further gap cases, it seems doubtful that this exception will be either explained or eliminated.

1. Jurisdiction by Residence

Jurisdiction over a member for purposes of a property division is often acquired by reason of the member's residence.[21] A court cannot obtain jurisdiction over a member solely because the member has a military assignment in the territorial jurisdiction of the court.[22] In this common situation, the "something extra" needed for the court to obtain jurisdiction is evidence showing the member's intention to reside in the court's territorial jurisdiction for some reason other than military assignment. Some states use domicile for residence, and vice versa (and in some the two are synonymous), so the factors recited in the following section are applicable here as well.

2. Jurisdiction by Domicile

Any jurisdiction where a member has his or her domicile also qualifies as a competent jurisdiction.[23] A member's domicile is where the member has his or her true, fixed, and permanent home. That home would be the home to which, whenever the member is absent, he or she intends to return. This concept is fairly similar to that underlying each member's declared "home of record," which is usually the jurisdiction from which the member entered the military, and is the jurisdiction to which the member will return upon leaving the military unless a different location is subsequently declared.

Lewis v. Lewis, 695 F. Supp. 1089 (D. Nev. 1988); Delrie v. Harris, 962 F. Supp. 931 (W.D. La. 1997). These cases are discussed in Subsection 4 of this section.

21. 10 U.S.C. § 1408(c)(4).
22. *Id. In re* Marriage of Hattis, 196 Cal. App. 3d 1162, 242 Cal. Rptr. 410 (Ct. App. 1987).
23. 10 U.S.C. § 1408(c)(4).

Several state courts have noted the presumption that an established domicile in that state remains until proven to have been changed.[24] A member's stated residence on federal and state income tax returns or on service records, or the state where a member votes (or last voted) or has a driver's or other license, could help determine where a member resides or has a permanent domicile.

These factors are not certain to lead to predictable results, however. The question is one of fact, and determining where a member's "true domicile" might be is sometimes an elusive quest.[25]

Different states use different definitions for the concepts of residence and domicile, sometimes entirely reversing the meanings given above. The law of each state potentially involved in a case (especially in potential jurisdictional conflict cases) should be considered.

3. Jurisdiction by Consent

Even if a service member does not have a residence or domicile within the territorial jurisdiction of the court, the member can consent to such jurisdiction.[26] Most courts have held that such consent may be express or implied, but the circumstances in which consent will be found vary somewhat and the case law is not consistent.

It has been generally believed that a member who no longer lived in a jurisdiction in which an action to divide a military retirement was filed could object to the action by means of a "special appearance" at which the court's jurisdiction was contested.[27] Similarly, it has been generally believed that a member could "consent" within the meaning of the

---

24. *See, e.g.,* Gowins v. Gowins, 466 So. 2d 32 (La. 1985); *In re* Marriage of Hattis, 196 Cal. App. 3d 1162, 242 Cal. Rptr. 410 (Ct. App. 1987).
25. *See* McMahon v. McMahon, 31 Mass. App. Ct. 504, 579 N.E.2d 1379 (App. Ct. 1991) (trial court correctly found Massachusetts to be retired member's domicile when both parties raised and married in state, returned to state throughout service, bought a home there, and when member had himself assigned there from 1984 until his retirement—despite member's tax declaration of Florida as his domicile and his registration to vote in that other state).
26. *Id.*
27. *See, e.g.,* Barrett v. Barrett, 715 S.W.2d 110 (Tex. App. 1986).

USFSPA by making a "general appearance" in the case under state law.[28] That is still the approach taken in most places, but the analysis has been made less certain by a California appellate court that has adopted its own approach in a series of cases discussed in the next section.

It should be reemphasized that these jurisdictional requirements apply only to divisions of retired pay as property. A court may lack jurisdiction under the USFSPA to divide the retired pay as property but still have jurisdiction under its own law to issue other valid orders concerning the member (for example, child or spousal support orders). Those orders can then be applied against military retired pay. As démonstrated in the sample decree language included at the end of this book,[29] sometimes alimony can be substituted for a property division.

4. Cases of Significance Addressing Jurisdictional Questions

In *Kovacich v. Kovacich,*[30] a Texas intermediate appellate court examined the question of jurisdiction in the context of a partition action filed by the former spouse in the state that had rendered a divorce decree that silently omitted disposition of the military retirement benefits.[31] The court became the first in what would become a trend, holding that a state court lacks power to divide military retirement benefits if a military member does not satisfy the jurisdictional criteria at the time of commencement of the suit then before the court.

The court stressed that the former spouse was *entitled* to a portion of the military retirement benefits, but the court felt constrained to require her to go elsewhere to seek enforcement of her entitlement. Though finding it could not compel the former husband's presence in Texas, the court

---

28. *See, e.g.,* Kildea v. Kildea, ____ Wis. 2d ____ 420 N.W.2d 391 (Ct. App. 1988); *In re* Marriage of Parks, 48 Wash. App. 166, 737 P.2d 1316 (Ct. App. 1987); *In re* Marriage of Fairfull 161 Cal. App 3d 532, 207 Cal. Rptr. 523 (Ct. App. 1984). Even a botched "special appearance" can constitute a general appearance giving the court authority to divide retired pay under the act. *See* Seely v. Seely, 690 S.W.2d 626 (Tex. App. 1985).

29. See Section B, Chapter Eight.

30. 705 S.W.2d 281 (Tex. App. 1986).

31. For a fuller explanation of partition actions, see Section H, Chapter Seven.

cautioned that "this ruling in no way affects Barbara's continuing status as a tenant in common or joint owner of the military retirement benefits."[32]

In other words, the court differentiated between the *character* of the property (which it obviously thought the state with jurisdictional power would recognize as joint) and the *procedural* limitation of where the action could be brought.

Six months later, a California intermediate appellate court, again in a partition action, reached much the same conclusion. In *Tarvin v. Tarvin*,[33] the court acknowledged that the language from which it implied preemption stemmed from congressional "concerns about 'forum-shopping' spouses who might seek to divide the military pension in a state lacking substantial contacts with the pensioner." Despite its conclusion that the underlying purpose of the statute was not served by barring the state that granted the divorce from partitioning benefits omitted from the divorce decree, the court found that it was obligated to dismiss the case for lack of jurisdiction.

Courts that have felt bound to follow *Tarvin* have noted that the question is one of ascertaining congressional intent; in *Hattis v. Hattis*,[34] the court held that "there are strong arguments to commend the flexible minimum contacts approach. . . . The rights accorded by USFSPA to the spouses of military personnel may ring hollow if it is impossible or prohibitively expensive to enforce them."[35] Believing there to be no federal guidance to the contrary, however, the *Hattis* court felt obliged to hold that there was no personal jurisdiction over the defendant.

From a logical standpoint, the congressional objective of preventing forum shopping is not furthered by implying preemption of actions for partition in the court that rendered the divorce. No such implication was seen as a barrier in correction of *McCarty*-gap cases.[36] Nevertheless, other

---

32. *See Kovacich,* 705 S.W.2d at 283.
33. 187 Cal. App. 3d 56, 232 Cal. Rptr. 13 (Ct. App. 1986).
34. 196 Cal. App. 3d 1162, 242 Cal. Rptr. 410 (Ct. App. 1987).
35. *Id.* at 414–15 (Benke, J., concurring and dissenting).
36. The California intermediate appellate court examined this situation when it decided *In re Marriage of McDonough,* 183 Cal. App. 3d 45, 227 Cal. Rptr. 872 (Ct. App. 1986). In that case, the service member generally appeared in the pre-*McCarty* dissolution proceedings. The military retirement

courts in other states have reached the same conclusion as the courts of Texas and California in partition actions, making the *Kovacich-Tarvin* result an essentially unchallenged result in the state courts.[37]

A short contrary line of authority exists in the federal courts, based on a nonpartition case. In *Steel v. United States,*[38] the Ninth Circuit Court of Appeals was in the peculiar position of determining which of two competing divorce court orders should be honored. The court examined 10 U.S.C. § 1408(c)(1) and noted that

> [a] careful reading reveals that this provision is a limitation on subject-matter rather than personal jurisdiction. A court otherwise having jurisdiction of the parties is not allowed to invoke the powers of [USFSPA] unless personal jurisdiction has been acquired by domicile or consent or residence other than by military assignment.[39]

In 1987, Nevada enacted a specific statute permitting the partition of military retirement benefits omitted from decrees of divorce.[40] In *Lewis v.*

---

benefits were not explicitly in issue, although the court had jurisdiction over all property of the parties, including those benefits. *See* 183 Cal. App. 3d at 50–51, 227 Cal. Rptr. at 874–75. The service member modified the property division during the *McCarty* gap to award all military retirement benefits to him as his sole and separate property; he was then transferred out of state. *Id.*

Subsequently, the former spouse filed a motion under Cal. Civ. Code § 5124, but was denied relief in the lower court on the ground that 10 U.S.C. § 1408(c)(4) preempted the state's power to grant partition of the pension. In reversing, the appellate court found that the service member's consent to California's division of marital property gave the state continuing personal jurisdiction over him for the purpose of distributing that property, while subject matter jurisdiction was provided by Section 5124 and the USFSPA. 183 Cal. App. 3d at 52, 227 Cal. Rptr. at 876.

37. *See, e.g.,* Sparks v. Caldwell, 104 N.M. 475, 723 P.2d 244 (1986); Messner v. District Court, 104 Nev. 759, 766 P.2d 1320 (1988).

38. 813 F.2d 1545 (9th Cir. 1987).

39. *Steel,* 813 F.2d at 1552.

40. The statute was enacted as Nev. Rev. Stat. § 125.161. After a fierce lobbying campaign by former military members, the statute was repealed in 1989. *See* 1989 Nev. Stats. ch. 34, § 1, at 63; *see also* Willick, *Res Judicata in Nevada Divorce Law: An Invitation to Fraud,* 4 Nev. Fam. L. Rep., Spr. 1989, at 1.

Lewis,[41] a former spouse sought partition of military retirement benefits omitted from a Nevada decree against a member who had relocated to Utah. The partition case brought under the statute was removed to federal court, where the member sought dismissal on jurisdictional grounds.

Quoting the above language from *Steel,* the federal district court stated that because the USFSPA concerned only subject matter jurisdiction, the question of personal jurisdiction was one of state law. The court noted that the Nevada statute gave jurisdiction to the state trial courts for the partition action if at the time of divorce the court had properly exercised personal jurisdiction over the member.

The notable aspect of the *Lewis* case is that the federal court was perfectly willing to let the state exercise jurisdiction for partition when it had jurisdiction at the time of divorce, if the state wished to do so.[42] This reasoning mirrors that of the *McCarty*-gap cases, such as *McDonough,* discussed above.

Essentially the same conclusion was reached by another federal district court in *Delrie v. Harris,*[43] when the court approved the Louisiana long-arm statutory reach over a nonresident defendant under the concept of continuing jurisdiction from the divorce (which omitted division of the military retirement benefits) thirty-three years earlier. The court found that the jurisdictional limitations of 10 U.S.C. § 1408(c)(4) did not act as "heightened requirements for personal jurisdiction," but that the federal law was "a substantive requirement linked to 10 U.S.C. § 1408(c)(1), which goes to a court's initial 'treating' of military retired pay as property."[44]

However, having found no problem with personal jurisdiction, the *Delrie* court nevertheless found that the former spouse had no remedy, because the parties' 1963 divorce had not treated—or reserved jurisdiction to treat—the military retired pay as property, and the divorce preceded June 25, 1981.[45]

---

41. 695 F. Supp. 1089 (D. Nev. 1988).
42. It is worth noting that the decision in *Lewis* preceded that in *Messner,* which had a directly opposite holding and did not even acknowledge the existence of the *Lewis* opinion.
43. 962 F. Supp. 931 (W.D. La. 1997).
44. *Delrie,* 962 F. Supp. at 934.
45. The case hinged on the proper interpretation of 10 U.S.C. § 1408(c)(1), which provides (after the 1991 amendments) that a court lacks jurisdiction

The most recent significant developments in the jurisdictional area have been in California, where one appellate district has decided that the USFSPA essentially gives the member power to make a general appearance for all purposes under state law while still reserving the separate right to consent or not consent to the court's exercise of jurisdiction over the division of military retirement benefits. In *Tucker v. Tucker,*[46] the trial court was faced with an original divorce action in which the service member specifically requested that the court set aside the retirement benefits as his separate property. Child custody, visitation, and support were also in issue.

The member described his appearance as "special," despite his active participation in the contest of all other matters. The court nevertheless found that the member's presence in the jurisdiction was solely because of military assignment, and that he never formed the intent to make California his domicile. Turning to the issue of implied consent, the court perceived an ambiguity in the USFSPA, about what constitutes consent. Noting the judicial economy of litigating the retirement issues in the same jurisdiction as the custody and support issues, the court briefly acknowledged rulings from Louisiana, Texas, and another California appellate district holding that consent to litigation of the case constituted consent to litigation of the military retirement benefits.[47]

to treat disposable pay as property if the decree was issued before June 25, 1981, and did not treat, or reserve jurisdiction to treat, the retired pay as property. Specifically, the statutory language addresses the final decree, where it includes the parenthetical phrase "(including a court ordered, ratified, or approved property settlement incident to such decree)." The question was whether the parenthetical language illustrates the word "decree" or limits it. The former spouse argued that the language was limiting, and that because her divorce decree included no property settlement, the restriction did not apply to her. The federal court noted that at least one Louisiana state court had agreed with this interpretation (*Meche v. Meche,* 635 So. 2d 614 (La. Ct. App. 1994), but that two had not. *See* White v. White, 623 So. 2d 31 (La. Ct. App. 1993); Johnson v. Johnson, 605 So. 2d 1157 (La. Ct. App. 1994). The federal court ruled that the amendments to the USFSPA barred the partition suit, and that under *Mansell,* the courts were not to "eviscerate a federal statute in order to achieve a sympathetic result," regardless of the economic harm inflicted on former military spouses. *See also* Kemp v. Department of Defense, 857 F. Supp. 32 (W.D. La. 1994).

46. 226 Cal. App. 3d 1249, 277 Cal. Rptr. 403 (Ct. App. 1991).
47. *Tucker,* 226 Cal. App. 3d at 1255, 277 Cal. Rptr. at 406 (citing *In re* Mar-

The court chose instead to interpret its own earlier holding in *Hattis v. Hattis*[48] as a statement that a military member can simultaneously agree that a state "has jurisdiction over nonpension issues and at the same time argue [that a state] has no power to divide his or her military pension."[49] Going further, the court concluded that Section 1408(c)(4) of the USFSPA does not really address jurisdiction at all, but rather provides a defense analogous to the doctrine of forum non conveniens. In a final footnote, the court commented that a member's objection might be seen most properly as based on subject matter, rather than personal, jurisdiction.[50]

The *Tucker* court's analysis is not unprecedented,[51] but it is notable. The anti–forum-shopping rules were never really necessary, because no state permits division of any property rights without sufficient minimum contacts to satisfy constitutional concerns. Unfortunately, especially in cases such as *Tucker,* the jurisdictional limitations are producing exactly the harm they were intended to prevent, but in reverse—they provide a means for manipulation of otherwise adequate jurisdiction as a tactical weapon to prevent the proper court from hearing all aspects of a case that it should decide.

Since *Tucker,* no court has apparently been willing to embrace that court's litigate-everything-but-this holding, even when approvingly citing that court's earlier holding in *Hattis.* Later opinions, while noting the dispositional authority of the USFSPA on the question of jurisdiction, have more logically concluded that the mandate of the act is to require a finding of residence or domicile or consent.[52]

---

riage of Jacobson, 161 Cal. App. 3d 465, 207 Cal. Rptr. 512 (1984)); Gowins v. Gowins, 466 So. 2d 32 (La. 1985); Seeley v. Seeley, 690 S.W.2d 626 (Tex. App. 1985).

48. 196 Cal. App. 3d 1162, 242 Cal. Rptr. 410 (Ct. App. 1987).
49. *Tucker,* 226 Cal. App. 3d at 1256, 277 Cal. Rptr. at 407.
50. *Tucker,* 226 Cal. App. 3d at 1258 n.1, 277 Cal. Rptr. at 408 n.1.
51. In *McHugh v. McHugh,* 115 Idaho 198, 766 P.2d 133 (1988), a minority of the court would have held that bifurcation of divorce actions is required, so that all matters *except* that of military retirement can be resolved when the court has personal jurisdiction, but that one issue may be resolved only in the jurisdiction in which the member happens to live.
52. *See, e.g., In re* Akins, 932 P.2d 863 (Colo. Ct. App. 1997) (citing *Hattis,* ignoring *Tucker,* and holding that when out-of-state service member does not express consent to jurisdiction of court, question is whether domicile or residence can be established, or whether "consent" can be made out;

This seems to be one of those interpretive areas under the USFSPA that will ultimately require resolution by the U.S. Supreme Court if it is to be resolved at all. Until that time, the state courts can reasonably be expected to continue issuing conflicting opinions.

C. MISCELLANEOUS RESTRICTIONS AND LIMITATIONS

1. Courts of Competent Jurisdiction

A former spouse of a member must have been a party to a divorce, dissolution, annulment, or legal separation case in a court of competent jurisdiction to have an opportunity to receive retired pay benefits.[53] Courts of competent jurisdiction include those of the fifty states, the District of Columbia, the Commonwealth of Puerto Rico, Guam, American Samoa, the Virgin Islands, the Northern Mariana Islands, and the Trust Territory of the Pacific Islands.[54]

A court of competent jurisdiction also includes any court of the United States.[55] Although those courts do not have jurisdiction to enter divorces, military retirement cases have found their way into the federal courts.[56] United States courts include the Supreme Court of the United States, U.S. Courts of Appeals, U.S. District Courts, and other courts created by acts of Congress.[57]

Any court of competent jurisdiction of a foreign country would also be a court of competent jurisdiction, if an appropriate agreement between the United States and that foreign country was in place.[58] Such an agree-

---

such consent "is not whether the military member simply waived his right to contest personal jurisdiction under state procedural rules. Rather, the statutory language requires some form of affirmative conduct demonstrating express or implied consent to general in personam jurisdiction").

53. 10 U.S.C. § 1408(a)(1).
54. *Id.* § 1408(a)(1)(A); 32 C.F.R. § 63.3(d).
55. 10 U.S.C. § 1408(a)(1)(B).
56. *See, e.g.,* Kirby v. Mellenger, 830 F.2d 176 (11th Cir. 1987).
57. 28 U.S.C. § 451.
58. 10 U.S.C. § 1408(a)(1)(C). It does not appear that any country has such a treaty with the United States. If it is possible to interpret an existing treaty as providing for such recognition, it does not appear that any U.S. court has so held.

ment would require the United States to honor orders from that country's courts relating to child support, alimony, or property division incident to divorce, dissolution, annulment, or legal separation proceedings.[59] It does not appear that, at this time, there is any country with which the United States has such an agreement or treaty.

The competent-jurisdiction requirement is entirely distinct from the necessity of having federal jurisdiction over the member. The former is required for any order seeking to invoke the USFSPA,[60] while the latter is required only for a division of retired pay as property.[61]

2. Nonappealability

To be an effective court order, a decree of divorce, dissolution, annulment, or legal separation must be final.[62] A decree is final if

- no appeal may be taken from it, or no appeal has been taken within the time allowed under applicable law for the taking of an appeal, or
- a timely appeal was taken and finally decided.

EXAMPLE

Judy and David are divorced in accordance with state law, and Judy is granted alimony. Judy applies for direct payment of the alimony from the military pay center, but David appeals the entry of the decree within the time limit for appeals. The divorce decree would not qualify as a court order until a decision on the appeal was entered.

Even if Judy had been granted a *temporary* support order, she could not get direct payment under the USFSPA. Though such a temporary order is probably nonappealable, it does not fulfill the USFSPA's requirement that a court order be a final decree. Of course, her inability

---

59. *Id.* § 1408(a)(1)(C).
60. *Id.* § 1408(b)(2)(A).
61. *Id.* § 1408(c)(4).
62. *Id.* §§ 1408(a)(2)–(3).

to proceed during the appeal under the USFSPA does not mean that Judy is without remedies.[63]

The service secretaries will not independently research whether an order, which on its face appears to be a valid decree, is in fact valid.[64] To satisfy the requirement of being issued "in accordance with the laws of the jurisdiction," the order must simply have nothing on its face providing reasonable notice that it is *not* valid.[65]

D. THE CONUNDRUM OF "DISPOSABLE" PAY

The language of the USFSPA provides that a portion of only *disposable* retired pay be paid to a former spouse. "Disposable retired pay" is defined in three different ways, depending upon the date of the final decree. The time periods are (1) from passage of the USFSPA until the *Mansell* decision (May 30, 1989), (2) from that decision until the 1990 amendments became effective (February 4, 1991), and (3) thereafter, each of which is discussed at length below. The concept of disposable pay is central to a complete understanding of this area of the law.

It should be remembered that resolving the question of how much pay is "disposable" may not be the end of a collection analysis. The amount of disposable pay may not be identical to the cash actually received; if state law restricts collection to a portion of cash actually reaching the member, collection could be less. At least for decrees final on or after May 30, 1989, a member's current or future claim of a disability rating could alter the disposable pay available to the spouse. The lawyer for the spouse (who is the party at risk) has a burden of careful drafting in anticipation of such a change in status.[66]

---

63. If David was still on active duty, Judy could request a statutory support allotment under 42 U.S.C. § 665. If David was already retired, Judy might have to reduce any arrears to judgment and then apply for garnishment. The procedures for garnishment are discussed in Subsection 3, Section D, Chapter Five.
64. The process by which a member or former spouse can object to a determination by the service secretary is explained in Section J, Chapter Seven.
65. 32 C.F.R. §§ 63.6(c)(1)–(2).
66. See Subsection 4, Section B, Chapter Seven.

1. Decrees Final before May 30, 1989

For divorces in which the court order became effective *before* February 4, 1991, disposable pay is defined[67] as the total monthly retired pay to which the member is entitled, less the following amounts:

- amounts owed by the member to the United States,[68]
- amounts that are required to be, and are, deducted from retired pay, including fines and forfeitures ordered by courts-martial or for federal employment taxes,[69] and amounts waived to receive compensation under Title 5[70] or Title 38,[71]
- amounts that are properly withheld for federal, state, and local income taxes, if authorized or required by law,[72] and amounts withheld under 26 U.S.C. § 3402(i),[73]
- for court orders issued before November 14, 1986, payments for government life insurance premiums,[74]

---

67. 10 U.S.C. § 1408(a)(4) (as it existed before the 1991 amendments). The "effective dates" section of the 1991 amendments specified that the changes embodied in the definition of "disposable retired pay" apply only to divorces, dissolutions of marriage, annulments, and legal separations that become effective after the end of the ninety-day period beginning on the date of the enactment of the amendments (that is, ninety days after November 5, 1990, or February 4, 1991).
68. 10 U.S.C. § 1408(a)(4)(A).
69. *Id.* § 1408(a)(4)(B).
70. *Id.;* the waiver referenced would be intended to allow collection of benefits payable under a civil service retirement; *see* 5 U.S.C. §§ 8331 *et seq.,* 8401 *et seq.*
71. 10 U.S.C. § 1408(a)(4)(B); the waiver referenced would be intended to allow collection of benefits payable through the Veteran's Administration; *see* 38 U.S.C. § 314.
72. The deduction from gross retired pay is authorized "to the extent such amounts withheld are not greater than would be authorized if such member claimed all dependents to which he was entitled." 10 U.S.C. § 1408(a)(4)(C).
73. Withholdings under this subsection are deducted from gross pay in figuring disposable pay only if the member "presents evidence of a tax obligation which supports such withholding." *Id.* § 1408(a)(4)(D).
74. *Id.* § 1408(a)(4)(E) (as it existed before November, 1986).

- for court orders issued on or after November 14, 1986, for a member retired for disability, the amount payable to the member under 10 U.S.C. § 61 computed on the basis of the percentage of the member's disability on the date when the member was retired (or placed on the temporary disability retirement list,[75] and
- deductions to provide a survivor's benefits for the *same* person to whom payment is being made pursuant to the court order.[76]

Within this first time period, there is another distinction made for cases involving members retiring for disability under Chapter 61 (10 U.S.C. § 61). The critical date is November 14, 1986, the effective date of the 1986 amendments. The USFSPA, before those amendments, characterized all pay received by such members as disability pay, even though only a portion of the retired pay received by the member was *for* the disability. Because such pay was not considered part of disposable pay, there was effectively *no* division of retired pay if a member was retired for disability under Chapter 61 before November 14, 1986.

Before May 30, 1989, the courts of several states considered the exclusion of disability retired pay to be merely a payment limitation, rather than a jurisdictional limitation, and awarded spouses the share of the regular retired pay that *would have* been available if the member had not waived it in favor of obtaining disability retired pay.[77]

The drafters of the 1986 amendments intended to permit former spouses in such situations to obtain new orders dividing the *nondisability portion* of the retirement benefits as defined in the 1986 amendments.[78] The regulations seem to provide otherwise, however, and at least some of the military pay centers did not honor such new orders. Nothing would

---

75. *Id.* § 1408(a)(4)(E) (as it existed before the 1991 amendments); 32 C.F.R. § 63.6(e)(2)(vi).
76. 10 U.S.C. § 1408(a)(4)(F) (which was redesignated as Section 1408(a)(4)(D) by the 1991 amendments). The Survivor's Benefit Plan is discussed in greater detail in Chapter Six.
77. *See, e.g., In re* Marriage of Mastropaolo, 166 Cal. App. 3d 953, 213 Cal. Rptr. 26 (Ct. App.), *cert. denied,* 475 U.S. 1011 (1985); Campbell v. Campbell, 474 So. 2d 1339 (La. Ct. App. 1985).
78. Letter from U.S. Representative Les Aspin to U.S. Representative Bill Cobey (June 12, 1986).

appear to be gained, therefore, by getting a reissued order dividing the nondisability portion of retired pay. Spouses seeking to enforce such awards are apparently restricted to using state law remedies, such as contempt, in seeking enforcement. Further congressional clarification on this point is warranted.

Former spouses who were awarded a portion of retired pay as property after November 14, 1986, can get direct payments from the appropriate service secretary—even if the member is receiving a combination of disability and nondisability retirement—up to the allowable maximum percentage of (nondisability) disposable pay.[79]

That "allowable maximum percentage" of 50 percent applied to *all* court orders served on the service secretaries, whether for child support, alimony, or division of the retired pay as property. The structure of the USFSPA, however, has previously led several courts to conclude that the 50 percent limitation was merely a *direct pay* limitation, and not a restriction on the jurisdiction of state courts to consider the gross amount of retired pay in dividing property between spouses.[80]

The pre-1991 system remains in place for final orders issued before February 4, 1991.[81] Accordingly, the only way for a former spouse divorced before that date to get more than 50 percent of disposable pay is through garnishment.[82] A couple examples illustrate how the calculations were done before and after the 1991 amendments.

EXAMPLE (OLD SYSTEM)

Bob is a military retiree entitled to $1,400 per month in gross retired pay; his authorized deductions for all required purposes total $300. Bob's "disposable retired pay" is therefore $1,100 per month. Alice was Bob's second wife. Under the divorce decree, the maximum amount that may be paid directly to Alice for alimony, child support, property division, or for all three combined, is $550 per month.

---

79. 10 U.S.C. § 1408(a)(4)(C).
80. *See, e.g.,* Casas v. Thompson, 42 Cal. 3d 131, 720 P.2d 921, 228 Cal. Rptr. 33 (1986), *cert. denied,* 479 U.S. 1012 (1987).
81. *See* Pub. L. No. 101-510, § 555(e)(2), 104 Stat. 1485, 1570 (1990).
82. See Subsection 3, Section D, Chapter Five.

If an additional amount of $100 is withheld for payment of premiums to the Survivor's Benefit Plan (SBP) of which Carol, Bob's first wife, is a beneficiary, the total disposable retired pay *as to Alice* is still $1,100. The maximum amount available for direct payment to Alice would still be $550.

If, however, Alice was the designated SBP beneficiary and the same $100 was withheld, the maximum amount available for direct payment to Alice would be $500, because $1,100 (disposable) minus $100 (SBP premium) equals $1,000, and 50 percent of $1,000 is $500.

EXAMPLE (NEW SYSTEM)

The gross monthly retired pay of Donald, a military retiree, is $1,000 per month. Donald's former spouse Daisy is the beneficiary of the SBP pursuant to the divorce court's order. The SBP premium reduces Donald's disposable pay by $100 as to Daisy, but the taxes he has withheld are irrelevant. The total disposable retired pay as to Daisy is $900. The decree requires payments to Daisy of $400 per month as a division of retired pay as property. The designated agent would make direct payments of $400 per month to Daisy, because the 50 percent limitation is not exceeded. The maximum amount that Daisy could have received is $450 per month (50 percent of $900).

---

2. *The* Mansell *Decision*

The significance of the term "disposable pay" was greatly changed by the U.S. Supreme Court on May 30, 1989, in *Mansell v. Mansell*.[83] The case itself addressed the impact of the USFSPA on a pre-*McCarty* property settlement agreement and divorce decree, which had awarded the former spouse an interest in the member's Veteran's Administration (VA) disability benefits.

At the time of divorce, the member had voluntarily waived a corresponding sum of regular retired pay to receive those VA payments, because the disability award was not taxable. In subsequent years, the mem-

---

83. 490 U.S. 581 (1989).

ber sought a court ruling that the former spouse could not share in the VA benefits because the USFSPA permitted division of only disposable pay, and disability benefits were defined in the USFSPA as excluded from disposable pay.

The majority of the Court held that Congress had intended to preempt state law, at least in part, and that the federal law acted to cut off the former spouse's interest in all sums labeled "disability," even if taken in lieu of an equal sum of normal retirement benefits. The Court concluded that as long as state law allowed the merits of the controversy to be reached,[84] federal law prohibited state court division of any more than half of disposable pay as defined by the USFSPA.

Though *Mansell* addressed only disability benefits, the decision stands for the proposition that the USFSPA preempts the power of state courts to *consider*[85] anything more than disposable pay in fixing the property rights of spouses.[86] In other words, the disposable-pay limitation of the USFSPA is a restriction on the subject matter jurisdiction of the state courts.

On remand, the California appellate court decided that the initial decree was res judicata and not subject to being changed under *Mansell*'s interpretation of federal law, despite the division of disability benefits.[87] Other courts have also refused to permit modifications to existing final decrees based on *Mansell*.[88] Thus, the case may have little or no effect on

---

84. The Court noted that whether it was proper to reopen a property settlement to reach the federal question, or whether that reopening should have been blocked by res judicata, was a question of state law over which the Court had no jurisdiction. *Mansell,* 490 U.S. at 586 n.5.

85. The term of art in the statute is "treat."

86. At the congressional hearings leading up to the 1990 amendments, Congress had before it proposed amendments that would have reversed the Supreme Court's interpretation of partial preemption. Although inferring legislative intent from a failure to act is always speculative, Congress may, by failing to act on those proposals, have impliedly concurred in the Court's determination that present law restricts the *substantive jurisdiction* of the state courts to treatment of only disposable pay, rather than gross retired pay.

87. *In re* Marriage of Mansell, 217 Cal. App. 3d 219, 265 Cal. Rptr. 227 (Ct. App. 1989).

88. *See, e.g.,* Toupal v. Toupal, 109 N.M. 774, 790 P.2d 1055 (1990); Berry v. Berry, 786 S.W.2d 672 (Tex. 1990).

the amounts held to be *due* under decrees entered before May 30, 1989, regardless of how much might actually be directly *paid* by the government under those decrees.[89]

During the interim between May 30, 1989, and February 4, 1991, however, *Mansell* prevented any allocation to former spouses of any amounts not included in the definition of disposable pay under the USFSPA, as a matter of limitation on courts' subject matter jurisdiction. Although that continued to be true after the 1990 amendments went into effect, the importance of the limitation was decreased, as explained below.

3. Decrees Final after February 4, 1991

In the 1990 amendments, Congress embraced the Court's *Mansell* analysis and expanded on it, drawing a distinction between the substantive limitation on state court jurisdiction to award a portion of retired pay as property, and the payment limitations found in other provisions of federal law.

Specifically, the 1990 amendments altered the reference limiting payments of disposable retired pay from Subsection (d), which governs all payments by the service secretaries, to Subsection (c), which governs division of retired pay as property.[90] This change removed orders for child support or alimony from the disposable pay limitation, apparently making it possible to obtain direct payment of those amounts even when those sums, in combination with any property award to the former spouse, exceed 50 percent of disposable pay. In other words, on the face of the statute, the 50 percent limitation now applies only to the maximum amount that can be paid to a former spouse by means of direct payment *for a division of retired pay as property.*

Simultaneously, Congress altered the definition of disposable pay in a way that enlarges the amount of gross pay within that definition. For decrees entered on or after February 4, 1991, disposable pay is defined[91]

---

89. It is well known that state courts can use contempt sanctions and other available remedies to enforce orders even when direct payment of sums cannot be diverted from a disabled member to a former spouse. *See* Rose v. Rose, 481 U.S. 619 (1987).

90. 10 U.S.C. § 1408(e)(1).

91. *Id.* § 1408(a)(4).

as the total monthly retired pay to which a member is entitled, less the
following amounts:

- amounts owed by the member to the United States for previous overpayments of retired pay and recoupments required by law resulting
  from entitlement to retired pay,[92]
- amounts deducted from retired pay as a result of forfeitures of retired
  pay ordered by a court martial or as a result of waiver of retired pay
  required by law to receive compensation under Title 5[93] or Title 38,[94]
- for a member retired for disability, amounts payable to the member
  under Chapter 61, computed on the basis of the percentage of the
  member's disability on the date the member retired or was put on the
  temporary disability retired list,[95] and
- amounts deducted to provide survivor's benefits for the *same* person
  to whom payment is being made pursuant to the court order.[96]

Notably removed from the list are taxes withheld. It is hard to over-
state the importance of this change to the lifetime payments to individuals.
For each divorce case before February 4, 1991, the military pay center
withheld taxes from the gross retired pay, divided the posttax amount
between the member and the spouse pursuant to court order, and sent a
check to each. At the end of each year, the member was eligible to claim
a tax credit for amounts withheld on sums ultimately paid to the former
spouse, and the former spouse owed a tax liability for any amounts she
received.

The bottom line of this procedure was to always pay more actual
money to the member, and less to the former spouse, than was shown on
the face of a simple percentage division of the retirement benefits. Many

---

92. *Id.* § 1408(a)(4)(A).
93. *Id.* § 1408(a)(4)(B); the waiver referenced would be intended to allow col-
    lection of benefits payable under a civil service retirement; *see* 5 U.S.C.
    §§ 8331 *et seq.,* 8401 *et seq.*
94. 10 U.S.C. § 1408(a)(4)(B); the waiver referenced would be intended to
    allow collection of benefits payable through the VA; *see* 38 U.S.C. § 314.
95. 10 U.S.C. § 1408(a)(4)(C).
96. *Id.* § 1408(a)(4)(D). The SBP is discussed in greater detail in Section B,
    Chapter Six.

former spouses, not receiving a Form 1099 or W-2P, thought the money they received was "tax free," not realizing that it was their responsibility to account for, and pay taxes on, all sums they received.[97] Many members did not realize they had a yearly tax credit coming (which usually took an accountant to figure out). Most courts were unaware that the payments ordered were being skewed by the phrasing of the act and the tax code.

The amendments, effective for divorces on or after February 4, 1991, addressed all those problems. The change, embodied at 10 U.S.C. § 1408(a)(4), altered the definition of "disposable pay" so that taxes were no longer taken "off the top" before the retirement benefits were divided between spouses. Both spouses are now sent a W-2P form, reflecting what they received during the year and allowing for reasonable tax planning, and courts are permitted to divide what is essentially the gross sums of benefits, which is what most judges thought they had been dividing all along.

EXAMPLE

Linus and Gretchen married before Linus entered military service, and remained married until after Linus retired in 1982. Upon divorce, Gretchen was awarded 50 percent of the disposable retired pay as a division of property, which she has received ever since by direct payment. Subsequently, Linus married Loretta, and they divorced some years later. If Loretta was awarded a portion of the retired pay as property, she would be unable to enforce it by means of direct payment from the pay center, because there was no overlap between the marriage and Linus's military service.

If Loretta was awarded alimony, however, the 1990 amendments may allow payment to her of the amount awarded by the court, despite the payments to Gretchen. The limiting language of 10 U.S.C. § 1408(e)(1) (concerning the maximum amount of disposable retired pay that may be paid under court orders) now restricts only court orders dividing retired pay as property. Additionally, the definition of "disposable pay" has been changed so that taxes are no longer deducted from gross retired pay in determining disposable pay. (See 10 U.S.C. § 1408(a)(4).) Thus, it is particularly likely that Loretta will be able to

---

97. *See* Eatinger v. Commissioner, T.C. 310 (1990).

enforce the decree, at least to some extent, because a larger percentage of gross retired pay is considered "disposable" under the newer definition.

The actual impact of these changes on amounts paid by the government to some former spouses might be limited. All court orders, for direct payment or garnishment, still have a payment limitation of 65 percent, but Congress changed the sum to which the 65 percent applies from "disposable pay" to "remuneration for employment that is payable by the United States."[98] The ramifications of this change are explored below.[99]

For the purpose of this discussion, however, it should be noted that there may be little or no difference in a given case between 50 percent of disposable (even without tax withholdings deducted, because any spousal share is not counted at all) and 65 percent of remuneration for employment (because tax withholdings are deducted, and the spousal share still is not counted at all).

Practitioners are faced with determining the amount that *should* be paid under the disposable analysis, and then seeking to collect it by other (state law) means if it is not actually paid by the military pay center. Cautious practitioners representing former spouses will probably seek reservations of jurisdiction over spousal support even more often, in an effort to cope with the uncertainties created by the USFSPA.

Under both the older and newer versions of the 50 percent of disposable limitation, military retirement is not treated like civilian or other government retirement plans. Under most state and federal laws, a domestic relations court can order up to 100 percent of the retirement benefits to be paid to the former spouse.[100]

E. THE "TEN-YEAR" COMPROMISE AND ITS RAMIFICATIONS

1. What the Rule Is and How It Works

The USFSPA expressly permits state courts to treat military retired pay payable to a member after June 25, 1981, either as property solely of

---

98. 10 U.S.C. § 1408(e)(4)(B).

99. See Subsection 3, Section D, Chapter Five.

100. *See, e.g.,* Employee Retirement Income Security Act, Pub. L. No. 98-397 (1974).

the member or as community or marital property.[101] If the requirements of the USFSPA are fulfilled, the military will honor final decrees that award a portion of retired pay as a division of property by making direct payment of that monthly portion to the former spouse.[102] A court order that divides retired pay as property, however, may be enforced by direct payment to the former spouse only if the parties were married for at least ten years during which the member performed at least ten years of creditable military service.[103] This is often called the 20/10/10 rule.[104]

A spouse's right to compel the military pay center to make direct payment under a court order does not accrue ratably during the required ten years. Rather, if a former spouse was married to a member for one day less than ten years of creditable service, the spouse could not require the military pay center to make direct payments of sums owed under a property settlement or award. Instead, the former spouse would be required to find some other means to collect the sums owed.

Put another way, the military is prohibited from making direct payment of a property division to a former spouse if the member and former spouse were married for fewer than ten years of the time the member performed creditable service. In such cases, the burden of collection falls on the former spouse. No other federal retirement system has such a limitation.

It is important to remember that this restriction is upon direct payment *only*, and not upon the substantive right of the former spouse under state law to a portion of the retired pay as property.[105] If the marriage lasted fewer than ten years during active duty, the retired pay could still be treated as marital property by the court in balancing the property awards to each spouse, but no award to the former spouse of a portion of that retired pay could be enforced by obtaining direct payment from the military pay center. The 20/10/10 rule is *not* a limitation upon the subject matter jurisdiction of the state courts.

---

101. 10 U.S.C. § 1408(c)(1).
102. *Id.* § 1408(d)(1).
103. *Id.* § 1408(d)(2); 32 C.F.R. §§ 63.6(a)(1)–(2).
104. For years of service needed to reach retirement/years of marriage of the parties/years of overlap between service and marriage.
105. *See, e.g.,* LeVine v. Spickelmier, 109 Idaho 341, 707 P.2d 452 (1985); Oxelgren v. Oxelgren, 670 S.W.2d 411 (Tex. App. 1984).

Though the rule provides no restriction on the substantive right of a former spouse, its practical effect is often the same as a legal bar. A former spouse in possession of an order that does not satisfy the rule must rely on whatever enforcement mechanisms are available under state law. Merely reducing the arrearages to judgment will not help; the military pay centers are barred from garnishing any such arrearages just as they are barred from making the payments directly in the first place.[106]

A former spouse in possession of an order that does not satisfy the rule must file a motion to reduce arrears to judgment in state court. Once the arrearage is established, property other than the military retired pay could be attached, and the judgment could be recorded to cause payment if the member tried to sell real estate in later years. Assuming these measures are inadequate, the former spouse can rely only upon the threat of contempt sanctions both to enforce the property award prospectively, and to collect whatever arrearages are reduced to judgment.

Experience has shown that such mechanisms are often inadequate. There is often no other property against which to garnish, and the member might have no real estate in the member's name. The civil contempt powers of many courts are limited to fairly short jail time impositions, which some members have endured rather than begin payments to their former spouses. Even if garnishment is successful, it applies only to amounts already past due and reduced to judgment, requiring repeated trips to court for that purpose.

Counsel may convince state courts to order members to execute allotments for prospective payments, especially when a substantial arrearage has accrued or payments have been very inconsistent. If the member nonetheless cancels the allotment once the court proceeding is finished, the former spouse must start all over again in the state court with a new motion. Enforcement of orders in such a case becomes a war of attrition, in which the former spouse is forced to incur attorney's fees for each return to court, and the member hopes to have enough delay between court appearances to make cancellation of the allotment financially worthwhile.

Attorney's fees awarded to the former spouse in such a proceeding can be garnished from the stream of military retired pay, but this is of

---

106. *See* 10 U.S.C. § 1408(d)(5). Note that the pay center *will* pay under a garnishment to collect any sums awarded to the former spouse *other than* accrued arrearages in military retired pay.

little value if the sum awarded is less than the cost of the proceeding, or if the amount owed to the spouse each month is so close to the maximum amount payable that the garnishment itself is not financially reasonable to pursue.

The conclusion should not be drawn, however, that a spousal interest in a less-than-ten-year-overlap case is not worth pursuing just because the member resists enforcement. By its own terms, the USFSPA does not provide any substantive bar to former spouses seeking to enforce court orders running afoul of the ten-year rule.[107] Members who choose to rely on this procedural limitation to frustrate collection by their former spouses turn themselves into judgment debtors, with all the usual disadvantages of such a status in our increasingly computerized and cross-indexed society. These disadvantages include bad credit reports, interminable proceedings seeking examination of the judgment debtor, garnishment of second-career income, contempt orders resulting in jail time, or other emotionally or fiscally destructive outcomes. Nor should members who defy court orders to make payments expect much sympathy or assistance from the federal or bankruptcy courts; though members in some jurisdictions may be able to discharge accrued arrearages, each month of nonpayment under a court order causes a new arrearage to come into existence.[108]

There is not even consistency among those affected, because some members may be essentially "judgment-proof" and thus in no danger of secondary collection, while those members who do most to improve their stations in life and establish ties to communities are least likely to find any real advantage in the rule's practical result.

---

107. "Nothing in this section shall be construed to relieve a member of liability for the payment of alimony, child support, *or other payments required by a court order* on the grounds that payments made out of disposable retired pay under this section have been made in the maximum amount permitted. . . . Any such unsatisfied obligation of a member may be enforced by any means available under law other than the means provided under this section. . . ." 10 U.S.C. § 1408(e)(6) (*emphasis added*).

108. See the bankruptcy discussion in Section F of this chapter. For a review of the policy analyses likely to be used by other reviewing federal courts, see *Fern v. United States*, 15 Cl. Ct. 580 (1988) (denying retirees' attempts to circumvent judgments in favor of their former spouses in three different categories of military retirement benefits cases), *aff'd*, 908 F.2d 955 (Fed. Cir. 1990).

All these problems are exacerbated in interstate cases, because it is extraordinarily difficult to enforce an interstate civil contempt. When the member is not in the jurisdiction of the court order, the former spouse is usually required to have the judgment domesticated in the state to which the member has moved, and engage counsel in the new state in an attempt to enforce it.

It is simply not economically feasible for many former spouses to pursue these cases; as a matter of course, the monthly amount ordered paid to a spouse in a less-than-ten-year-overlap case is smaller than it would be in other cases. Thus, if counsel fails to note the payment restriction, the end result may well be a judgment that for all practical purposes is unenforceable, raising malpractice concerns. It is possible that the malpractice risk might be ameliorated (in those jurisdictions that permit it) by including language requiring the member to pay all attorney's fees and other costs of collection, if made necessary. Of course, if the member is truly judgment-proof, that will not be much help.

Practitioners must be clear in advising their clients about what the 20/10/10 rule does *not* affect. Court orders providing for payment of alimony or child support are not limited by the 20/10/10 rule.[109] Similarly, the rule has no application to a court's power to nominate the former spouse as beneficiary of the SBP.[110]

Given all these problems for everyone involved in cases affected by the ten-year rule, it can be said that the rule serves no constituency well, and inflicts hardships on many persons without any commensurate benefit. In the last major round of congressional hearings on this issue, an ABA committee of experts in this area concluded as follows:

> The ABA position is that state court awards should be enforceable. The ten-year direct pay limitation is a wholly artificial bar to collection that only serves to prevent enforcement of valid state court orders. It often makes a sham of state court orders, and has been interpreted in some states as a jurisdictional limitation on the power of the state court to consider military retirement benefits where service and marriage over-

---

109. 32 C.F.R. § 63.6(a)(2).
110. *See* 10 U.S.C. §§ 1448(d)(3), 1450(f)(4). Some courts are less willing, however, to order such a beneficiary designation when the overlap of service and marriage is of comparatively short duration.

lapped by less than ten years. Finally, it unjustly penalizes spouses in some states which lack alimony laws. It should be eliminated.[111]

2. Coping with the Rule in a Less-Than-Ten-Year-Overlap Case

A practitioner representing a former spouse who was married to a member for fewer than ten years during active-duty service faces special difficulties due to the enforcement problems discussed above. Such a practitioner does, however, have certain options.

If the former spouse's interest is truly a small one, the present value of that interest could be determined and offset against other marital property or cash to be paid off.[112]

More problematic is the case involving a substantial putative former spouse share when the parties have insufficient assets to permit an offset.[113] The options available to a former spouse's lawyer are then reduced to bargaining a reduced interest in exchange for a stipulation adequate to secure that interest, or attempting to persuade the court to impose an irrevocable alimony obligation. Both options have drawbacks.

In the classic nine-year-overlap case, the former spouse has a putative 22.5 percent interest.[114] Most jurisdictions permit almost any sort of stip-

---

111. *See* 1993–1994 ABA Policy and Procedures Handbook at 202 (ABA 1993), noting 1979 and 1982 resolutions approved by the House of Delegates of the ABA. The 1982 resolution, in the wake of *McCarty,* urged Congress to enact legislation making all deferred compensation derived from federal employment subject to state property and divorce laws, except where specifically exempted by explicit federal legislation. *See also* Proposed Amendments to the Uniformed Services Former Spouses Protection Act, 1990: Hearings on H.R. 3776, H.R. 2277, H.R. 2300, and H.R. 572 Before the Subcomm. on Military Personnel and Compensation of the House Comm. on Arned Services, 101st Cong., 2nd Sess. (1990) (Statement of Marshal S. Willick, Chairman of Subcommittee on Federal and Military Pension Legislation, Committee on Federal Legislation and Procedures, Section of Family Law, on behalf of the American Bar Association, April 4, 1990, at 5).

112. See Subsection 3, Section B, Chapter Three.

113. Even in the hypothetical nine-year-overlap case involving a staff sergeant, the present value of the former spouse's putative share was over $20,000. Such a sum is typically outside the realm of possible trade-offs or payoffs for individuals so situated.

114. That is, nine divided by twenty, multiplied by one-half.

ulated settlement reached during "arm's-length" negotiations, and it might be in the interests of both the member and the former spouse, given the uncertainties of trial and the certain expenses of litigation, to trade a few percentage points of value for a stipulated award of irrevocable alimony (or secured stream of payments characterized in some other way).

The basis of such a settlement is an award to the former spouse of irrevocable, unmodifiable alimony in an amount measured by the military retirement benefits, in exchange for a waiver by the former spouse of any property interest in the retirement benefits themselves. There is no reason why cost of living adjustments and similar items cannot be included in such an award.

The downside to such an arrangement for the former spouse in an alimony substitution case is that some members have sought court orders revoking such bargained-for "irrevocable" awards, usually based on the changed circumstances of one party or the other. Even when the former spouse prevails against the member's attempt to cut off such payments, there is a substantial expense to such litigation.[115] Less onerously, alimony can be provided only as a reserved possibility if the retirement cannot be divided as provided in the decree or the member fails to make payments.

If a nonalimony resolution is desired, it is difficult in most cases to come up with sufficient security with which such a lifetime stream of payments can be secured. This causes problems particularly in jurisdictions such as Texas, which have formal or informal barriers to establishment of alimony awards. And, of course, the problems associated with bankruptcy remain as a factor in any form of exchange for the former spouse's putative share.[116]

The history of the congressional compromise that gave rise to the ten-year rule is discussed in the following subsection, but those who are seeking some practical means of coping with the problems created by the rule should review the options set forth above, and the implementation of those options in the model clauses at the end of this book.[117]

It is acknowledged that these work-arounds to the ten-year rule are philosophically awkward, in that they attempt to satisfy the underlying purpose of the entire USFSPA by circumventing one of its limitations. It would not be surprising if courts squarely addressing the practices rec-

---

115. *See* Waltz v. Waltz, 110 Nev. 605, 877 P.2d 501 (1994).
116. See Section F of this chapter.
117. See Section B, Chapter Eight.

ommended in this subsection gave differing opinions of their permissibility. Eventually, another trip to the U.S. Supreme Court (or a congressional revisiting of the issue) may well be necessary to eliminate the problem in the future.

3. Historical Background of the Ten-Year Rule

Those interested in explaining the reason for this peculiar rule to a disbelieving judge or intransigent opposing counsel may require some of the history behind it. This rather odd restriction on collection, but not on substantive right, came about as a political compromise in Congress.

During the rush to enact the USFSPA following *McCarty,* the House and Senate came up with different provisions. The House version was far more restrictive, and would have limited the states' right to treat military retirement benefits as property to those marriages in which there had been a ten-year overlap of the marriage with active-duty service.[118] The Senate committee had considered and rejected such a provision.[119]

When the bills went to conference committee, the conferees agreed to remove the House's substantive restriction in exchange for a limitation on use of the federal direct-pay mechanism to cases in which there had been such a ten-year service and marriage overlap.[120] The U.S. Supreme Court has recognized the fact of the political compromise and its result in an entirely procedural payment limitation, which the court has used in contrast to other, substantive portions of the USFSPA.[121]

Since that time, there have been efforts to change the provision. As noted above, the ABA's subcommittee has attacked the rule as "artificial" and "unjust." Various bills have been introduced in Congress to eliminate the direct-payment limitation,[122] but none have been approved. It is likely that this is due to the relatively small number of persons affected, the comparative modesty of the sums at stake in such cases, and the congressional desire to avoid making any changes in this subject area unless forced to do so.

---

118. *See* H.R. CONF. REP. NO. 749, at 165 (1982) (97th Cong., 2d Sess.).
119. *See* S. REP. NO. 502, at 9–11 (1982) (97th Cong., 2d Sess.)
120. *See* H.R. CONF. REP. NO. 749, at 166–67 (1982) (97th Cong., 2d Sess.).
121. *See* Mansell v. Mansell, 490 U.S. 581, 591–92 n.13 (1989).
122. *See, e.g.,* H.R. 3776, 101st Cong., 1st Sess., 135 CONG. REC. H9154-06
     § 3(b)(1989).

F. BANKRUPTCY: DIVORCE LAW
THROUGH THE LOOKING GLASS

The intersection between the fields of divorce law and bankruptcy law is less like the meshing of gears than like an automobile accident. Most authors writing about both fields speak of their "collision."[123] This is largely the result of inconsistent objectives.

From a property standpoint, the goal of equitable division or community property law might be said to be the fair and equitable division of assets and liabilities between the parties in light of their individual and mutual histories and their respective status and potentials upon divorce. The bankruptcy code exists, however, to serve the policy decision that "it is better to allow someone with overwhelming debt to pay all creditors fairly to the extent possible but to leave the debtor with the means to start over. This is the debtor's 'fresh start.' "[124]

Because the rights of former spouses under the current statutory scheme are derivative of those of the member, the first question must be the impact of filing a bankruptcy petition upon the right of a member to begin or continue receiving retired pay. A member declaring bankruptcy does not lose the right to receive future retired pay based upon prior or future military service. Although there does not appear to be a case on point, it seems to be universal practice to treat the time-in-service of a member who has not yet reached eligibility for retirement as a mere contingent expectancy for bankruptcy purposes, and not an "asset" that could be seized and liquidated by the bankruptcy court. One recent case buttresses this analysis; when the former spouse declared bankruptcy, the former spouse's right to a future share of the member's retired pay was not an asset of the bankruptcy estate, because (1) it could not be accelerated or transferred, (2) the former spouse had no vested claim to any amount until each particular month's payment came due, and (3) payment of any amount at all was subject to the member's survival at the beginning of each future month.[125]

---

123. *See, e.g.,* E. Allen Riegesehl, *The Ethics Dilemma,* FAM. ADVOC., Winter 1992, at 34.
124. *See* H. SOMMER & M. MCGARITY, COLLIER FAMILY LAW AND THE BANKRUPTCY CODE 1-4 (L. King ed., 1991).
125. *See* Stackhouse v. Kotz (*In re* Kotz), 146 B.R. 669 (Bankr. E.D. Va. 1992).

The bankruptcy code exempts "a veterans' benefit" from inclusion in the bankruptcy estate, but does not define what is meant by that term.[126] At least one federal circuit court has ruled that military retirement benefits are not property of the bankruptcy estate because they constitute reduced compensation for ongoing reduced services imposed on the military retiree.[127] The continuing viability of this case (or at least its reasoning) is in some doubt, however, now that the U.S. Supreme Court has criticized that characterization in the tax field.[128]

A distinction should be drawn based upon the timing of the bankruptcy vis-à-vis the divorce. At least one textbook concludes that when the bankruptcy petition is filed during the pendency of the divorce, the vesting of the spousal interest could vary depending on the law of the state of divorce, thus rendering any spousal claim to a portion of retired pay as property dependent on persuading the court that the funds to be obtained would be in the nature of, and necessary for the nondebtor's (former spouse's), support.[129]

The law regarding this first circumstance (that is, the member's filing of a bankruptcy petition *during* the divorce and before the former spouse's interest is ruled upon by the divorce court) is substantially undeveloped, and could well turn in several different directions, depending upon what is given priority—technicality or equity, bankruptcy law or family law, or federal or state interests. At least in the meantime, however, it appears to be a strategy through which a member could try to divest a former spouse of any interest merely by timing correctly the filing of a petition in bankruptcy. It is possible that amendments to bankruptcy law in 1994, discussed below, could prevent such divestment.

More is known about the effect of a member's filing a bankruptcy petition *after* a divorce court has ruled that a former spouse is entitled to a portion of the retired pay.

In cases before enactment of the USFSPA, an order to pay a portion of retired pay to a former spouse (or a sum of money in lieu of such a portion)

---

126. *See* 11 U.S.C. § 522(d)(10)(B).
127. *See In re* Haynes, 679 F.2d 718 (7th Cir. 1982).
128. *See* Barker v. Kansas 503 U.S. 594 (1992); *see also* Subsection 3, Section K, Chapter Seven.
129. *See* SOMMER & MCGARITY, *supra* note 124, ¶ 2.02[6] (citing RUTKIN, FAMILY LAW AND PRACTICE § 46.03[4][b] (1990), and MCCAHEY, VALUATION AND DISTRIBUTION OF MARTIAL PROPERTY § 23.02[6] (1990)).

was often considered a "debt" dischargeable in bankruptcy rather than a property interest.[130] There does not appear to be much in the way of currently useful precedent before 1982, and practitioners are cautioned not to be deceived by any effort by an opponent to use this outdated case law.

Since passage of the USFSPA, courts have generally tilted toward nondischargeability of an award of a portion of military retired pay to a former spouse. The Fifth Circuit has simply held that an award of a portion of the retired pay as property made it the former spouse's separate property from that day forward, leaving no "debt" to be discharged or otherwise addressed by the bankruptcy court.[131]

The Ninth and Eight Circuits have generally agreed with this principle, although their opinions diverge on the question of arrearages. Probably the most widely cited case is *In re Teichman*,[132] in which the Ninth Circuit confirmed the nondischargeability of the former spouse's future interest in payments to her of military retired pay to be paid after the date of the bankruptcy petition. By split decision, however, the court termed amounts previously paid to the member (despite the divorce court order awarding those to the former spouse) as a "debt" to her that could be discharged. The court rejected the former spouse's claim that the debt should be found nondischargeable on the basis of a tortious violation of the member's fiduciary duty to remit the funds to the former spouse. Instead, the court found that the member could at most be considered a constructive trustee, whose breach of duty was not sufficient to prevent discharge.[133] Thus, due to the bankruptcy, the former spouse received the future sums owed pursuant to the decree, but the member was able to retain all sums that he *should* have previously paid to the former spouse under the state court order (that is, the arrearages). Lower courts have

---

130. *See* SOMMER & MCGARITY, *supra* note 124, ¶ 6.05[8].
131. *See In re* Chandler, 805 F.2d 555 (5th Cir. 1986), *cert. denied*, 481 U.S. 1049 (1987). Note that the former spouse had achieved direct payment of her portion of the retired pay from the military pay center, a fact that is meaningless in equity, but apparently was considered important to the more technicality-oriented bankruptcy court. This appears as a factor in other bankruptcy cases as well. *See, e.g., In re* Manners, 62 B.R. 656 (Bankr. D. Mont. 1986).
132. *In re* Teichman, 774 F.2d 1395 (9th Cir. 1985).
133. *See* 11 U.S.C. § 523(a)(4).

used similar language in discharging arrearages when they concluded that the former spouses did not act quickly enough in seeking arrearages.[134]

Five years later, the Eighth Circuit in *Bush v. Taylor*[135] concurred regarding the nondischargeability of the former spouse's future interest in payments to the former spouse, but held that any sums paid to the member and kept rather than being paid to the former spouse were retained by the member wrongfully, and he remained liable—despite the bankruptcy—for the full amount of payments that should have, but were not, made to the former spouse. Thus, the bankruptcy had no impact on the former spouse's rights, prospectively or retrospectively from the time of the bankruptcy petition.

The Seventh Circuit reached much the same result, but only by means of the tenuous finding that military retirement benefits are not part of the bankruptcy estate because postpetition services are required of the member, making the benefits postpetition wages.[136]

Various lower bankruptcy courts have issued opinions along the same lines.[137] When divorce counsel for a former spouse had the foresight to include language indicating that any sums paid to the member that should, under the decree, have been paid to the former spouse would be considered subject to an express trust, the court enforced the award to the former spouse as a nondischargeable debt.[138]

---

134. *See, e.g.,* Albert v. Albert (*In re* Albert), 187 B.R. 697 (Bankr. D. Kan. 1995).

135. Bush v. Taylor, 912 F.2d 989, (8th Cir. 1990), *vacating* 893 F.2d 962 (8th Cir. 1990).

136. *See In re* Haynes, 679 F.2d 718 (7th Cir.), *cert. denied,* 459 U.S. 970 (1982).

137. *See In re* Hall, 51 B.R. 1002 (Bankr. S.D. Ga. 1985). Some cases hold generally that the former spouse's share of a retirement interest was such that the debtor retained no interest. *See, e.g., In re* Stolp, 116 B.R. 131 (Bankr. W.D. Wis. 1990); *In re* Farrow, 116 B.R. 131 (Bankr. M.D. Ga. 1990); *In re* Manners, 62 B.R. 656 (Bankr. D. Mont. 1986). Other cases follow the constructive-trust reasoning. *See In re* Sommerville, 122 B.R. 446 (Bankr. M.D. Ala. 1990); *see also In re* Tidwell, 117 B.R. 739 (Bankr. S.D. Fla. 1990); *In re* McNierney, 97 B.R. 648 (Bankr. S.D. Fla. 1989); *In re* Mace 82 B.R. 864 (Bankr. S.D. Ohio 1987); *In re* Thomas, 47 B.R. 27 (Bankr. W.D.N.C. 1984).

138. *See In re* Dahlin, 94 B.R. 79 (Bankr. E.D. Va. 1988); *see also In re* Eichelberger, 100 B.R. 861 (Bankr. S.D. Tex. 1989). The editors of one text,

In at least one case, a bankruptcy court has simply dismissed a Chapter 13 case altogether.[139] The order for dismissal said little, but the underlying facts are illuminating. The member in the case had gone to extraordinary lengths in attempting to prevent his former spouse from obtaining an interest in the retired pay. First, he filed for divorce in Nevada, although both parties resided in Virginia.[140] During litigation of the divorce, he attempted unsuccessfully to prevent any spousal claim, or at least to prevent any claim until after actual retirement, despite Nevada case law permitting a spousal claim upon eligibility for retirement.[141]

After the divorce decree was entered, he changed lawyers and attempted an appeal to the Nevada Supreme Court, which was subsequently dismissed.[142] He then filed the bankruptcy action. After the former spouse moved to dismiss the bankruptcy action, the member attempted to solicit the former spouse's murder, but he was apprehended and ultimately sentenced on reduced charges.[143] All this information was brought to the attention of the bankruptcy court, which apparently had sufficient information in front of it to conclude that the filing was not made in good faith for the purpose of reorganization. Other bankruptcy courts, in other contexts, have ruled that a Chapter 7 bankruptcy can be dismissed for having been filed in "bad faith," when a debtor files a bankruptcy petition to frustrate a divorce decree and to push a former spouse into bankruptcy.[144]

---

however, have cautioned that the result would have been different in a Chapter 13 bankruptcy, because debts for breach of fiduciary duties are apparently dischargeable under that section of the bankruptcy code. *See* Sommer & McGarity, *supra* note 124, ¶ 6.05[8] n.132.

139. *See In re* Hazlett, No. BK-N-91-0659 (D. Nev. Jan. 23, 1992).

140. The statutory or case law of many jurisdictions allows members to maintain residency despite absence from the jurisdiction. *See, e.g.,* 340 Op. Nev. Att'y Gen. (1954); 78 Op. Nev. Att'y Gen. (1972).

141. *See* Gemma v. Gemma, 105 Nev. 458, 778 P.2d 429 (1989); Fondi v. Fondi, 106 Nev. 856, 802 P.2d 1264 (1990). Also see the discussion of distribution to former spouses upon eligibility for retirement in Section C, Chapter Seven.

142. *See* Hazlett v. Hazlett, No. 21231 (Nev. Sup. Ct. Mar. 28, 1991) (order dismissing appeal).

143. *See* United States v. Hazlett, CR 91-140-N---01 (D.C. E.D. Va., Feb. 14, 1992) (judgment of conviction for violation of Title 18 U.S.C. §§ 922(m), 924(a)(3)(B), possession of unregistered automatic rifle).

144. *See* Huckfeldt v. Huckfeldt, 39 F.3d 829 (8th Cir. 1994) (surgeon husband

Some courts have "saved" the allocation to the former spouse only by finding it to be, at root, "in the nature of" some form of alimony or maintenance.[145] At least one state supreme court has simply ignored its own usual rules of stare decisis and held that trial courts can order alimony once a debtor discharges an obligation in bankruptcy that was important to the negotiated divorce decree.[146]

This is not to say that the case law has uniformly favored former spouses. When counsel for the former spouse was not sufficiently careful in drafting the language of the decree, when the funds paid to the former spouse were not a portion of the retired pay but a sum meant to compensate the former spouse for the spousal interest in the retired pay, and when no argument could be successfully made that the funds were necessary for the support of the former spouse, the former spouse's interest has been found to be dischargeable.[147] Again, such cases tend to predate the recent amendments to the bankruptcy laws.

Government pay centers have expressed some uncertainty and confusion when served with both pay orders and notices of bankruptcy. In a case in which the military retired pay had been merged into a civil service retirement, and sums were being paid to the former spouse, the Office of Personnel Management (OPM) refused to pay the former spouse any further sums until it received some word from the bankruptcy court regarding status.[148] The former spouse filed a motion to lift the stay, obtaining an order to strike her motion because the case was closed and the automatic stay was no longer in effect.[149] Because the OPM was concerned only with

---

took low-paying job after completing his education to cause his creditors to chase his former spouse, with "deliberate intention of unloading debt, particularly to [his former spouse], which he could shortly begin to repay"); *see also In re* Brown, 21 F. Supp. 935 (D. Iowa 1938).

145. *See* Love v. Love, 116 B.R. 267 (Bankr. D. Kan. 1990); *In re* Anderson, 21 B.R. 335 (Bankr. S.D. Cal. 1982); Erspan v. Badgett, 647 F.2d 550 (5th Cir. 1981); *In re* Corrigan, 93 B.R. 81 (Bankr. E.D. Va. 1988).

146. *See* Martin v. Martin, 108 Nev. 384, 832 P.2d 390 (1992) (credit-card debts).

147. *See In re* Neely, 59 B.R. 189 (Bankr. D. S.D. 1986); *In re* Heck, 53 B.R. 402 (Bankr. S.D. Ohio 1985) (nonmilitary case).

148. *See In re* Endsley, No. 92-04317-8P7 (Bankr. M.D. Fla. Nov. 23, 1992) (order striking motion to lift stay).

149. *Id.*

the automatic stay (the bankruptcy discharge not affecting the federal retirement benefits), the former spouse obtained the order she needed to
have the flow of payments to her restored.[150]

It is also possible for a former spouse to contest the discharge in
bankruptcy of an obligation to remit to the former spouse a portion of
retired pay, by attacking it as a "fraud while acting in a fiduciary capacity"
or a tortious "debt for willful and malicious injury."[151] The cases are few,
but litigation in bankruptcy court has at least sometimes caused the bankruptcy court to carry into effect the divorce court's orders.[152] At least one
court has held that a decree-incorporated designation of the former spouse
as the SBP beneficiary is an irrevocable, nondischargeable transfer and
not a "debt" subject to discharge in bankruptcy.[153]

Not all bankruptcy courts are blind to the damage caused to equity by
uncritical application of traditional bankruptcy principles to the domestic
relations field. One bankruptcy court has commented as follows:

---

150. This is another of those cases that has wended its way through multiple
courts, leaving odd products in its wake. Because the spouse did not file an
answer to the member's bankruptcy complaint, the bankruptcy court ruled
that her Louisiana judgment awarding a portion of the civil service retirement attributable to military service was "rendered legally unenforceable."
Later, the government attempted to recoup from the member all amounts
paid to the former spouse. The bankruptcy court ultimately ruled that the
government should have never paid anything to the former spouse in the
first place, and denied the government's request, in *United States v. Endsley,*
204 B.R. 242 (Bankr. M.D. Fla. 1996). The court stretched a bit to reach a
result sympathetic to the member, citing overruled Nevada cases, and perhaps accidentally creating quite a bit of dicta that could cause uncertainty
for many years in that district about the meaning of an order "incident to"
a decree of divorce. The court appeared to state indirectly that one court
cannot enter a decree of divorce in a partition suit that could be considered
"incident to" a decree of divorce entered elsewhere. That result, if honored,
would make suspect the Eleventh Circuit's earlier holding of exactly the
result criticized, in *Kirby v. Mellenger,* 830 F.2d 176 (11th Cir. 1987).
151. *See* 11 U.S.C. §§ 523(a)(4), 523(a)(6).
152. *See In re* Thomas, 47 B.R. 27 (Bankr. S.D. Cal. 1984); *In re* Wood, 96 B.R.
993 (Bankr. 9th Cir. 1988) (nonmilitary case).
153. *See In re* Anderson, No. X86-02033F, 1988 WL 122983 (Bankr. N.D. Iowa
Nov. 15, 1988).

We are increasingly troubled by the trend of parties to leave divorce court with an agreement that settles property and alimony matters, only to immediately walk down the street to the federal courthouse and attempt to relitigate those issues. Such actions call into question the good faith of the parties and their counsel and raise thorny issues of comity and finality of judgments, to say nothing of attempting to make the bankruptcy court into some type of appellate divorce court. We do not think Congress intended this result when it enacted § 523(a)(5). While we recognize that certain marital debts and obligations are and should be dischargeable, we do not believe that § 523(a)(5) gives one spouse carte blanche to retain marital property at the other spouse's expense.[154]

The preceding paragraphs show part of the problem in this area. When a member chooses to try defeating the divorce court's order by resort to bankruptcy court, the only guarantee is significantly greater expenses for both parties and a great deal of further litigation. ABA committee recommendations to Congress to legislate the nondischargeability of division of retirement benefits (and other aspects of divorce decrees) were apparently responsible in part for the new Subsection (a)(15) exceptions to discharge; a detailed exploration of those provisions is beyond the scope of these materials.

After the most recent changes in the bankruptcy laws, spouses now have at least a somewhat better shot at preventing discharge of arrearages in military retirement benefits, as well as saving future payments, even if the property division is treated as a property division. Still, it would be valuable for the military and other federal pay centers to devise consistent and fair regulations sufficient to govern procedure in this all too common situation. This is still an area where the lawyers for both parties (but particularly the lawyer for the former spouse, who bears the greatest risk) must be wary.

G. "EARLY OUTS": VSI, SSB, AND EARLY RETIREMENT

The military drawdown in the wake of the collapse of the Soviet Union led to significant numbers of members seeking early separation or

---

154. McGraw v. McGraw (*In re* McGraw), 176 B.R. 149 (Bankr. S.D. Ohio 1994) (finding that divorce decree made member husband the constructive trustee of all military retirement benefits intended by that decree to be paid to former spouse).

essentially being forced out of service. At least three separate programs for encouraging early retirements from service were created in the 1990s to spare large numbers of service members from facing selective early-retirement boards (among other alternatives) as the only means of pruning the military population. First, the programs will be briefly explained, after which their treatment in divorce litigation will be discussed.

The Variable Separation Incentive (VSI) and Special Separation Benefit (SSB) programs were created by Congress[155] in 1992. The programs were given to each of the services as tools for reducing the force size without sacrificing force readiness; it was up to each service to decide how to apply the programs. The basic requirements were fairly nonrestrictive—the programs could be offered to members in "selected job specialties" who had accrued between six and twenty years of service. Some were required to serve in reserve units, as well, after leaving active duty.

The following year, Congress created an early-retirement program whereby the services could offer early retirement for members with more than fifteen but fewer than twenty years of service. Retirement under this program is similar to "regular" military retirement, except that the sum paid contains a penalty. The formula is 2.5 percent of monthly base pay, multiplied by years of creditable service, less 1 percent for each year short of twenty that the member was in service at the time of retirement.

All three of these programs were later extended to be effective until 1999.[156] Similar programs were offered to National Guard and reserve members.

1. Voluntary Separation Incentive

The VSI pays members annual payments equal to 2.5 percent of their annual basic pay multiplied by the number of years of accrued service, for twice the years of service served. A master sergeant (E-8) with over ten years in 1995 would have had an annual basic pay of $33,149. Such an individual, electing VSI, would receive twenty annual payments of

---

155. Pub. L. No. 102-190, div. A, tit. X, pt. E, § 1061(a)(7), 105 Stat. 1472 (1991). This was part of the Defense Authorization Act.
156. Pub. L. No. 103-160, div. A, tit. V, subtit. E, §§ 555(a), 555(b), tit. XI, subtit. H, § 1182(a)(2), 107 Stat. 1666, 1771 (1993). Again, this was part of the Defense Authorization Act.

$8,287.25, totaling $165,745. The unpaid portions constitute a property interest that a member can bequeath if the member's death precedes all payments, an attribute that "normal" military retirement does not share. Still, the benefit is treated by most courts as a substitute for retirement, rather than as a form of "severance pay," as discussed below.

2. *Special Separation Benefit*

The SSB pays a single lump sum of 15 percent of annual basic pay multiplied by accrued years of service. The hypothetical 1995 master sergeant discussed above would have received $49,723.50. Obviously, the total received would be considerably less, but the lure of "money now" has proven irresistible to many,[157] despite the significant hammer that all payments are taxed in the year received. In other words, while VSI payments have the effect of increasing annual income a bit for some time, an SSB payment is much more likely to push a member into a higher tax bracket, increasing the tax bite and lowering still further the sum actually paid to the member.

3. *"Fifteen-Year" Retirement*

As of September 30, 1997, 48,000 members had taken early retirement under the Temporary Early Retirement Authority (TERA).[158] In all ways other than sums paid, the members electing TERA retirements are treated just like any other retirees. There is a significant difference in how their spouses and former spouses are treated, however. Because, by definition, no member taking a TERA retirement ever stays on active duty for twenty years, it is not possible for a spouse of such a member to ever have twenty

---

157. *See* Grant Willis, *SSB's Quick Cash Is Favorite of Bonus Takers,* AIR FORCE TIMES, Mar. 16, 1992, at 6 (reporting six-to-one ratio of SSB to VSI participants in the air force and marines, and four-to-one ratios in the army and navy, despite the fact that according to at least one Pentagon official, the preference for SSB makes no sense from an economic and fiscal point of view).

158. OFFICE OF THE ACTUARY, DEP'T OF DEFENSE, FY 1997 DOD STATISTICAL REPORT ON THE MILITARY RETIREMENT SYSTEM 4 (1998).

years of marriage during active duty, and therefore to be a 20/20/20 former spouse entitled to lifetime medical and other benefits.

This creates the situation whereby a *current* spouse of a TERA retiree is treated just like the spouse of any other retired member, but the *former* spouse of a TERA retiree (regardless of the timing of the divorce and the retirement) has none of the ancillary benefits that the former spouse of a "regular" retiree would have. As in similar situations described elsewhere in this book, this reality creates a double-edged sword upon divorce, because most divorce courts must consider "the condition in which the parties will be left" by the divorce, and could therefore award the former spouse of a TERA retiree greater property or alimony to compensate for the loss of medical and other benefits. Despite this, anecdotal accounts suggest that since inception of the program, a number of members have elected TERA retirements for the specific purpose of reducing or eliminating postdivorce benefits to their former spouses.

4. Treatment of "Early-Outs" in Divorce and Postdivorce Cases

Almost all the cases dealing with the three programs discussed above have mentioned the paucity of evidence of legislative intent regarding divorce in the underlying legislation. The courts, being left primarily to their own devices, have reasoned by analogy to regular retirement, and to other employment separation programs.

There have been few enough cases in this subject area that it would be unwise to consider the issue closed. The consensus of case law to date, however, is that the benefits are generally considered as divisible as the retirements that were foregone by election of the early-out benefits, despite the lack (for SSB and VSI) of a federal mechanism for direct payment to the former spouse.

In re McElroy[159] was a case involving SSB, in which the member chose the early-out after sixteen years. The court, examining the available legislative history, stated that its examination of the programs showed no congressional intent to preempt state court divisions, and that the program in substance was more analogous to deferred compensation than severance pay, and was therefore marital property. That court found persuasive the

---

159. 905 P.2d 1016 (Colo. Ct. App. 1995).

program provision that required repayment of the sums received if the member ever returned to service and received a "regular" retirement.

The same court reached the same conclusion about the VSI program in *In re Shevlin.*[160] Both opinions have been approved and reiterated.[161] Other courts throughout the country have used similar language or reasoning to reach the same result regarding both programs, as shown in *Kulscar v. Kulscar,*[162] *In re Crawford,*[163] *Marsh v. Wallace,*[164] *Abernathy v. Fishkin,*[165] *Blair v. Blair,*[166] and *Fisher v. Fisher.*[167] A few courts have reached the opposite result, such as in *McClure v. McClure.*[168] Most decisions finding the benefits to be nondivisible were either reversed on appeal, or specifically restricted to narrow findings of special circumstances. Examples of this include the decisions in *Kelson v. Kelson,*[169] *Baer v. Baer,*[170] *In re Kuzmiak,*[171] and *In re Anderson.*[172]

---

160. 903 P.2d 1227 (Colo Ct. App. 1995) (same result in same court, same day, addressing VSI payments).
161. *In re* Heupel, 936 P.2d 561 (Colo. 1997).
162. 896 P.2d 1206 (Okla. Ct. App. 1995) (SSB divisible in place of military retirement divided in divorce, refusing to allow "one party to retain all the compensation for unilaterally altering a retirement plan asset in which the other party has a court-decreed interest").
163. 180 Ariz. 324, 884 P.2d 210 (Ct. App. 1994) (same holding).
164. 924 S.W.2d 423 (Tex. App. 1996).
165. 638 So. 2d 160 (Fla. Dist. Ct. App. 1994) (VSI divided in accordance with time-rule formula).
166. 271 Mont. 196, 894 P.2d 958 (1995) (same holding).
167. 319 S.C. 500, 462 S.E.2d 303 (Ct. App. 1995) (VSI divided in accordance with time rule; early discharge under VSI program analogous to early retirement, and resulting benefits are as divisible as retirement benefits they replace; there is no federal preemption of state court division of these benefits).
168. 98 Ohio App. 3d 27, 647 N.E.2d 832 (Ct. App. 1994).
169. 647 So. 2d 959 (Fla. Dist. Ct. App. 1994) (VSI held not divisible in split opinion), *overruled,* 675 So. 2d 1370 (Fla. 1996).
170. 657 So. 2d 899 (Fla. Dist. Ct. App. 1995) (when service member given ultimatum to accept VSI or be immediately involuntarily terminated, VSI payments were severance pay rather than retirement pay, and not divisible).
171. 176 Cal. App. 3d 1152, 222 Cal. Rptr. 644 (Ct. App. 1986) (pre-SSB/VSI case; separation pay received upon involuntary discharge preempted state court division).
172. 541 N.W.2d 838 (Wisc. 1995) (table; text only at 1995 WL 551241; not selected for official publication; no precedental value).

At least for the time being, there is no enforcement mechanism beyond normal state court enforcement (such as contempt) for court-ordered divisions of VSI and SSB benefits, whereas TERA retirements may be divided by application for direct payment, just as a "normal" twenty-year retirement would be. Though the decisions published to date do not give much insight into the practicalities of collection, it can reasonably be supposed that collection is as easy, or as difficult, as with any other money judgment between former spouses.

It is simply not possible to predict every change that might be made to the military retirement programs, and that the property settlement agreement or divorce decree should be crafted with demonstrations of intent (and reservations of jurisdiction, if necessary) sufficient to allow a reviewing court at some later date to discern whether the parties had an agreement intended to transcend recharacterization of the benefits addressed and, if so, what that intent was. The form provided at the end of this book provides a statement of such intention in its definition of the benefits at issue. It also provides alimony conversion clauses and other language to allow the practitioner facing such a situation to develop some means of actually enforcing any order obtained.

Chapter Five

PROCEDURAL LIMITATIONS AND COLLECTION METHODS

A. CHECKLIST OF REQUIREMENTS FOR OBTAINING AN ENFORCEABLE ORDER

A qualifying "court order" is necessary to obtain payment of military retirement benefits to a former spouse, or to provide survivor's benefits. There are only six basic requirements—provided by the Uniformed Services Former Spouses Protection Act (USFSPA), applicable state law, and certain military regulations—that must be satisfied for a court order to be qualified. If a qualifying court order is obtained, the USFSPA provides for direct payments to a spouse or former spouse from retired pay for child support or alimony, or as a division of property.[1]

Though practitioners should be aware, of course, that there are a host of qualifications, exceptions, and secondary considerations for most of these requirements, the checklist of the six basic requirements is helpful to keep in mind:

1. The order must be issued by a court of competent jurisdiction.[2]
2. The order must be a final decree of divorce, dissolution, annulment, or legal separation issued by a court in accordance with the laws of the jurisdiction in which the court is located,[3] from which no further appeal can be taken.[4] The order may also be a court ordered, ratified, or approved property settlement "incident to" such a final decree,[5] or a final decree modifying the terms of a previously issued decree or

---

1. 10 U.S.C. § 1408(d)(1).
2. *Id.* § 1408(a)(1); 32 C.F.R. § 63.3(d).
3. 10 U.S.C. § 1408(a)(2)(A).
4. *Id.* §§ 1408(a)(2)–(3). A final decree is defined further as one from which no appeal may be taken, or one from which no appeal has been taken within the time allowed for such appeals under applicable law, or one from which an appeal was taken and has been decided.
5. *Id.* § 1408(a)(2); 32 C.F.R. §§ 63.3(e), 63.3(c)(3).

property settlement. A modifying decree must also meet the requirements of an order.[6]

3. The order must provide for the payment of child support, alimony, or
    a division of property. For alimony or child support, it is necessary
    only that the court order set an amount payable by the member.[7] In
    the case of a division of property, however, the order must specifically
    provide for an amount, "expressed in dollars or as a percentage of
    disposable retired pay, from the disposable retired pay of a member."[8]

4. If the order seeks to divide retired pay as property, it must indicate
    that the court had federal jurisdiction over the service member[9] and,
    if issued while the member was on active duty, that the provisions of
    the Soldiers' and Sailors' Civil Relief Act of 1940 (50 U.S.C. App.
    § 501 *et seq.*) were followed.[10]

5. If the order seeks to divide retired pay as property to be paid directly
    by the military pay center, the former spouse must have been married
    to the service member during ten years of the member's creditable
    service. The order should identify the dates of marriage, service, and
    marriage/service overlap).[11]

---

6. 10 U.S.C. § 1408(a)(2). The modifying decree qualifies as a court order if
    it continues in effect an earlier decree that, as modified, meets all the re-
    quirements of a court order.

7. *Id.* § 1408(a)(2)(B); 32 C.F.R. § 63.3(e). For further discussion of the dif-
    ferences between division of retired pay as property and use of retired pay
    as a source for payments of child support or alimony, see Section A, Chapter
    Four.

8. 10 U.S.C. § 1408(a)(2)(C). A court order that uses a formula whose ele-
    ments are ambiguous will not be honored unless clarified by the court. The
    regulations require the elements of the formula to be specifically set forth
    or readily apparent on the face of the order. 32 C.F.R. § 63.6(c)(8). For
    further discussion of disposable pay, and the arguments concerning division
    of gross and net pay, see Section D, Chapter Four. The enforceability of an
    order providing for payment of a certain dollar sum, *plus* a percentage of
    future cost of living adjustments, is uncertain. Previously, the air force ap-
    parently honored such orders, while the army did not. The consolidated pay
    center apparently went with the policy to not honor them as written. See
    the discussion under Subsection 4(a), Section C of this chapter.

9. 10 U.S.C. § 1408(b)(2).

10. *Id.* § 1408(b)(1)(D).

11. *Id.* § 1408(d)(2). This is not to say that a valid order dividing retired pay

6. The order must sufficiently identify the member[12] and be certified and properly served upon the military authorities.[13]

B. PROCEDURES TO BE FOLLOWED TO ENFORCE AN ORDER

The USFSPA has four basic requirements for effective service of a court order on the secretary of the service concerned (or the secretary's designated agent):

1. Service must be made either in person or by certified or registered mail, return receipt requested.[14] In reality, all service is made by certified mail. (Documents sent by overnight service or regular mail will be returned as improperly served.)
2. The order must be regular on its face. A court order is regular on its face if it (1) is issued by a court of competent jurisdiction, (2) is legal in form, and (3) includes nothing on its face that provides reasonable notice that it is issued without authority of law.[15]
3. The order (or accompanying documents) must identify the member concerned and, if possible, include the member's Social Security number.[16]
4. If the member is still on active duty, the order (or accompanying documents) must certify that the member's rights under the Soldiers' and Sailors' Civil Relief Act were observed.

The regulations further require that the order be authenticated or certified by the issuing court within ninety days immediately preceding ser-

---

as property cannot be entered if there are fewer than ten years of overlap between the marriage and the military service, but only that direct *payment* is restricted under those circumstances. For an extended discussion of this topic, see Section E, Chapter Four.

12. 10 U.S.C. § 1408(b)(1)(C); 32 C.F.R. §§ 63.6(b)(1)(iv)–(v).
13. 32 C.F.R. §§ 63.6(b), 63.6(c)(2), 63.6(c)(5).
14. 10 U.S.C. § 1408(b)(1)(A). The designated agents to receive service of garnishment orders are the same. 50 U.S.C. App. § 510; 32 C.F.R. § 63.6(d)(2).
15. 10 U.S.C. § 1408(b)(2).
16. *Id.* § 1408(b)(1)(C).

vice on the secretary or designated agent.[17] An information statement should also be submitted along with the order (see explanation below).

If the conditions of the USFSPA are met, the service secretaries are required to honor orders to make direct payments to former spouses from retired pay.[18] The affected member's retired pay is reduced by any amount paid to the former spouse.

A designated agent is obligated to respond to an application by a former spouse within ninety days of effective service of a court order. In the real world, responses sometime take longer. If the order will be honored, the response will inform the former spouse of the date payments should begin, and the amount of gross pay, deductions, and disposable retired pay, or that full payment of a court-ordered fixed amount will be made. If the order will not be honored, the response will explain the reasons.[19]

The designated agent also is obligated to notify the member of receipt of an order within thirty days after effective service of a court order or garnishment action.[20] The member will receive from the agent a copy of the order, an explanation of the limitations on direct payment, and information about the amount to be deducted from retired pay for the former spouse. The member will also be requested to advise the designated agent if the court order has been amended, superseded, or set aside. The member has thirty days from the date the notice is mailed to respond with information or valid reasons why the court order should not be honored. Failure of the member to respond will result in payments to the spouse as provided in the notice.[21]

A request for payment of sums pursuant to the USFSPA may be made on DD form 2293, "Application for Former Spouse Payments from Retired Pay," which can be obtained from the appropriate designated agent.[22]

---

17. 32 C.F.R. § 63.6(c)(2).
18. 10 U.S.C. § 1408(c)(4).
19. 32 C.F.R. § 63.6(b)(4).
20. *Id.* § 63.6(f)(1).
21. *Id.* §§ 63.6(f)(2)–(3).
22. *Id.* § 63.6(b). A copy is included as Exhibit 3, Appendix F. Presumably, those portions of the regulations calling for requirements no longer necessary under the terms of the act itself will be formally eliminated when the new, proposed regulations are finalized as law. *See* Appendix D.

Use of the form is not required. The designated agent must accept a signed statement signed personally by the former spouse[23] as long as the following information is enclosed:

- Notice to make direct payment to the former spouse from the member's retired pay.
- A copy of the court order and accompanying documents that provide for payment of child support, alimony, or property division; these documents must be certified by an official of the issuing court.
- A statement that the order has not been amended, superseded, or set aside.
- Sufficient identifying information about the member; at least the member's full name, Social Security number, and branch of service should be given.
- The full name, Social Security number, and address of the former spouse.
- A personal agreement by the former spouse that any future overpayments to the former spouse are recoverable and subject to involuntary collection from the spouse or his or her estate.
- A personal agreement by the former spouse (as a condition precedent to payment) to notify the designated agent if the court order is vacated, modified, or set aside, if the former spouse remarries (if the order provides for payment of alimony), or if a child receiving child support by direct payment dies, is emancipated, is adopted, or attains majority.
- If the court order divides retired pay as property, a representation (accompanied by either a court order so stating or some accompanying documentation) that the parties were married for at least ten years during the member's creditable service; the better practice is to recite this fact in the decree itself.

C. LIMITATIONS

1. Soldiers' and Sailors' Civil Relief Act

Since 1940, certain additional federal restrictions have bound civil practitioners who attempt to bring actions against active-duty service

---

23. Note that counsel cannot sign the application for this benefit in place of the former spouse; even when counsel is doing the paperwork, always be sure that the former spouse signs a request for direct payment.

members. They are set forth in a federal statute frequently referred to as the Soldiers' and Sailors' Civil Relief Act of 1940 (Civil Relief Act), although it has been amended since then.[24] This act is much misunderstood.

Essentially, the law postpones or suspends certain civil obligations; a member's request for a stay of proceedings will be granted *unless* military service does *not* materially affect the member's ability to defend the action.[25] Counsel can be appointed to invoke rights under the Civil Relief Act before default will be entered, and the member may request that any default against him or her be set aside if

- no appearance was made,
- there is some meritorious defense, and
- military service adversely affected the member's ability to defend the action.[26]

A judgment or garnishment may be stayed or vacated, unless military service did or does not materially affect the member's ability to comply.[27] A special appearance made just to invoke the protections of the Civil Relief Act does not constitute a general appearance.[28]

The U.S. Supreme Court has issued vague guidance that the law should be "liberally construed to protect those who have been obligated to . . . take up the burdens of the nation."[29] Normal civil procedure questions may or may not be resolved differently when the Civil Relief Act is implicated. There is authority that the normal rules for making a general appearance may apply, at least when a member signs papers, and affirmatively seeks relief in the court.[30] Though simply accomplishing service of process on a defendant in the territorial jurisdiction of the court is normally adequate to give the court authority to proceed,[31] a divorce de-

---

24. *See* 50 U.S.C. App. § 500 *et seq.* (1991).
25. *Id.* § 521.
26. *Id.* §§ 521, 520(4).
27. *Id.* § 523.
28. *See* O'Neill v. O'Neill, 515 So. 2d 1208 (Miss. 1987); *In re* Brown, 225 Ill. App. 3d 733, 587 N.E.2d 648 (App. Ct. 1992).
29. Boone v. Lightner, 319 U.S. 561 (1943).
30. *See* Roqueplot v. Roqueplot, 88 Ill. App. 3d 59, 410 N.E.2d 441 (App. Ct. 1980).
31. *See, e.g.,* Cariaga v. District Court, 104 Nev. 544, 762 P.2d 886 (1988).

cree may be set aside, and further proceedings stayed on appeal, when the individual served was shipped out of the United States by military orders after service of process upon him.[32]

In the special context of actions involving an active-duty member in which a former spouse seeks to apply the USFSPA, the former spouse must ensure that the final court order "or other documents served with the court order" certify that the rights of the member under the Civil Relief Act were observed.[33] The better practice is to recite that fact explicitly on the face of the court order. (An example is in the form at the end of this book.)

Applicability of the Civil Relief Act, in practice, often appears to hinge on very minor distinctions perceived by individual decision makers, at least in the divorce context, and it is difficult to frame a test that would likely be reliable in light of the existing case authority.[34] There is at least an implied, if not a stated, duty of due diligence on the part of the member to try to participate in the proceedings.[35] Further, the stays are not for the duration of military service, necessarily, but only for that period necessary to allow participation in the proceedings.[36]

There is some question about satisfaction of this procedural requirement in cases in which the divorce decree preceded passage of the

---

32. Kramer v. Kramer 668 S.W.2d 457 (Tex. App. 1984).

33. 10 U.S.C. § 1408(b)(1)(D).

34. For example, a stay for eight months of hearings on matters including child custody, alimony, and attorney's fees until a member's return to the United States, was upheld in *Coburn v. Coburn,* 412 So. 2d 947 (Fla. Dist. Ct. App. 1982), but the availability to another member of thirty days' annual leave, which he chose not to use, was taken as evidence that he could have defended against a divorce suit if he chose to do so, and so a stay was denied in *Cromer v. Cromer,* 49 N.C. App. 403, 271 S.E.2d 541 (Ct. App. 1980). Courts can, and have, taken judicial notice of the availability of such leave. *See* Underhill v. Barnes, 288 S.E.2d 905 (1982) (161 Ga. A. 776).

35. *See* Palo v. Palo, 299 N.W.2d 577 (S.D. 1980) (when member wife was able to find her way from Germany to South Dakota for hearings, member husband was found unwilling rather than unable to attend hearing; both had been posted at same location).

36. *See* Plesniak v. Wiegand, 31 Ill. App. 3d 923, 335 N.E.2d 131 (App. Ct. 1975) (member's fourth requested stay over four years turned down, and denial of stay upheld on appeal, as member had not made "reasonable effort" to make himself available).

USFSPA. Anecdotal accounts indicate that in some cases, the military pay center has required issuance of a "clarifying" order from the original issuing courts that the Civil Relief Act was satisfied. In other cases, some evidence that the provisions of the act were followed has been required (for example, showing a general appearance and evidence that under relevant case law, such an appearance constitutes consent for a case to go forward). In still others, such administrative requirements have been disregarded for divorce decrees issued before June 26, 1981. The passage of time, of course, continually decreases the number of such cases.

2. Multiple and Conflicting Orders

Experienced litigators know that the real world of litigation can be "messy"; cases are not always resolved in a single order entered at the close of linear proceedings. Frequently, prejudgment orders are entered, or motions are filed after judgment to amend, construe, modify, or correct problems in the original judgment. Procedures have been established to deal with multiple and conflicting court orders directing payment to one or more former spouses of a member.[37]

If a service secretary receives effective service of more than one court order directing payment to a spouse and one or more former spouses, or to more than one former spouse, the secretary must treat the orders on a first-come, first-served basis, up to the 50 percent limitation.[38] The 1990 amendments may have altered this analysis, however, if successive orders are for different types of payments.[39]

The military retirement system is a first-to-file system, not a first-judgment system. The key time is that of receipt of an order by the secretary, not the time when the order is entered by the court. As explained in greater detail in the following subsections, the inadequacy of available retired pay to satisfy a court-ordered payment to a former spouse does not relieve a member of liability, it merely requires the former spouse to resort to other remedies.[40]

---

37. 10 U.S.C. §§ 1408(e)(2)–(3); 32 C.F.R. §§ 63.6(h)(4)–(6).
38. 10 U.S.C. § 1408(e)(2); 32 C.F.R. § 63.6(h)(4). This provision is similar to those related to garnishment of federal employee pay. *See* 42 U.S.C. § 661(c).
39. See Section D, Chapter Four.
40. 10 U.S.C. § 1408(e)(6).

If a court of competent jurisdiction issues a stay of execution, the designated agent is supposed to suspend payments of any disputed amounts until the dispute has been resolved.[41] There is no time limit on how long the agent may withhold payments pending resolution of the dispute.

In the case of conflicting court orders directing payment of different monthly amounts to the same former spouse, the designated agent must pay the *least* amount ordered under the conflicting orders until the conflict is resolved. The agent will retain the lesser of

- the difference between the largest amount required by the conflicting court orders and the least amount ordered, and
- the amount of disposable retired pay that remains available for payment of any conflicting court order.[42]

As demonstrated in the following example, this can be quite confusing to all those involved in such a situation, even if the military pay center makes no mistakes in applying the statute and regulations.[43]

EXAMPLE

Frank and Annette are divorced. Annette is beneficiary of Frank's Survivor's Benefit Plan (SBP). Frank's disposable retired pay of $1,000 per month is reduced by the $100 monthly SBP premium. As to Annette, Frank's disposable retired pay is $900. The designated agent is effectively served with one court order to pay Annette $200 per month, and a conflicting court order to pay Annette $425 per month. The agent will make direct monthly payments to Annette of $200, because that is the lower figure.

To determine how much to retain, the agent must determine the lesser of two sums. First, the agent must find the difference between the largest amount required by court order ($425) and the least amount

---

41. 32 C.F.R. § 63.6(h)(6).
42. 10 U.S.C. § 1408(e)(3); 32 C.F.R. § 63.6(h)(5).
43. 10 U.S.C. § 1408(e)(3); 32 C.F.R. § 63.6(h)(5).

payable by court order ($200). That difference is $225 ($425 minus $200). Next the agent must determine the amount of disposable retired pay that remains available to pay any court order. In this case, 50 percent of $900 is $450, and $450 minus $200 equals $250 available. The first method yields the lesser amount, so the agent will retain $225 each month. The agent will pay Frank $475 per month, that being the $900 disposable, less the $200 paid to Annette, less the $225 retained.

Suppose that after four months with the above arrangement in place, the agent received a third court order directing payment of $350 per month to Annette, and both Frank and Annette certify the new order to be valid. The agent had retained $900 ($225 multiplied by four months).

The agent will pay the $900 retained as follows: Annette would receive $600 ($150 for each of the four months that the agent paid her $200 per month instead of the correct amount of $350 per month); Frank would receive $300 ($75 for each of the four months, as the agent withheld $225 per month and will pay Annette only $150 for each month). Subsequently, the agent will pay $350 to Annette and $550 to Frank each month.

Another problem that can cause consternation is how the pay centers apply the requirement of "first come, first served."[44] If the pay center receives both a garnishment order under the Social Security Act and a direct-pay order, it will honor the earlier order until satisfaction of the order or exhaustion of available pay, and then turn to the second order.

In many states, however, garnishments may be established only for limited times, after which new garnishments must be processed and served. If an earlier former spouse was collecting alimony under such a garnishment, and a later former spouse then served a direct-pay order that could only be partially satisfied, the former spouses would reverse priority when the garnishment expired and had to be renewed, because a direct-pay order need only be served once. Thus, it appears that the statute permits a previously established garnishment to be supplanted for collection purposes by a later direct-pay order.

---

44. 10 U.S.C. § 1408(e)(4).

3. *Miscellaneous Limitations on Payments to Former Spouses*

A former spouse cannot sell, assign, transfer, or otherwise dispose of an award of retired pay, including by inheritance.[45] This is theoretically sound, because a former spouse's rights are derivative of a member's rights, and members are likewise restrained from hypothecating their rights to receive retired pay.[46] Once a former spouse receives a portion of retired pay, however, there are no restrictions under the USFSPA on the uses that may be made of that money.

Former spouses may not require that they be paid on any particular schedule; retired pay is sent to former spouses on the same monthly cycle as payments are made to members.[47] If a member is entitled to receive retired pay on the date of service of a court order requiring payments to a former spouse, payments will begin within ninety days thereafter.[48] If the member is not yet eligible for retired pay on the date of service, payments will begin within ninety days of the date on which the member first becomes entitled to receive retired pay.[49]

A former spouse who applies for direct payment must agree, as a condition precedent to payment, to notify the designated agent promptly if the court order under which application is made is vacated, modified, or set aside. The applicant must also agree to provide notice of any subsequent remarriage, if any part of the payment is for alimony,[50] or of a change in a child's eligibility, if any part of the payment is for child support.[51]

The order must state whether the former spouse is to receive a percentage of the retired pay or some particular sum of dollars out of it. As discussed in greater detail in the following section, there were some unresolved conflicts among the pay centers in their treatment of orders calling for divisions of retired pay that referenced *both* a percentage and a specific dollar figure.

---

45. *Id.* § 1408(c)(2).
46. *See* S. Rep. No. 97-502, at 16 (1982).
47. 32 C.F.R. § 63.6(h)(2).
48. 10 U.S.C. § 1408(d)(1).
49. 32 C.F.R. § 63.6(h)(1).
50. Presumably, this would be true only if applicable state law provided that any of the payments must terminate upon remarriage.
51. 32 C.F.R. § 63.6(b)(1)(vii).

Payments to a former spouse terminate on the earliest to occur of the former spouse's death, the member's death, or the termination date (if any) in the court order.[52] To be assured of lifetime benefits, a former spouse must become the beneficiary of the SBP,[53] because the member could die before the former spouse.

If an award of retired pay as property is not collected in the month when it is payable, it is lost to the former spouse insofar as the federal collection mechanisms are concerned. There is no facility under the USFSPA to recover arrearages in property distributions *of the retired pay as property* that are not made by direct payment. This is often confusing, because the USFSPA does provide for garnishment of any other unsatisfied property distribution order.[54]

EXAMPLE

Gomez and Morticia are divorced after ten years of marriage during service. The decree awards Morticia 25 percent of the retired pay as her sole and separate property, and $1,000 for her share of retired pay that Gomez received but did not share with her. She is also awarded $1,000 to equalize other property distributions, but Gomez does not pay it to her. If Morticia returns to court and obtains a garnishment order for the $1,000 arrearage in retired pay and the $1,000 in other property, the military pay center will garnish only in satisfaction of the "other property" award. She must enforce the retired pay property arrearage in some other way under state law.

---

4. Service Peculiarities and Distinctions

a. Enforceability of Dollars Plus Future Percentage Awards

The relevant portion of the USFSPA defines an enforceable court order for the division of property, in part, as an order that "specifically

---

52. 10 U.S.C. § 1408(d)(4).
53. See Section B, Chapter Six.
54. 10 U.S.C. § 1408(d)(5); 32 C.F.R. § 63.6(d)(1).

provides for the payment of an amount, expressed in dollars or as a percentage of disposable retired pay, from the disposable retired pay of a member to the spouse or former spouse of that member."[55]

If payments to a former spouse are based on an order that calls simply for the payment of some exact number of dollars, the order will be honored (within the payment limitations of federal law) regardless of changes to the sum of retirement benefits paid to the member—in other words, the former spouse will continue getting the $250 (or whatever amount specified), despite any cost of living adjustment (COLA) increases in the retirement benefits from which the former spouse is being paid.

If payments to a former spouse are based on a percentage rather than a fixed dollar sum, however, the amount paid will change proportionately beginning on the effective date of future COLAs.[56] In other words, if the retirement benefits were $1,000 and the former spouse's 25 percent was $250, then a 3 percent COLA would cause the former spouse's share to rise to $257.50.

One way practitioners have dealt with other issues in a divorce (for example, a small but recognized right to spousal support under state law) is to use the retirement as a resource. If some additional sum should be paid to the spouse, the spouse's share of the retired pay might be stated as somewhat above the precise mathematical percentage to which the spouse might be entitled. Likewise, if some sum is owed to the member, in the settlement, the spouse's share of the retirement could be stated as somewhat below what the spouse might mathematically be entitled to receive.

Usually, such a "modified" spousal share would be followed by a means of increasing that sum in the future as COLAs accrued.[57] There is

---

55. 10 U.S.C. § 1408(a)(2)(C).

56. 32 C.F.R. § 63.6(h)(2). The pay centers were divided about whether they will enforce the COLA provisions of orders providing for payment of a fixed amount *plus* a certain percentage of future COLAs. As explained in note 59, that dispute has been resolved, to some degree.

57. When a "dollar certain" order is *silent* about COLAs, it could theoretically be argued that such an order was intended to limit the former spouse to exactly that sum of dollars, regardless of future inflation. It could also be argued that the sum reached was necessarily in relation to the entire sum of retired pay payable to the member, and was implicitly to remain proportional so it would not become reduced by inflation. The pay center will

some question about whether orders calling for payment of a fixed sum plus a given percentage of future COLAs are enforceable. Orders so structured are frequently an attractive way of balancing other aspects of decrees.[58]

Before consolidation of the pay centers, the air force pay center had (informally) declared that it *would* honor such orders, the navy pay center had declared that it would *not* do so, and the remaining pay centers either did not express a policy or were inconsistent in honoring such orders. Because the consolidation of the military pay centers left responsibility for administering military retirement benefits payments with the Cleveland center, it appears (in the short run, at least) that such orders will not be honored and should not, therefore, be drafted or submitted.[59] Like all such informal policies, of course, that decision could be changed at any time.

The air force policy appeared grounded in the opinion that if the statute allows either form of benefit award, it must allow them both; because the parties' (or the court's) intentions were clear and simple to enforce, the orders were honored. Navy policy was apparently to honor the dollar

---

simply presume that silence means no increases to a dollar sum order, and will presume that COLAs *do* accrue to percentage orders. Presumably, each jurisdiction will have its own rules of reasonable interpretation of such orders, but to avoid confusion and failure of expectations, the better practice is to specify what effect, if any, future COLAs will have on the award.

58. If, for example, the parties had negotiated the SBP beneficiary designation as irrevocably belonging to the former spouse, but had also negotiated that the former spouse should bear the entire cost of the premium, the parties could deduct the dollar cost of the half of the premium that the member would otherwise bear from the dollar sum yielded by the former spouse's percentage. This is discussed in greater detail in Subsection 5, Section B, Chapter Six.

59. As for such orders already in existence, there is reason to believe that orders being honored will continue to be honored. The Director of Defense Finance and Accounting Service (DFAS), on October 28, 1993, decided that all orders accepted by any of the prior pay centers on or before that date that provided for fixed dollar sums with COLA increases would be "grandfathered" to continued implementation. *See* Letter from M.W. McCarthy, Esq., private practitioner, to Joel Rosson, Esq., Chief Counsel, DFAS-Cleveland (Dec. 21, 1993) (memorializing conversation verifying DFAS policy).

sum set forth in the order, and simply disregard the COLA percentage language as surplusage. This policy was seemingly grounded in some administrative conclusion of "inclusio unius est exclusio alterius"[60]— because the statute says an order should be expressed as dollars *or* a percentage, such an order may not refer to dollars *and* a percentage.

It should be possible to achieve the desired result indirectly, even if the military pay center in a particular case refuses to allow a "dollar plus percentage" form of order, or if such a form is ultimately determined by the courts to be unacceptable under the USFSPA. The practitioner must simply determine the percentage equivalent of the dollar sum negotiated, and place that percentage in the order.[61]

It is uncertain how any pay center might interpret an order having two different percentage figures in it, but there does not appear to be anything in the USFSPA preventing such an order. Given the history on this matter however, it seems possible that some military bureaucrats could fixate on the "a" in the phrase "a percentage of disposable retired pay" and deny enforcement to that sort of order as well. As long as those charged with enforcing the USFSPA seem more concerned with frustrating the intentions of the parties and the courts than in carrying their wishes into effect, such problems are inevitable.

b. Enforcement of Clauses Calling for Only the Former Spouse (or Only the Member) to Pay the SBP Premium

As a matter of negotiation or order, there are times when the SBP is awarded to the former spouse, but the former spouse is ordered to pay the entire premium for that benefit. Such stipulations or orders are analyzed much the same as the "dollar plus percentage" form of retirement benefits awards discussed above. In some cases, trial courts want the member to pay all or some part of the SBP premium as part of the division of rights and obligations in the divorce. In others, courts want to allocate the SBP benefits to the former spouse (or give the former spouse the option to have

---

60. Literally, "The inclusion of one implies the exclusion of the other." *See* BLACK'S LAW DICTIONARY 906 (4th ed. 1968).
61. Instead of awarding the former spouse $435 per month, the order could award the former spouse 43.5 percent of the retirement benefits then payable ($1,000), plus a like percentage of all future COLAs.

them in place) only if the former spouse makes full payment of the SBP premium.

Under present law, if the court order deems the election of the former spouse as beneficiary (or if the member does so with or without court order), and the retirement benefits are divided with the same person, the military will deduct the SBP premium from the gross sum of the benefits before division of the retirement benefits into shares to the member and former spouse.[62]

The practical effect of this "default" provision is to split the cost of the SBP premium between the member and former spouse in the same proportion as the benefits are divided. If the former spouse was awarded 50 percent of the retirement benefits, then each will pay half the cost of the SBP premium; if the former spouse was awarded only 25 percent of the retirement benefits, then the member will pay three-quarters of the cost of the SBP premium. This is illustrated in the following example.

EXAMPLE

Roy and Dale divorce after being married for exactly fifteen years of Roy's thirty-year military career. Dale is entitled to her time-rule percentage—25 percent—of the military retirement benefits (that is, one-half of the marital half of the service time). If the total retirement benefit is $1,000 per month, then (without considering the SBP) Roy would get $750 and Dale would get $250. If the SBP is in effect with Dale as the named beneficiary, however, the pay center will take $65 off the top for the premium. Of the remaining $935 per month, Roy will get $701.25 (that is, 75 percent), and Dale will get $233.75. The bottom line is that Roy's payments were reduced by $48.75, and Dale's by $16.25—Roy would have effectively paid three-quarters of the premium. If Dale's share of the retirement benefits was even smaller, Roy would "pay" an accordingly higher percentage of the SBP premium.

This automatic allocation of a part of the cost of the SBP premium to the member has caused some courts to attempt to shift the burden for the

---

62. 10 U.S.C. § 1408(a)(4)(D).

premium payments, entirely or in part, from the member to the former spouse. Other courts have tried to order members to maintain the SBP at the member's own cost. Presently, there is no statute or regulation specifically facilitating such a shift in either direction, and there is no official or uniform policy regarding whether or how such a clause would be honored by the military pay centers. Anecdotal accounts suggest that generally, at least, such clauses are *not* presently being honored.

As with the "dollar plus percentage" matter discussed above, it *is* possible to do indirectly what is not readily accomplished directly. As discussed elsewhere,[63] the SBP premium amount at any given time can be ascertained. It is possible to deduct the cost of that premium from the award to the former spouse (either directly in dollars, or indirectly as a percentage), thus allocating the entire cost to either the member or the former spouse. This should even hold the relative spousal interests consistent after future COLAs.

EXAMPLE

Walter and June divorce just after Walter's retirement; they were married for 100 percent of the military service time and the retirement is $1,000. The total SBP premium is $65. In negotiation, the parties agree on many things, including June's continuation as the SBP beneficiary, and her payment of the entire premium. Walter's half of the post-SBP deduction amount is therefore increased by $32.50 to $500, while June's is reduced to $435. As a percentage of the total $1,000, Walter's 50 percent was thus raised to 53.48 percent, and June's was reduced to 46.52 percent. (For the purpose of this example, ignore any distinctions about whether the spousal interest is stated as a percentage or in dollars.)[64]

Assume a 5 percent COLA, increasing the gross retired pay from $1,000 to $1,050. The SBP premium, charged at 6.5 percent, increases from $65 to $68.25, leaving $981.75 in disposable pay. Walter's 53.48 percent of the total retired pay less SBP yields $525.04,

---

63. See Subsection 5, Section B, Chapter Six.
64. For a detailed explanation of how this can be made to work, see Subsection 5, Section B, Chapter Six.

and June's 46.52 percent of the total retired pay less SBP yields $456.71. Note that Walter has gained 4¢ at June's expense (because Walter's actual 50 percent of gross would have been only $525).[65]

The proposed model divorce decree at the end of this book includes alternate provisions intended to shift the SBP premium burden to the former spouse. Because the adjustment is made by drafting counsel in the section providing for the sum of retired pay payable to the spouse, there is nothing in the SBP section itself that provides for this payment if the percentage adjustment method is used. This method has the advantage of not requiring the pay center to be involved in the process at all.

The model also includes currently unenforceable alternative clauses for asking the pay center to deduct the premium from the former spouse's full share, and a "fallback" provision, in the event this method is chosen, requiring direct reimbursement by the former spouse to the member if the military pay center fails to take the money out of the former spouse's portion.[66]

The downside to the fallback clause is that it requires a monthly flow of checks, with all the usual problems of continuing interaction, enforcement, and so on—in this case the member's enforcement of a clause requiring payments from the former spouse. The direct percentage deduction is a preferable method in cases in which it is decided that the former spouse should bear the SBP premium cost. It would probably be a good idea to reflect somewhere on the face of the order that this is what was

---

65. This trivial change does not expand much over time, and is subject to the vagaries of rounding (both the military's elimination of all sums less than a dollar, and rounding each party's percentage in dollars and cents). If there is another 5 percent COLA the following year, the gross retired pay increases from $1,050 to $1,102.50. The military rounds down any sums less than a dollar, leaving $1,102. The 6.5 percent COLA costs $71.63, leaving $1,030.37 to be divided. Walter's 53.48 percent yields $551.04, and June's 46.52 percent yields $479.33. Walter still is receiving only 4 cents more than a straight 50 percent of the gross pay. If the next year another 5 percent COLA accrues, Walter would get $578.55, and June would get $502.25; Walter would be receiving 5 cents more than a straight 50 percent of the gross pay.
66. See Section B, Chapter Eight.

done, to ensure that any later proceedings are clear on why the spousal share was increased or decreased from what the time-rule percentage otherwise would have been.

c. Inquiry into Accuracy of Members' Claims regarding Tax Withholding

The amount of disposable pay for orders entered before February 4, 1991, varies in accordance with the number of exemptions claimed by the member, and therefore the taxes withheld from the gross pay as part of the calculation of disposable pay. The ramifications of this variation are explained in greater detail below.[67]

The military pay center does not appear to have a formal policy for dealing with the matter. The Comptroller General issued a ruling in 1984 generally prohibiting the withholding of an amount greater than that intended to cover the tax liability on the military retirement itself,[68] but it has proven difficult for former spouses who suspect such abuse to prevent the practice.

The implementing regulations call for the pay centers to honor a withholding request that "is consistent with the member's tax liability . . . when the member presents evidence to the satisfaction of the designated agent. . . ."[69] There is no guidance, however, for determination of the amount of state income tax due, whether the pay center should seek verification of a claim of the member being single or remarried, or whether there is any retroactive effect to a determination that improper withholding had led to an incorrect division of retired pay.

---

67. See Section K, Chapter Seven.
68. Matter of Uniformed Services Former Spouses Protection Act, Apr. 25, 1984 (*In re* Flynn), 63 Comp. Gen. 322 (1984) (Comptroller General's Decision No. B-213895, Apr. 25, 1984). A retired air force colonel had nearly all his retired pay withheld for federal income taxes, thus reducing the sums available as disposable pay for division with his former spouse. The ruling found that practice impermissible, and withholding for purposes of figuring disposable pay was limited to amounts necessary to cover the retired pay itself and amounts for which the member "presents evidence of a tax obligation which supports such withholding."
69. 32 C.F.R. § 63.6(e)(2)(iv).

By 1996, however, the Defense Finance and Accounting Service (DFAS) had apparently generated an internal policy governing reviews of member requests for additional withholding. The *Krone* case[70] involved a 1976 Nevada divorce. The former spouse only received a fixed sum—corresponding to a percentage of the retirement payable at that time—for almost twenty years, while the retirement itself had increased dramatically because of COLAs. The former spouse eventually discovered that she should have been receiving increases during that time, applied for direct payments from DFAS, and sought an order from state court clarifying that she was entitled to a share of all COLAs.[71]

The member, another retired air force colonel, had gone to great lengths to restrict payments being made by DFAS under the USFSPA to his former spouse. After losing in state trial court (after the former spouse put in an application for direct payment and it was honored), and while the matter remained on appeal, he tried to convince DFAS to withhold $1,400 from his retired pay before calculating the spousal share; he had his accountant send in information claiming that "the marginal tax rate" on his military retired pay was 28 percent, and that he must therefore have $1,040 withheld to cover federal taxes, and an additional $250 to cover state taxes.

Using the calculation methodology developed in the 1984 case, DFAS declined his request, finding that the colonel's "projected effective tax rate" was only 12.2382 percent, so that only $446.65 could be deducted before calculating the former spouse's share. DFAS also determined that only $107 of the $250 requested could legitimately be withheld for state taxes before calculating the spousal share.

The colonel filed a request for an advance decision from the Comptroller General's office. The decision stated that DFAS was entirely correct, and that in calculating the amount of disposable retired pay subject to apportionment with a former spouse, the deductions of federal income

---

70. Matter of Colonel Robert M. Krone, USAF (ret.); Federal Income Tax Withholding from Military Retired Pay for Former Spouse Protection Act Purposes (*In re* Krone), 75 Comp. Gen. ____ (1996) (Comptroller General's Decision No. B-271052, Aug. 6, 1996).

71. Bryan (f/k/a Krone) v. Krone, No. D 176240 (8th Jud. Dist. Ct., Clark County, May 23, 1994); Order Dismissing Appeal (Nev. Sup. Ct. No. 27235, May 20, 1998).

tax withholdings from gross retired pay may not be fixed at a percentage rate exceeding the member's projected effective tax rate (that is, the ratio of the member's anticipated total income tax to his anticipated total gross income from all sources).[72] If nothing else, the *Krone* case is a good reminder of the rationale for the 1991 change in the law to permit dividing the member's and former spouse's shares before calculation of taxes.

Again, there is little reliable data about what actually happens in the military pay centers when a member requests additional withholding or a former spouse complains that a member is claiming excessive exemptions for the purpose of raising the amount withheld and, ultimately, decreasing the sum divided with the former spouse. For now, counsel for former spouses believing such to be the case can do little except watch for unexplained reductions in the sum being paid to the former spouse, and either file a motion in local court, seeking discovery, or subpoena the records from the military pay center. The proposed model language at the end of this book includes a waiver for release of information necessary to obtain or enforce a payment order, and such language might be sufficient to allow counsel's inquiry without further court orders.

d. Enforcement of Award of Retired Pay at Particular Rank and Grade When That Status Varies from Actual Retirement

This matter concerns the situation in which the divorce precedes the retirement, and the parties agree (or the court orders) that the spousal share be determined as a portion of the retired pay payable to the member as if retirement had occurred on the date of divorce. At least one state has expressly limited its courts to dividing retired pay based upon the rank held by the member on the date of divorce.[73]

---

72. *In re* Krone, 75 Comp. Gen. ___ (1996) (Comptroller General's Decision No. B-271052, Aug. 6, 1996, at 3–4).

73. *See, e.g.,* Grier v. Grier, 731 S.W.2d 931 (Tex. 1987). In *Grier,* the 1975 decree of divorce omitted mention of the military retirement benefits, but a 1983 partition judgment awarded the former spouse a share based upon the length of marriage during service, at the rate of retired pay the member attained after divorce. Mr. Grier had been on the promotion list to lieutenant colonel at the time of divorce, but was not actually promoted from major until eight months afterward. The Texas Supreme Court held that granting

As with the above matters, there appears to be no uniform policy, and anecdotal accounts vary considerably about whether and how such orders are honored. The solution for this sort of case is an adequate reservation of jurisdiction in the trial court to fashion the actual award in a way that satisfies the state's law and military regulations. For example, if a court in such a state mandated division as if the member was a major with twenty years, and the member retires as a lieutenant colonel with twenty-five years, the court could simply enter an order after actual retirement awarding a sum equal to what the court wanted paid to the former spouse (phrased as a dollar sum or as a lesser percentage of the higher rank that would be equivalent in dollars to the percentage of the lower rank).

The problem in all these matters is much the same. To the degree that the military pay centers do not comply with a court's division, by sending to the former spouse either more or less than the court intended, they create the kind of enforcement and contempt problems that have exacerbated postdivorce litigation in the state courts.

D. COLLECTION METHODS

1. Voluntary Assignment

Especially in older cases (when this was the only method of obtaining payments to a former spouse), decrees commonly stated that "the member shall pay to the former spouse" a share of the retired pay. The typical method of accomplishing such payments was for the member to execute an allotment form for some portion of retired pay, naming the former

---

the former spouse a percentage of the retired pay based on the rank ultimately attained by the member would "impermissibly invade" the member's separate property. The court went on to hold that the former spouse should receive the mathematical percentage of gross retired pay "based on the rank of major which is currently payable to such officer who would have retired with 20 years service in September 1975 together with increases which may occur other than increases attributable to elevation in rank or services rendered by the military spouse after the date of divorce." 731 S.W.2d at 933. In other words, it became the burden of counsel to figure COLA adjustments from the date of divorce based on a hypothetical retirement, and then to fashion a form of order sufficient to allow the military pay center to pay it.

spouse as recipient. Members are free to execute allotments to anyone or anything they choose, and in any amount up to the entirety of disposable pay; if an allotment is submitted, the military pay center will send the money as directed by the member.

Allotments are still necessary as a payment mechanism in certain cases, such as those in which there is less than a ten-year overlap between service and marriage and the alimony alternative cannot be used.[74] There are also cases in which the final settlement calls for payments to the former spouse from the military retired pay in a sum greater than can be accomplished under the direct-pay provisions of the USFSPA. In those cases, where the parties mutually wish to avoid further court proceedings, an allotment may be submitted for the difference between the ordered sum and the sum paid directly.

There were many problems with this procedure in divorce cases. All control was in the hands of the member before direct payments could be ordered, and it was not at all uncommon for members to demand "take-backs" from the other provisions of decrees in exchange for keeping the allotment in place. Because members are free to change voluntary allotments at any time, another recurrent problem with allotments was with members who executed allotments, then later revoked them. The usual enforcement mechanism for the spouse was a contempt motion in state court, but that was cumbersome and expensive, especially if the member had relocated (requiring domestication, two lawyers, and much delay).

A third and very common problem with the allotment procedure was the near-universal habit of phrasing the spousal share as a fixed dollar sum (even if it was based on a percentage), causing its continual inflationary erosion over time as inflation crept but COLAs did not accrue to the spousal share. Anecdotal accounts indicate that some pay centers did accept spousal *percentage* allotments over the years, but that others did not (currently, percentage allotments are not accepted). This problem required the annual updating of allotments to reflect the increased spousal share from a fixed percentage, which many divorcing couples were unable, or unwilling, to do.

Problems with the pre-USFSPA allotment procedure were highlighted when *McCarty* was issued. Although there do not appear to be any reliable numbers compiled by anyone, there is no doubt that many hundreds, if not thousands, of members canceled spousal share allotments when the

---

74. See Subsection 2, Section E, Chapter Four.

opinion was issued in 1981, in part generating the backlash by the spouses that led to the various state "open-window" laws, and the USFSPA itself. Because the peculiarities of the USFSPA make arrearages in military retired pay noncollectible from future retired pay, the state courts were left with the task of ascertaining and enforcing collection of arrearages through other methods.

About the only way to enforce an order calling for execution of an allotment is the filing of an "order to show cause" regarding contempt (this procedure is known by many different names throughout the country), asking that the member be jailed until the contempt is purged by execution of the proper allotment form. Ancillary remedies include examination of the judgment debtor (once arrears have been determined) and recordation of arrearage judgments for payment upon the sale of real estate in the jurisdiction of the court. These awkward enforcement mechanisms often led to extended games of cat-and-mouse for embittered ex-spouses, where members executed allotments to get out of jail and then revoked or reduced the allotments once released, effectively daring the former spouses to spend the time and money to start the process over again.

At least one state has laws seeking to make such collection battles a little simpler. Texas has a statutory "turnover" mechanism whereby a court can place an obligation on an individual to turn over sums, even if exempt from direct execution until payment, on pain of contempt. The Texas Civil Code provides that a judgment creditor can reach the property, including "future rights to property," owned by a judgment debtor if the property "cannot be readily attached or levied on by ordinary legal process."[75] The courts are empowered to appoint receivers, order turnover to the debtor's control, or "otherwise apply the property to the satisfaction of the judgment." Contempt powers, as well as costs and attorney's fees recovery, are built in to the statute.

The essential reasoning behind the statute is that retired pay, once received, loses any kind of exempt character it might otherwise have; because the order is directed to the judgment debtor and not the military pay center, the Texas courts do not believe that federal law is offended by an order requiring *any or all* sums of retired pay to be turned over after receipt by a member.[76]

---

75. TEX. CIV. PRAC. & REM. CODE ANN. § 31.002 (West 1987 & Supp. 1992).
76. Cain v. Cain, 746 S.W.2d 861 (Tex. App. 1988). This holding may require

"Voluntary assignment" by means of allotment remains a useful mechanism for certain cases, when the facts leave it as the only means of accomplishing payment. Its practical and enforcement difficulties, however, make it a tool that should be used only when necessary, and only with due consideration of the later costs to both parties should anything go wrong.

2. Statutory Support Allotments

Despite its name, a statutory support allotment is a creature of garnishment, rather than allotment. Essentially, it is a product of a change of heart by Congress in 1982, when federal paychecks became subject to execution for state-court-ordered child (or child and spousal) support.[77] An "allotment" for current support becomes mandatory when a member of the uniformed services is at least two full months delinquent in such an obligation.[78] The law applies only to members on active duty for more than thirty days, whose support obligation has been ordered by a Title IV-D agency (essentially, under the Uniform Reciprocal Enforcement of Support Act (URESA), the Uniform Interstate Family Support Act (UIFSA), or one of their successors) or a court authorized to order support.

To obtain such an "allotment," formal written notice must be sent to the proper military pay center and include the following:[79]

- A request for initiation of the allotment under the statute, specifying the name and Social Security number of the member and the name and address of the person to whom the support is to be paid
- A certified copy of the underlying support order
- A statement explaining (1) that support payments are in arrears in an amount equal to at least two full months of support, and (if relevant) that payments are twelve weeks in arrears, (2) what (if any) limitations

---

revision in light of the U.S. Supreme Court decision in *Mansell v. Mansell*, 490 U.S. 581 (1989) (limitations in USFSPA go to substantive jurisdiction of state courts, and not merely their collection mechanisms).

77. The Tax Equity and Fiscal Responsibility Act of 1982, Pub. L. No. 97-248, § 172, 96 Stat. 324, 401 (1982).

78. 42 U.S.C. § 665(a)(1).

79. *Id.* § 665(a); 32 C.F.R. § 54.6 (1986).

have been placed on the duration of payments, and (3) what sum should be paid for current support (as well as how much, if any, of an amount is to be applied toward arrearages)
- Certification that the person sending the notice is an "authorized person" under the law, meaning a Title IV-D state official, or a court having authority to issue a support order

There are various limitations on what can be paid under this procedure. There must be some component of child support (that is, a spousal support award may be collected under this statute only if child support is *also* being collected).[80] A payment limitation of 60 percent of disposable earnings is in place, unless the member is providing current support to a different dependent child or spouse, in which case the limitation is 50 percent; in either case, if payments are twelve weeks or more in arrears, the respective limitation is raised by 5 percent.[81] It should be noted that the definition of "disposable earnings" is that under the Social Security laws, not the USFSPA, so the calculation of the sums in question include a deduction for tax liabilities, much like calculations of disposable pay before the USFSPA amendments of 1991.

3. Garnishments under the USFSPA and the Social Security Act

a. Under the USFSPA

A former spouse may use the garnishment provision of the USFSPA[82] if the member does not fully satisfy orders for payment of alimony, child support, or property (other than a division of retired pay as property).[83] If the designated agent receives court orders[84] not only for direct payment of alimony, child support, and/or property division, but also for garnishment, the orders will be satisfied on a first-come, first-served basis.[85]

---

80. 42 U.S.C. § 665(a)(1); 32 C.F.R. §§ 54.3(b)(e), 54.4 (1986).
81. 32 C.F.R. § 54.6(a)(5) (1986); 15 U.S.C. § 1673(b).
82. 10 U.S.C. § 1408(d)(5).
83. *Id.* § 1408(e)(4).
84. Only one foreign country, the Federal Republic of Germany, had an agreement with the United States for allowing garnishment of members' retired pay. That treaty presumably remains effective after German reunification.
85. 10 U.S.C. § 1408(e)(4)(A).

There is currently no provision in the federal law for a former spouse to garnish or otherwise recover payments—of a portion of retired pay as property—that were not made when ordered. The lack of an enforcement mechanism is procedural, not substantive or jurisdictional; these sums remain collectible by means of state court remedies, if any are available. Some courts impose limitations on arrearage awards under state or federal law to no earlier than certain cutoff dates, typically 1981 (*McCarty* and the retroactive effective date of the USFSPA) or 1983 (the actual passage and effective date of the USFSPA), but sometimes earlier or later.

The 1990 amendments made changes concerning the limitations on payments when there are both direct payment and garnishment orders. As with the direct-pay provisions, however, the 1990 amendments were prospective only, leading to a two-tier garnishment law dependent upon the date of the underlying final decree.

For final orders after the effective date of the 1990 amendments (that is, after February 4, 1991), the limitation is not 65 percent of disposable retired pay, but 65 percent of the amount of retired pay that is considered "remuneration for employment that is payable by the United States" under the Social Security Act.[86] A separate provision of the 1990 amendments specifically excludes amounts, paid to a former spouse under a property division, from the definition of "amounts received as retired pay for service in the uniformed services."[87] In combination, the amendments should sometimes increase and sometimes decrease the amounts available for decrees issued after February 4, 1991.[88]

There are circumstances in which computations using the definitions within the Social Security Act yield different results from those expected under a "disposable pay" analysis. For example, 42 U.S.C. § 662(f) has a sweeping definition of when the entitlement of an individual to money is deemed "based upon remuneration for employment." Among the items included are periodic benefits, including payments to individuals of pensions, retirement, or retired pay.

---

86. *Id.* § 1408(e)(4)(B).

87. *Id.* § 1408(c)(2).

88. At the time of publication of this book, the entire following discussion remained somewhat theoretical. The Cleveland pay center personnel stated by phone that they continue to use disposable retired pay as the sum to which the 65 percent limit applies. They declined to confirm that policy in writing.

Specifically *excluded* from the definition of remuneration for employment are certain federal death and disability benefits. There is, however, an *exception to the exception* for amounts—paid by the Veteran's Administration (VA) to a former member of the armed forces—obtained by waiver of retired pay.[89]

Thus, one example of a different result under the new rules would be the situation in which a member receives a partial VA disability benefit. Under the new rules, sums would be available for garnishment of child support and alimony arrearages that would not have been available under the former rules, which required having disposable pay available.

EXAMPLE

Fred and Wilma divorce, with Wilma awarded $250 of Fred's $1,200 retired pay as a division of property, and $500 per month in child support, which Fred does not pay.

Assume the order was issued *before* the 1990 amendments. Wilma would receive her $250 by direct payment, and could seek to garnish for arrears in child support. Presuming $200 in tax withholding, Fred's disposable pay would be calculated as follows: $1,200 (retired pay), minus $200 (tax withholding), equals $1,000. Wilma's $250 direct pay would be 25 percent of that $1,000, leaving 40 percent ($400) available for garnishment.

Presume the order was issued *after* the 1990 amendments. Wilma would receive her $250 by direct payment, and could seek to garnish for arrears in child support. Tax withholding and disposable pay would not be relevant. Wilma's $250 would not count as part of Fred's "remuneration for employment" under 42 U.S.C. § 662, so he would have $950 in that category. Assuming that Fred had a total annual income of $60,000 and an effective tax rate of 19.07 percent, he would be

---

89. The enforcing regulations, 5 C.F.R. § 581.103, state that "disability retired pay" is subject to garnishment proceedings. Presumably, this means that sums received under Chapter 61 (that is, when the member retired for disability) may be reached to the same extent as sums received under Chapter 38 (that is, postretirement disability sums received after application to the VA).

found to withhold properly against the military retired pay only in the same percentage, leaving him $768.84 in calculated "disposable." Wilma could obtain only 65 percent of that sum by both direct pay and garnishment, or $499.74. After subtracting her $250 direct payment, only $249.74 would be available for the child support garnishment.

EXAMPLE

In the above example, then, if Fred received $400 of his total monthly retired pay as VA disability payments, the whole analysis would change.

Under the pre-1991 rules, the amount garnishable would be calculated as follows: $1,200 (retired pay), minus $200 (tax withholding), minus $400 (disability retired pay), equals $600 (disposable pay). Wilma's $250 direct pay would be 41.67 percent of that $600, leaving only 23.33 percent ($139.98) available for garnishment.

Under the new rules, the amount garnishable would be as follows: $1,200 (retired pay), minus $250 (Wilma's direct pay), leaving $950 total available. Wilma could still obtain only 65 percent of that sum by both direct pay and garnishment, or $617.50. After subtracting her $250 direct payment, the same $367.50 would be available for the child support garnishment. In other words, under the new rules, a disability award on facts such as these has no effect on a garnishment.

The committee report accompanying the 1990 amendments indicated that no change in the rules surrounding disability retired pay was intended. It is therefore not certain that Congress realized that pursuant to the amendments spouses would have less available for garnishment in many instances, but comparatively *more* available if the member has a disability. It is also uncertain at this time how the military pay center will apply these changes, and whether the regulations will be rewritten to put these rules into practice, or whether some attempt will be made to divine the intention underlying the language used.[90] To further confuse matters, a

---

90. The implementation of new rules through the regulations has precedent. The "certified within ninety days" rule, for example (discussed in the procedural section), is not found in the act, but only in the regulations at 32 C.F.R. § 63.6(c)(2).

separate limitation of 25 percent of disposable pay applies to garnishments for property (that is, non-child support and non-spousal support).[91]

It may be in the best interest of the former spouse to *not* request present payment of certain kinds of payments due from the pay center; total collections can be increased by taking a strategic approach toward submission of orders. Generally, the former spouse should try to maximize direct payment from the military pay center of each month's property award.

> ✒ **Practice Tip:** When spousal or child support has been ordered, in addition to a division of retired pay as property, but the sum of disposable retired pay is inadequate to provide all sums owed to the former spouse, it may be better to request payment of *only* the property award from the military pay center. Child support is generally easier to collect in other forums and through other mechanisms, and accrued arrearages in child support can be garnished against the military retired pay. It is more difficult to collect a property award through, for example, garnishment against a second career's paychecks, and arrearages in retired pay may not be collected through garnishment of retired pay.

Child or spousal support payments could be allowed to slip into arrears, to be later reduced to judgment and garnished.[92] If there had been sufficient funds to pay the property award, but not all the child support owed, collection by garnishment of the arrears could begin once the child has attained majority and is no longer receiving present support.

When the award is for spousal support (or child support if the property award left no portion of the child support collectible as present payments), deferring collection of the support may still allow collection. Child and spousal support payments tend to be static, or at least not fully indexed to inflation, while COLAs will make the total sum of disposable retired pay larger on an ongoing basis. Eventually, these processes should allow for garnishment of old support arrearages.

As an alternative strategy, support payments could be allowed to slip into arrears and collected by garnishment from the member's postservice

---

91. 15 U.S.C. § 1673(a) (1977).
92. Obviously, any practitioner attempting these strategies must have a detailed command of the intricacies of the laws of the applicable jurisdictions concerning arrearages, interest, collections, executions, and statutes of limitations. Optimum strategy may well vary from state to state.

private-sector employers. In most states, priority for garnishments is given to child support (or child and spousal support). In terms of collectibility, it is difficult to imagine a fact pattern that would justify collecting support and deferring collection of property payments.[93]

b. Under the Social Security Act

The USFSPA is not necessarily directly relevant to collections of past-due child support (or spousal and child support). Service of a relevant court order, showing the existence of an arrearage equal to at least two full months of support, should be made on the proper military pay center, by certified mail, return receipt requested, along with whatever legal process (writ of garnishment by sheriff or writ of attachment, for example) is required under state law. The pay centers have proven fairly helpful in assisting private counsel with internal requirements. Again, the procedures ultimately resulting from the consolidation process may not be known for some years.

As noted above, the Social Security Act now allows for the involuntary assignment of a portion of an active-duty member's pay, at least when child support is in issue. Garnishment against federal pay of any sort was first authorized by the Social Services Amendments of 1974.[94] The new law waived sovereign immunity by the United States to allow the enforcement of state court orders against active duty and retired military members, among others. The waiver went to debts for child support or alimony, and is generally considered to have been passed for the purpose of allowing garnishment of salaries of federal employees who did not make support payments.[95]

Three years later, Congress fleshed out the law with some procedural guidance and directives about how to resolve conflicts between federal

---

93. There could be other reasons for doing so. Though presumably a property award would accrue interest if unpaid, like any other civil judgment, some states have not always allowed interest to run on support payments. Texas, for example, only began allowing interest on support payments on September 1, 1991.

94. Pub. L. No. 93-647, § 101(a), 88 Stat. 2337, 2357 (1974) (codified as amended at 42 U.S.C. § 659(a)).

95. *See, e.g.,* Parker v. Parker, 335 Pa. Super. 348, 484 A.2d 168 (Super. Ct. 1984).

and state law.[96] Other congressional acts the same year[97] limited collections by garnishment to the 50 percent (if there are other spousal or child dependents) or 60 percent (if not), plus 5 percent extra if more than twelve weeks in arrears, that were discussed in the immediately preceding section.

Congress essentially made all federal employees subject to garnishment for *any* debt by adding a new Section 5520a to Title 5 of the United States Code.[98] Pursuant to the new provision, any writ, order, or summons "in the nature of a garnishment" for *any* debt is to be withheld from the "pay"[99] of any "employee" of the executive, legislative, or judicial branches of government. By its own terms, the new law makes garnishment thereunder secondary to collection of child support or alimony under the Social Security Act.[100]

The military is specifically addressed in Subsection k of the new act, which directs the secretaries of "the Executive departments concerned" to promulgate regulations applying to military members by April 4, 1994.[101] Provisions were to be made for the Soldiers' and Sailors' Civil Relief Act.

The new provision could lead to reversal of many of the existing conclusions about what is collectible, and what position members and spouses take regarding "reduced present pay for reduced services." An order for arrearages in military retirement payable as a division of property is certainly as valid as any other civil debt. Therefore, it would appear that garnishment under the new law would be possible for such sums, as long as military retired pay is "pay" as defined in the legislation.

The usual positions are thus reversed: spouses will want to assert that military retired pay is "pay" (that is, compensation paid for personal services) under the new law, and retired members will certainly assert that retired pay is a pension, and therefore not pay garnishable under the act.

---

96. Pub. L. No. 95-30, § 501, 91 Stat. 126, 157 (1977) (codified as amended at 42 U.S.C. § 659, 661–62).
97. Pub. L. No. 95-30, § 501(e), 91 Stat. 126, 161 (1977) (codified as amended at 15 U.S.C. § 1673(b)).
98. Pub. L. No. 103-94, § 9, 107 Stat. 1007 (1993).
99. Including basic, premium, severance, back, sick, or incentive pay, "and any other compensation paid or payable for personal services, whether such compensation is denominated as wages, salary, commission, bonus pay or otherwise." 5 U.S.C. § 5520(a)(4)(A).
100. *Id.* §§ 5520a(h)(2), 5520a(i).
101. *Id.* § 5520a(k)(1).

It seems inevitable that this matter will require further legislative guidance or, more likely, a series of court decisions to determine if it has altered the scope of what is actually collectible, as developed in decisions reached under the USFSPA.

c. Requirement of Election of Mechanism

A garnishment or direct-pay order submitted to the military pay center should indicate clearly on its face what is being sought, and the authority under which it is being sought. Because there are different limitations on collection under each of the possible statutory mechanisms for obtaining payment, practitioners should plan the order of collections in a way that maximizes sums payable (in both the short and long run) as discussed above. It is quite possible that collection of one amount due might have to be put off entirely until a different category of debt has been satisfied.

Chapter Six
MILITARY-RELATED BENEFITS

A. MEDICAL BENEFITS

For some years, dependents of retired members of the uniformed services have been entitled to medical benefits on essentially the same basis as dependents of active-duty members.[1] The original Uniformed Services Former Spouses Protection Act (USFSPA) provided that certain former spouses were eligible for certain medical benefits available to dependents of retired members of the uniformed services. The medical benefits available to qualified spouses are for treatment at uniformed services medical facilities, and benefits under the Civilian Health and Medical Program of the Uniformed Services (CHAMPUS), explained below.

Former spouses who meet the eligibility tests set forth below may be provided health care at any uniformed services medical facility. The health care available to eligible former spouses is the same as that available to dependents of active-duty members.[2] Medical care is provided to various categories of eligible persons in the order of priority established by the facility, however, and in practice this usually means that few services are ever provided at such facilities.

The 1985 amendments to the USFSPA expanded the groups of former spouses qualified to receive medical benefits.[3] The 1986 amendments extended the "open period" during which certain spouses could get medical benefits.[4] The 1989 and 1990 military authorization acts extended these periods further.

---

1. Pub. L. No. 89-614, 80 Stat. 862 (1966).
2. Beneficiaries who use any uniformed service medical facility are subject to the capabilities of the professional staff and the availability of space and facilities. 32 C.F.R. § 728.3.
3. Pub. L. No. 98-525, § 645, 98 Stat. 2492 (1984).
4. Pub. L. No. 99-661, § 646, 100 Stat. 3816 (1986).

1. *Eligibility and Limitations*

Three categories of former spouses are eligible for these benefits, depending upon three criteria:

- the number of years of creditable service performed by the member,
- the number of years the former spouse was married to the member, and
- the number of years during which the marriage overlapped the creditable service.

This is usually expressed as a three part number (for example, 20/20/20).

a. 20/20/20 Former Spouses

A former spouse is eligible for lifetime medical benefits if, on the date of the final decree of divorce, dissolution, or annulment, the following criteria are fulfilled:

- the former spouse had been married for at least twenty years to a member of the uniformed services, and
- the member of the uniformed services had performed at least twenty years of creditable service, and
- at least twenty years of that marriage were during the member's creditable service.[5]

A former spouse can meet this test regardless of the date of divorce.[6] It is irrelevant whether the divorce decree specifies any such benefit, or whether the parties contemplated the benefit. Like Social Security, medical

---

5. 10 U.S.C. § 1072(2)(F).

6. Pub. L. No. 98-525, § 645(a)(3) (1984) amended the original act (Pub. L. No. 97-252 (1982)) by opening this category to any former spouse who meets these three criteria regardless of the date of divorce. The original legislation required that the final decree be dated after February 1, 1983, for the former spouse to qualify. Former spouses divorced before February 1, 1983, were therefore covered only for care received on or after January 1, 1985.

benefits for former spouses in this category who fulfill the legislative criteria have a statutory entitlement separate from the rights and obligations accruing to the member. They cost the member nothing.

b. 20/20/15 Former Spouses Divorced before April 1, 1985

Former spouses in this category are also eligible for lifetime medical benefits. Qualification for this second category requires fulfilling the following criteria:

*   the former spouse was married to a member of the uniformed services for at least twenty years, and
*   the member had performed at least twenty years of creditable service, and
*   the marriage overlapped the creditable service by at least fifteen but fewer than twenty years, and
*   the decree of divorce, dissolution, or annulment was entered before April 1, 1985.[7]

c. 20/20/15 Former Spouses Divorced on or after April 1, 1985

Former spouses in this third category must meet the same 20/20/15 criteria as required for the second category. If, however, the decree of divorce, dissolution, or annulment was entered on or after April 1, 1985, then the former spouse loses the medical coverage within two years after the date of the decree.[8]

If the decree was entered between April 1, 1985, and September 29, 1988, then the former spouse had benefits through the later of December 31, 1988, and two years from the date of the decree. For a decree entered on or after September 29, 1988, the former spouse receives medical benefits for only *one* year following the date of the decree.[9] A former spouse

---

7. 10 U.S.C. § 1072(2)(G). This category was added to the statute in Pub. L. No. 98-525, § 645(a), 98 Stat. 2435 (1984). This "magic date" was the effective date of the implementing legislation.
8. 10 U.S.C. § 1072(2)(G); 32 C.F.R. § 199.3(b)(2)(ii)(D)(2)(*ii*).
9. Pub. L. No. 100-456, § 651(a), 102 Stat. 1990 (1988) (creating 10 U.S.C. § 1076(f)).

purchasing coverage under the Uniformed Services Voluntary Insurance Plan or its successor programs (described below), however, retains some CHAMPUS coverage for an additional year, to the extent preexisting conditions are excluded from that voluntary insurance plan.[10]

d. Reservists' Former Spouses

The medical benefits for reservists and National Guard members are generally reflective of the distinct pattern of retirement benefits for those services. Benefits generally are deferred until the member reaches age sixty, at which time medical care is available at military facilities for the member and the member's dependents.

"Dependents" include current spouses and unremarried widows or widowers, as well as children under age twenty-one (or those under twenty-three who are full-time students). Also included are parents and parents-in-law who are dependent upon a member for over half their support and reside in the member's household, and persons who met this criteria at the time of the member's death.

Former spouses of such members have rights that echo those of former spouses of regular members. The following applies to former spouses of "active, retired, or deceased" members; in other words, while the member is on active duty, or after turning sixty and becoming eligible to retire, or if the member died while serving more than thirty days active duty.

Former spouses who are 20/20/20 former spouses are eligible for lifetime benefits. If they are 20/20/15 former spouses, and divorced before April 1, 1985, they are eligible for lifetime medical benefits. If they are 20/20/15 former spouses, and divorced after April 1, 1985, but before September 29, 1988, they get two years of carry-over coverage, and if divorced after September 29, 1988, they get one year.

For all the above, marriage during service "on active reserve status creditable for retirement" is "service during marriage" for purposes of the statutory test.

---

10. 10 U.S.C. § 1076(f)(7). Because of the length of time it took to set up this program, any former spouse eligible for conversion to the Uniformed Services Voluntary Insurance Program under prior law continued to qualify despite the passage of years from the divorce until the election to enroll in that insurance program. Pub. L. No. 100-456, § 651(c), 102 Stat. 1990 (1988).

e. Restrictions on Rights of Former Spouses

There are restrictions to the rights of former spouses who are eligible for medical benefits as 20/20/20 or 20/20/15 former spouses (the same restrictions apply to former spouses of reservists or members of the National Guard). Those restrictions are as follows:

- The former spouse must not remarry.[11] Eligibility for health benefits ceases upon remarriage and is *not* regained even if the subsequent marriage terminates.
- The former spouse must not be covered by an employer-sponsored health care plan.[12] If there is such a plan, however, and coverage thereunder is terminated (voluntarily or otherwise), eligibility for benefits is restored.
- The former spouse must not yet be age sixty-five. Upon eligibility for Medicare (Part A), CHAMPUS eligibility ends.

f. Extending Benefits by Separation Rather Than Divorce

Counsel should be aware that it is possible in some cases to extend medical coverage for a former spouse while still dividing the military retirement benefits. This is so because the USFSPA permits military retired pay to be divided by an order of "divorce, dissolution, annulment, or legal separation," while the statute governing CHAMPUS eligibility (and the regulations thereunder) speak only of "final decree of divorce, dissolution, or annulment."[13]

If the court enters a decree of separate maintenance (known in some states as a legal separation) rather than a divorce, it is thus possible to preserve the "marriage" for purposes of current and future medical coverage, while entering a final order for division of the military retired pay.

---

11. 10 U.S.C. §§ 1072(2)(F)–(G).
12. *Id.*
13. *Compare* 10 U.S.C. § 1408(a)(2) *with* 32 C.F.R. § 199.3(b)(2)(ii)(C) (eligibility of former spouse requires being unremarried, not being covered by an employer-sponsored health plan, and having been married to a member during twenty years of creditable service).

This can be beneficial for both parties, such as in situations when the member is not yet eligible for retirement, the former spouse is in questionable or ill health, and the member faces a substantial alimony claim intended to provide for those medical costs.

Of course, like most such items, this sword has two edges. Whereas a former spouse might bargain away some part of an alimony claim to secure continuing insurance benefits, the predilection of the local judiciary to grant alimony to compensate for anticipated medical costs (that would be covered but for the actions of the opposing party) might well determine which party benefits from this bargaining chip.

Most states today have "one-party" or "no-fault" divorce, so a divorce decree can be entered even over the active opposition of the opposing party. Thus, use of this strategy might require cooperation of the parties, or at least agreement to delay entry of a formal divorce until satisfaction of the former spouse's eligibility for medical benefits. It is in the best interest of both parties to cooperate in a way in which their mutual exposure to liability can be lessened, but it is too often true that the parties are too embittered toward one another to cooperate even for their mutual benefit.

There are also cases in which the cooperation would have to be extended indefinitely to be useful. The above strategy presupposes that the parties have been married during the entirety of military service, so that at some future date, the former spouse's potential lifetime medical benefits would vest. If the parties married after the member started service, and the member is set to retire before the vesting of the former spouse's medical benefits, a delay in the divorce will be helpful only during the delay itself, because the former spouse's potential benefits will *never* vest.

In these cases, the only options are to remain "married" although legally separated until the former spouse is eligible for Medicare, or until some other event occurs (remarriage to a covered individual or a certain term of years, for example) Still, when a particular medical condition of the former spouse exists at the time of the potential dissolution, preservation of the technical marriage during completion of treatment has substantial value.

2. CHAMPUS

Former spouses who are eligible for beneficiary health benefits may use CHAMPUS. CHAMPUS is a supplemental program to the uniformed services medical care system. One of the primary functions of CHAMPUS is to provide financial assistance to beneficiaries for certain prescribed medical care obtained from civilian sources.[14] CHAMPUS pays for some medically necessary services and supplies used in the diagnosis and treatment of illness or injury. Beneficiaries must obtain CHAMPUS certification on their military identification cards before using CHAMPUS. Though CHAMPUS has a copay requirement, there are a number of CHAMPUS supplement plans available from military-related organizations.

Further information on the details of the CHAMPUS program can be obtained in the *CHAMPUS Handbook,* a general program guide available to all CHAMPUS beneficiaries from the Patient Affairs Office at any uniformed services facility. The facility can also direct interested persons to a CHAMPUS Health Benefits Advisor (HBA), an appointed advisor who may assist beneficiaries in applying for benefits and in preparing claims. Further information and claims forms are available through the Office of CHAMPUS, Aurora, CO 80045-6900.

3. The US-VIP Program and Its Successors

From time to time, there have been efforts to provide transitional health care coverage to former spouses; historically, they have been abandoned by the underwriting insurance companies, sometimes unexpectedly, and the availability of coverage has not been reliably predictable. Probably the longest lasting of these was established for former spouses who were married to members for at least one year, and who were automatically eligible for a private health insurance plan known as the Uniformed Services Voluntary Insurance Plan (US-VIP), administered by the Mutual of Omaha Insurance Company. There was no federal regulation of how the premiums for this coverage should be paid; in the absence of a court order, the cost will have to be borne by the former spouse.[15] The plan also covered dependent children.

The name of this program is sometimes still used, although it collapsed around 1992. The version of the program current in 1996 goes by

---

14. 32 C.F.R. § 199.4(a).

15. It was anticipated by framers of the amendment to the act that the divorce decree would make some provision about who was to pay the premiums. H.R. Conf. Rep. No. 98-1080, at 302 (Sept. 26, 1984).

the unpronounceable acronym CHCBP, for Continued Health Care Benefit Program, and provides coverage for eligible former members, their dependent children, and unremarried former spouses.[16] It was established by the National Defense Authorization Act for fiscal year 1993, and basically follows most of the same rules and procedures as the CHAMPUS program, although it is not technically affiliated in any way with that program.

Obviously, 20/20/20 former spouses have no need for this program because they are covered under CHAMPUS, although they apparently retain this eligibility (within the plan's application time limits) if they become ineligible for CHAMPUS benefits. Former spouses who do not satisfy even the 20/20/15 test are still eligible to enroll in the carryover coverage plans, as long as the marriage lasted at least one year. They do not, however, receive any postdivorce CHAMPUS coverage for preexisting condition coverage if they purchase such coverage. (Preexisting conditions were covered by US-VIP after one year, but it is not certain that the successor program also provides this benefit.)

B. SURVIVOR'S BENEFITS

1. The Survivor's Benefit Plan and Its Predecessors

The Survivor's Benefit Plan (SBP) was created in 1972 to provide a monthly annuity to certain spouses and dependents of retired members of any of the uniformed services. It largely replaced an earlier survivor's plan known as the RSFPP (the Retired Serviceman's Family Protection Plan),[17] which is of little importance here because there was no provision under that plan for making a former spouse a beneficiary of a survivorship

---

16. Program details are available from the CHCBP Administrator, P.O. Box 1608, Rockville, MD 20849-1608; 800/809-6119.

17. The RSFPP was originally known as the Uniformed Services Contingency Option Plan of 1953, enacted by Pub. L. No. 83-239, 67 Stat. 501 (1953). The name was changed by Pub. L. No. 87-381, 75 Stat. 810 (1961). The RSFPP is described at 10 U.S.C. § 1431 *et seq.* That program was generally considered a failure due to the very low participation rate of eligible members. The USFSPA had no effect on the RSFPP. Neither former spouses nor retired members who had elected benefits under the RSFPP are affected by any of the benefits described in this section of the book.

benefit. Members entitled to retired pay are eligible to participate in the SBP.[18] Under the plan, a survivor's annuity is payable after a member's death.[19]

Some members retired *before* 1972 are nevertheless participants in the SBP, because Congress has provided a number of "open enrollment periods" or "open seasons" during which nonparticipants could join the program, and those who had selected less than the full amount of benefits could increase their level of participation.

In 1982, SBP coverage was extended to former spouses at the election of the member.[20] Subsequent legislation (some of which is discussed in greater detail below) revised the types and attributes of available SBP coverage. In 1983, members already retired were permitted to cover their former spouses during an open enrollment ending September 23, 1984.[21] In 1984, court orders noting a member's voluntary election to make a former spouse the SBP beneficiary were made enforceable.[22] In 1985, the cost of former spouse coverage was made identical to present spouse coverage, and coverage for children by a former spouse was made possible.[23] In 1986, state courts were allowed to order that former spouses be members' beneficiaries.[24] An open season for both the SBP and the Supplemental Survivor's Benefit Plan (see explanation below) was put into place from April 1, 1992, through March 31, 1993.[25]

Those choosing to begin or increase their participation in the SBP program during an open season were also faced with paying a premium. The form of the premium is an additional percentage of the base amount covered by the SBP. For those first enrolling, the premium is charged against the entirety of the base amount selected. For those only increasing coverage, the premium applies against only the increase in the base

18. 10 U.S.C. § 1448(a)(1)(A).
19. *Id.* § 1447 *et seq.*
20. Pub. L. No. 97-252, 96 Stat. 735 (1982).
21. Pub. L. No. 98-94, 97 Stat. 614 (1983).
22. Pub. L. No. 98-525, 98 Stat. 2492 (1984). The spouse has a time limit of one year from the date of the court order to request that the election be "deemed" made by the member by application to the proper finance center.
23. Pub. L. No. 99-145, 99 Stat. 583 (1985).
24. Pub. L. No. 99-661, 100 Stat. 3816 (1986).
25. *See* Pub. L. No. 101-189, 103 Stat. 1352 (1989).

amount. In both cases, the additional premium set at the last open season was as follows:

YEARS RETIRED	ADDITIONAL PREMIUM RATE	YEARS RETIRED	ADDITIONAL PREMIUM RATE
0–1	0%	9–10	1.8%
1–2	.2%	10–11	2.1%
2–3	.4%	11–12	2.4%
3–4	.6%	12–13	2.7%
4–5	.8%	13–14	3.0%
5–6	1.0%	14–15	3.3%
5–6	1.2%	15–16	3.6%
6–7	1.4%	16–17	3.9%
7–8	1.6%	17–18	4.2%
8–9	1.8%	18 +	4.5%

It should be noted that the open season legislation to date has not included "deemed election" language, but rather required that the member "voluntarily" sign the necessary form—even if that "voluntary" signature was on threat of contempt for failing to do so. The model decree language at the end of this book includes an "open season" clause for inclusion in decrees when the facts warrant it; such a clause should be sufficient to permit the divorce court to later threaten or impose contempt sanctions to obtain the requisite signature.

a. Eligibility and Calculations

To be eligible to participate in the SBP, a member must be either entitled to retired pay or eligible for retired pay for nonregular service because he or she is under age sixty.[26] The SBP is not divisible. As explained below, it can be made to cover more than one person in certain circumstances (such as a spouse and dependent child), but it cannot be divided between a spouse and former spouse, or between two former spouses.[27]

---

26. 10 U.S.C. § 1448(a)(1). Eligibility for retired pay for nonregular service is defined in 10 U.S.C. § 1331 *et seq.*

27. The military retirement system has no provision for division of a survivor-

The SBP is funded by contributions taken out of the member's retired pay. As discussed in greater detail below, it is possible to allocate the burden of those premiums by adjusting the percentages of the retirement benefits paid to each party.[28] For members entering service before March 1, 1990, premiums are the lesser of the amount computed by two tests. The first test is 2.5 percent of the first $446 of the base amount,[29] plus 10 percent of the remaining base amount. The second test is 6.5 percent of the base amount. Members entering service on or after March 1, 1990, have no choice; for them, SBP premiums are 6.5 percent of the base amount.

The maximum amount of the standard SBP annuity for a beneficiary under age sixty-two or a dependent child is 55 percent of the elected amount of the member's base retired pay,[30] as adjusted from time to time for cost of living increases.[31] SBP payments are reduced for a beneficiary who is age sixty-two or older.[32] After the 1985 amendments to the USFSPA, existing beneficiaries receive the greater amount available under two tests.

First, under the older "Social Security offset" test, SBP benefits are offset, dollar for dollar, by any Social Security benefits received by the beneficiary because of credit earned by the member while on active duty.[33]

---

ship interest. The absence of such a provision works hardships of unjust enrichment and dispossession. At the 1990 hearings on the USFSPA, the members' political pressure groups, the former spouses' political pressure groups, the Pentagon representative, and the ABA representatives all agreed that this required correction, but Congress has taken no action to date.

28. See Subsection 5, Section B, of this chapter.
29. Amount effective as of January 1, 1998.
30. As computed under 10 U.S.C. §§ 1401–1401a.
31. 10 U.S.C. § 1451(a)(1)(A).
32. For "children only" designations, the benefits continue only until the child is eighteen years old (or twenty-two if a full-time student). 10 U.S.C. § 1447(5).
33. Thus, if the Social Security benefits were based entirely on *non*military Social Security credits, there would be no offset. *See* 53 Comp. Gen. 733 (1974) (explaining why only the military service covered by Social Security was considered for the offset, even if the member also had civilian earnings covered by Social Security). Similarly, there would be no offset for a beneficiary who remained employed and earned too much money to receive

Under the second test, benefits are reduced from 55 percent to 35 percent of the elected amount of the member's base retired pay at age sixty-two (again, as adjusted for cost of living increases). Beneficiaries first eligible after October 1, 1985, automatically fall under the second of the two tests.

Criticism of the lowering of benefits at age 62 led to the development of a "high option" supplement known as the Supplemental Survivor's Benefit Plan (SSBP).[34] Under the supplement program, payment of additional premiums could increase the survivor's benefits by 5 percent for each SSBP unit purchased.

Unlike the SBP itself,[35] the SSBP was designed to be actuarially neutral—that is, the program was designed to neither save nor cost the government any money. Thus, the increased coverage comes at a significantly increased cost. The cost of each unit is a percentage of gross retired pay, which is different depending upon the age of the member enrolling in the program. Essentially, the percentage goes up as age goes up, as illustrated below.

Age of Election	Premium	Age of Election	Premium	Age of Election	Premium	Age of Election	Premium
17	.70%	33	1.27%	49	1.67%	65	3.46%
18	.72%	34	1.33%	50	1.74%	66	3.62%
19	.75%	35	1.36%	51	1.80%	67	3.80%
20	.77%	36	1.19%	52	1.88%	68	3.95%
21	.80%	37	1.12%	53	1.97%	69	4.13%
22	.83%	38	1.13%	54	2.07%	70	4.30%
23	.86%	39	1.17%	55	2.17%	71	4.50%
24	.89%	40	1.22%	56	2.27%	72	4.74%
25	.93%	41	1.27%	57	2.37%	73	4.95%
26	.97%	42	1.28%	58	2.48%	74	5.18%
27	1.00%	43	1.31%	59	2.60%	75	5.38%

(continued)

Social Security payments, although this has the counterintuitive effect of making larger payments go to beneficiaries who have larger incomes.

34. *See* Pub. L. No. 101-189, 103 Stat. 1352 (1989). The plan was to become effective October 1, 1991, but various factors caused modifications by legislation. *See* Pub. L. No. 101-510, 104 Stat. 1485 (1990); Pub. L. No. 102-190, 105 Stat. 1290 (1991).

35. Theoretically, the government subsidizes the SBP program to the extent of 40 percent, with the other 60 percent paid by means of the premiums collected from the military retired pay of those participating.

Age of Election	Premium	Age of Election	Premium	Age of Election	Premium	Age of Election	Premium
28	1.04%	44	1.37%	60	2.62%	76	5.64%
29	1.08%	45	1.43%	61	2.87%	77	5.90%
30	1.13%	46	1.49%	62	3.02%	78	6.13%
31	1.18%	47	1.56%	63	3.16%	79	6.42%
32	1.23%	48	1.62%	64	3.31%	80	6.68%

Because the amount of any particular member's total SBP and SSBP premiums are dependent upon factors of age and total gross pay, they must be individually calculated to be accurately determined.

b. DIC and Other Reductions in Benefits

There are other reductions in SBP benefits as well. Since 1956, Dependency and Indemnity Compensation (DIC) payments under 38 U.S.C. § 1311(a) have been payable to the survivors of any veteran who dies after December 31, 1956, from a service-connected or compensable disability.[36] DIC payments are not made to persons divorced from members.

If an SBP beneficiary is entitled to DIC, the DIC payment is a dollar-for-dollar offset from the SBP payment.[37] However, certain supplemental amounts to the DIC benefits, attributable to the support of a dependent child by the recipient or the recipient's satisfaction of certain enumerated disability qualifications, do *not* get offset against SBP.[38] DIC payments are not taxed; like disability payments made to members instead of regular retired pay, they are therefore more valuable than the (taxable) SBP payments that would otherwise go to the survivor.

If the widow or widower of a member remarries, DIC payments are terminated. There was some confusion about whether the benefits would be reinstated if the second marriage ended. A 1990 amendment, however, clarified that the remarriage of the DIC recipient permanently terminates any entitlement, even if the new marriage ends by death or divorce of the new spouse.[39] This change was, apparently, intended to be prospective

---

36. 38 U.S.C. § 410(a). *See* Pub. L. No. 84-881, 70 Stat. 862, 867 (1956).
37. 10 U.S.C. § 1451(c)(2).
38. *See* 38 U.S.C. §§ 411(b)–(d).
39. Pub. L. No. 101-508, § 8004, 104 Stat. 1388-343 (1990).

only. Further, if the remarriage occurred when the former spouse was over fifty-five, the SBP payment is apparently to be increased to the full amount. (In other words, the DIC offset is replaced by additional SBP dollars, leaving the only effect one of taxes.)

One very common reduction in SBP benefits should be highlighted, as it provides planning opportunities for lawyers involved in these cases. A beneficiary receives a smaller annuity if a member elects less than the entire base retired pay for computing the SBP annuity. Note that the spouse of a married member must consent to any election of less than the entire base retired pay, unless a former spouse is made the SBP beneficiary. If the member makes no election, or if the member's spouse does not consent (when required), the entire amount of the member's base retired pay is used to calculate the SBP.

The reduced amount can be from $300, indexed from 1986,[40] up to the member's full gross retired pay. Subsequent cost of living adjustments (COLAs) will increase a reduced base amount to keep it proportionally the same as the amount initially selected.

The planning opportunity stems from the reality that the former spouse is often set to receive less than half the military retired pay. If the SBP is calculated on the full base amount, the former spouse would actually receive an *increase* in monthly payments upon the death of the member, a result that may not have been anticipated by anyone involved, or that could be specifically negotiated. An example is useful.

EXAMPLE

If the total retired pay is $1,000, and the full base amount is selected, the 6.5 percent premium cost would be $65, and would provide a benefit of $550 (that is, $1,000 multiplied by 55 percent). If the spouse had been receiving half of retired pay, the spouse would receive a $50 per month increase upon the member's death. To have the former spouse continue receiving only $500, the base amount would have to be ad-

---

40. The fiscal year 1986 Department of Defense Authorization Act provided that the $300 base was to be indexed to COLAs accruing to post-October 1, 1985, basic pay. As of January 1, 1998, the indexed base is $446.

justed from $1,000 to $909.09. It is worth noting that the premium in this example would shrink from $65 to $59.09.

If, on the other hand, the particulars of the deal reached (or order entered) in a given case *require* that the former spouse receive a larger death benefit than her amount of lifetime payments, it may be reasonable to leave the base amount at the maximum, even if the former spouse is receiving less than half the retired pay. Appropriate circumstances could include lifetime payments arranged so that the former spouse is paying for the SBP in whole or part, or the former spouse's receipt of alimony or other benefits terminable upon the member's death.

c. Treatment of Reservists

Members entitled to a reserve-component annuity are those who would be eligible for retired pay based on reserve service.[41] The amount of the survivor's annuity based on a member's reserve service might be calculated differently from that of members who retire after twenty or more years of active duty, although the same rules regarding extent of coverage, automatic coverage unless coverage is specifically declined, and so on, apply.

The Reserve Component Survivor Benefit Plan (RCSBP) was established to provide annuities to beneficiaries of reservists who completed the requirements for eligibility for retired pay at age sixty but died before reaching that age.[42] Before 1978, reservists could not elect participation in their SBP program until they were eligible to draw retired pay (that is, at age sixty). That year, legislation granted them the power to elect participation upon notification of eligibility for retirement, which generally is long before they reach age sixty.[43]

There are three options available to reservists upon notification for eligibility. Option A declines coverage until age sixty. Presuming survival

---

41. See Section D, Chapter Three.
42. *See* Pub. L. No. 95-397, 92 Stat. 843 (1978).
43. *See id.*

to that time, this option has the same costs and benefits as the active-duty SBP program. Option B provides coverage so that payments begin on the later of (1) the date of the retiree's death, or (2) the date the retiree would have turned sixty. Option C provides coverage so that payments begin immediately after the retiree dies, regardless of age. Options B and C are actuarially adjusted so that premiums are higher, benefits are smaller, and the lesser risk is otherwise reflected in the benefits payable.

As of 1983, it was possible for reservists to designate former spouses as their SBP recipients.[44] The amount of the reserve-component annuity payable to a beneficiary is calculated by a formula that apparently ensures that a reserve-component annuity is always less than a corresponding standard annuity.[45]

The regulations establishing the formula take into account the age of the member electing to provide the annuity at the time of election; the difference in age between the member and the beneficiary of the annuity; whether the member provided for the annuity to become effective upon the member's death before age sixty, on the day after death, or on the sixtieth anniversary of the member's birth; appropriate group annuity tables; and other factors the secretary of defense considers relevant.[46]

SBP benefits based on reserve-component service have a reduction similar to that for regular retirement SBP benefits after a beneficiary turns age sixty-two. Members and surviving beneficiaries can obtain further information about reserve-component SBP benefits by contacting the Defense Finance and Accounting Service (DFAS).

2. *Application and Litigation; Voluntary and Deemed Elections*

The SBP applies automatically to a member who is married or has at least one dependent child at the time the member becomes entitled to retired pay, unless the member affirmatively elects not to participate in the SBP.[47] The member's spouse must consent to any election not to participate in the SBP, to an annuity for that spouse at less than the maximum level, or to an annuity for a dependent child but not for the spouse.[48] When

---

44. *See* Pub. L. No. 98-94, 97 Stat. 614 (1983).
45. 10 U.S.C. §§ 1451(a)(2), 1451(f).
46. *Id.* § 1451(f).
47. *Id.* § 1448(a)(2).
48. *Id.* § 1448(a)(3)(A).

the spouse does not consent to noncoverage, and none of the special circumstances noted below (the spouse cannot be found, for example) are
present, the spouse can petition for instatement of the benefits later, even
after the member's death.[49] The spouse can be named SBP beneficiary
even when he or she has little or no time-rule percentage of the retired
pay itself.[50] The spouse's consent is not required (1) if the spouse cannot
be located, (2) if, due to exceptional circumstances, requiring the member
to seek the spouse's consent would otherwise be inappropriate, or (3) if
the member elects to provide the SBP annuity for a former spouse (and/
or dependent children).[51]

A member may elect to provide the SBP annuity to a former spouse,
whether or not the member is presently married. If a married member
provides an annuity for a former spouse, the member's current spouse and
dependent children of that spouse cannot be beneficiaries of the member's
SBP annuity.[52] Former spouses, regardless of when they were divorced,
became eligible to be SBP beneficiaries after February 1, 1983.[53]

A former spouse is normally eligible to be made the SBP beneficiary
as a former spouse based on the above only if he or she is *already* a
former spouse when the member becomes eligible to retire.[54] In other
words, a married member cannot elect to make a spouse a "former spouse"
SBP beneficiary if the member was still married to that person when the
member became eligible to participate in the SBP. There does not appear
to be any data about how, if at all, this is verified by the military pay
center.

If the member married after becoming eligible for retired pay, and
then divorced that person, the now former spouse may not be made the
SBP beneficiary, unless the member was married to that former spouse
for at least one year or the former spouse is the parent of children by that

---

49. *See* McCarthy v. United States, 10 Cl. Ct. 573 (1986), *aff'd,* 826 F.2d 1049
(Fed. Cir. 1987).
50. *See* Matthews v. Matthews, 336 Md. 241, 647 A.2d 812 (1994).
51. 10 U.S.C. §§ 1448(a)(3)(C)–(D).
52. *Id.* § 1448(b)(2). The finance center will notify the member's spouse of the
election to make the member's former spouse the SBP beneficiary, but the
current spouse's consent is not required. *Id.* § 1448(b)(3)(D).
53. Pub. L. No. 97-252, §§ 1003(b)(1), 1006(c), 96 Stat. 718 (1982).
54. 10 U.S.C. § 1448(b)(2).

marriage.[55] In other words, a spouse who is acquired after retirement may not be made the SBP beneficiary unless *either* the marriage lasted a year or longer, *or* the marriage produced a child.

Generally, an election to make a former spouse (or former spouse and child) the SBP beneficiary is not revocable. If the original designation of the former spouse was voluntary, however, the member may change the election to provide an annuity to a new spouse or dependent child (within one year of acquiring the new beneficiary); if the election was pursuant to court order, the member will require a superseding court order to effect the change of election.[56]

A dependent child can be an SBP beneficiary only if (1) he or she is the child of the former spouse who is the beneficiary, or (2) he or she is the child of a current spouse who is the beneficiary, or who has consented to provide the benefit to the child only, or (3) the previously named former spouse beneficiary is no longer still alive.[57]

An unmarried member without a dependent child may elect to provide an SBP annuity to any natural person who has an insurable interest in the member.[58]

Beginning with the amendments to the USFSPA effective November 14, 1986, courts were able to order members to elect (or to enter agreements to elect) to provide SBP annuities to former spouses (or former spouses and dependent children).[59] Before that date, such court orders were unenforceable.

If a member enters a written agreement to provide an SBP annuity to a former spouse or if a court order requires the designation of a former spouse as the SBP beneficiary and the member fails or refuses to make the election, then the member may be deemed to have made the election. To initiate such a "deemed election," the former spouse must file a written request with the appropriate service secretary requesting that the election be deemed to have been made. The written request must be filed within

---

55. *Id.* § 1448(b)(3)(B).
56. *Id.* §§ 1450(f)(1)–(2). If the election was pursuant to an agreement not incorporated in a court order, the member need only provide a statement signed by the former spouse agreeing to the change. *Id.* § 1450(f)(2)(B).
57. *Id.* § 1448(b)(4).
58. *Id.* § 1448(b)(1).
59. Pub. L. No. 99-661, 100 Stat. 3816 (1986).

one year of the date of the court order,[60] and must be signed by the former spouse.[61] The request should be accompanied by a copy of the pertinent court order (if the election is pursuant to court order), regular on its face, or a copy of the agreement to elect and a statement from the clerk of the court stating that the agreement has been filed with the court in accordance with the applicable state law.[62]

When a former spouse makes a deemed election request, the member may be able to save a little money by sending to the pay center a request for former spouse coverage. Current policy appears to be that premiums will be assessed as of the date of the court order if made pursuant to the deemed election alone, but will be assessed only as of the month following the month of the request if made pursuant to member request. Depending upon the date of the order in question, the member could save up to eleven months of premiums by sending in the request for former spouse coverage.

> **Practice Tip:** Although there is no rule requiring transmission by certified mail, sending the deemed election by certified mail, or by overnight courier, is a means of preserving proof of transmission to the pay center within one year. Though there has not been any court case indicating such, current pay center practice indicates that the one-year date may apply as of the date of receipt at the proper pay center office, and not the mailing date; thus, it is a good idea to avoid being too close to the deadline when sending a deemed election.

The survivors of members who died while still on active duty are not necessarily excluded from participating in the SBP. The finance centers will honor a member's election to treat a former spouse as the SBP beneficiary if the member died after becoming eligible to receive retired pay; qualifying for retired pay but not having yet applied for or been granted

---

60. 10 U.S.C. § 1450(f)(3)(B).
61. The services were at one time in disagreement about whether the request could be signed by the former spouse's lawyer or legal representative. Though various service centers during the consolidation have given assurances that DFAS policy allows for a lawyer's signature for a deemed election request, prudent practice suggests having the former spouse sign the request, lest a further change of interpretation within the bureaucracy make the critical deemed election worthless or untimely.
62. 10 U.S.C. § 1450(f)(3)(A).

that pay; or completing twenty years of service, but not yet completing ten years of active *commissioned* service needed for retirement as a commissioned officer.[63] The procedural requirements are the same as in other cases.

> ✎ **Practice Tip:** Practitioners should note the existence of some uncertainty in the pay centers about when applications should or must be made (that is, after the divorce, or after retirement, if the divorce is from a member still on active duty). The statute appears to indicate (and some pay centers have ruled) that a deemed election must be made within one year of the court order, even if the member's retirement is several years in the future. As a matter of prudence, if the divorce occurs while the member is on active duty, provision should be made for the SBP in the divorce decree, the deemed election should be made immediately thereafter, and counsel for the former spouse should ensure that either counsel or the former spouse checks back with the finance center sometime shortly after the member's retirement to ensure that the military recognizes the SBP designation.[64] If there is a problem, checking with the military within the first year after the divorce could allow for correction of otherwise disastrous errors, some varieties of which are explored below.

3. Special Timing Rules and Malpractice Traps: The SBP "Time Bomb"

If the designation of a former spouse as beneficiary is made by a member, it must be written, signed by the member, and received by DFAS within one year after the date of the decree of divorce, dissolution, or annulment.[65]

As a practical matter, however, the services have been quite liberal in granting "administrative corrections" upon the requests of members, even

---

63. *Id.* § 1448(d)(1).
64. Anecdotal accounts indicate that some of the clerks at some of the pay centers have told practitioners that *reapplication* would be required after retirement if the divorce, and beneficiary designation, was before retirement.
65. 10 U.S.C. § 1448(b)(3)(A).

years after a divorce, when spouse coverage was in effect rather than "former spouse" coverage, but premiums were paid and the members claimed that they "mistakenly assumed that [the former spouse] remained the covered beneficiary following the divorce since SBP costs continued to be withheld."[66]

As for court orders, the rules for making the election may differ between married and unmarried members. For example, an unmarried member who elects to treat a former spouse as an SBP beneficiary need not have the written election incorporated in, ratified, or approved by a court order.

At the time of the election, the member must submit a written statement to the appropriate service secretary. The statement must be signed by both the former spouse and the member, and state whether the election is being made pursuant to the requirements of a court order or a written voluntary agreement previously entered by the member as a part of or incident to a divorce, dissolution, or annulment proceeding. If pursuant to a written agreement, the statement must state whether such a voluntary agreement was incorporated in, ratified, or approved by a court order.[67]

In prior years, it was widely believed that the one-year period in which a former spouse must request a deemed election ran concurrently with the one-year period in which a member must make the election after the divorce. It was therefore thought that the former spouse risked losing the SBP designation entirely if he or she waited until the member's one-year election period ended. Subsequent developments, however, made this rule slightly more flexible, much more complicated, and a bit illogical in application.

The spouse might be able to extend the period within which he or she can request a deemed election by returning to court after the divorce and

---

66. *See, e.g.,* Memorandum from Gary F. Smith, Chief, Army Retirement Services, on behalf of the Secretary of the Army, to Director, DFAS (Feb. 20, 1997) (entitled "Administrative Correction of SBP Election—Johnson, Alfred H. III," noting a 1994 divorce decree requiring member to maintain coverage for his former spouse, noting the member's 1997 request for a change in the SBP election from "spouse" to "former spouse," and directing collection of the cost refund that was paid to the member, and that the records be corrected to show former spouse coverage).

67. 10 U.S.C. § 1448(b)(5).

obtaining an order stating that the spouse is to be deemed the SBP beneficiary. This is because the *member* is obliged to make the election "within one year after the date of the decree of divorce, dissolution, or annulment,"[68] whereas the *former spouse* must make the request "within one year of the date of the court order or filing involved."

If there was no previous order giving a valid right to the former spouse to be the SBP beneficiary, the one-year deemed election period runs from the date of a postdivorce order concerning the SBP.[69] This is true for orders that were issued before the effective date of the SBP deemed beneficiary law, as well as orders that inadequately attempted to provide for the SBP, or omitted all mention of the benefit.[70] However, once a valid court order is issued requiring coverage, the one-year period begins to run, and any subsequent court order that merely reiterates, restates, or confirms the right of coverage as SBP beneficiary cannot be used to start a new one-year election period.[71]

This is where the complications and illogic come in. Assume three identical divorces on the same day: In the first case, the lawyer, who knew almost nothing about military retirement benefits law, did not even know there was an SBP to allocate. The second knew that something had to be done, and so put a statement in the order verifying that the former spouse was the irrevocable beneficiary of the benefit. The third not only knew to secure the right, but knew about the deemed election procedure, sent the required notice, and so on.

One year and one day after the divorce, the third former spouse's rights would be secure. The first former spouse could go back to court at

---

68. *Id.* § 1448(b)(3)(A).
69. *See, e.g.,* Comp. Gen. B-232319 (*In re* Minier, Mar. 23, 1990); Comp. Gen. B-226563 (*In re* Early, Mar. 2, 1990); Comp. Gen. B-247508 (Sept. 2, 1992).
70. As an aside, this is true even when the divorce court is unsure how to characterize the benefit. In one case, the court made a point of saying that it could not tell if the SBP was a property right, an alimony allocation, or some kind of insurance, but in any event it was valuable, and the benefit was to be secured to the former spouse, even though she did not qualify to receive a portion of the military retirement benefits themselves because the marriage did not overlap the military service. *See* Matthews v. Matthews, 336 Md. 241, 647 A.2d 812 (1994).
71. Comp. Gen. B-244101 (*In re* Driggers, Aug. 3, 1992); 71 Comp. Gen. 475, 478 (1992).

any time (before the member's death) to get a valid order for SBP beneficiary status, and then serve the pay center. The second former spouse, however, whose rights were supposed to be "secured" by the judgment, would be entirely without a remedy (except a malpractice claim against the divorce lawyer).

It makes little sense for the law to protect the putative rights of those who do not even try to secure rights upon divorce, while denying any protection to those who believe they have already litigated and received a valid court order protecting those same rights, but that is the bottom line of the law as it now stands. Even the Department of Defense has recognized the unnecessarily harsh results that are produced by the current law,[72] but Congress has not yet taken any action to correct the situation.

4. Limitations on the Benefit

In addition to the conditions explained in the above three subsections, there are various limitations that practitioners should keep in mind when dealing with the SBP.

An annuity payable to a widow, widower, or former spouse is suspended if the beneficiary remarries before age fifty-five.[73] If the remarriage occurred before November 14, 1986, benefits were suspended if the former spouse was not yet age sixty.[74]

The suspension is effective as of the first day of the month in which the beneficiary remarries. Payments to the beneficiary may resume if the later marriage ends by death, annulment, or divorce. If the beneficiary

---

72. A memorandum to Congress in 1991 recommended extending the period in which application could be made from one year to five. *See* "DoD Report on the Survivor Benefit Plan, August, 1991," under cover entitled "A Review of the Uniformed Services Survivor Benefit Plan (SBP) and Report on the Pending Supplemental Plan and Open Enrollment Period, Prepared by Department of Defense, October, 1991," in turn attached to correspondence dated October 1, 1991, from Christopher Jehn, Assistant Secretary of Defense, to Hon. Les Aspin, Chairman, House Armed Services Committee.

73. 10 U.S.C. § 1450(b).

74. Pub. L. No. 99-661, § 643(a) (1986) reduced the remarriage benefit termination age from sixty to fifty-five for remarriages that occurred on or after the date of enactment.

obtains SBP benefits from the second marriage, he or she must choose between the annuities.

5. *How to Shift the Entire Premium Cost for the SBP to a Former Spouse, or to a Member*

Under current law, there is no direct way to shift the premium cost for the SBP to the former spouse or to the member. The "default" is that the SBP premium is taken "off the top," ultimately resulting in the parties paying the SBP premium in the exact proportions that they divide the military retirement benefits. To adjust who pays what, it is necessary to adjust the percentage or dollars payable to reflect the fact of deduction of the expense from the desired party. An example may help illustrate the process.

EXAMPLE

Lieutenant Colonel (O-5) Hiram retired in 1997, with twenty years of service. He was married to Lois for the entire length of service. His monthly nondisability retired pay was $2,477 per month. The parties agreed in negotiations that Lois would bear the entire SBP premium. Without considering the SBP, Lois would receive 50 percent, while Hiram would keep the other 50 percent, or $1,238.50. Assuming the lowest-cost premium option available is 6.5 percent of the base amount, and figuring the full sum of the retirement *as* the base amount yields an SBP premium of $161 per month. What would be simple, but *cannot be done,* is to have the military simply deduct that sum from *Lois's share* of the military retirement benefits. This would leave her with $1,077.50, pay the SBP premium, and leave Hiram's portion unchanged at $1,238.50.

Because that cannot be done under current law, Lois's share must be adjusted to achieve the same result. It would *not* be adequate to just subtract the 6.5 percent from Lois's 50 percent share, leaving her with 43.5 percent. It must be remembered that the military will not know or care about this adjustment, and will still simply take the SBP premium off the top, and then divide the remaining $2,316 by the stated percentages; the result would be Lois receiving $1,007.46, and Hiram receiving $1,308.54 per month. In other words, the spouse would get too little, and the member too much.

Instead, it is necessary to reduce the spousal percentage by a percentage sufficient to yield the correct dollar sum. First, figure the spouse's correct sum; as shown above, in this case the formula is as follows: $Y = .50X$ minus $.065X$ (where $Y =$ spouse's share, and $X =$ the military retirement benefits). Using the numbers recited above, the formula reads $Y = \$1,238.50$ minus $\$161 = \$1,077.50$. To solve for the correct percentage, divide that sum—the amount the spouse *should* be receiving—by the amount of the total military retirement benefits less the SBP premium cost: $\$1,077.50 \div (\$2,477$ minus $\$161)$ $= .4652417$, or about 46.52 percent. This amount is the percentage that the spouse would be awarded if she was to pay the entire SBP premium.

The military pay center will pay the SBP premium "off the top"; the remaining $2,316 will be divided with 46.52 percent to Lois, paying $1,077.40, and 53.48 percent to Hiram, paying $1,238.60. The 10¢ variation from ideal is due to rounding.[75] The result is that Hiram will receive the same money that he would have received if there was no SBP at all, which was the intended result.

Note that in this example the difference from the spouse's original percentage is *not* 6.5 percent, but only 3.48 percent, which is the mathematical ratio for reduction of the spousal share to provide for SBP, in this case. The percentage will vary, depending upon the original spousal shares, whether the full retirement is chosen as the base amount for the SBP, and whether the cost of the SBP is figured as 6.5 percent of the base amount or under the alternative formula that some members can use.

The following table can be used to "translate" a spousal percentage of the entire military retired pay into a reduced percentage that will result in the spouse paying for the entire SBP premium.

---

75. It could be almost eliminated by bringing the percentages out another decimal point, but rounding to the nearest cent will always create a very minor variation.

Spousal Percentage Intended (Time Rule or Other)	Spousal Percentage Resulting If Spouse Pays Entire SBP Premium
50%	46.52%
49%	45.45%
48%	44.39%
47%	43.32%
46%	42.25%
45%	41.18%
44%	40.11%
43%	39.04%
42%	37.97%
41%	36.90%
40%	35.83%
39%	34.76%
38%	33.69%
37%	32.62%
36%	31.55%
35%	30.48%
34%	29.41%
33%	28.34%
32%	27.27%
31%	26.20%
30%	25.13%
29%	24.06%
28%	22.99%
27%	21.93%
26%	20.86%
25%	19.79%
24%	18.72%
23%	17.65%
22%	16.58%
21%	15.51%
20%	14.44%
19%	13.37%
18%	12.30%
17%	11.23%
16%	10.16%
15%	9.09%
14%	8.02%
13%	6.95%

(continued)

Spousal Percentage Intended (Time Rule or Other)	Spousal Percentage Resulting If Spouse Pays Entire SBP Premium
12%	5.88%
11%	4.81%
10%	3.74%
9%	2.67%
8%	1.60%
7%	0.53%
6–1%	Here and below, the spousal share is a negative number.

To verify the calculations, pick a number for the total military retired pay (the *actual* numbers in the case would be useful) and rerun the same calculations. If the total disposable pay was $1,000 (for example), the spouse would receive $500 without SBP being considered, leaving $500 to the member. The SBP premium, at 6.5 percent of the $1,000 total, would be $65. What the military would *not* do is subtract that $65 from the spouse's $500, leaving her $435. By altering her percentage to 46.52 percent, the military would do the math as follows: $1,000 − $65 = $935 × 46.52% = $434.96. This is the same amount that she *should* be receiving per the simple calculation that the military pay center will not do (the 4¢ difference is due to rounding).

The same sort of calculations can be done for translating the spousal percentage into what it would have to be for the *member* to pay the entire SBP premium. If that was the desired result, of course, the spousal percentage would have to be *increased* instead of decreased, to maintain the spousal share of the benefits, as set forth in the following table.

Spousal Percentage Intended (Time Rule or Other)	Spousal Percentage Resulting If Member Pays Entire SBP Premium
50%	53.48% (not permitted under 10 U.S.C. § 1408)
49%	52.41% (not permitted under 10 U.S.C. § 1408)
48%	51.34% (not permitted under 10 U.S.C. § 1408)
47%	50.27% (not permitted under 10 U.S.C. § 1408)
46%	49.20%
45%	48.13%

(continued)

Spousal Percentage Intended (Time Rule or Other)	Spousal Percentage Resulting If Member Pays Entire SBP Premium
44%	47.06%
43%	45.99%
42%	44.92%
41%	43.85%
40%	42.78%
39%	41.71%
38%	40.64%
37%	39.57%
36%	38.50%
35%	37.43%
34%	36.36%
33%	35.29%
32%	34.22%
31%	33.16%
30%	32.09%
29%	31.02%
28%	29.95%
27%	28.88%
26%	27.81%
25%	26.74%
24%	25.67%
23%	24.60%
22%	23.53%
21%	22.46%
20%	21.39%
19%	20.32%
18%	19.25%
17%	18.18%
16%	17.11%
15%	16.04%
14%	14.97%
13%	13.90%
12%	12.83%
11%	11.76%
10%	10.70%
9%	9.63%
8%	8.56%
7%	7.49%

(*continued*)

Spousal Percentage Intended (Time Rule or Other)	Spousal Percentage Resulting If Member Pays Entire SBP Premium
6%	6.42%
5%	5.35%
4%	4.28%
3%	3.21%
2%	2.14%
1%	1.07%

Note that under 10 U.S.C. § 1408(e)(1), it is not permissible to pay the former spouse more than 50 percent of the military retired pay. Thus, if it is intended that the former spouse receive more than about 46 percent, and that the member is to pay the SBP premium, some mechanism other than the shifting set forth above will be needed to effect that end.

C. SERVICE LIFE INSURANCE

A mistake frequently made in the course of negotiation or litigation is the effort to compel (or trade assets to receive) beneficiary status for a former spouse in a member's National Service Life Insurance (NSLI), or its active-duty counterpart, Serviceman's Group Life Insurance (SGLI).

This is a mistake because any such stipulation or court order is simply unenforceable—a court order compelling beneficiary status cannot be enforced. Under the laws setting up these insurance plans,[76] the insured has complete freedom to designate or redesignate the intended beneficiary of the program. The federal courts, early and forcefully, held that the programs were "the congressional mode of affording a uniform and comprehensive system of life insurance for members and veterans of the armed forces of the United States," and the resulting benefits were therefore immune from state court division, even when community property was the source of the premiums paying for the policy.[77] A host of similar programs have been established, and expired, since 1919.

---

76. *See* 38 U.S.C. § 1917; Pub. L. No. 85-857, § 717, 72 Stat. 1152 (1958) (as amended).

77. *See* Wissner v. Wissner 338 U.S. 657, 658 (1949); *see also* Estate of Allie, 50 Cal. 2d 794, 329 P.2d 903 (1958); 6 C.J.S. *Armed Services* § 226 (1975).

A former spouse who negotiated beneficiary status in exchange for giving up other rights, or was ordered to receive beneficiary status, thus has no direct remedy if the member dies having named someone else anyway; a member is free to change beneficiaries, and the named beneficiaries are free from suits from the former spouse for a portion of the proceeds.[78]

However, a former spouse who has been thus deceived is apparently not prohibited from proceeding against the member (at least while everyone is still alive). Such a suit would not be interfering with the protected insurance policy, but punishing the contemptuous act of duplicity by the member. As with other matters involved in these cases, the key is adequate vigilance, especially by the former spouse, to be sure that what was negotiated or ordered was actually put into place.

Far better than trying to fix the problems would be to avoid them altogether, of course. Preferable mechanisms by which payments after the member's death could be accomplished include private life insurance (with the intended beneficiary as owner), or beneficiary status under the SBP.

D. COMMISSARY, EXCHANGE, AND MISCELLANEOUS

Former spouses who are 20/20/20 former spouses[79] enjoy lifetime commissary and post exchange privileges.[80] Those privileges terminate

---

78. The key case is *Ridgway v. Ridgway,* 454 U.S. 48 (1981). Cases since then have cited it for the proposition that there is simply nothing they can do for defrauded former spouses. *See, e.g.,* Kaminski v. Kaminski, Civil Action No. 1278, 1995 WL 106497 (Del. Ch. Ct. New Castle, Feb. 24, 1995). In that case, the member had promised in his stipulated divorce decree to name his daughter from his first marriage as his irrevocable beneficiary. When he died leaving his second wife as sole beneficiary, the first wife's action seeking a constructive trust for the daughter was dismissed. The court said that the "narrow exception" for fraud was restricted to an "extreme factual situation," unlike simple breach of contract.

79. That is, former spouses who were married at least twenty years to members of the uniformed services who had at least twenty years of creditable service, and for whom twenty years of marriage overlapped twenty years of creditable service.

80. *See* 10 U.S.C. §§ 1062, 1065, 1072(2)(F), 1072(2)(G). Section 1005 of Pub. L. No. 97-252 (1982) directed the secretary of defense to prescribe regu-

upon the former spouse's remarriage. There are anecdotal accounts of reinstatement of these privileges after termination of a later marriage, but this does not seem correct, given that the same language is used for this section ("an unremarried former spouse") as was used for medical benefits. In any event, 20/20/15 former spouses[81] who were divorced between April 1, 1985, and September 29, 1988, have the same rights and privileges as 20/20/20 former spouses.

Commissary and exchange privileges are available upon presentation of a valid military identification (ID) card. Available benefits include access to officer, noncommissioned-officer (NCO), and enlisted clubs; commissaries, exchange stores, family centers, theaters, clothing stores, recreation services, open messes, laundry and dry cleaning stores, consolidated package stores, libraries, chapels, transient quarters, certain legal assistance, and casualty assistance.

E. THE NECESSITY OF OBTAINING A MILITARY ID CARD

The former spouse must have a valid military ID card to obtain health and medical care. To obtain an ID card, a former spouse should follow the procedures below.

1. Obtain DD Form 1172 (Application for Uniformed Services Identification and Privilege Card) from any military installation.
2. Appear in person (or send certified mail) to the ID-card-issuing office at any military installation. Present the completed Form 1172, copies of the certificate of marriage to the member, the final court order of divorce or annulment, a notarized statement that the former spouse has not remarried, and a notarized statement that the former spouse is *not* covered by a civilian employer-sponsored health plan (if seeking health benefits). A copy of the former spouse's birth certificate might

---

lations entitling former spouses who meet the 20/20/20 criteria to commissary and post exchange privileges to the same extent and on the same basis as surviving spouses of retired members of the uniformed services.

81. That is, former spouses who were married at least twenty years to members of the uniformed services who had at least twenty years of creditable service, and for whom fifteen years of marriage overlapped creditable service.

be needed. The navy apparently requires certified copies of the marriage certificate and divorce decree.

3. Sufficient identifying information of the member should be made available to the ID-card-issuing office to allow verification of the member's identity and status. (Provide at least the member's full name, branch of service, and Social Security number.)

4. The verifying official will get the member's service record to verify the twenty years of creditable service requirement.

5. If the request for an ID card was by mail, the former spouse will receive a letter once eligibility is verified. The letter can be taken to the ID-card-issuing office at any military facility for issuance of a dependent's ID card (DD Form 1173).

6. Dependent ID cards generally expire after three years. Depending upon the category of benefits for which the former spouse is qualified, the ID card will be restricted on its face concerning the benefits for which it can be used.

Chapter Seven

LITIGATION IN THE REAL WORLD:
TIPS AND TRAPS

A. GETTING INFORMATION FROM THE MILITARY PAY CENTERS

The member is almost always in a superior position regarding the information available about retirement matters at the time of divorce, because the information is sent directly to the member, and the member has a measure of control over various aspects of the process (when to apply for retirement, for example). Certain information required for valuation and apportionment of retired pay and other benefits is discoverable from the former spouse as well, of course (for example, dates of marriage and, if applicable, separation of the parties). Spouses often have access to retirement orders, Forms DD-214, or other relevant documents. Obviously, all available information should be gathered from the client directly before requesting information from the military.

Upon request, the military pay centers will usually provide certain information concerning military members without formal interrogatories, including the following:[1]

- Full name, rank, and date of rank
- Gross salary, including gross retired pay, and (if the member is retired) gross retired pay amounts from the date of retirement to the present[2]
- Past and present duty assignments, future assignments that are officially established, and telephone numbers for office of duty
- Source of commission and promotion sequence number, awards and decorations, and attendance at professional military schools
- Duty status at any given time

---

1. 32 C.F.R. § 286a(2); Dep't of Defense Reg. 5400.11-R (1997).
2. In 1991, for reasons not altogether clear, technicians at some pay centers began denying this information for active-duty members, while releasing it for retired members, citing "internal policy changes."

It is advisable to make the request for any of this information in writing. An example retired pay request letter is provided at the end of this book.[3] It is not uncommon for pay center technicians to tell lawyers that they cannot release any information about any member, citing only "the Privacy Act" as authority. Practitioners running into this sort of stone-walling should consult with the legal office at the pay center involved, where they are likely to obtain a better-informed response, and assistance in obtaining the release of appropriate information.

In some cases, the practitioner will require other information that can be obtained by means of interrogatories directed to the proper designated agent for receipt of court orders. The agent must respond within thirty days or within the period prescribed by state law, whichever is longer, and will disclose any of the following items:[4]

- The dates of the member's creditable service
- The dates of the member's eligibility for retirement and mandatory retirement
- The basis for computation of retired pay
- Whether the member has elected the Survivor's Benefit Plan (SBP) and, if so, the designation of beneficiaries
- If the member is retired, the amount of disposable retired pay and all deductions from gross retired pay
- If the member is retired, the date on which cost of living adjustments (COLAs) have been made

B. ANTICIPATING CHANGES IN STATUS

Altogether too often, divorce lawyers and divorce courts presume that their expectations regarding the availability and continuation of the career of the military member are destined to occur. A noncritical examination of the factual basis for what is most likely the primary asset of the marriage is naive. There are a number of ways, by the choices of a member, or through institutional decisions by Congress or the military, that the mem-

---

3. See Exhibit 4, Appendix F.
4. 32 C.F.R. § 63.6(g)(4).

ber's expected career path could be radically altered, if not entirely abandoned. The following sections discuss a few of those possibilities.

1. Variations in Planned Retirement Date

Anecdotal evidence suggests that a large amount of postdivorce litigation is caused by divorce decrees containing silent assumptions that turn out not to be true. Most common of these, perhaps, is the assumption that the member will serve for exactly 240 months, and then retire, at a particular rank. These assumptions are dangerous to both parties.

a. Service after Divorce or beyond Eligibility for Retirement

Whenever the member remains on active duty after the date of divorce, there is a degree of uncertainty to any award to the former spouse predicated on the member's anticipated retirement at the earliest possible date for regular retirement (twenty years). Essentially, the uncertainties fall into the categories of "when" and "how much."

For the "when" question, the issue can be stated as whether the former spouse will get money only if and when the member receives actual retirement funds, or will receive the spousal share of the retirement upon the member's *eligibility* to receive funds, whether or not the member actually chooses to retire. There is a burden to be borne in either direction.

If the former spouse receives nothing until the time of actual retirement, then payments to the former spouse are completely dependent upon an election over which the former spouse has no control—the spousal share is, in effect, held hostage. As discussed below,[5] some states have determined that it is inherently inequitable to prevent nonemployee spouses from realizing sums that are payable and would be paid but for the choice of the employee spouses. Except in the extremely rare circumstance in which extraordinary changes in rank are anticipated, the mathematical projections set forth below[6] show that it would almost always be a mistake for a spouse to defer collection past first eligibility. Of course, for the same reason, it is in a member's best interest to tie the spouse's receipt of benefits to the member's actual retirement, a move which, if

---

5. See Section C of this chapter.
6. *Id.*

successful, reduces the spousal share by at least 13 percent. Informed practitioners will include this reality in their bargaining positions (with deference to the law of the state in question, of course), and treat this timing point as an item of value, whichever way it is decided.

The "how much" question appears to depend almost entirely on the happenstance of the law of the state making the decision. Practitioners should be sure they know which way their state goes, and anticipate the possibility of any change to that interpretation. The two camps can be divided into the "rank at divorce" and "building block" states.

The "rank at divorce" approach is exemplified by the decision of the Supreme Court of Texas in *Grier v. Grier*.[7] The case was actually a declaratory judgment action brought by the husband in Texas eight years after the parties divorced. The court did not state where the divorce had been entered, but noted that the benefits were not divisible community property at the time of the decree. The husband had filed in reaction to the wife's filing in California of an action seeking partition of the military retirement benefits as omitted assets.

The husband was a major when the Griers divorced, but he had already been placed on a promotion list for lieutenant colonel (which rank he pinned on eight months after the divorce). The trial court used the time rule to find a spousal percentage of the gross retirement benefits based on the husband's rank at retirement (lieutenant colonel). The court of appeals reversed, and awarded the same percentage, but applied that percentage against the disposable retired pay that would have been paid to a major.

The Texas Supreme Court, starting from the precept that the benefits to be apportioned were based on the value of the community's interest at the time of divorce, held that the valuation of military retirement benefits is to be done according to the rank actually held by the service spouse on the date of the divorce, because granting the former spouse a percentage of the retired pay based on the rank ultimately attained by the member would "impermissibly invade" the member's separate property. The sum to be awarded, therefore, was the mathematical percentage of gross retired pay "based on the rank of major which is currently payable to such officer who would have retired with 20 years service in September 1975 together with increases which may occur other than increases attributable to ele-

---

7. Grier v. Grier, 731 S.W.2d 931 (Tex. 1987).

vation in rank or services rendered by the military spouse after the date of divorce."[8] The court found, however, that the sum against which the spousal percentage was to be applied was gross retired pay, rather than disposable pay.[9]

One justice, concurring and dissenting, agreed to the application of the spousal percentage to gross retired pay. That justice, however, would have held the applicable rank to that of lieutenant colonel, noting the husband's placement on the promotion list occurred during the marriage, and reasoning that valuation as of the date of divorce should include rank for which qualification was met but not yet formalized, and that the majority opinion exalted form over substance.

Other courts have attempted to be more philosophically analytical. Instead of focusing on a catchphrase or label, they have first attempted to understand the nature of the asset being divided, and then focused on how to accomplish an equitable division of that asset. The decisions of these courts can be labeled the "building block" cases. The decisions of several states seem to presume simply that the rank at retirement is the appropriate measure, and contain little analysis of why this is so.[10]

Explanations of the reasoning involved can be found in nonmilitary pension cases from these states, which were used as the basis of decision in military cases. One example is *Fondi v. Fondi,*[11] in which the Nevada Supreme Court found that a "wait and see" approach is mandated in pension cases, through which the community has an interest in the pension ultimately received, not just the pension as it exists on the date of divorce. That court has since emphasized that the "wait and see" approach is defined as ensuring that the spousal share of the pension is based on the value of the pension ultimately received by the worker, *rather than* a portion of the pension that would have been received if the worker retired on the date of divorce.[12]

---

8. *Id.* at 933.
9. This case was pre-*Mansell,* and this conclusion was based on Texas law.
10. *See, e.g.,* Casas v. Thompson 42 Cal. 3d 131, 720 P.2d 921, 228 Cal. Rptr. 33 (1986), *cert. denied,* 479 U.S. 1012 (1987).
11. Fondi v. Fondi, 106 Nev. 856, 802 P.2d 1264 (1990) (retirement under state public employees retirement system).
12. Sertic v. Sertic, 111 Nev. 1192, 901 P.2d 148 (1995) (Civil Service Retirement System (federal) retirement).

Some courts have explained what they are doing as adhering to the "qualitative" view of spousal contributions to retirement accrual.[13] In other words, though a pension may be based on the "highest salary earned," and the highest earning years are usually the last years of employment, all the years of work leading up to retirement are considered equally necessary to attain that status. Two consecutive spouses, during the first and last halves of a twenty-year military career, would be treated equally under the qualitative approach.

Perhaps the clearest expositions of the reasoning behind the two approaches are found in those cases in which a reviewing court splits about which interpretation is most correct. The Iowa Supreme Court faced such a conflict in the case of *In re Benson*.[14] The trial court had used a time-rule approach, with the wife's percentage to be applied to the sum the husband actually received, whenever he actually retired.

The reviewing court restated the question as being the time of valuation, with the choices being the sum the husband would have been able to receive if he had retired at divorce, or the sum payable at retirement. The court acknowledged that the longer the husband worked after divorce, the smaller the wife's portion became. The court accepted the wife's position that to "lock in" the value of the wife's interest to the value at divorce, while delaying payment to actual retirement, prevented the wife from earning a reasonable return on her interest.

Quoting at length from a law review article analyzing the mathematics of the situation, the court found that acceptance of the husband's argument would have required allowing him to collect the entirety of the accumulating "earnings" on the property accumulated by both parties. Three judges, dissenting, argued that the majority's approach "does violence" to the principle that marriage partners are entitled to a just and equitable share of the property accumulated through their *joint* efforts, and the principle that the court divides property the parties owned at the time of dissolution, not property they may acquire after dissolution. The Iowa court did not appear to even consider the possibility of beginning to pay the wife's interest at first eligibility for employment, "freezing" it at that point, and letting the husband enjoy all accumulations after that time. Presumably, this is because that possibility was not litigated at the trial level.

---

13. Stouffer v. Stouffer, 10 Haw. App. 267, 867 P.2d 226 (Ct. App. 1994).
14. *In re* Benson, 545 N.W.2d 252 (Iowa 1996).

Thus, it can be seen that the questions of "when" and "how much" are related, with some courts using many of the same arguments to support their conclusions, and apparently not even considering the arguments relating to one set of possibilities when deciding the other. Further, and worse, there seems to be very little effort to get beyond labels and rhetoric to consider, mathematically, the actual impact of the decisions being made. It can only be hoped that as the field of retirement division in divorce litigation matures, consensus founded on more rigorous analyses will begin to form in the courts.

b. Early Retirement, Voluntary Separation Incentive, Special Separation Benefit, and Separation Pay

The practitioner litigating a divorce involving a member still in service and not yet eligible for retirement should consider the possibility of the member's separation from service—voluntary or involuntary—before the anticipated regular retirement date. The programs currently known, and the cases involving disputes over the benefits paid through those programs, have been previously discussed.[15]

The lesson to be learned from those cases, however, is the difficulty of anticipating how Congress might alter the form and variety of military retirement programs, and the legal incidents of those programs. At the very least, if a divorce is contemplated while a member is on active duty and not yet eligible for regular retirement, thought must be given to the possibility that the member might not stay in service for the anticipated length of time, and decrees casually premised on "240 months of service" or "upon retirement" are an invitation to trouble.

The cautious practitioner will therefore build into whatever agreements or decrees are filed in each case sufficient safeguards, helping to ensure that the actual intention of the parties (and the court, in finalizing the case) can be kept in place regardless of the changing environment created by Congress, by the military pay centers, and by a changing world. The form at the end of this book attempts to do that.

2. Remarriage and Tax Withholding

There are two parts to this discussion—the impact of the member's remarriage, and the impact of the former spouse's remarriage. The mem-

---

15. See Section G, Chapter Four.

ber's remarriage is relevant only for divorces before February 4, 1991, and the former spouse's remarriage is not relevant at all under current law, although certain special-interest groups have for years sought to change the law to make that event relevant; it is possible that it will be of importance in the future.

As explained in an earlier section of this book,[16] the member has some freedom to alter the tax withholdings on the retired pay by claiming different numbers of dependents. A member remarrying, who would normally have an additional dependent (or more, with children) and who claimed them as such would have less withheld. This would have the effect of increasing the disposable pay available for division with the former spouse, and thus leave less to pay the expenses (and taxes) of the member and the new family.[17] It is also counterintuitive, because the very idea of lower withholdings is that less tax will be due, and therefore more money is to be made available to an individual who claims additional dependents.

Although it is now too late to do planning in this regard (because all affected decrees would have been entered before February 4, 1991), a former spouse who finds that the member has manipulated withholdings by claiming a false tax status should probably first try to bring that to the attention of the military pay center involved. Anecdotal accounts suggest very mixed results with this approach.

Alternatively, a motion could be brought in state court indicating that arrearages are due, because the amount that was to be paid under the court's earlier order has been artificially reduced by misrepresentation of tax status. Unfortunately, getting the information necessary for such a motion would probably require both knowledge of the member's current status, and a subpoena to the pay center to find out what was being claimed. As long as any monetary sanctions imposed against the member are *not* categorized as arrearages in military retired pay, however, they should prove garnishable from the military pay center.[18] For further information, see the general tax section of this book.[19]

---

16. See Subsection 4(c), Section C, Chapter Five.
17. It must be remembered that under the old system, the member received 100 percent of the benefit of all sums withheld from gross before disposable pay was determined.
18. 10 U.S.C. § 1408(d)(5).
19. Section K of this chapter.

Under present law, remarriage by a former spouse has no effect whatsoever on a division of retired pay between a member and a former spouse. Advocates for members' groups, however, have long argued that the division of retired pay in military members is somehow analogous to an award of alimony. Whether this is the cause of, or a rationalization for, the effort, such advocates have been trying for some time to terminate payments to a former spouse upon the former spouse's remarriage. For example, in 1990, Representative Dornan of California introduced H.R. 572, which would have had the effect, if it had been enacted, of simply terminating all spousal interests in military retired pay in the event of the former spouse's remarriage, for previously decided cases as well as prospective cases. Substantially identical efforts have been launched in Congress every year since then.

It is always difficult to predict which way the political winds might blow in Congress. A prudent practitioner, therefore, must simply accept the uncertainty and structure settlement agreements and decrees with the thought in mind that the law might change. The model decree, for example, contains both a clause indicating the parties' intent to have the benefits payable during the parties' joint lives and regardless of their marital status, and a reservation of jurisdiction that presumably would allow the divorce court to enter further orders adjusting the rights of the parties if there was such a dramatic change in federal law.

3. Postretirement Civil Service Employment

There are two matters to consider here—reduction in retired pay during actual civil service employment, and the disposition of the military retirement benefits if a civil service retirement is sought by the member.

a. Reduction in Retired Pay during Civil Service Employment

The "dual receipt" prohibition in federal law has long been a source of troubling inequities in military retirement benefits cases. The full history of the dual compensation rules[20] are beyond the scope of this book. The short version is that retired pay is reduced for retired military members who work for the federal government as civilians. Under current law,

---

20. 5 U.S.C. § 5532(b); 10 U.S.C. § 1408(a)(4)(B).

retired officers and enlisted members receive their full civilian pay, but only a portion of their military retired pay plus 50 percent of any remainder. As of December 1, 1997, that sum was $10,316.65[21] of military retired pay, and then half of all amounts beyond that sum.

From one perspective, the election of a civil service career after retirement from the military is simply a decision to invest in a greatly enhanced future retirement combining military and civilian service. The purpose of the law could be seen as preventing retired military members from receiving their full military retirement now, and then using the same service again for the enhanced civil service pension into which they can roll over their military pay.

Obviously, any external factor that causes a reduction in the amount of retired pay payable to a member affects the spousal interest as well. Theoretically, two different analogies seem possible. The same arguments could be made about spousal benefits here as in the disability area (discussed above and in the following subsection). If that analogy held, the spouse could theoretically make a claim against the member for the sum of military retired pay that would have been payable to the former spouse if the member had not taken a position that lowered the retired pay. If the Voluntary Separation Incentive (VSI) and Special Separation Benefit (SSB) cases (also discussed above) are found to be a more apt analogy, however, the former spouse would presumably share in the benefits actually received by the member, regardless of the role of his actions in reducing the benefit payable.

The case law seems to indicate that courts in the real world do not have a clear theoretical model that they are attempting to follow. Some meaning can be drawn from the sparse case authority, however. Two Texas cases primarily distinguished what a court (in Texas, anyway) should do when faced with a current divorce proceeding on the one hand, and a contempt enforcement proceeding on the other. A North Dakota case focused on the necessity, in a contempt proceeding, for the underlying decree to specify just what it is that the former spouse was to receive. Finally, a case from Arizona appears to represent a maturing of the analysis on this point.

---

21. The amount changes annually, essentially pacing inflation. *See* R.S. Hunter, G.L. Smith and D.M. Gordon (Eds.) 1998 RETIRED MILITARY ALMANAC 199–200 (1998).

Gallegos v. Gallegos[22] was a direct appeal of a divorce decree just entered by the trial court. The parties had stipulated to all provisions *except* the retirement, which was resolved by order. The lower court had directly granted the wife a portion of both the retirement benefits waived by the member in favor of Veteran's Administration (VA) benefits, and the retirement benefits waived by the member under the dual compensation law when he took a civil service job.[23]

The San Antonio intermediate appellate court looked to the then-new case of *Mansell v. Mansell,* 490 U.S. 581 (1989) (divorce courts are limited to direct division of disposable retired pay, and VA benefits are not included in that definition) and a then-recent case from a sister intermediate court.[24] The San Antonio court concluded that the trial court had exceeded its jurisdiction, because the Supreme Court case restricted divorce divisions to only disposable pay. The court therefore found that the trial court could neither divide the retired pay waived for VA benefits, nor divide the sums waived under the dual compensation law.[25]

The case was entirely dependent upon the appellate court's reading of the strictures imposed by *Mansell.*[26] The court's opinion had no direct

---

22. Gallegos v. Gallegos, 788 S.W.2d 158 (Tex. App. 1990).
23. The courts of Texas and California were at that time wrestling with the "gross versus disposable" question, and this court came down on the side of gross pay being what there was to divide. It goes beyond the scope of this issue, but essentially, state courts had long divided the gross amount of all benefits payable, while the wording of the federal statute addressed only "disposable pay." *See, e.g.,* Casas v. Thompson, 42 Cal. 3d 131, 720 P.2d 921, 228 Cal. Rptr. 33 (1986) (state courts should divide gross sum of retirement benefits; federal limitation is a procedural bar only), *cert. denied,* 479 U.S. 1012 (1987). Ultimately, the other view would prevail. *See* Mansell v. Mansell, 490 U.S. 581 (1989), *remanded,* 217 Cal. App. 3d 219, 265 Cal. Rptr. 227 (Ct. App. 1989).
24. This case was *Berry v. Berry,* 780 S.W.2d 846 (Tex. App. 1989). Of course, the San Antonio court could not have known that *Berry* would be reversed on appeal to the Texas Supreme Court. *See* Berry v. Berry, 786 S.W.2d 672 (Tex. 1990). It also could not know that *Mansell* itself would be highly restricted by the Texas Supreme Court and other reviewing courts, and that courts throughout the country would hold that spouses are to be compensated for any reductions in military retired pay caused by VA waivers.
25. The court called this "partial defeasance."
26. *See Gallegos,* 788 S.W.2d at 161.

guidance for the trial court in correcting the inequity created, because at that time, Texas did not have any provision for alimony. One of the three justices, however, included directions at the end of the case. Starting with the statement, "There is no doubt now, after *Mansell v. Mansell, . . .* that disability benefits from the VA must be excluded at the time of the division," Justice Butts went on:

> While this procedure bestows on some military retirees the control of what becomes "disposable" pay for purposes of division of community property, it nevertheless follows as a corollary of *Mansell.* Civil service employment and pay is governed by title 5 of the United States Code. Therefore, I reluctantly concur, pointing out that any change in the status of "waived" military retired pay would be brought to the attention of the trial court by motion to modify.[27]

Justice Butts concluded by being even more direct in asking the lower court to compensate the wife:

> Moreover, when the community estate is divided again on retrial, nothing in this opinion prevents the trial court from considering the size of the parties' separate estates and any differences in their earning capacities, including the disability income and civil service income at issue in this appeal, in making a just and right division. See *Murff v. Murff*, 615 S.W.2d 696, 699 (Tex. 1981).[28]

The case to which the trial court was directed (*Murff*) was an extremely widely cited opinion of the Texas Supreme Court.[29] The page to which the lower court was directed (699) states that "community property need not be equally divided" and directs the trial court to correct any injustice to the party not at fault by dividing other property to make a "just and right" division. This included figuring out what the parties would actually receive in the way of benefits from pensions that had accrued during the marriage.[30] Again, the Texas courts were required to go through

---

27. *Id.* at 162.
28. *Id.*
29. Shepards reveals pages of "followed" cites, approving citations from other states, and multiple annotations and articles.
30. Murff v. Murff, 615 S.W.2d 696, 699–700 (Tex. 1981).

this somewhat convoluted analysis because of the lack of any statutory power (at that time) to award compensatory or other forms of alimony.

Any doubt about the intention of the San Antonio court was resolved almost exactly five years later, when it issued its opinion in *Jones v. Jones.*[31] That case involved a husband's postdivorce efforts to avoid enforcement of the terms of a decree of divorce.

In *Jones,* the parties had married in 1978 and divorced in 1988. They stipulated to terms, which the court entered as a consent decree. The terms included a provision whereby the husband was to pay to the wife, "if, as, and when retirement is received" by him, a sum equal to 25 percent of the sum payable to a retired major with twenty years of service.[32] The husband retired in 1991, but sought and obtained a 40 percent disability rating, the receipt of which required him to waive an equivalent amount of retired pay. The trial court ordered that the sum waived was "not subject to division" as community property under the Uniformed Services Former Spouses Protection Act (USFSPA), and that the wife therefore could not compel him to compensate her for the loss of her share of funds.

The San Antonio court began its analysis by noting that the husband's effort to prevent enforcement of the terms of the decree was "a collateral attack on a final and unappealed judgment, thereby raising the issue of res judicata."[33] The court noted that the issue is one of state law.

In the course of its discussion, the San Antonio court explained that the *Berry* case, on which it had relied in *Gallegos,* had been overturned by the Texas Supreme Court and that *Berry* involved a wife's contempt action against a husband for nonpayment of a portion of military retirement benefits that he claimed were exempt by reason of his waiver of retired pay in favor of disability benefits.[34] Ultimately, the wife was

---

31. Jones v. Jones, 900 S.W.2d 786 (Tex. App. 1995).
32. Though not discussed in the case, it is nearly certain that the language used was an effort to comply with yet another Texas case that, based on state law, restricts retired pay to the rank and grade the member had at the time of divorce, if he continues service thereafter. *See* Grier v. Grier, 731 S.W.2d 931 (Tex. 1987) (1975 decree of divorce omitted mention of military retirement benefits, but 1983 partition judgment awarded former spouse a share based upon length of marriage during service).
33. *Jones,* 900 S.W.2d at 787.
34. In the intervening years, it had become common knowledge that in *Mansell* itself, on remand, the wife was permitted to enforce the terms of the decree

allowed to collect against the husband all sums that were ordered in the decree but which the husband had sought to recharacterize as disability.[35]

Finding that the divorce court had demonstrated jurisdiction over the parties and the subject matter, the appellate court held that the divorce decree was final and not subject to collateral attack:

> Similarly, here we have no findings of fact or conclusions of law and a final unappealed divorce decree which the [husband] attempted to collaterally attack in response to the motion to enforce the decree. Under Texas law, res judicata bars this collateral attack, and the trial court's judgment should be upheld. . . .[36]

Finally, the San Antonio court rejected the husband's attempt to rely on the earlier *Gallegos* opinion. The court found *Gallegos* "clearly distinguishable" because it was a direct appeal, timely brought, from a divorce decree, while *Jones* was a contempt enforcement proceeding relating to an already final, unappealable, decree of divorce. Accordingly, the appellate court directed the trial court to enforce that decree, and require the husband to make the wife whole by paying her the sum to which she was entitled under the terms of the decree, regardless of any amounts the husband had waived for VA disability or any other purpose.[37]

The North Dakota case provides an illustration of why the model decree at the end of this book contains so many antifraud fallback clauses. In *Knoop v. Knoop*,[38] the appellate court reviewed a proceeding in which the wife had sought to hold the husband in contempt for failure to comply with the payment terms of a decree. The parties had divorced while the husband was on active duty. The decree required alimony payments for five years, and called for a division of the military retirement benefits in accordance with the time rule, adding that the husband "shall make the necessary arrangements so that the retirement benefits to be paid to [the wife] shall be by allotment."[39]

---

against the husband. *See* Mansell v. Mansell, 490 U.S. 581 (1989), *remanded*, 217 Cal. App. 3d 219, 265 Cal. Rptr. 227 (Ct. App. 1989).

35. The Texas court joined the clear majority of courts in so holding.

36. *Jones*, 900 S.W.2d at 788.

37. *Id.*

38. Knoop v. Knoop, 542 N.W.2d 114 (N.D. 1996).

39. *Id.* at 115. This was a technical mistake, of course, and shows the dangers

When the husband retired and the wife did not immediately begin receiving her portion of the retired pay, she brought a contempt action, which was resolved by stipulation to an amended judgment that showed a specific percentage to which the wife was entitled, but added language making the intent unclear:

> [The wife] shall be entitled to 36.5% of [the husband's] retirement pay remaining after deduction of federal withholding made in accordance with a W-4 form which accurately reflects [the husband's] income tax filing status.[40]

The stipulated order also repeated the error requiring payments by allotment.

A year thereafter, the husband obtained a civil service job, which lowered the payments to the wife. The wife again sought a contempt order, claiming that the husband had paid neither the alimony nor the required share of military retired pay. Apparently, the husband then paid the full alimony arrearage.[41] The remaining claim of the wife was dismissed and she appealed.

The focus of the appellate court was on the North Dakota state law requirement that contempt must be proven by "clear and satisfactory proof" of willful and inexcusable intent to violate a court order. The appellate court found this to be within the sound discretion of the trial court, and that the core of the dispute was the precise language used in the amended decree. After reciting the history of military retired pay law, from *McCarty* through *Mansell,* and noting that the definition of "disposable retired pay" excludes amounts waived for VA disability benefits or under the dual compensation act, the court opined that the two should be treated similarly.[42] The appellate court noted that

> the same judge who ordered entry of the amended judgment presided over the contempt proceeding and concluded that "retirement pay," as

---

> of having decrees prepared for division of military retired pay that are not designed with the technical requirements of the military pay system in mind.

40. *Id.* at 116.
41. *Id.*
42. *Id.* at 116–17.

used in the amended judgment, had to mean "disposable retired pay" as defined by the Former Spouses Act and *Mansell*.[43]

The appellate court then ruled that the interpretation of the amended judgment was a question of law that it could review, noting its intent to defer to the trial court's construction if the language was ambiguous, unless the lower court misapplied the law in interpreting the decree.

The appellate court then reversed the lower court, holding that the law did not "require the trial court to import a given definition into the amended judgment; [the law] merely limited the size of the pie from which the trial court could cut in determining a property division."[44] The court found that wife's share of 36.5 percent was not meaningful in determining what the court could use to enforce the judgment, but only "half of disposable pay," meaning that the lower court could use whatever was left after the dual compensation offset.

The appellate court did the math, and noted that after the dual compensation offset, there was more than enough money in "50 percent of the member's disposable retired pay" to satisfy the original payment amount.[45] The court then reiterated its prior holding in *Vitko v. Vitko*,[46] that *Mansell* is to be "construed narrowly to allow trial courts to consider parties' ultimate economic circumstances in dividing their marital property."[47]

The appellate court agreed, however, that contempt should not lie, because the amended decree at issue in that case was not clear about how much the husband was to pay (its reference to "retirement pay remaining after deduction of federal withholding") and the requirement for payment by allotment "suggests" that the parties had some unclearly expressed intention modifying the sum payable. The ambiguity did not allow a con-

---

43. *Id.* at 117.
44. *Id.*
45. *Id.* at 118.
46. Vitko v. Vitko, 524 N.W.2d 102 (N.D. 1994).
47. *Knoop*, 542 N.W.2d at 118. This holding is remarkable in the way it mirrors the directions of the Texas Supreme Court in *Murff*, discussed above. The national consensus appears to be that *Mansell* is to be read as strictly limited as possible, to keep spouses from being cheated out of their share of benefits as provided in state court divorce decrees. See the discussion in the following section dealing with VA disability waivers.

tempt sanction, because the party to be held in contempt could not reliably tell what he was to pay.[48]

The appellate court therefore remanded the case to the trial court, with instructions to clean up the language of the judgment and apply the sums available under law to satisfy the wife's claims. Of course, the *Knoop* court did not have before it a decree specifically calling for imposition of alimony sufficient to neutralize any reduction in military retired pay that the husband managed to obtain. It appears the court would have seized upon a decree like the model at the end of this book to satisfy the intended award to the former spouse.

On August 14, 1997, the Arizona Supreme Court issued a decision entitled *In re Gaddis*.[49] The parties divorced after a twenty-eight-year marriage, and the member had retired about a year before the divorce. The wife apparently had waived her interest in the retirement, but timely moved to set aside that decree; she was ultimately awarded one-half of her husband's military retirement benefits as of February 1994. The award was affirmed on appeal.[50]

From the decision, it appears that as of the time of the award, the husband already had disability benefits totaling some $1,000, making the disposable pay about $1,359 to $1,870, and making the former spouse's share some $750 to $785.

The husband then went to work for the civil service. The dual compensation offset reduced the husband's disposable retired pay to only $680 per month, which he divided with the former spouse. She filed a petition for order to show cause why he should not be held in contempt. The trial court held that the wife's preexisting award was not reduced by virtue of her husband's obtaining government employment and the implication of the dual compensation offset.

The Arizona appellate court selected as the key question whether the reductions in retired pay existed when the award to the former spouse was made.[51] The court viewed the proscription of *Mansell*—that the USFSPA

---

48. *Id.*
49. *In re* Gaddis (Ariz. 957 P.2d 1010, 250 Ariz. Adv. Rep. 21 1997).
50. Gaddis v. Gaddis, No. 2 CA-CV 94-0337 (Ariz. Ct. App. Mar. 31, 1995) (memo. decision).
51. This mirrors the reasoning of several courts deciding the disability cases, discussed above and below this section.

"does not grant state courts the power to treat as property divisible upon divorce military retired pay that has been waived to receive veterans' disability payments"—as a call for state courts to take a "snapshot" when the award to the spouse is made. If sums of disposable retired pay have been waived up to that point, they are not divisible.

The court rejected, however, the husband's claim that the law called for the former spouse's interest to be "automatically reduced" by the sum he waived to receive civil service compensation, despite the fact that the waiver occurred after the final dissolution decree. The court found that Arizona law does not permit, and federal law does not require, such an outcome.

In the court's view, the husband was attempting a "de facto modification" of a final property award, which state law did not permit. Noting that the reduction would have been caused by "a post-decree change in circumstances unilaterally imposed" by the husband, the court specifically analogized the dual compensation waiver to a waiver of benefits used to claim SSB or VSI benefits, which the court had already held allowed tracing of the spousal interest to the substituted benefit.[52] In support of its conclusion, the Arizona court quoted—without attribution—exactly the same language from the California cases of *Luciano* and *Gillmore* relied upon elsewhere relating to VSI, SSB, and disability cases.[53] Specifically, the court held as follows:

> At the time of the decree, there was no dual compensation offset because husband had not yet obtained civil service employment. When he subsequently did, the decree already had established wife's fixed interest in the military retirement benefits.[54]

The court found that because the decree "protected wife's right to receive the property she had been allocated, or its value, without specifying an

---

52. *See* Crawford v. Crawford, 180 Ariz. 324, 884 P.2d 210 (Ct. App. 1994).

53. The court specifically quoted and analogized to *In re Marriage of Strassner,* 895 S.W.2d 614 (Mo. Ct. App. 1995), which is discussed in the following section addressing disability benefits. The Arizona court held that in this situation, like that one, the spousal interest had been "finally determined" on the date of the decree, and enforcing that order in the face of a postdecree recharacterization by the member did not violate *Mansell.*

54. *Id.* at 1013.

improper source of funds for indemnification," it did not so much "prospectively divide [waived] benefits" as provide "a manner of enforcing the property division contained in the original decree."[55] The Arizona court rejected the husband's "misplaced" reliance on the Texas holding in *Gallegos* discussed above, because the court in that case attempted to divide exempt property specifically.

The bottom line to these cases is that there is just not much authority regarding dual compensation matters. When it has been addressed in litigation about current divorces, some courts have held that actual division of the retired pay is limited to disposable pay, with any shortfall to the spouse to be compensated by other means. When postdecree enforcement has been at issue, however, the courts appear to require that the member compensate the spouse for any action taken by the member that lowers sums payable to the spouse.

This provides a nice "bright line" for practitioners, but it heightens the need for counsel for spouses to be alert in two ways. First, counsel must be aware of any unilateral changes in the retirement benefits divisible at the time of divorce, and consider whether an alimony or other award to compensate for the waived property interest is appropriate. Second, counsel must take care in the drafting of decrees to make clear that the award to the spouse is absolute, and may not be reduced by any kind of postdivorce recharacterization that the member might attempt.

b. Military Retirement Benefits Component
of a Civil Service Retirement

Perhaps ironically, there have been situations in which the dual receipt rules have resulted in former spouses receiving shares of military retirement benefits from which they otherwise would have been barred. In one post-*McCarty*-gap case, brought under a state window statute, the court "traced" the spousal share of the military service, even though the member had been awarded all the interest in the retirement in a divorce during the *McCarty* gap, *and* had subsequently obtained a 100 percent VA disability rating, because he waived all those awards to roll his military service into a later civil service retirement.[56]

---

55. *Id.*
56. Leatherman v. Leatherman, 122 Idaho 247, 833 P.2d 105 (1992).

This approach, known as the "source of the benefit" method, would be repeated in later years by courts trying to decide whether former spouses had an interest in SSB or VSI benefits. The reasoning, which is pretty straightforward, states that if one spouse derives an economic benefit attributable to services performed during the marriage, and there is not a specific legal prohibition on sharing that benefit with the former spouse, then the benefit should be divided in accordance with normal marital property law.

Notably, Congress itself appears to have adopted the reasoning of this theory in amendments that went into effect in 1997 for both Civil Service Retirement System (CSRS) and Federal Employees Retirement System (FERS) retirements, but only to waivers made on or after January 1, 1997. Under those rules, if a military member waives military retired pay to take a civil service retirement, the former spouse must be paid what she would have received from the military for the waiver to be accepted by the Office of Personnel Management (OPM).[57]

This modification was apparently designed to address one inequity noted by the ABA Committee representatives at the 1990 hearings—under prior law, an order for division of military retirement benefits was not enforceable by the OPM, and was not sufficient to divide civil service retirement benefits, which often caused postdivorce litigation between those affected.[58]

The OPM has published a guidebook for lawyers who are drafting retirement orders for CSRS or FERS retirement benefits.[59] That guide includes model paragraphs, including one entitled "Protecting a former spouse entitled to military retired pay" (paragraph 111). It reads as follows:

---

57. Pub. L. 104-201, Div. A, Title VI, Subtitle D, § 637, 110 Stat. 2579 (1996).
58. *See* 5 C.F.R. Part 8331, Subpart Q, App. A § V-D.
59. Retirement and Insurance Group, U.S. Office of Personnel Management, A Handbook for Attorneys on Court-Ordered Retirement, Health Benefits, and Life Insurance under the Civil Service Retirement System, Federal Employees Retirement System, Federal Employees Health Benefits Program, and Federal Employees Group Life Insurance Program (rev. ed. 1995). This book can be obtained from the Government Printing Office, Superintendent of Documents, P.O. Box 371954, Pittsburgh, PA 15250-7954. It is identified as S/N 006-000-01408-9, and costs $14 per copy, which includes all forms on computer disk. ISBN 0-16-045511-1.

Using the following paragraph will protect the former spouse interest in military retired pay in the event that the employee waives the military retired pay to allow crediting the military service under CSRS or FERS. The paragraph should only be used if the former spouse is awarded a portion of the military retired pay. "If [employee] waives military retired pay to credit military service under the Civil Service Retirement System, [insert language for computing the former spouse's share from 200 series of this appendix.]. The United States Office of Personnel Management is directed to pay [former spouse]'s share directly to [former spouse].[60]

When a postmilitary civil service career seems likely, allocation of the retirement benefits from that service should probably be explicitly set forth. When (as in most cases) it is only one possibility among many, the standard form clauses at the end of this book (allowing for issuance of a further order tracing the military retired pay and entry of a further order) are probably adequate.

4. Postdivorce Disability Application by the Member

A retired member may seek the VA's evaluation of whether the member has suffered a service-connected disability, or reevaluation of a disability rating previously granted.[61] The U.S. Supreme Court has indicated that this right is not to be infringed upon by the state courts. On the other hand, state divorce courts have traditionally had the power to award spousal support (alimony) based on the economic realities of the parties, and to adjust such an award based on the parties' changing circumstances after divorce.

Before *Mansell,* there was little question that counsel for a former spouse should probably have sought a reservation of jurisdiction to seek an alimony award in case a share of the retired pay as property was cut off. The basis for the request would have been the (generally correct) assumption that the court's nonaward of alimony, or the size of any award that was granted, necessarily took into account the military retirement benefits flowing to the former spouse. The cutoff of those payments, by the member's action of applying for and being granted nondivisible dis-

---

60. *Id.* ¶ 111.
61. *See, e.g.,* Mansell v. Mansell, 490 U.S. 581 (1989), *remanded,* 217 Cal. App. 3d 219, 265 Cal. Rptr. 227 (Ct. App. 1989).

ability payments, constitutes a change in the parties' circumstances that warrants a review of the alimony award.[62]

After *Mansell,* however, there would appear to be at least some doubt about the constitutionality of that strategy. To receive tax-free disability pay upon retirement for disability, a member must waive an equivalent portion of retired pay. Such waived pay is excluded from the definition of "disposable" pay that may be split with a former spouse in accordance with a court order. Ultimately, any disability claim increases the money flowing to the retiree at the expense of the former spouse, even to the point of eliminating the spousal share entirely.[63]

After *Mansell,* some believed that any disability award existing on the date of divorce simply could not be considered by a divorce court, and some courts stopped their analysis at the finding that the sums waived are excluded from division as marital property.[64] It has proven not entirely correct, however, that they "cannot be considered." Military disability pay *may* be considered as a factor in awarding to the former spouse a disproportionate amount of community property, or otherwise considered as part

---

62. *See In re* Marriage of McGhee, 131 Cal. App. 3d 408, 182 Cal. Rptr. 456 (Ct. App. 1982) (compensation by means of alimony, as set forth in agreement between parties, used by dissolution court when member halted flow of military retirement benefits to former spouse after *McCarty* decision; court termed use of such "backup" clauses as making the property award "supportified"); *In re* Marriage of Sheldon, 124 Cal. App. 3d 371, 177 Cal. Rptr. 380 (Ct. App. 1981) (noting "close relationship between the amount of a property division and the entitlement, if any, of a spouse to spousal support"); *In re* Marriage of Mastropaolo, 166 Cal. App. 3d 953, 213 Cal. Rptr. 26 (Ct. App. 1985) ("conditionally" reversing alimony award "on condition" that court's affirmance of retirement division became final); Austin (Scott) v. Austin, No. 92-015818 (Mich. Ct. App. ____) (unpublished intermediate court opinion), *review denied,* 451 Mich. 857, 546 N.W.2d 255 (1996) (alimony, previously reserved, but only until remarriage, instituted for wife in lieu of pension share lost because of member's transfer to VA disability status; court approval given to post-remarriage alimony when alimony compensates for distribution of pension earned during marriage, under *Arnholt v. Arnholt,* 129 Mich. App. 810, 343 N.W.2d 214 (Ct. App. 1983) (nonmilitary case)).

63. *See* Mansell v. Mansell, 490 U.S. 581 (1989).

64. *See, e.g.,* Davis v. Davis, 777 S.W.2d 230 (Ky. 1989).

of the present and future "economic circumstances" of parties.[65] At least when the parties have agreed that the spouse is to receive half the retirement, courts have expressed a willingness to enforce that agreement by requiring the member, who applied for disability at the time of divorce, to divide the disability benefits as well.[66] This logic would appear to apply equally to cases in which there was a court order rather than an agreement.

When the disability is claimed *after* the divorce, it has the inevitable result of reducing the spousal share of retirement benefits paid to the former spouse as a share of marital property, unless precautions are taken in the phrasing of the decree, or a court is willing to take steps to enforce the original division of assets.

Some courts have gone to considerable lengths to invoke their equitable powers to protect former spouses from postdivorce status changes by members that would have had the effect of partially or completely divesting the spouses.[67] In *Mansell* itself, the court—upon remand—refused to allow the ruling in that case to affect the preexisting division of dollars between the parties.[68] This logic was followed by other courts examining pre-*Mansell* divorces.[69]

For divorces occurring after the appellate *Mansell* decision, the same result has been ordered, but sometimes with different logic. Safeguard clauses and indemnification for reduction clauses are permissible, and have the result of protecting the spouse from the member's unilateral reclassification of benefits. The theory appears to be one of constructive trust; once the divorce goes through, the retirement money is considered no longer the member's property to convert.[70]

---

65. *In re* Kraft, 119 Wash. 2d 438, 832 P.2d 871 (1992) (citing many other cases); *In re* Brown, ___ Mont. ___, 892 P.2d 572 (*aff'd* Jan. 18, 1995).
66. Hisgen v. Hisgen, 554 N.W.2d 494 (S.D. 1996).
67. *In re* Marriage of Stier, 178 Cal. App. 3d 42, 223 Cal. Rptr. 599 (Ct. App. 1986) (disability irrelevant to attempted equal division of retirement benefits in pre-*McCarty* divorce); *In re* Marriage of Briltz, 141 Cal. App. 3d 17, 189 Cal. Rptr. 893 (Ct. App. 1983) (nonmilitary case).
68. *In re* Marriage of Mansell, 217 Cal. App. 3d 219, 265 Cal. Rptr. 227 (Ct. App. 1989), *on remand from* 490 U.S. 581 (1989).
69. *See* Toupal v. Toupal, 109 N.M. 774, 790 P.2d 1055 (1990); Berry v. Berry, 786 S.W.2d 672 (Tex. 1990); Maxwell v. Maxwell, 796 P.2d 403 (Utah Ct. App. 1990); MacMeeken v. MacMeeken, 117 B.R. 642 (Bankr. D. Kan. 1990).
70. *See In re* Strassner, 895 S.W.2d 614 (Mo. Ct. App. 1995). *See also* Owen

Courts have been clearest about protecting the bargained-for expectations of the parties in those cases in which the property settlement agreement ratified by the divorce decree contained an explicit consideration of the possibility of disability application, and stated the parties' intention to divide the resulting disability benefits as they had the retirement benefits that were replaced.[71] The form at the end of this book contains clauses that are intended to permit reviewing courts to find that intention and make that interpretation.

Some courts have simply redistributed other property. In *Torwich (Abrom) v. Torwich*,[72] the member's application for a disability award, reducing the wife's share of the military retirement from $249 to $97 per month, was termed "exceptional and compelling circumstances" sufficient to allow redistribution of property four years after the divorce. This case has been relied upon for the proposition that *Mansell* permits "other adjustments to be made" to take into account a reduction in a spousal share resulting from a disability claim by the member.[73] Probably the most

---

v. Owen, 14 Va. App. 623, 419 S.E.2d 267 (Ct. App. 1992) (explicit indemnification; husband's subsequent disability retirement and reduction in retired pay to wife required husband to pay subtracted sums to wife and did not violate *Mansell* in any way); Dexter v. Dexter, 105 Md. App. 678, 661 A.2d 171 (Ct. Spec. App. 1995) (implicit indemnification; wife entitled to benefit of bargain reached at divorce); McHugh v. McHugh, 124 Idaho 543, 861 P.2d 113 (Ct. App. 1993).

71. *See In re* Stone, 274 Mont. 331, 908 P.2d 670 (1996) (support award based on total of retirement and disability pay); Abernethy v. Abernethy, 670 So. 2d 1027 (Fla. Dist. Ct. App. 1996) (property division upheld against disability award), *aff'd*, 699 So. 2d 235 (Fla. 1997) (overruling lower court's holding that disability benefits could be assigned by property settlement agreement, but holding that if final judgment guarantees stream of payments to former spouse measured by military retired pay, and requires member to indemnify or guarantee those payments to former spouse, any VA disability or other conversion or reduction in disposable retired pay is irrelevant— what is owed to former spouse is guaranteed stream of payments, as defined in underlying court order); *contra*, Kutzke v. Kutzke, No. 95 CA 66 (Ohio Ct. App. Apr. 12, 1996), 22 Fam. L. Rep. (BNA) 1291 (Apr. 30, 1996) (unpublished slip opinion).

72. Torwich (Abrom) v. Torwich, 282 N. J. Super. 524, 660 A.2d 1214 (Super. Ct. App. Div. 1995).

73. Clauson v. Clauson, 831 P.2d 1257 (Alaska 1992); McMahan v. McMahan, 567 So. 2d 976 (Fla. Dist. Ct. App. 1990).

straightforward such "adjustment" is a change to any ongoing alimony payments, because the recharacterization will almost always result in a "change in the parties' relative financial conditions."[74]

This is not to say that the result is universal. Some courts have refused, on the basis of state laws prohibiting postdivorce amendments to property divisions, to compensate the former spouse in any way at all for a post-divorce conversion of military retired pay into disability pay, even if that conversion altered the anticipated equitable division.[75]

Recitations of intent and reliance upon compensatory awards of alimony by reviewing courts are not perfect solutions; they necessarily involve further litigation, and some uncertainty. Still, it is hard to conceive of any strategy that would suffice to absolutely protect the former spouse's interest in a future income stream, unless there was sufficient other property in a case that the court could grant a mortgage or lien to protect the actuarial equivalent of the former spouse's share.

The bottom line to these cases is that it is incumbent upon the lawyers, particularly the lawyer for the spouse, to anticipate postdivorce status changes and build that anticipation into the decree.

C. DIVISION OF BENEFITS UPON ELIGIBILITY (DESPITE THE MEMBER'S CONTINUING SERVICE)

Several state courts have held that the interest of a former spouse in military retired pay is realized at vesting (that is, after twenty years of creditable service), theoretically entitling the spouse to collect a portion of what the member *could* get at that time, regardless of whether the member actually retires.[76] If a member is eligible for retirement at the time

---

74. *See* Kramer v. Kramer, 567 N.W.2d 100 (Nebr. 1997) (discussing rationale of collected cases).

75. *See* Gilliland v. Stanley, Appeal No. 02A01-9603-GS-00056, 1997 WL 180587 (Tenn. Ct. App. Western Section, at Jackson, April 16, 1997).

76. *See In re* Marriage of Luciano, 104 Cal. App. 3d 956, 164 Cal. Rptr. 93 (Ct. Appl. 1980); *In re* Marriage of Gillmore, 29 Cal. 3d 418, 629 P.2d 1, 174 Cal. Rptr. 493 (1981); *In re* Marriage of Scott, 156 Cal. App. 3d 251, 202 Cal. Rptr. 716 (Ct. App. 1984); Gemma v. Gemma, 105 Nev. 458, 778 P.2d 429 (1989); Koelsch v. Koelsch, 148 Ariz. 176, 713 P.2d 1234 (1986); Ruggles v. Ruggles, 116 N.M. 52, 860 P.2d 182 (1993); Balderson v. Balderson, 127 Idaho 48, 896 P.2d 956 (1994); Blake v. Blake, 807 P.2d 1211 (Colo. Ct. App. 1990).

of divorce, the *Luciano/Gillmore* analysis gives the former spouse an election to begin collecting his or her percentage share immediately.[77] Those cases made clear that in California a spouse has to make an "irrevocable election" at the time of divorce concerning whether to begin receiving the spousal share of the retirement benefits upon maturity (eligibility for regular retirement), or to wait until the wage earner actually retires, thus enjoying a "smaller piece of a larger pie" by getting a shrinking percentage of a retirement based upon postdivorce increases in the wage earner's salary and years in service.

A spouse making an election to receive benefits upon eligibility should also receive the imputed COLAs that *would have* accrued if the member had retired, but the former spouse would *not* share in any actual later increases in rank, or benefit from additional years in service.

Courts typically figure spousal shares as percentages, the numerator of which is time in service during marriage, and the denominator of which is total time in service (all multiplied by one-half). If the spouse elected to wait until actual retirement, he or she would receive a "smaller share of a larger pie." Not all state courts follow this analysis.[78] This is likely to be an area that will see significant further development in the courts.

EXAMPLE

George and Jane divorce in 1991 in California just as George, a major, completes twenty years of active-duty service. Although he could retire and obtain $1,794 per month in retired pay, he elects to remain in service. If all service occurred during the marriage, and there were no applicable deductions, Jane could request $897 per month, starting at

---

77. The theory underlying the analysis is that the former spouse should be able to decide when benefits that are due and payable will actually commence, and that the "employee spouse cannot by election defeat the nonemployee spouse's interest in the community property by relying on a condition within the employee spouse's control." *In re* Marriage of Luciano, 104 Cal. App. 3d 956, 960, 164 Cal. Rptr. 93, 95 (Ct. App. 1980).

78. *See, e.g.,* Grier v. Grier, 731 S.W.2d 931 (Tex. 1987). The court held that *actual* rank at the time of divorce was the rank at which calculations were to be performed.

the time of divorce, as her community property share of the retirement for which George was eligible.

If Jane chooses to wait the additional three years until George actually retires, George could obtain $2,063 in retired pay as a major, because his multiplier would be for twenty-three years of service rather than just twenty (all figures presume constant 1991 dollars). In this scenario, Jane would have been married to George for only 86.96 percent of his active-duty service, instead of the entire service time, so her spousal share would shrink from 50 percent to 43.48 percent. Her portion of the retired pay would *still* be $897 per month ($2,063 multiplied by 43.48 percent, multiplied by one-half), and she would have received nothing for the three years of payments she might have received (three multiplied by twelve, multiplied by $897, equals $32,292).

The situation is somewhat different if George advances in rank, however. Under the same facts, if George was promoted to lieutenant colonel after twenty-three years, he could receive $2,467 in retired pay. Jane's 43.48 percent would be $1,073 per month. The extra $176 per month she would receive for waiting would "make up" the $32,292 she did *not* get in about fifteen years, if everyone lived long enough.

The concern expressed by those courts trying to preserve the spousal right to payment at eligibility for retirement is warranted by an analysis of the loss that would be suffered. If, for example, a master sergeant (E-8) divorced in 1997 at exactly twenty years of service, having been married for the full time of service, the sum payable would be $1,319 per month ($15,828 per year).[79] The parties would each have a 50 percent putative interest in the retirement benefits accrued through that time. Assuming they were married when the member was twenty years old[80] and the former spouse was eighteen, they would be forty and thirty-eight, respectively, at the time of divorce. If the former spouse immediately

79. OFFICE OF THE ACTUARY, DEP'T OF DEFENSE, FY 1996 DOD STATISTICAL REPORT ON THE MILITARY RETIREMENT SYSTEM 284–85 (1997) [hereinafter FY 1996 REPORT].
80. The Department of Defense Actuary makes that assumption when building the lump-sum equivalency table. *See* FY 1996 REPORT, *supra* note 79 at 287.

began receiving 50 percent of the sum payable at that time, the payments would be $659.50 per month, or $7,914 per year. Actuarially, the former spouse would receive benefits during the member's lifetime, which at age forty is about thirty-six more years, and thus receive approximately $288,228.[81]

By waiting for collection of the spousal share for another ten years, until actual retirement at thirty years of service, it is true that the "pie" will have grown to $2,329 per month ($27,948 per year), and the spousal share (33.33 percent at the thirty-year mark) will have grown to $776.26 per month ($9,315 per year).[82] However, by that time both parties will be ten years older, and the member's life expectancy will be about twenty-seven years, making the estimated lifetime collection about $252,995.[83]

For the spouse, the approximate lifetime collection difference is about 13 percent. This approximate ratio holds true across ranks. For example, using the Office of the Actuary standard of service entry at age twenty-three for an officer, and using the above facts for a divorce after twenty years, with retirement after thirty years, the former spouse would have lifetime collections of about $592,532 if payments of the spousal share started at eligibility, and only $508,851 if the larger dollar sum started being paid at thirty years.

The difference is more dramatic if the people involved are any older than those above, because there is less actuarial time for the later-starting-but-higher sum to make up for the lack of collection in earlier years. Just adding five years to the age of service entry in the above hypotheticals

---

81. This hypothetical uses a military-specific, nondisability retired life expectation chart published by the Department of the Actuary, and makes assumptions based on the life of the *member*, because the benefits end when the member dies. *See* FY 1996 REPORT, *supra* note 79, at 288. Survivorship benefits are not included, for clarity, but would not change the conclusions reached. These calculations are given in 1997 dollars for simplicity; it is presumed that salaries, and therefore retirements, would keep pace with inflation.

82. FY 1996 REPORT, *supra* note 79, at 284–85.

83. All this assumes that the former spouse receives a share of the retirement benefits ultimately payable. If the Texas-style restriction to the rank and grade at the time of divorce is adopted, then the decrease in value of the spousal share would be greatly accelerated. There does not appear to be any actuarial justification to the Texas-style analysis.

makes the difference in the former spouse's lifetime collections drop by another 3 to 5 percent.[84]

Thus, there is no doubt that deferring spousal collection until actual retirement leads to significantly less return to the spouse from the spouse's time investment in the member's career. On the other hand, employee spouses often express the feeling that it is not possible for them to continue with employment to achieve the largest possible retirement if they are required to divert from current earnings a sum equal to the spousal portion of the retirement that would have been received had employment been terminated at eligibility. In other words, members have stated that to allow payment of the spousal share at eligibility essentially forces them to retire.

This argument does not appear to be logical, because the actual cash flow to members will always be *greater* before retirement than after (current wages are always greater than the sum of the retirement), so that the same flow of cash to the former spouse is a lesser share of the total cash otherwise flowing to the member before retirement than after retirement. More likely, the position is based in perceptions, because postdivorce direct payments by the pay center to a former spouse simply make the payments to the member smaller, while payments to the former spouse from the member while service continues appear to be a large expenditure. In either event, there is apparently no hard data available to substantiate that any members were "forced" to retire as a result of spousal share payments beginning upon eligibility.

As briefly discussed above, the bottom line is that, given the realities of finite life expectancies, the spouse would usually not live long enough to realize a benefit to waiting for collection, and this is even more certain when the time value of money is added to the calculation (that is, investment/interest/present value calculations). Lawyers for spouses should seek collection at first eligibility in virtually every case (and, of course, ask for the hypothetical COLAs that would have accrued if/as/when retirement had been taken at first eligibility). Lawyers for members should seek to delay spousal payments to the extent possible.

---

84. For those who wish to replicate the calculations, an E-8 member at age 48 has a life expectancy of 28.86 years, making the spousal share $227,590; at age 58, the life expectancy is 20.39, yielding $184,407, a ratio of 81 percent. For the O-6 member, at age 45, life expectancy is 35.22, yielding a spousal share of $561,900, and at age 55, the life expectancy is 26.01 and the spousal share is $476,035, a ratio of 84.72 percent.

There are some practical considerations on this point. There is no mechanism to enforce a preretirement allocation to the former spouse of a "due and payable" amount of retired pay. In practice, if a former spouse wishes immediate payments, but a member is unwilling or unable to pay the portion upon divorce, settlement is sometimes reached by calculating the member's share of equity in other assets, and offsetting the former spouse's monthly putative share as a pay-down of the member's interest in those assets. In other words, the former spouse may buy out the member's interest in, say, the marital residence, by *non*receipt of the spousal share payable at the member's eligibility for retirement. This is sometimes a more satisfactory resolution than having any money actually change hands.

In the hearings leading up to the 1990 amendments to the USFSPA, there was some effort to broaden the current law (which prohibits courts from ordering members to retire[85]) to encompass a prohibition on *Luciano*-type orders. The proposals died in committee but could, of course, resurface at a later date. The effect of such a change would be the devaluation of spousal shares in all cases in which the divorce preceded actual retirement.

D. DEFAULT DIVORCES

The short version, at least for spouse's lawyers, is "DON'T." No matter which party files for divorce, default divorces can cause many inequitable results.

The former spouse who files may present a dilemma for the member, but both parties are put in a position of some danger. If a divorce action is validly brought under state law against a member who does not wish that state to apply its law in providing for disposition of the military retirement benefits, the member's choice of response is critical, because the existence of the retirement issue does not limit the jurisdiction of the state court concerning other matters.

A member's opposition to any portion of the relief sought may well be construed by the state court as a general appearance, giving the court authority to dispose of the retirement benefits because of the member's

---

85. 10 U.S.C. § 1408(c)(3).

consent to jurisdiction.[86] The member may have to choose between not opposing an adverse ruling on custody, alimony, or other property issues, on the one hand, or allowing the court to dispose of the military retirement benefits, on the other.

The results in such a situation are often unfair to the spouse as well. If the member did not appear, and the state court order purported to dispose of the retirement benefits despite lack of "federal jurisdiction" to do so, the spouse would have an unenforceable order. If the state that had jurisdiction over the military retirement benefits under the USFSPA did not allow partition actions, the spouse would have no recourse.

Thus, a member may prevent any state court from addressing the retirement simply by refusing to appear and allowing default to be taken. Even spouses who are fully informed face the unpleasant choice of remaining involuntarily married, or suffering a grossly inequitable property distribution.

At least two solutions to these problems were presented to Congress in 1990 by the ABA Committee, but Congress has acted on neither.

The USFSPA could specifically allow for subsequent actions, in whatever state did have jurisdiction over the retirement benefits, to consider their division. If it is feared that spouses might be over-compensated, the statute could direct the later court to take into account any compensation that may have been awarded to the spouse in the divorce to try to compensate for that earlier court's lack of jurisdiction over the retirement.

A more economical solution would be to amend the jurisdictional limitations to require simply that the divorce state apply the substantive law—concerning military retirement benefits division—of the state in which the member is a legal resident. This would allow for consideration of all assets in a single proceeding and lower the likelihood of disproportionate asset division, while assuring that no member's retirement benefits could be disposed of by the law of a jurisdiction where the member was present solely by military order.

It should be noted, however, that both these solutions are necessary only to accommodate the apparent congressional intent to partially preempt state law in this field. Whenever one asset is treated "specially" in a divorce property division, there is the danger that the equities sought by the trier of fact will be distorted.

---

86. This is explored in greater detail in Section B, Chapter Four.

There is also a significant danger to the former spouse when the *member* files for divorce and a default is possible against the former spouse (even, or perhaps especially, when the member files in a jurisdiction remote from the former spouse by virtue of military assignment or by retained jurisdiction). In such a suit, the member might list the retired pay as an asset and ask the court to award it solely to the member, or might omit it entirely.

If the asset was listed, it is imperative for the former spouse to make an appearance in the action, either to request division of the asset or to challenge the jurisdiction of the court to proceed with the divorce on whatever grounds are applicable. Failure to do so, once apprised of the existence of the divorce action and the claim to the retirement benefits by the member, will probably preclude later challenge to the divorce court's disposition of the asset.

If the military retirement benefits were not noted as an asset for division by the divorce court, the results might be the same. Silence in a decree effectively divests the former spouse of any interest in the military retirement benefits; there is no presumed share for former spouses in the military system, so the absence of a provision for division is treated by the pay centers the same way as an affirmative award to the member of the entirety of the benefit.

Anecdotal accounts show that many members, by design or happenstance, have obtained simple, default divorces (without providing for division of the military retirement benefits, or sometimes any property division at all) and relocated to states that do not partition assets omitted from decrees of divorce. Such states provide safe havens for members, even if the members purposefully effected fraud, making it impossible for any court to ever make an equitable distribution of property.

For those states that allow the remedy of partition, silent omission of the retired pay might be corrected by a subsequent partition suit, but there is often a question of why the former spouse did not oppose the silent divestment when notified of the divorce, and courts have had mixed responses to claims by former spouses that they were emotionally devastated, financially unable to oppose the action wherever it proceeded, or not informed that the absence of disposition was equivalent to divestment.[87]

---

87. See Section H of this chapter for a fuller explanation of partition actions.

E. VESTEDNESS AND MATURITY

The leading case in the United States (if not the earliest case so holding[88]) is *In re Marriage of Brown.*[89] The case itself concerned a private pension, not military retirement benefits, and was primarily intended to reverse a 1941 opinion in which the court had ruled that nonvested retirement benefits were a "mere expectancy." The case led, however, to a string of cases establishing the practical universality of division—in the California courts—of all interests in pension benefits, including military retirement benefits.

Several other states, especially in community property jurisdictions, followed suit, resulting in opinions stating the general proposition that retirement benefits were generally divisible, to the extent they were based on services performed during the marriage, whether or not those benefits were payable at the time of divorce.[90] Eventually, nearly all states recognized that the "vestedness" or "contingency" of retirement benefits has nothing to do with their marital character, and have divided the benefits, contingencies and all, between the parties to the degree the benefits were earned during marriage. This has extended even to jurisdictions that have appeared indifferent or hostile to spousal interests in retirement benefits.[91]

Before these cases, and continuing in those states that do not recognize unvested or unmatured retirement benefits as marital property subject to division, an employee (or military member) could entirely dispossess a spouse, even after decades of marriage while the benefits were being earned, by the simple expedient of divorcing (or, in some jurisdictions, merely separating or filing for divorce) just before vesting or maturity.[92]

---

88. The New Mexico Supreme Court addressed vested, nonmature retired pay in *LeClert v. LeClert,* 80 N.M. 235, 453 P.2d 755 (1969). Two years later, the Washington Intermediate Court of Appeals held that nonvested retirement benefits constituted community property, in *DeRevere v. DeRevere,* 5 Wash. App. 741, 491 P.2d 249 (Ct. App. 1971).

89. *In re* Marriage of Brown, 15 Cal. 3d 838, 544 P.2d 561, 126 Cal. Rptr. 251 (1976).

90. *See, e.g.,* Forrest v. Forrest, 99 Nev. 602, 668 P.2d 275 (1983).

91. *See In re* Grode, 543 N.W.2d 795 (S.D. 1996) (noting majority of cases following *Brown*); Abrams v. Abrams, 516 N.W.2d 352 (S.D. 1994).

92. *See, e.g.,* Skirvin v. Skirvin, 560 N.E.2d 1263 (Ind. Ct. App. 1990); Durham v. Durham, 289 Ark. 3, 708 S.W.2d 618 (1986); Note, *Retirement Pay: A Divorce in Time Saved Mine,* 24 HASTINGS L. REV. 347 (1973).

Anecdotal accounts indicate that some employees did just that, some even remarrying their former spouses after the effective date of the pension benefits, once the members' unilateral control of those funds was thus assured.

There is some question about how "vested" a member really might be. There is some protection for regular officers with at least eighteen years of service, who cannot be discharged for being passed over for promotion twice consecutively if on the proposed date of discharge they are within two years of qualifying for retirement.[93] This has caused some state courts that still focus on the "vestedness" distinction to redraw the line for divisibility at eighteen years.[94] Reserve officers have even greater protection. They are protected, not just from discharge from being passed over for promotion, but from any involuntary discharge, when it occurs within two years of "becoming eligible for retired pay under a purely military retirement system."[95]

There may be some distinctions among the service branches in this area. Army regulations require "review" of any discharge of any soldier who has completed eighteen years of service.[96] Air force regulations call for "special consideration" in favor of retaining people with at least sixteen years of creditable service.[97] As a matter of tradition, the services have been reluctant to discharge members approaching retirement, especially those with over eighteen years of service, absent a court martial offense or other misconduct.

All this has an interplay with the divorce law of those few states still recognizing lack of "vestedness" as a barrier to division of a retirement interest. Even in those states, it would appear that a military retirement should be considered a divisible asset at the eighteen-year mark, or perhaps the sixteen-year mark if the member is in the air force. Anecdotal accounts suggest that the courts in such states do indeed make such rulings, which may vary depending on the evidence presented about how "secure" the individual member is perceived to be.

---

93. 10 U.S.C. § 632.
94. *See, e.g.,* Milam v. Milam 92 N.C. App. 105, 373 S.E.2d 459 (Ct. App. 1988).
95. 10 U.S.C. § 1163.
96. Army Regulation 635-200, 1-21 (1994).
97. Air Force Regulation 39-10, 6-35 (1995).

Obviously, all such variability lessens the predictability and uniformity that would be most helpful to lawyers counseling clients on both sides of these cases, and increases the opportunities for gamesmanship and inequitable results. Presumably, current trends will continue—"vestedness" will be seen as meaningful in an ever-shrinking number of states; those states that were the latest to recognize *any* property interest in retirement benefits will eventually join the rest of the country in dividing those assets, matured or not, and vested or not, that accrued during the marriage.

F. MULTISTATE AND INTERNATIONAL LITIGATION

Several other sections of this book discuss cases involving more than one state, and no effort will be made here to repeat or cross-reference them extensively; the reader should reference the substantive subject area that the cases involve, or (if a case name is known) the table of cases at the end of this book. This discussion is restricted to a recap of the peculiar problems to think about whenever the courts of more than one state are involved, and the international aspect of military retirement benefits cases.

1. Multiple State Recap

At the very beginning of every case, whether brought at the time of divorce or as part of a postdivorce enforcement or modification proceeding, the lawyers on both sides should examine the jurisdictional aspects.

It may be that the state court has insufficient "federal jurisdiction" over the member to effect a successful division of the retired pay as property, leading to additional choices between proceeding on an alternate theory (alimony, for example), or abandoning the action and proceeding where the member can be served. If one side or the other does not appear and a default is contemplated, a host of other dangers arise.[98] Even if there is sufficient federal jurisdiction, or the other party could be compelled to make a general appearance, there still might be a choice to make: the law concerning military retirement benefits could differ in some subtle way— such as whether division of retired pay upon eligibility is permitted— which could tip the balance between possibly attractive venues.

---

98. See Section D of this chapter.

If there is any realistic possibility that the parties will live in different states after divorce, it becomes even more important for the spouse to make sure the order is directly enforceable through the military pay center, because interstate enforcement by contempt is so difficult (see following subsection).

2. Divorces Involving the Courts of More Than One Country

Military-related divorce cases involving a court of some other country, as well as the federal and state law applicable to these cases, illustrate the principle of "the danger of unintended consequences."[99] Given the enormous number of American service personnel stationed abroad in the past fifty years,[100] it seems almost certain that the number of actual persons affected is far higher than the relatively few published cases would indicate. Examining the facts of such a case can be highly instructive.

Jill Prevost married Tom Harms, a career military officer, in 1967. By 1984, when their marriage ended, they were living separately in Germany. Jill filed for divorce in Illinois (Tom's legal residence) in March, 1984.[101] In May, Tom requested a stay pursuant to the Soldiers and Sailors Civil Relief Act. Tom filed a new action in the German court with jurisdiction over divorce actions at about that time, and the German court proceeded to judgment on questions of custody, visitation, support, and property division.

The German court, apparently aware of the USFSPA and its legal proscription against foreign-court division of military retirement, stated as follows:

> The parties have agreed that a pension equalization shall proceed between the parties by way of the law of obligations (contracts). A regu-

---

99. This principle—that the ultimate application of any action or rule, however well intentioned, may create a worse harm than the rule was designed to address—is sometimes referred to as a branch of "applied Murphology."

100. Even in the post–cold war, post-drawdown world, there were about 295,000 personnel in foreign countries, and over 10,000 in U.S. territories or "special locations." Given these numbers, it would be remarkable if there were *not* a large number of marriages, and divorces, involving persons from more than one country, and possibly involving the courts of more than one country.

101. Case No. 84-C-290, Champaign County, Illinois.

lation under U.S. law that possibly put the wife into a better position is specifically reserved to the wife. This agreement is appropriate and reserves to the parties their rights for pension equalization, it therefore was agreed to by the Family Court.

In 1987, the Illinois court dismissed the filed-but-never-completed Illinois divorce action. Jill filed a "registration petition" in 1990, trying to get the Illinois court to act on the reservation of rights in the German divorce decree. Counsel focused on the reservation clause, instead of seeking an Illinois judgment recognizing and enforcing the German settlement dividing the retirement.

The lower court eventually dismissed Jill's petition, finding that it had no subject matter jurisdiction to entertain a claim for division of a military retirement, because in the absence of a current existing marriage, it had no provision under state law permitting it to hear a case between these persons. In other words, the court found that the fact of a completed (German) divorce prevented the state court from acting.

Jill appealed. The intermediate appellate court affirmed the lower court's dismissal on February 20, 1992.[102] That court found that under the Illinois constitution, the lower courts could hear actions for division of property only when the state legislature had explicitly given authority to do so, and that judgments of foreign countries could not be registered under the Uniform Enforcement of Foreign Judgments Act. The court rebuffed Jill's claim of jurisdiction under the USFSPA, without clearly explaining its reasoning. It expressed "concern" that its decision "leads to an inequitable result," but advocated only that "those who prepare uniform law proposals" should consider an enactment for undivided military retirement benefits.[103] Jill did not, or could not, appeal to the Illinois Supreme Court.

Tom retired in September, 1992, but did not send any portion of the retired pay to Jill. In 1994, Jill filed a federal court action through counsel

---

102. *In re* Brown, 225 Ill. App. 3d 733, 587 N.E.2d 648 (App. Ct. 1992).
103. Obviously unknown to the court, the officials at the National Commission on Uniform State Laws (NCUSL) had refused to do any such thing when asked to do so in 1988, claiming that the problem was too "state specific" to be the subject of any uniform law proposal, and that state courts "clearly" had the power to deal with such situations.

in Virginia,[104] which is where both she and Tom then lived. The federal district court found "no federal jurisdiction, expressed or implied," to adjudicate the partition action Jill had brought.[105] The district court judge, obviously reluctant to say anything that might even imply an expansion of the role of the federal courts, held that the USFSPA allows courts only to apply state divorce laws to military pensions. The court distinguished *Kirby v. Mellenger*[106] (discussed elsewhere at length) as having been decided in quite different circumstances, because it was a diversity case instead of a federal question case. The court rather obliquely remarked that the result it reached "may be lamentable," but found dismissal was required as a matter of federal question jurisdiction.[107]

Next, Jill tried state court. She filed an action for partition of the retirement, adding a state court action for enforcement of the parties' contract to divide retirement. The Virginia trial court dismissed the action, finding that the German decree did not constitute a written contract because it was not signed by the parties, in accordance with German procedure, and if it was an oral contract, the statute of limitations for its enforcement had run.

The Virginia Supreme Court affirmed the "no written contract" finding, but reversed the lower court's finding that litigation was barred by the statute of limitations on the oral contract embodied in that decree, finding that the Illinois court simply lacked subject matter jurisdiction and that the breach had not occurred until Tom retired in 1992.[108] The case was remanded.

---

104. Phillip Schwartz, Esq., Schwartz & Ellis, 6950 North Fairfax Drive, Arlington, VA 22213, 703/532-9300.

105. Brown v. Harms, 863 F. Supp. 278 (E.D. Va. 1994).

106. Kirby v. Mellenger, 830 F.2d 176 (11th Cir. 1987).

107. The same result has been reached by other federal district courts in reasonably similar circumstances. *See, e.g.,* Miller v. Umfleet, No. SA-88-CA-769 (W.D. Tex. Sept. 1, 1991) (when military member had been transferred from Texas to another state by military orders, federal district court found no subject matter jurisdiction to exist under USFSPA or the Federal Declaratory Judgments Act, 28 U.S.C. § 2201, and a failure of "complete diversity"; the court further opined that the case would fit within the domestic relations exception to federal jurisdiction even if such jurisdiction had been established, although dismissal was self-described as done "not lightly").

108. Brown (Harms) v. Harms, 251 Va. 301, 467 S.E.2d 805 (1996).

On remand, through other counsel,[109] the case was transformed back into a domestic relations and equity case; motions were filed in chancery seeking specific performance of the oral contract expressed in the German decree, and in law, seeking damages. At the time of this writing, proceedings remain pending in Virginia state court. There is no way to tell how much longer the case will proceed, or how or where it will eventually end.

An obvious lesson of the *Harms* case is to showcase the vulnerability of the legal position of overseas spouses. If they choose to defend themselves in foreign divorce actions, and litigate retirement issues, they will receive orders unenforceable under U.S. federal law, and have to face res judicata arguments as well. If they try to "reserve" the question, they might not ever be able to get state courts to find they have jurisdiction to enforce the "reserved" rights. And if they ignore the action, members will be able to take judgments against them on all contested issues, by default (again, with res judicata possibilities looming).

Harms is remarkable, among other things, for the sheer tenacity of its litigants. Many similar cases are apparently resolved quickly and quietly, at least when one party does not oppose a correction to what is apparently conceded to be an inequitable result. For example, in *Stewart v. Gomez*,[110] the parties had been divorced in 1987 in England. The member, who arranged for the British divorce, had specifically assured the former spouse that he was looking out for the best interest of the spouse and their children and specifically promised that when he retired, the former spouse would receive a portion of the military retirement benefits. The member subsequently retired and moved to Nevada, but did nothing to ensure payments to the former spouse. The former spouse moved to South Carolina. She filed a "Complaint for Partition of Omitted Property and Enforcement of Express Contract" in the Nevada courts. The member essentially ignored the action; default was granted, and the former spouse began receiving the promised share of the military retirement benefits.

---

109. By the time of the appeal, Jill was represented by Timothy Hyland, now of Lefler, Hyland & Thompson, 11320 Random Mills Road, Suite 540, Fairfax, VA 22030-7499, 703/293-9300. On remand, she was represented by David L. Duff, Esq., 11320 Random Hills Road, Suite 525, Fairfax, VA 22030.

110. Stewart v. Gomez, Case No. D 156799 (8th Jud. Dist. Ct., Clark County, Nev. Nov. 22, 1992).

The lessons to be learned from *Harms* on the one hand, and *Gomez* on the other, vary depending on one's perspective. Both certainly stand for the proposition that a former spouse must move quickly and in a court with apparent jurisdiction, if a divorce looms in any foreign jurisdiction. *Harms* could also be interpreted as standing for the proposition that a member can divest a spouse by arranging to have a divorce decree entered while out of the country, and ensuring that he remains outside the personal jurisdiction of any state that has procedures for dividing omitted marital property. From the spouse's perspective, the case highlights the danger of not being sure there is an enforceable order in place at the time of divorce. *Gomez*, from the member's perspective, could be taken as nothing more than an illustration of the danger of not fully asserting all possible procedural and technical defenses, given the decade in which Tom Harms staved off collection by Jill (now Brown).

About the only tactical advice that can be offered to spouses of members who are overseas is to ensure that any divorce proceeds through the U.S. courts, with the member clearly consenting to litigation in that jurisdiction. If, for whatever reason, that is impossible, it seems that the spouse would be prudent to begin American proceedings simultaneously with any foreign divorce, in whatever state the member had last established residence or domicile, by way of declaratory judgment or partition. Though this is not obvious, and is inconvenient and expensive, it is the closest thing to some assurance of protection of the spousal share that appears to be available under current law.

G. USE OF STATE COURT REMEDIES

There are many circumstances in which the federal law as it now exists can lead to a party having a right but lacking a remedy. The most obvious example is the "ten-year" case, where the marriage and service have overlapped by a bit less than ten years, and the state court awards the spouse a percentage of the retired pay as property.[111]

---

111. For further information on the ten-year problem, see Section E, Chapter Four.

If payments that were to be made directly by the member to the spouse are not forthcoming, the practitioner is left only with those remedies that are available in the court that issued the underlying decree or order. In virtually all cases, this will be a state dissolution court.[112] In several contexts, it is now established that the federal courts will not intervene to prevent the states from using their contempt powers to fine or imprison members who refuse to comply with state court judgments for payments of retired pay, even when there is no federal mechanism by which the spouse can *directly* obtain payment of those funds.

The U.S. Supreme Court has ruled that a member can be imprisoned for failing to pay child support, despite his claim that payments could be made only from his VA disability award, which was exempt from execution.[113] The Fifth Circuit has approved the use of sanctions, including incarceration, for contempt of court for a member's refusal to pay a portion of retired pay as property.[114]

Experienced domestic practitioners are well aware of the limitations of civil contempt as a remedy in interstate cases. Still, it now appears that sufficient pressure can be applied by the state courts to justify the substantial expense and difficulty of domesticating a state court judgment in whatever jurisdiction a member can be found in these circumstances.

---

112. The federal courts have been consistently resistant to becoming involved in divorce matters under the guise of peril to some federally protected interest. *See, e.g.,* Silva v. Silva, 680 F. Supp. 1479 (D. Colo. 1988) (upholding dismissal of action by member seeking to strike down unappealed state court division of disability retired pay); Fern v. United States, 15 Cl. Ct. 580 (1988), *aff'd,* 908 F.2d 955 (Fed. Cir. 1990). This is not to say that sometimes an order dividing retired pay as property might not be issued by a federal court. *See, e.g.,* Kirby v. Mellenger, 830 F.2d 176 (11th Cir. 1987).
113. *See* Rose v. Rose, 481 U.S. 619 (1987).
114. *See* Goad v. Rollins, 921 F.2d 69 (5th Cir.), *cert. denied,* 500 U.S. 905 (1991). The lengths to which the involved individuals were willing to go is illustrative. Mr. Goad fought contempt at every turn, even trying to sue the judge who found him in contempt (and his bailiff), the jailors who held him, and the friend who lent his ex-wife the filing fee to get to court. Eventually, his case was dismissed with prejudice, monetary sanctions in favor of all those he sued were assessed against him, and he was forbidden from filing anything on any subject involving military retired pay without permission of the district or appellate courts.

H. PARTITION OF PREVIOUSLY OMITTED RETIREMENT BENEFITS

The domestic relations laws of many states permit former spouses to return to court for partition of assets not disposed of in the original divorce proceeding, typically as a "tenant in common" of the omitted assets.[115]

The 1990 amendments to the USFSPA were largely concerned with partition cases, so some time will be spent discussing the effect of those amendments before turning to more general concerns in partition cases. The amendments codified the practice of honoring partition judgments from actions relating to divorces after passage of the USFSPA, but not partition judgments from actions relating to divorces before that date.[116] The military pay centers will honor orders resulting from partition actions, if the original divorce decree was entered on or after June 25, 1981.

The 1990 amendments appear to prohibit partition actions if the original decree was entered before *McCarty* and the divorce court did not divide the retired pay as property (or reserve jurisdiction to do so in the future).[117] The House Committee Report claimed that the new amendments were an attempt to make a public policy judgment "consistent with the balancing of state and federal interests that has been the hallmark of this law since its inception." Adopting the view of the minority of courts that have examined the issue, the committee declared that the retroactive effect of the USFSPA was expressly limited to the day before the *McCarty* decision; that is, June 25, 1981.[118]

---

115. *See, e.g.,* Henn v. Henn, 26 Cal. 3d 323, 605 P.2d 10, 161 Cal. Rptr. 502 (1980).

116. *See* 10 U.S.C. § 1408(c)(1).

117. 10 U.S.C. § 1408(c)(1). The amendment altered 10 U.S.C. § 1408(c)(1) to include a two-part test for orders dividing or partitioning retired pay that would *not* be honored. The proceeding is barred if the final decree (1) was issued before June 25, 1981, and (2) did not treat (or reserve to treat) any amount of the member's retired pay as property of the member and the member's spouse or former spouse.

118. It should be noted that at least one federal court has found that such statements of intention do not mean much. Noting a line of U.S. Supreme Court holdings, the Claims Court commented, "Such statements or views by members of a subsequent Congress specifying the intent of a prior Congress in passing legislation are entitled to little, if any weight." Fern v. United States,

The original bill would have immediately cut off all sums payable under state court partition orders, and would have forbidden any new such actions from being filed. When the proposal went to conference committee, however, it was tempered. As passed, the amendments still appear to prohibit new partition actions (or motions to reopen) that address pre-*McCarty* decrees.

The conference committee inserted language, however, extending the cutoff of payments to such spouses under *existing* partition judgments addressing pre-*McCarty* decrees for an additional two years (until November 5, 1992). The amendment has *no effect* on pre-*McCarty* divorces that did divide military retirement benefits, or on partition judgments that addressed divorces finalized on or after June 25, 1981.

Based on the precedent of *Mansell,* it appears that the congressional bar on partition actions was intended to be interpreted as a substantive limitation on the subject matter jurisdiction of the state courts, and not merely a limitation on use of the federal collection mechanisms in enforcement of otherwise valid state court judgments.[119] In actuality, many states have provided the remedy of partition of omitted assets since long before the military retirement benefits issues arose, and merely treated those assets like any other.[120] And some states, at least, have found ways of resisting this restriction on their equitable powers.

It was thought on passage that the "no partition" bar was fairly complete. At least one Texas court, however, has elected to disregard it, holding that the underlying state law constituted a *built-in* "reservation of jurisdiction" to divide any omitted asset, including military retirement benefits.[121] The court reasoned that Texas courts automatically treat, or reserve jurisdiction to treat, any amount of military retirement pay in accordance with the laws governing ownership of undivided property, so an ex-wife's action to partition military retirement benefits of her ex-husband who retired from service in 1981, following a 1976 divorce, was not affected by the 1990 amendment to the USFSPA making partition not avail-

---

15 Cl. Ct. 580, 587 (Ct. Cl. 1988) (citations omitted); *see also* Rainwater v. United States 356, U.S. 590, 593 (1958).

119. This is the view expressed by at least some reviewing courts. *See* Curtis v. Curtis, 7 Cal. App. 4th 1, 9 Cal. Rptr. 2d 145 (Ct. App. 1992).

120. *See, e.g.,* Bank v. Wolff, 66 Nev. 51, 202 P.2d 878 (1949).

121. *See* Lee v. Walton, 888 S.W.2d 604 (Tex. App. 1994).

able (sometimes called the Section 555 amendments). Opinions from intermediate appellate courts in California[122] and New Mexico,[123] however, indicate that at this point those states are unwilling to reach such a conclusion.

Some lawyers have voiced constitutional concerns about the ability of Congress to cut off payments established by courts after litigation of exactly the same issue. If anything, however, the history of litigation in this field has shown a vast deference by the state and federal courts to congressional line drawing, and an unwillingness to allow either side to establish a constitutional claim.[124] Additionally, it should be remembered that the effect of this amendment is limited to former military spouses who were divorced before June 25, 1981. If the law as amended remains in place for just a few years, the ever-declining number of persons affected by it will probably make it permanent.[125]

As an aside, it should be noted that arrears that accrued for benefits not paid to the former spouse probably remain fully enforceable despite the cutoff, as long as the court issued an order of the spouse's entitlement to those payments before the congressional cutoff.[126]

This is not to say that all questions revolving around the partition of omitted military retirement benefits from pre-*McCarty* divorces are an-

---

122. Curtis v. Curtis, *supra* note 119.
123. Hennessy v. Duryea, 1998 N.M.CA. 36, 955 P.2d 683 (N.M. Ct. App. 1998).
124. *See, e.g.,* Brannon v. Randmaa, 736 S.W.2d 175 (Tex. App. 1987), *cert. denied,* 486 U.S. 1019 (1988); Fern v. United States, 15 Cl. Ct. 580 (1988), *aff'd,* 908 F.2d 955 (Fed. Cir. 1990).
125. The congressional deal making and interest balancing that went on in trying to give something to "both sides" in 1990 had a few unfortunate results. It is well known that, especially until recently, spouses of military personnel were effectively limited in, or barred from, working outside the home— spouses of enlisted personnel often could not find work, and officers' wives were expected to be available for various volunteer tasks as a normal part of the officers' careers. It was not until recently that more than half of military spouses had outside jobs. *See Married to the Military,* AIR FORCE TIMES SUPP., May 20, 1996 (noting that 54.5 percent of "military wives" worked outside the home). Arguably, the ability to receive a share of the pension benefits earned during marriage was *most* critical for the earlier "war brides" and other former spouses who are at this point elderly, and least likely to have received an education or job training.
126. *See* Curtis v. Curtis, *supra* note 119.

swered. For example, as a matter of impairment of contracts, there is some doubt whether those cases in which (during suit or upon threat of suit) the parties stipulated to amend their decrees of divorce can be so summarily undone.

An enforceability question is raised by the very fact that a partition case is an independent proceeding. At least one federal court has held that a judgment in a partition action is not a "court order" within the meaning of the similar civil service statutes, because it is independent from, and therefore not "incident to," a decree of divorce.[127] This may have become moot, however, by the very restrictions placed in the USFSPA by Congress. When it constricted the jurisdiction of courts to treat retired pay as property in the 1990 amendments to 10 U.S.C. § 1408(c)(1), Congress specifically referenced partition actions, and "defined out" only those affecting decrees issued before June 25, 1981. Application of the ancient doctrine of "inclusio unis est exclusio alterias"[128] would seem to indicate congressional approval of partition actions *other than* those barred. Although there are many quirks in the law in this area, it would seem at least questionable to interpret the statute in such a way that partition actions were permitted, but enforcement of the resulting orders were prevented.[129]

Another unresolved matter concerns partition actions in which the military member waived military retired pay for the purpose of merging service with some other retirement system (most commonly, civil service). Arguably, the waiver of military retired pay waived application of the 1990 amendments, working to the former spouse's benefit here as such a waiver works to the member's benefit in the cases concerning waivers for disability. At least for the moment, OPM appears to ignore the 1990 amendments in applications for division of civil service pay, even if part or all the benefits to be divided are attributable to military service during marriage.[130]

---

127. Carmody v. Secretary of Navy, 886 F.2d 678, 681 (4th Cir. 1989).
128. "The inclusion of one implies the exclusion of the other." *See* BLACK'S LAW DICTIONARY 906 (4th ed. 1968).
129. But see the discussion of the "ten-year compromise" in Section E, Chapter Four.
130. *See* United States v. Endsley, 204 B.R. 242 (Bankr. M.D. Fla. 1996) (noting facts of partition case tracing military retirement benefits through civil ser-

To be enforceable, partition actions must be brought with sufficient federal jurisdiction under 10 U.S.C. § 1408, as well as adequate state court jurisdiction.[131] When the partition action is brought in a state different from the one that granted the divorce, some courts have applied the partition law of the former matrimonial domicile,[132] while others have elected to use the law of the forum where the suit is heard.[133]

The rationales for these choices differ. Some cases indicate that the jurisdictional limitations of the federal law can be avoided if partition is sought by way of a motion in the original divorce action rather than by means of a separate action.[134] Under this reasoning, if the divorce court had jurisdiction under federal law at the time of the divorce, then it would have jurisdiction to enter a postdivorce order of partition.

Although the case law is not entirely uniform, it is usually held that general "residuary" clauses disposing of all other assets "in the possession" of a party are *not* sufficient to divest a former spouse of a putative interest in military retired pay, leaving it subject to a later suit for partition. At least in the community property states that have considered the issue, the asset must be *specifically* awarded to the member spouse to defeat a later partition action.[135] Statutes of limitation are generally construed to bar collection of only those individual payments that are beyond the relevant cutoff date, not to bar the partition actions themselves,[136] but this interpretation is not uniform.[137] Case law is thin, but at least in some

---

vice benefits despite phrasing of 10 U.S.C. § 1408(c)(1)); Leatherman v. Leatherman, 122 Idaho 247, 833 P.2d 105 (1992) (court traced spousal share of military service even though member had been awarded all the interest in the retirement, and had subsequently obtained a 100 percent VA disability rating, because he waived all those awards to roll his military service into a later civil service retirement).

131. See Section A, Chapter Four.
132. Kirby v. Mellenger, 830 F.2d 176 (11th Cir. 1987).
133. Fransen v. Fransen, 142 Cal. App. 3d 419, 190 Cal. Rptr. 885 (Ct. App. 1983).
134. *In re* Marriage of Parks, 48 Wash. App. 166, 737 P.2d 1316 (Ct. App. 1987).
135. *See, e.g.,* Brannon v. Randmaa, 736 S.W.2d 175 (Tex. App. 1987), *cert. denied,* 486 U.S. 1019 (1988); Casas v. Thompson, 42 Cal. 3d 131, 720 P.2d 921, 228 Cal. Rptr. 33 (1986), *cert. denied,* 479 U.S. 1012 (1987).
136. *See, e.g.,* Mooney v. Glasspool, 602 S.W.2d 364 (Tex. App. 1980).
137. *See* Grieshaber v. Grieshaber, 793 S.W.2d 161 (Mo. Ct. App. 1990) (when

places, predivorce separation is not generally seen as a limitation on the right of the former spouse to request a share of the military retirement benefits accruing during separation.[138]

I. DISABILITY PERCENTAGES AND THEIR MEANING

The forms of disability retirement that might be at issue in military cases are discussed in the introductory chapter of this book and again in the section dealing with anticipating changes of status. The practitioner should note that it is possible for a retired member to seek a reevaluation of the disability rating granted by the VA.[139] Because of this, as noted above, counsel for the former spouse should probably seek a reservation of jurisdiction to seek an alimony award in the event of a cutoff of the former spouse's share of the retired pay as property.

> **Practice Tip:** It may be in the best interest of the former spouse to *not* request present payment of certain sums when there is a VA disability involved in a property and support case. When child support has been ordered, but the sum of disposable retired pay is inadequate to provide all sums owed to the former spouse (for example, division of retired pay as property and a child support award), the former spouse might be better served by evaluating what strategy would maximize total collections.

As discussed above, it is sometimes best to collect property awards at the expense of support awards.[140] When a child is in the household of the former spouse and is still under the age of majority, there is another possibility. The VA is permitted, but not required, to make payments to

---

wife failed to file petition to divide pension for fourteen years, despite knowing of its existence, and husband died in interim, laches barred spousal claim to partition omitted military retirement benefits).

138. *See, e.g.,* Ewing v. Ewing, 901 S.W.2d 330 (Mo. Ct. App. 1995) (when parties separated for lengthy period—twenty years—before either party sought divorce, laches did not bar claim to pension accrued during period of separation).

139. *See* Mansell v. Mansell, 490 U.S. 581 (1989), *remanded,* 217 Cal. App. 3d 219, 265 Cal. Rptr. 227 (Ct. App. 1989).

140. See the discussion of collection by garnishment in Subsection 3, Section D, Chapter Five.

the custodian of a minor if a child support award is not being satisfied by a veteran receiving VA disability benefits.

J. APPEALING AN ADVERSE DECISION

The regulations provide for reconsideration of a designated agent's response to an application for payments, upon request of the former spouse or the member.[141] The party making the request must identify those issues he or she believes were determined incorrectly. The agent's response will provide an explanation of the determination reached.

Though the regulations do not specify a route for appeal, ultimate recourse is apparently to the counsel for the Department of Defense Secretary.[142]

K. TAXATION OF RETIREMENT BENEFITS AND SBP PAYMENTS

When military retired pay is used as a source for child support or alimony payments, the usual tax consequences remain. (That is, child support is nondeductible to the payor and nontaxable to the recipient, whereas alimony is deductible to the payor and taxable to the recipient.)

Nondisability retired pay is treated as wages and is subject to federal income tax withholding.[143] The division of military retired pay as property in a court order is not a "taxable event" in tax parlance—the order dividing the benefits does not in itself trigger any tax liability. Instead, only the payment of retirement benefits triggers taxes.

There was significant confusion in prior years about who owed those taxes once triggered. The Internal Revenue Service (IRS) determined that

141. 32 C.F.R. § 63.6(i).
142. Anecdotal accounts from government sources indicate that appeals are reviewed quite thoroughly and are sometimes successful. A specific lawyer is assigned to a case upon receipt of a court order and works with the case until reaching a final decision. If one of the parties requests reconsideration, the decision is reviewed by a different lawyer at that center. The Chief Attorney and Commander of the center reviews the decision. If the parties still disagree with the center's decision, the case can be reviewed in Washington, D.C., by the counsel to the Department of Defense Secretary, although no specific procedure for that review is set forth in the regulations.
143. I.R.C. § 3401.

former spouses were taxed on the share of military retirement benefits paid directly to them from the government,[144] but the Tax Court initially held that payments under a division of military benefits were *not* taxable to the former spouse, because the military benefits were part of a property settlement.[145] Later, the Tax Court ruled that a community property share of the retirement to the former spouse, whether received from the government or the member, was income to the former spouse.[146]

Since the 1989 decision of the U.S. Supreme Court in *Mansell*[147] and the 1990 amendments to the USFSPA, however, it has seemed increasingly clear that the intent of Congress is for the former spouse to bear all responsibility for taxes on sums paid to her or him, while the member is responsible for all taxes on the amounts actually paid to the member. This clear intention has had a somewhat crooked path toward resolution.

Under the pre-1991 rules, in part just to avoid confusion about who would bear what tax burden, it was reasonably common for former spouses to negotiate divorce settlements waiving rights to retired pay in exchange for either normal or irrevocable alimony, which was sometimes pegged to COLAs to the retirement. Of course, this method of allocation was not possible in states that did not permit alimony (for example, Texas).

The 1990 amendments to the disposable pay sections of the USFSPA apply only to divorces, dissolutions of marriage, annulments, and legal separations that become effective after February 4, 1991. It is therefore necessary to analyze cases differently, depending on whether the relevant court order was issued before or after that date.

1. Divorces Entered before February 4, 1991

Before the effective date of the 1990 amendments, all deductions from retired pay, including amounts deducted for payment to a former spouse,

---

144. Priv. Ltr. Rul. 86-05007 (October 30, 1985). The IRS also ruled that the former spouse is to be taxed on his or her portion of the benefits even if the entire payment was made to the member, and the member then paid a part to the former spouse. Priv. Ltr. Rul. 86-29030 April 18, 1986).
145. Mildred R. Ficchi, 86,191 PH Mem OTC.
146. Eatinger v. Commissioner, 1990 T.C. Memo No. 310 (June 20, 1990). This was consistent with the position that evolved within the IRS that did *not* classify payments of military retirement benefits as a division of property under Section 1041. *See* Priv. Ltr. Rul. 88-13023 (1987 PRL Lexis 4201).
147. Mansell v. Mansell, 490 U.S. 581 (1989).

were still considered part of the retired member's wages for withholding purposes.[148] As a practical matter, the member had income withheld on the entire gross amount, the resulting "disposable" pay was divided, and then the member was entitled to a refund of taxes withheld on amounts paid to the former spouse. The former spouse paid the full taxes on the portion of the disposable pay received. Because withholding preceded division, any percentage division of retirement benefits under the former law increased property distribution to the member and reduced it to the former spouse as a matter of course.[149]

The amounts withheld were based on the member's pay and exemptions. This led to widespread anecdotal accounts of abuse by members, who manipulated their tax status to maximize withholding and minimize disposable income available for division with former spouses. As discussed above, there has been an administrative ruling from the Comptroller General prohibiting this practice since 1984, but enforcement of the prohibition has been uneven, because the pay centers had no uniform policy on how to handle accusations of such manipulation.[150]

This situation could be resolved by congressional passage of new legislation intended to apply the 1990 amendments to those divorced before the effective date of that legislation.[151] Instead of solving the actual

---

148. Treas. Reg. § 31.3401(a)-(1)(b)(5).

149. Reports by the General Accounting Office and Congressional Research Service in 1984 and 1989 found that court orders purporting to divide military retirement benefits on a "50/50" basis actually effected a split of "55.4 percent/44.6 percent" to "58.4 percent/41.6 percent"—always in favor of the former military member—after the impact of tax withholdings was considered. CONGRESSIONAL RESEARCH SERVICE, REPORT FOR CONGRESS: MILITARY BENEFITS FOR FORMER SPOUSES: LEGISLATION AND POLICY ISSUES (Mar. 20, 1989). *See also* CONGRESSIONAL RESEARCH SERVICE, REPORT FOR CONGRESS 88-512 A: TREATMENT OF FORMER SPOUSES UNDER VARIOUS FEDERAL RETIREMENT SYSTEMS (July 25, 1988).

150. 63 Comp. Gen. 322 (1984) (Comptroller General's Decision No. B-213895, Apr. 25, 1984), discussed above in Subsection 4(c), Section C, Chapter Five.

151. It has been tried previously. As early as 1991, Representative Patricia Schroeder of Colorado attempted to carry the redefining language of the 1990 amendments backward to encompass all prior decisions. To date, all such efforts have been unsuccessful.

problem, however, the government simply changed its tax procedures. In 1994, the IRS revised the reporting and withholding requirements for division of property payments in divorces occurring before February 4, 1991.[152] The division inequity noted by the Congressional Research Service (CRS) remained (see note below), but starting in 1995, former spouses began having taxes on the reduced share that they received withheld.

2. Divorces Entered on or after February 4, 1991

For divisions of retired pay as property pursuant to decrees entered on or after February 4, 1991, the tax consequences are much simpler, and much more similar to those in other retirement systems. Portions of a member's retired pay awarded to a former spouse explicitly "may not be treated as amounts received as retired pay for service in the uniformed services."[153]

Therefore, there should be no withholding of taxes (before division of retired pay) on amounts paid to a former spouse when the divorce occurred on or after February 4, 1991. Instead, both the member and the former spouse have tax withheld on their respective shares of the pretax "new disposable" pay.

The former spouse is taxed on SBP payments as he or she would be for other payments from an annuity.[154] The payments to the former spouse are considered taxable income.

3. Explanation of the Policy Debate Underlying the Arguments in This Area

It is more important than it might seem to have an understanding of the policy debates that underlie decisions about taxability of the benefits.

---

152. As with many developments in this area, implementation followed the decision by a matter of years. *See* Memorandum from Jerry E. Holmes, Chief, Branch 2, Office of the Assistant Chief Counsel, Department of the Treasury, to John P. Springett, Principal Deputy Director, DFAS (Oct. 9, 1991) (Reference number CC:EE:2—TR-45-1666-91). The memorandum requested a 1992 implementation. The Defense Finance and Accounting Service subsequently requested and obtained a delay until 1994.

153. 10 U.S.C. § 1408(c)(2).

154. 26 U.S.C. § 72.

The rationales for the taxation conclusions form the framework within which many other questions have been held to rise and fall—including some that could make the benefits themselves divisible or not.

In 1989, the CRS reported to Congress on legislative and policy issues in the military retirement benefits area.[155] In addressing the definitions of military retired pay, the author found that only two of the four reasons for the existence of military retirement benefits (as set forth by the Department of Defense) supported treating military retirement benefits as a pension that could be justifiably treated as divisible property in a divorce. Those two factors were competing for qualified employees and providing economic security to employees.[156]

The CRS report found that two of the Defense Department's stated reasons for having retirement benefits were unique to the military. They were ensuring that promotion opportunities were open to "young and able" members, and ensuring the existence of a pool of experienced personnel subject to recall to active duty during time of war or national emergency. The author quoted from the U.S. Supreme Court's *McCarty* opinion at some length, and concluded that these factors justified a conclusion that "military retired pay may not be treated as property for any other purpose [than as an asset in divorce cases, by virtue of the USFSPA]."[157]

In the world of civilian employment, however, reasonable parallels could be found to the first of these allegedly "unique" factors, because a retirement plan always provides some incentive for senior employees to leave employment, thus opening positions to the "young and able." The second factor, that members could be subject to recall, is actually the basis most seized upon in the debate about whether military retirement benefits are (or should be) different from pensions for many purposes, including taxation.

The study's author found the military retirement system to be "non-contributory," because no specific portion of active-duty pay (or "employer" contribution during service) goes into a separate retirement account.[158] In the private sector, however, the same can be said of virtually

---

155. CONGRESSIONAL RESEARCH SERVICE, REPORT FOR CONGRESS 89-187 F: MILITARY BENEFITS FOR FORMER SPOUSES: LEGISLATION AND POLICY IS-SUES (Mar. 20, 1989).

156. *Id.* at 7.

157. *Id.* at 10.

158. *Id.* at 8.

any defined-benefit type of plan, as opposed to a defined-contribution plan.[159] It should be noted that the most recent amendments to the formula for determining the amount of military retired pay to be paid have caused the system to even more closely resemble a standard defined-benefit sort of pension plan.[160]

Additionally, the concern about "contributions" seems overstated. The military retirement compensation package is widely used by recruiters as an incentive to enlist, much the way any company's retirement system and other "perks" are used in recruitment of desired personnel. The way in which the money is ultimately provided seems entirely irrelevant to whether the retirement benefits should be considered to be what they are touted as being upon enlistment—an additional payment for active-duty service, over and above the regular pay received, to be made after retirement.

The definitional uncertainty eventually percolated through the courts as an income tax case. It is interesting—but not surprising—to note that

---

159. In the former, the employee obtains a right to a payment after retirement, usually for life. Often, the benefit is determined by a formula taking into account the highest salary received and the total number of years worked for the employer (such as a "high-three" or "high-five" plan). For example, a plan might pay one-tenth of an employee's average monthly salary over the three years before retirement, multiplied by one-fourth the number of years that the employee worked. A twenty-year employee earning an average of $2,000 per month during his last years would get $1,000 per month (that is, $2,000 multiplied by 0.1, multiplied by 20, multiplied by 0.25).

    In contrast, a defined contribution plan is one in which the employee has an individual account made up of contributions made by the employee (and, if any, by the employer), plus investment gains. Employers are not required by law to contribute, although many such plans contractually bind the employer to add some formula percentage of the amount the employee puts into the plan. *See* 29 U.S.C. § 1002(34). These plans come in many varieties, including profit sharing plans (employer contributions vary according to company performance), stock bonus plans (the plan invests in the securities of the company itself), 401k plans (employee chooses either taxable salary or nontaxable contribution to the plan), and money purchase plans (like profit sharing, but with a fixed employer contribution).

160. See the explanation of the military's post-1986 retirement system in Chapter One.

the legal arguments of the affected groups shifted 180 degrees, depending on the economic impact upon their members.

Traditionally, advocates for members have argued that military retired pay is reduced pay for reduced services, and therefore is immune from state court division as a "pension" in divorce cases.[161] That argument has been completely reversed in the debate over the tax treatment of military retirement benefits. Advocates for members have argued that because the retirement benefits *are* divisible in divorce cases as pensions, the states are precluded from taxing that income as wages.[162]

In *Barker v. Kansas*,[163] the U.S. Supreme Court struck down the tax imposed by the state of Kansas on military retirement benefits paid to retirees, because the state did not similarly tax retirees under the Kansas Public Employees Retirement System. Previously, in *Davis v. Michigan Department of Treasury*, the Court had ruled that a state could not tax federal civil service retirees if it did not also tax recipients of state retirement benefits.[164] Under the standard set forth in *Davis*, the question was whether taxation on the federal, but not the state, retirees was "directly related to, and justified by, 'significant differences between the two classes.' "[165]

The Kansas Supreme Court had found such "significant differences"[166] when it decided the case at the state level. Specifically, the court found six distinctions:

> (1) [F]ederal military retirees remain members of the armed forces of the United States after they retire from active duty; they are retired from active duty only; (2) federal military retirees are subject to the Uniform Code of Military Justice (UCMJ) and may be court martialed for offenses committed after retirement; (3) they are subject to restrictions on civilian employment after retirement; (4) federal military retirees are subject to involuntary recall; (5) federal military retirement benefits are not deferred compensation but current pay for continued readiness to return to

---

161. *See, e.g.,* Casas v. Thompson, 42 Cal. 3d 131, 720 P.2d 921, 228 Cal. Rptr. 33 (1986), *cert. denied,* 479 U.S. 1012 (1987).

162. *See* Barker v. Kansas, 503 U.S. 594 (1992).

163. *Id.*

164. *See* Davis v. Michigan Dep't of Treasury, 489 U.S. 803 (1989).

165. *Id.* at 816 (as quoted in *Barker,* 503 U.S. at 598).

166. *See* Barker v. Kansas, 249 Kan. 186, 815 P.2d 46 (1991).

duty; and (6) the federal military retirement system is noncontributory and funded by annual appropriations from Congress; thus, all benefits received by military retirees have never been subject to tax.[167]

The U.S. Supreme Court began with congressional intent. Noting that *McCarty* was promptly overturned by passage of the USFSPA, the Court observed that a finding that retired pay is divisible marital property is "inconsistent with the notion that military retirement pay should be treated as indistinguishable from compensation for reduced current services."[168]

Turning to state and federal tax laws, the Court observed that military retirement benefits are treated as deferred compensation for purposes of determining deductibility of individual retirement account (IRA) contributions.[169] The Court found "unpersuasive" the Kansas court's conclusion that such tax treatment was limited to the context of IRA contributions.

The Court never did specifically address the six grounds cited by the Kansas court. Rather, the Court mentioned the factors discussed above, and simply concluded that for purposes of 4 U.S.C. § 111, military retirement benefits are to be considered deferred pay for past services. The structure of the holding left open the possibility that the Court *could* find that military retirement benefits are something else "for purposes of" some other statute or dispute.

Nothing can be considered permanent in the field of tax law. Even more precarious is any legal generalization about the character of military retirement benefits based upon the tax treatment accorded those benefits in a tax case. At least for the moment, however, the U.S. Supreme Court has interpreted the tax laws to be in accord with the arguments that military retired pay is deferred compensation.

4. An Aside regarding Settlements and Taxes

There are several reasons that it might be appropriate to settle a spousal interest in military retirement benefits in exchange for cash. It is not uncommon in short service-marriage overlap cases, or when arrearages

---

167. *Barker,* 249 Kan. at 196, 815 P.2d at 53 (as quoted in *Barker,* 503 U.S. at 598).
168. *Barker,* 503 U.S. at 603.
169. *Id.* at 604.

are owing in an underpayment or partition case. Sometimes, especially when arrearages are in issue, the possibility of appeal or a bankruptcy filing and its attendant risks can cause both parties to desire a cash settlement, usually at something less than the full sum computed.

It appears that the U.S. Tax Court has come down on the side of the position that even between *former* spouses, such exchanges of community property rights to pension payments (past, present, or future) are "transfers of property between spouses or incident to divorce" and therefore exempt from tax under Section 1041 of the Internal Revenue Code.[170] The little authority that exists on this subject also seems to suggest that state courts are sympathetic to requests by service members in partition cases to divide only the sum of military retirement net-after-taxes, to avoid ordering members to pay out money that they did not actually receive.[171]

Anecdotal accounts, however, suggest that the IRS has nevertheless attempted, in several arrearage-settlement cases, to assess the former spouse for taxes on the entire settlement amount, treating the sum received as taxable income in the year received, or as an "anticipatory assignment," which is the label the tax court rejected in *Balding*.[172]

The lesson for lawyers on both sides of any settlement seems clear. The anticipated tax results of the settlement should be recited within the agreement or stipulation, to decrease the likelihood of any disagreements about intent and to provide a means of recourse if those expectations prove unfounded given the shifting sands of taxation effects. It is worth going to some pains to prevent the parties from taking inconsistent positions (such as the member seeking reimbursement for past taxes while the former spouse was treating the money received as a nontaxable transfer under Section 1041), as such inconsistent positions would seem an invitation to a protracted battle with the IRS that both parties could lose.

L. THE SPECTER OF MALPRACTICE

This examination of military retirement benefits in divorce litigation has come full circle, and it seems appropriate to remind practitioners (especially the busy ones who skipped the introduction and are looking up

---

170. Balding v. Commissioner, 98 T.C. 368 (1992).
171. *See In re* Schoning, 106 Or. App. 399, 807 P.2d 820 (Ct. App. 1991).
172. Balding v. Commissioner, 98 T.C. 368 (1992).

this section because it is the problem they face) of some of the road signs on the malpractice trail, so they can avoid repeating those errors.

To reiterate, the military retirement is frequently more valuable than all other assets combined, *including* the equity in the marital residence. Neglecting to provide for that asset can constitute malpractice.

Courts have, for over a decade, held lawyers who handle divorces to knowing the intricacies of the retirement system involved in their cases.[173] The scope of damages that are at stake is the value of whatever benefit the client lost—which could be the entire retirement benefits payable to the client.[174] Even guessing "right" by happenstance may not save a lawyer from liability, which can be imposed primarily for not doing the research to find out *whether* benefits are payable.[175]

All lawyers practicing divorce law will be held responsible for knowing about the existence, value, and methodology of division of whatever actual or potential retirement (and survivor's) benefits might exist. The potential losses to the client—whether the member or the former spouse—are catastrophic, and the resulting risks to counsel are enormous.

The bottom line for litigators is that they must either have, learn, or hire sufficient expertise to deal competently with this species of asset. A lawyer who does not do so, and continues to handle these cases, will sooner or later make an error that cannot be corrected.

---

173. *See* Aloy v. Mash, 38 Cal. 3d 413, 696 P.2d 656, 212 Cal. Rptr. 162 (1985).
174. *See* Bross v. Denny, 791 S.W.2d 416 (Mo. Ct. App. 1990) ($108,000 malpractice award against trial lawyer for not knowing he could seek division of military retirement after change in law; lawyer's original advice was correct (the retirement was nondivisible under *McCarty*), but when USFSPA passed just days before the separation agreement was signed, he missed it).
175. *See* Smith v. Lewis, 13 Cal. 3d 349, 530 P.2d 589, 118 Cal. Rptr. 621 (1975). In this malpractice case, involving an underlying divorce that concerned a National Guard retirement, liability against counsel was predicated on the legal duty to perform a "reasonable amount" of research even when the legal question was in a field known to be unsettled. Here, counsel guessed correctly (without any research to verify) that the asset was not divisible at that time, and did not assert a claim based on that belief. The retirement benefits later became divisible when the law changed, but the failure to assert the claim prevented the former spouse from returning to court upon that change. The former spouse was awarded some $100,000 in damages against the lawyer.

Chapter Eight
FORMS AND DRAFTING AIDS

A. APPLICATION FOR DIRECT PAYMENT UNDER USFSPA

It should be noted that the official application form is somewhat out of date, in that the addresses for the pay centers are no longer correct. For the moment, at least, all applications for direct payment under the Uniformed Services Former Spouses Protection Act (USFSPA) are to be sent as follows:

- Army, Navy, Air Force and Marine Corps:
  Defense Finance and Accounting Service
  Cleveland Center (Code LF)
  P.O. Box 998002
  Cleveland, OH 44199-8002
- Coast Guard:
  United States Coast Guard
  Commanding Officer (L)
  Pay and Personnel Center
  444 Quincy Street
  Topeka, KS 66683-3591
- Public Health Service:
  Offices of General Counsel
  Department of Health and Human Services
  Room 5362
  330 Independence Avenue, SW
  Washington, DC 20201

B. SAMPLE DECREE LANGUAGE

In most cases, the following language should be adaptable for the purpose of building an enforceable court order. Note that many of the clauses that follow are *alternatives* to one another, and that use of one may therefore preclude use of another.

As with any form, caution is warranted in its use. Drafting an order is a complex venture, replete with traps by omission and commission. *Slavish copying of any form is an invitation to disaster.* Unless the case receives personal attention in taking care of all contingencies, it might be most economical in the long run to enlist expert assistance.

Marshal S. Willick, Esq.
3551 East Bonanza Road, Suite 101
Las Vegas, NV 89110-2198
702/438-4100
Nevada Bar #2515
Attorney for [NAME]

DISTRICT COURT
CLARK COUNTY, NEVADA

[NAME],	)	
	)	
Plaintiff,	)	
	)	
vs.	)	
	)	
[NAME],	)	CASE NO.
	)	DEPARTMENT
Defendant	)	DOCKET

DECREE OF DIVORCE

TO USERS OF THIS FORM: Do a "search and replace" from "MEMBER" and "SPOUSE" to whatever is required by local rules—"Plaintiff" and "Defendant" or the parties' names as appropriate to the case. Be careful, though; sometimes, the words "member" or "spouse" are used descriptively below, and so should not be eliminated. Note that the "for more than ten years" in the paragraph below should be eliminated if such is not true in the case in question.

The above-entitled cause coming on regularly for trial on _____, 19__, before the above-entitled court; Plaintiff appearing in person and with Plaintiff's attorney, _____, ESQ., and the Defendant appearing by and through Defendant's attorney, _____, ESQ., and the parties having each waived the making, filing, and service of Findings of Fact and Conclusions of Law, and written notice of entry of Judgment, and the parties consenting to the jurisdiction of this court and the trial of this action, and the Court being fully advised in the premises, and finding that Plaintiff is a bona fide resident of the State of Nevada, and that this Court has jurisdiction over both the parties hereto and this action under both Chapter 125 of the Nevada Revised Statutes and 10 U.S.C. § 1408 *et seq.,* and that all applicable portions of the Soldier's and Sailor's Civil Relief Act of 1940 have been complied with by waiver or otherwise, and that _____ is entitled to the relief prayed for in said _____ upon the grounds therein, and that the parties were married on [Date of Marriage], in [Place of Marriage], and that they remained married for more than ten years during MEMBER's creditable military service.

The following paragraph provides the Social Security numbers necessary under the USFSPA.

NOW, THEREFORE, IT IS HEREBY ORDERED, ADJUDGED, AND DECREED that the bonds of matrimony heretofore and now existing between Plaintiff, [name], SSN _____, and Defendant, [name], SSN _____ be, and the same are hereby wholly dissolved, and an absolute Decree of Divorce is hereby granted, and the parties are hereby restored to the status of single, unmarried persons.

"All Military Retirement Benefits" (MRB) language ignores the limits of *Mansell* in defining the intent of the parties and the court; use the paragraph below for either preretirement or postretirement divorces, but note that the early retirement language is not necessary for postretirement cases. For the "beginning" blank, use "upon first eligibility for retirement," OR a specific date, OR negotiate some other triggering condition.

IT IS FURTHER ORDERED, ADJUDGED, AND DECREED that, beginning _____, SPOUSE shall receive [ALT1 the sum of $____] [ALT2 ____ percent] per month from MEMBER's military retirement as SPOUSE's sole and separate property, payable from MEMBER's disposable retired or retainer pay, and that SPOUSE shall further receive __ percent of any future cost of living increases in said retired or retainer pay, computed from the gross sum thereof. For the purpose of interpreting this Court's intention in making the division set forth in this Order, "military retirement" includes retired pay paid or to which MEMBER would be entitled for longevity of active duty and/or reserve component military service and all payments paid or payable under the provisions of Chapter 38 or Chapter 61 of Title 10 of the United States Code, before any statutory, regulatory, or elective deductions are applied (except for deductions because of an election to provide a survivor benefit annuity to SPOUSE). It also includes all amounts of retired pay MEMBER actually or constructively waives or forfeits in any manner and for any reason or purpose, including but not limited to any waiver made to qualify for Veterans Administration benefits, or reduction in pay or benefits because of other federal employment, and any waiver arising from MEMBER electing not to retire despite being qualified to retire. It also includes any sum taken by MEMBER in addition to or in lieu of retirement benefits, including but not limited to exit bonuses, voluntary separation incentive pay, special separation benefit, or any other form of compensation attributable to separation from military service instead of or in addition to payment of the military retirement benefits normally payable to a retired member, except that the percentage of such benefits payable to SPOUSE will have to be recalculated to take into account that fewer than 240 months of total service have accrued. All sums payable to SPOUSE as a portion of military retirement shall be payable from MEMBER's disposable retired or retainer pay to the extent that it is so restricted by law.

Use for *Mansell* compliance in a nonvested case. Lawyers for spouses should omit the "when and if they vest" language. Member's lawyers should delete the language including waived retirement benefits within the definition. Whether or not the "or which would have accrued" language is proper depends on whether state law in the issuing state provides for payment of benefits upon eligibility for retirement.

[ALT] IT IS FURTHER ORDERED, ADJUDGED, AND DECREED that SPOUSE has an interest in the military retirement benefits accruing to MEMBER as a result of his service in the United States Armed Forces, when and if they vest, as her sole and separate property, equal to _____ percent (one half of _____ months of military service performed during marriage divided by 240 months of MEMBER's military service) of the sum payable at that time, plus a like percentage of all cost of living adjustment increases that accrue to said military retirement benefits thereafter, or which would have accrued if the retirement had been elected. For the purpose of interpreting this Court's intention in making the division set forth in this Order, "military retirement" means disposable retired pay as defined in 10 U.S.C. § 1408, and includes all amounts of retired pay MEMBER actually or constructively waives or forfeits by electing not to retire despite being qualified to retire, or reduction in pay or benefits because of other federal employment. It also includes any sum taken by MEMBER in lieu of retirement benefits, including but not limited to exit bonuses, voluntary separation incentive pay, special separation benefit, or any other form of compensation attributable to separation from military service instead of or in addition to payment of the military retirement benefits normally payable to a retired member, except that the percentage of such benefits payable to SPOUSE will have to be recalculated to take into account that fewer than 240 months of total service have accrued. All sums payable to SPOUSE as a portion of military retirement shall be payable from MEMBER's disposable retired or retainer pay to the extent that it is so restricted by law.

The next two paragraphs establish an alternative of substituting alimony in lieu of MRBs. Note that the language used in these paragraphs varies depending upon whether the Member has already attained eligibility for retirement.

IT IS FURTHER ORDERED, ADJUDGED, AND DECREED that SPOUSE has a putative interest in the military retirement benefits accruing to MEMBER as a result of his service in the United States Armed Forces, as her sole and separate property, equal to _____ percent (one half of _____ months of military service performed during marriage divided by _____ months of MEMBER's military service) of the sum payable to MEMBER upon eligibility for retirement, plus a like percentage of all cost of living adjustment increases that accrue to said military retirement benefits thereafter, computed from the gross sum thereof. For the purpose of interpreting this Court's intention in making the division set forth in this Order, "military retirement" includes retired pay paid or to which MEMBER would be entitled for longevity of active duty and/or reserve component military service and all payments paid or payable under the provisions of Chapter 38 or Chapter 61 of Title 10 of the United States Code, before any statutory, regulatory, or elective deductions are applied (except for deductions because of an election to provide a survivor benefit annuity to SPOUSE). It also includes all amounts of retired pay MEMBER actually or constructively waives or forfeits in any manner and for any reason or purpose, including but not limited to any waiver made to qualify for Veterans Administration benefits, or reduction in pay or benefits because of other federal employment, and any waiver arising from MEM-BER electing not to retire despite being qualified to retire. It also includes any sum taken by MEMBER in addition to or in lieu of retirement benefits, including but not limited to exit bonuses, voluntary separation incentive pay, special separation benefit, or any other form of compensation attributable to separation from military service instead of or in addition to payment of the military retirement benefits normally payable to a retired member, except that the percentage of such benefits payable to SPOUSE will have to be [ALT would have had to have been] recalculated to take into account that fewer than 240 months of total service have accrued.

IT IS FURTHER ORDERED, ADJUDGED, AND DECREED that, pursuant to the stipulation of the parties, SPOUSE shall have no interest whatsoever in said military retirement benefits as community property or her separate property, having waived said rights on condition and in exchange for a stipulated Order of this Court for an award of unmodifiable alimony for her support, beginning the first day of the first month following MEMBER's retirement or attainment of eligibility for retirement (or any other form of compensation attributable to separation from military service), [ALT beginning the first day of the first month following entry of this decree,] in an amount equal to _____ percent of the military retirement benefits to which MEMBER is or would be eligible upon retirement or eligibility therefor, [ALT2 in the sum of $____ per month,] plus ____ percent of all cost of living adjustment increases that accrue to said military retirement benefits thereafter (or which would accrue if such benefits were elected upon eligibility), which support obligation shall not be dischargeable in bankruptcy or otherwise. If MEMBER departs service before the accrual of 240 months of creditable service, the percentage payable to SPOUSE shall be recalculated to take into account that fewer than 240 months of total creditable service accrued.

The following paragraph states that cost of living adjustments are specifically contemplated, and accrue to both the Member's and the Spouse's portions of the benefits.

IT IS FURTHER ORDERED, ADJUDGED, AND DECREED that the amount called for herein shall not be modifiable by the direct or indirect action of either party hereto, either by way of increase or decrease, except as expressly set forth herein. It is contemplated that future cost of living adjustments will be granted by the United States government, by means of which the gross military retirement benefits specified above will increase, thus raising the amount being paid to SPOUSE.

The following paragraph states the intention to provide a lifelong benefit as a property settlement, which could be critical if the federal law is changed to otherwise allow for termination upon remarriage.

IT IS FURTHER ORDERED, ADJUDGED, AND DECREED that the payments called for herein from MEMBER's retired or retainer pay shall continue during the joint lives of the parties, and regardless of the future marital status of either of them; they shall terminate only upon the death of either SPOUSE or MEMBER.

This provision provides for simultaneous payments to the Member and Spouse, and states an intention to comply with federal law.

IT IS FURTHER ORDERED, ADJUDGED, AND DECREED that the appropriate military pay center shall pay the sums called for above directly to SPOUSE, to the extent permitted by law, at the same times as MEMBER receives his retired or retainer pay, and that this Decree is intended to qualify under the Uniformed Services Former Spouses Protection Act, 10 U.S.C. § 1408 *et seq.,* with all provisions to be interpreted to make the Decree qualify.

The following paragraph is not strictly necessary, but tends to make the Member feel better and clarifies intentions.

IT IS FURTHER ORDERED, ADJUDGED, AND DECREED that with the exception of the amounts specifically awarded to SPOUSE, the balance of MEMBER's retired or retainer pay is awarded to MEMBER as his sole and separate property.

First fallback provision; payments by allotment if direct payment is not made or is insufficient.

IT IS FURTHER ORDERED, ADJUDGED, AND DECREED that if the amount paid by the military pay center to SPOUSE is less than the amount specified above, MEMBER shall initiate an allotment to SPOUSE in the amount of any such difference, to be paid from any federal entitlements due MEMBER, with said allotment to be initiated by MEMBER immediately upon notice of such difference, and making up any arrearages in installments not less in amount or longer in term than the arrearages accrued.

Second fallback provision; direct payment by Member for any month in which the order is not yet in effect, or in which the pay center fails to provide the contemplated payment and allotment is not possible.

IT IS FURTHER ORDERED, ADJUDGED, AND DECREED that if in any month direct payment is not made to SPOUSE by the military pay center, and no federal entitlement exists against which such an allotment may be initiated, or for whatever reason full payment by allotment is not made in that month, or if the amount paid through the allotment is insufficient to pay the difference specified above, MEMBER shall pay the amounts called for above herein directly to SPOUSE by the fifth day of each month in which the military pay center and/or allotment fails to do so, beginning [ALT1 in _____, 19__] [ALT2 upon MEMBER's eligibility for retirement].

Third fallback provision; if the military retirement merged with another retirement program, that other retirement program should honor this order to the extent possible.

IT IS FURTHER ORDERED, ADJUDGED, AND DECREED that if MEMBER takes any steps to merge his military pension with another retirement program of any kind, that retirement system, program, or plan is directed to honor this court order to the extent of SPOUSE's interest as set forth above, to the extent that the military retirement is used as a basis of payments or benefits under such other retirement system, program, or plan.

Fourth fallback provision; if the Member's actions cause a decrease of payments to the Spouse, the Member must make up the difference.

IT IS FURTHER ORDERED, ADJUDGED, AND DECREED that if MEMBER takes any action that prevents, decreases, or limits the collection by SPOUSE of the sums to be paid hereunder (by application for or award of disability compensation, combination of benefits with any other retired pay, waiver for any reason, including as a result of other federal service, or in any other way), he shall make payments to SPOUSE directly in an amount sufficient to neutralize, as to SPOUSE, the effects of the action taken by MEMBER. Any sums paid to MEMBER that this court order provides are to be paid to SPOUSE shall be held by MEMBER in constructive trust until actual payment to SPOUSE.

Fifth fallback provision, reservation of jurisdiction by the court to enter further, construing, or enforcing orders as required. For cases in which alimony in lieu of retirement benefits was awarded, substitute "sums" for "military retirement benefits" in the first sentence, and phrase the reservation of jurisdiction to make a further award of alimony in the event the Member does not comply with the terms as set forth.

IT IS FURTHER ORDERED, ADJUDGED, AND DECREED that the Court shall retain jurisdiction to enter such further orders as are necessary to enforce the award to SPOUSE of the military retirement benefits awarded herein, including the recharacterization thereof as a division of Civil Service or other retirement benefits, or to make an award of alimony (in the sum of benefits payable plus future cost of living adjustments) in the event that MEMBER fails to comply with the provisions contained above requiring said payments to SPOUSE by any means, including the application for a disability award or filing of bankruptcy, or if military or government regulations or other restrictions interfere with payments to SPOUSE as set forth herein, or if MEMBER fails to comply with the provisions contained above requiring said payments to SPOUSE.

The following paragraph is a safeguard paragraph intended to allow relatively painless discovery from the military pay center in the event further information is necessary to come up with an enforceable order. It is probably necessary only in cases in which the Member is still in service on the date of divorce, so that some information is not known at that time.

IT IS FURTHER ORDERED, ADJUDGED, AND DECREED that MEMBER has waived any privacy or other rights as may be required for SPOUSE to obtain information relating to MEMBER's date of retirement, last unit assignment, final rank, grade, and pay, present or past retired pay, or other such information as may be required to enforce the award made herein, or required to revise this order to make it enforceable.

The following boilerplate paragraph is required by the federal act.

IT IS FURTHER ORDERED, ADJUDGED, AND DECREED that all applicable portions of the Soldier's and Sailor's Civil Relief Act of 1940, as to division of retired or retainer pay, have been complied with by waiver of MEMBER or otherwise.

The following paragraph elects the Spouse as the irrevocable beneficiary of the Survivor's Benefit Plan (SBP) benefits at the full base amount.

IT IS FURTHER ORDERED, ADJUDGED, AND DECREED that SPOUSE is and shall be deemed as the irrevocable beneficiary of the survivor's benefit plan (SBP) through MEMBER's military retirement as the former spouse of MEMBER, and MEMBER shall execute such paperwork as is required to make or extend the election of SPOUSE as said beneficiary, and shall do nothing to reduce or eliminate that benefit to SPOUSE. MEMBER shall elect the former spouse-only option and shall select as the base amount the full amount of monthly retired pay.

The following paragraph elects the Spouse as the irrevocable beneficiary of the SBP benefits at a base amount sufficient to cover the spousal interest, but no more.

IT IS FURTHER ORDERED, ADJUDGED, AND DECREED that SPOUSE is and shall be deemed as the irrevocable beneficiary of the survivor's benefit plan (SBP) through MEMBER's military retirement as the former spouse of MEMBER, and MEMBER shall execute such paperwork as is required to make or extend the election of SPOUSE as said beneficiary, and shall do nothing to reduce or eliminate that benefit to SPOUSE. MEMBER shall elect the former spouse-only option and shall select as the base amount the higher of (1) the minimum permissible SBP amount, or (2) a sum of monthly retired pay that, when multiplied by 55 percent, will yield the same dollar sum as is paid to SPOUSE during the parties' lifetimes under the terms of this order.

The paragraph below attempts to allocate the cost of the SBP plan to the Spouse. It is *not* required, but may be used when the parties have negotiated, or the court has ordered, that the Spouse is to be responsible for the entire SBP premium. The primary clause is NOT currently considered enforceable by the Cleveland pay center, so its use may require the contemplated monthly reimbursements.

✐ **Practice Tip:** If you DO intend to allocate the cost of the SBP to the Spouse, consider, as an alternative to the paragraph set forth below, calculating the cost of the premium and deducting it from the Spouse's share of the retirement percentage or dollar sum directly. To do so, if the spousal share is a percentage, calculate the cost of desired coverage, establish the percentage of the total military retirement that the dollar sum equals, and then deduct the proper percentage from the spousal share. The remaining dollar sum of the total benefits can be expressed as a percentage that should remain constant despite future cost of living adjustments. This method of dealing with the problem is probably preferable in most cases: it does not require "reimbursements" and minimizes the parties' future direct financial dealings.

IT IS FURTHER ORDERED, ADJUDGED, AND DECREED that the premium for said SBP shall be deducted by the military pay center from the amounts otherwise payable to SPOUSE as her portion of the military retirement as specified above. Should said deduction be impossible, for whatever reason, SPOUSE shall reimburse MEMBER for the cost of SPOUSE's SBP coverage to the extent that MEMBER does not receive retired pay because of that coverage. Unless it is established that MEMBER pays a different sum for SPOUSE's coverage, the sum of reimbursement shall be calculated as follows: (The amount of the SBP premium) × (1 − [SPOUSE's percentage of the military retirement benefits]). The obligation for reimbursement shall exist for each month in which MEMBER incurs a cost for SPOUSE's SBP coverage, beginning ten days after SPOUSE is notified in writing that MEMBER has incurred the expense of maintaining SPOUSE as said irrevocable beneficiary.

The following is a paragraph intended to allow waiver of the SBP by the Spouse and its replacement by a private insurance policy when financially reasonable; the Member is required to cooperate. Note that, as written, the paragraph does not indicate who is to pay for such replacement coverage; presumably, counsel will have this term mirror the responsibility for the SBP premiums.

IT IS FURTHER ORDERED, ADJUDGED, AND DECREED that SPOUSE shall have the right to waive her interest in said SBP as specified in the immediately preceding paragraph, and shall be permitted to obtain other insurance coverage on MEMBER's life, in such sums as she deems appropriate to secure SPOUSE's insurable interest. In the event SPOUSE makes such an election, MEMBER shall sign such documents or perform such other acts as are necessary to allow SPOUSE to secure such insurance coverage on his life, including complying with a request for a physical examination, if necessary.

Use the following paragraph if (1) the Member has already retired, (2) the SBP was NOT elected at the time of retirement, (3) it is desired to have the SBP in effect for the Spouse in the future, if possible. Note that, as written, the following paragraph does not allocate the SBP premium cost (see comments above).

IT IS FURTHER ORDERED, ADJUDGED, AND DECREED that upon the next open enrollment period, if any, MEMBER shall elect the Survivor's Benefit Plan survivor benefit annuity associated with his military retirement and shall designate SPOUSE as the named beneficiary thereof.

After this point, the user should include whatever nonmilitary-related divorce clauses are necessary to the case.

C. SAMPLE DECREE LANGUAGE FOR MEMBERS' LAWYERS

There is language that, from the member's perspective, would be preferable, depending on what is allowable under statutory or case law authority in a given state. In addition to the alternatives set forth in the clause above, below are some tactical devices for members' lawyers to consider, and for former spouses' lawyers to note.

Probably most important, in terms of total economic impact, is whether (and if so, where) the law of the state of dissolution has come down on the question of whether the former spouse shares in a time-rule percentage of the ultimate rank and grade achieved by the service member, or is restricted to the rank and grade, as well as years of service, accrued at the relevant time (under state law, date of separation, filing, or actual divorce). The factors, theories, and relevant cases are discussed in the main text of this book at some length.

If state law permits restricting the former spouse's share, a clause such as the following can be substituted for the clause in the form awarding the former spouse a share of the military retirement benefits. Note that all clauses discussed above that would assist the former spouse (payment upon eligibility for retirement, for example) have been removed from the following paragraph to make its core intention easier to discern.

IT IS FURTHER ORDERED, ADJUDGED, AND DECREED that SPOUSE has an interest in the military retirement benefits accruing to MEMBER as a result of his service in the United States Armed Forces, when and if they vest, as her sole and separate property, equal to the following formula. One half, multiplied by a percentage in which the numerator is [INSERT MONTHS OF SERVICE DURING MARRIAGE] and the denominator is [INSERT TOTAL MONTHS OF SERVICE CREDITABLE FOR RETIREMENT[1]] multiplied by the military retired pay payable to a member retiring at the rank of [INSERT RANK AT APPLICABLE VALUATION DATE] who would have retired with twenty years service on [INSERT DATE AT WHICH MEMBER WILL OR DID

---

1. If unknown, recite "the total months of service creditable for retirement at the time of retirement."

REACH ELIGIBILITY FOR REGULAR RETIREMENT], together with all increases that did or would have occurred, other than increases attributable to elevation in rank or services rendered after said date, plus a like percentage of all cost of living adjustment increases that accrue to said military retirement benefits hereafter. For the purpose of interpreting this Court's intention in making the division set forth in this Order, "military retirement" means disposable retired pay as defined in 10 U.S.C. § 1408. All sums payable to SPOUSE as a portion of military retirement shall be payable from MEMBER's disposable retired or retainer pay to the extent that it is so restricted by law.

This formula should yield the kind of distribution ordered by the Texas Supreme Court in *Grier v. Grier,* 731 S.W.2d 931 (Tex. 1987).

D. SUMMARY CHECKLIST FOR HANDLING A MILITARY RETIREMENT CASE

CHECKLIST FOR MILITARY RETIREMENT BENEFITS CASES

1. Be familiar with the two federal rules that work with, and partly supersede, state law.
    - 10 U.S.C. § 1408.
    - 32 C.F.R. § 63.6.
2. Ensure that you have jurisdiction, *both* under your state law *and* under federal law.
    - Be aware that your state court must have jurisdiction over the service member by reason of residence (*other* than because of military assignment), domicile, or consent to the jurisdiction of the court.
        — Be aware of some differences among courts in what constitutes "consent"; for most it is any general appearance, but for at least one court it means consent to litigation of that particular asset.
    - NEVER take default against an out-of-state military member and seek to divide the retirement benefits; you will probably end up with an unenforceable order that may not be "fixable" in any court anywhere.

- Be sure the marriage *overlapped* the member's military service by at least ten years during creditable military service.
  — If not, you cannot get the military pay center to send the spousal share of a property award directly to the former spouse.
  — If you do not have a ten-year overlap of marriage and service, consider getting an alimony award instead, because that is directly payable regardless of the length of overlap.
3. Your order should recite certain necessary "magic language."
   - Compliance with the Soldier's and Sailor's Civil Relief Act must be noted.
   - Include the name and Social Security number of both the member and the former spouse.
4. Define "military retirement benefits" the way you really intend.
   - If you mean something other than the current definition of "disposable pay," say so.
   - Make sure that you clearly state your intention regarding future cost of living adjustment increases to the military retired pay.
   - State the spousal portion of the retired pay as a percentage of the total benefit or as a fixed dollar sum.
     — Be careful not to mix fixed dollar awards and percentages, and be aware that cost of living adjustments may not accrue to fixed dollar awards.
   - Realize that the definition of "disposable pay" is sometimes changed, and may or may not be what your state court *thinks* it is dividing.
5. Remember that military retired pay can be used for payment of child support and alimony, as well as be divided as property.
6. Follow up *after* the divorce by serving the order on the military pay center.
   - Service must be made *only* by certified or registered mail, return receipt requested, or by personal service.
   - The court order *must* be certified within ninety days of service on the military pay center.
7. If the member is still on active duty, provide for possible future contingencies.
   - Provide for what division will be made, and when, if the member takes an early retirement or elects an alternate benefit such as the

Special Separation Benefit, Variable Separation Incentive, or fifteen-year retirement.

- In states (such as California) that provide for division upon eligibility for retirement, provide for the member's possible service *after* eligibility for retirement by requiring personal payments by the member until actual retirement.
- Provide for whether alimony should be possible if the member takes a disability retirement and therefore reduces or eliminates the regular retired pay that could be divided.
  — This item also applies even if the member has *already* retired, because members can apply for postretirement disability ratings.
- If there is a disability, realize that a disability percentage does *not* directly translate into a percentage of total retired pay.
- Provide for the possibility of any military retired pay "rolled over" into civil service retirement or other pensions, including any "dual receipt" limitations involved in other federal service.
  — Again, this item also applies to divorces occurring after retirement.
- Provide for a reservation of jurisdiction to correct the form of order to comply with intentions in the event statutes change or the member's service takes an unexpected turn.

8. Ensure that you provide for disposition of the Survivor's Benefit Plan.
   - The benefit is *not* divisible between a present and former spouse; there can be only one beneficiary.
   - State courts have authority to determine whether the spouse is to remain a postdivorce beneficiary of the survivorship interest.
   - The *amount* of the benefit can be varied, by basing it upon the full base pay amount or some lesser sum.
   - Be sure you separately serve the proper office at the military pay center with a deemed election of the former spouse as beneficiary within one year of the date of divorce, or the spouse gets no survivorship benefits no matter what the decree says.

9. Obtain information regarding military-related benefits.
   - Identification cards, insurance benefits under the Civilian Health and Medical Program of the Uniformed Services, and base and commissary privileges are determined according to whether the member served for twenty years and was married for twenty years, and whether those two periods *overlapped* by twenty years.
   - If a former spouse remarries, the medical benefits are lost permanently, even if the later marriage ends.

CONCLUSION

Military retirement benefits are so central to any military-affected divorce that practitioners cannot afford to *not* know a great deal of the detail required to provide for their adequate disposition. It has become increasingly important for domestic relations practitioners to learn all aspects of relevant retirement plans, and to develop appropriate valuations for those assets, with thoughtful written contingencies for tax, survivorship, and related issues. Only then can counsel intelligently negotiate—or litigate—their clients' interests in such retirement benefits.

In the comparatively young field of military retirement benefits in divorce, the practitioner must be cautious to take nothing for granted; there have been too many policy reversals, changes of congressional sentiment, and retroactive enactments and holdings to feel very secure about any policy, decision, agreement, or decree. Still, the practitioner should not give up as hopeless the task of looking out for the client's present and future best interests. With care and attention to the pleadings, agreements, and orders, it is possible to fashion resolutions to military-related divorce matters that should withstand the test of time. It is my hope that this book will prove helpful to such efforts.

APPENDIX A

THE PRESENT STATE OF THE LAW: STATE-BY-STATE SUMMARY

It is impossible, of course, to be comprehensive in any book concerning the state of the law across the country on this topic. Practitioners are cautioned that the information below is not complete (due to the sheer number of cases) and is almost certainly not up-to-date, because all research for this book had cutoff dates before publication, and much was borrowed wholesale from another practitioner in this field.[1] The law in this area is evolving quickly and, at times, radically; perhaps in part because the subject area is less than twenty years old. Still, it is hoped that a summary history of case law will give some assistance to a practitioner seeking to determine the general approach of a state that might be involved in a case of this sort, at least by giving a relevant case from which to begin researching.

Alabama

Divisible. As of August, 1993, the Alabama Supreme Court held that disposable military retirement benefits accumulated during the course of the marriage are divisible as marital property. *Vaughn v. Vaughn,* 634 So. 2d 533 (Ala. 1993). *Kabaci v. Kabaci,* 373 So. 2d 1144 (Ala. Civ. App. 1979) and cases relying on it that are inconsistent with *Vaughn* are expressly overruled. Note that Alabama has previously awarded alimony from military retired pay. *Underwood v. Underwood,* 491 So. 2d 242 (Ala. Civ. App. 1986) (wife awarded alimony from husband's military disability retired pay); *Phillips v. Phillips,* 489 So. 2d 592 (Ala. Civ. App. 1986) (wife awarded 50 percent of husband's gross military pay as alimony).

---

1. My special thanks for the fifty-state summary text to lawyer Mark E. Sullivan, 1306 Hillsborough Street, Raleigh, NC 27605, 919/832-8507.

Alaska

Divisible. *Chase v. Chase,* 662 P.2d 944 (Alaska 1983), *overruling Cose v. Cose,* 592 P.2d 1230 (Alaska 1979), *cert. denied,* 453 U.S. 922 (1982). Nonvested retirement benefits are divisible. *Lang v. Lang,* 741 P.2d 649 (Alaska 1987). Note also *Morlan v. Morlan,* 720 P.2d 497 (Alaska 1986) (trial court ordered civilian employee to retire to ensure spouse received her share of pension—the pension would be suspended if employee continued working; on appeal, court held that employee should have been given option of continuing to work and periodically paying spouse the sums she would have received from retired pay; in reaching this result, court cited California *Gillmore* decision). Also see *Clausen v. Clausen,* 831 P.2d 1257 (Alaska 1992), which held that although *Mansell* precludes division of disability benefits received in lieu of retirement pay, it does not preclude *consideration* of these payments when making an equitable division of marital assets.

Arizona

Divisible. *DeGryse v. DeGryse,* 135 Ariz. 335, 661 P.2d 185 (1983); *Edsall v. Superior Court of Arizona,* 143 Ariz. 240, 693 P.2d 895 (1984); *Van Loan v. Van Loan,* 116 Ariz. 272, 569 P.2d 214 (1977) (nonvested military pension is community property). A civilian retirement plan case (*Koelsch v. Koelsch,* 148 Ariz. 176, 713 P.2d 1234 (1986)) held that if the employee is not eligible to retire at the time of the dissolution, the court *must* order that the spouse begin receiving the awarded share of retired pay when the employee becomes *eligible* to retire, whether or not he or she does retire at that point.

Arkansas

Divisible. *Young v. Young,* 288 Ark. 33, 701 S.W.2d 369 (1986); *but see Durham v. Durham,* 289 Ark. 3, 708 S.W.2d 618 (1986) (military retired pay not divisible when member had not served twenty years at time of divorce, and therefore military pension had not "vested"). *Also see Burns v. Burns,* 31 Ark. 61, 847 S.W.2d 23 (1993) (in accord with *Durham,* but strong dissent favors rejecting twenty years of service as prerequisite to "vesting" of military pension).

California

Divisible. *In re Fithian,* 10 Cal. 3d 592, 517 P.2d 449, 111 Cal. Rptr. 369 (1974); *In re Hopkins,* 142 Cal. App. 3d 350, 191 Cal. Rptr. 70 (Ct. App. 1983). A nonresident service member did not waive his right under the Uniformed Services Former Spouses Protection Act (USFSPA) to object to California's jurisdiction over his military pension by consenting to the court's jurisdiction over other marital and property issue. *Tucker v. Tucker,* 226 Cal. App. 3d 1249, 227 Cal. Rptr. 403 (Ct. App. 1991); *Hattis v. Hattis,* 196 Cal. App. 3d 1162, 242 Cal. Rptr. 410 (Ct. App. 1987). Nonvested pensions are divisible. *In re Brown,* 15 Cal. 3d 838, 544 P.2d 561, 126 Cal. Rptr. 633 (1976). In *In re Mansell,* 216 Cal. App. 3d 937, 265 Cal. Rptr. 227 (Ct. App. 1989) (on remand from *Mansell v. Mansell,* 490 U.S. 581 (1989)), the court held that gross retired pay was divisible because it was based on a stipulated property settlement to which res judicata had attached. State law has held that military disability retired pay is divisible to the extent it replaces what the retiree would have received as longevity retired pay (*In re Mastropaolo,* 166 Cal. App. 3d 953, 213 Cal. Rptr. 26 (Ct. App. 1985); *In re Mueller,* 70 Cal. App. 3d 66, 137 Cal. Rptr. 129 (Ct. App. 1977)), but the *Mansell* case raises doubt about the continued validity of this proposition. If the member is not retired at the time of the dissolution, the spouse can elect to begin receiving the award share of "retired pay" when the member becomes *eligible* to retire, or anytime thereafter, even if the member remains on active duty. *In re Luciano,* 104 Cal. App. 3d 956, 164 Cal. Rptr. 93 (Ct. App. 1980); *see also In re Gillmore,* 29 Cal. 3d 418, 629 P.2d 1, 174 Cal. Rptr. 493 (1981) (same principle applied to civilian pension plan).

Colorado

Divisible. *In re Marriage of Beckman and Holm,* 800 P.2d 1376 (Colo. 1990) (nonvested military retirement benefits constitute marital property subject to division pursuant to Colo. Rev. Stat. § 14-10-113 (1987 repl. vol. 6B)). *See also In re Hunt,* 909 P.2d 525, 19 BTR 1813 (Colo. Sup. Ct. Dec. 18, 1995) (holding that postdivorce increases in pay resulting from promotions are not marital property subject to division).

Connecticut

Probably divisible. Conn. Gen. Stat. § 46b-81 (1986) gives courts broad power to divide property. *Thompson v. Thompson,* 183 Conn. 96,

438 A.2d 839 (1981) (nonvested civilian pension is divisible). The Connecticut Supreme Court held in *Krafick v. Krafick,* 234 Conn. 783, 663 A.2d 365 (1995), that vested pension benefits are divisible as marital property in divorce.

Delaware

Divisible. *Smith v. Smith,* 458 A.2d 711 (Del. Fam. Ct. 1983). Nonvested pensions are divisible. *Donald R.R. v. Barbara S.R.,* 454 A.2d 1295 (Del. Super. Ct. 1982).

District of Columbia

Divisible. See *Barbour v. Barbour,* 464 A.2d 915 (D.C. 1983) (vested but unmatured civil service pension held divisible; dicta suggests that nonvested pensions also divisible).

Florida

Divisible. As of October 1, 1988, all vested and nonvested pension plans are treated as marital property to the extent they are accrued during the marriage. FLA. STAT. 61.075(3)(a)4 (1988); *see also* 1988 Fla. Sess. Law Serv. 342, § 3(1). These legislative changes appear to overrule the prior limitation in *Pastore v. Pastore,* 497 So. 2d 635 (Fla. 1986) (only vested military retired pay can be divided). This interpretation was recently adopted by the court in *Deloach v. Deloach,* 590 So. 2d 956 (Fla. Dist. Ct. App. 1991).

Georgia

Probably divisible. *Cf. Courtney v. Courtney,* 256 Ga. 97, 344 S.E.2d 421 (1986) (nonvested civilian pensions divisible); *Stumpf v. Stumpf,* 249 Ga. 759, 294 S.E.2d 488 (1982) (military retired pay may be considered in establishing alimony obligations); *see also Hall v. Hall,* 51 B.R. 1002 (Bankr. S.D. Ga. 1985) (Georgia divorce judgment awarding debtor's wife 38 percent of debtor's military retirement, payable directly from United States to wife, granted wife nondischargeable property interest in 38 percent of husband's military retirement); *Holler v. Holler,* 257 Ga. 27, 354 S.E.2d 140 (1987) (court "[a]ssum[ed] that vested and nonvested military retirement benefits acquired during the marriage are now marital property subject to equitable division," citing *Stumpf* and *Courtney,* but then deciding that military retired pay could not be divided retroactively if it was not subject to division at time of divorce).

Hawaii

Divisible. *Linson v. Linson,* 1 Haw. App. 272, 618 P.2d 748 (Ct. App. 1981); *Cassiday v. Cassiday,* 68 Haw. 383, 716 P.2d 1133 (1986). In *Wallace v. Wallace,* 5 Haw. App. 55, 677 P.2d 966 (Ct. App. 1984), the court ordered a Public Health Service employee (who is covered by the USFSPA) to pay a share of retired pay upon reaching retirement age whether or not he retires at that point. He argued that this amounted to an order to retire, violating 10 U.S.C. § 1408(c)(3), but the court affirmed the order. In *Jones v. Jones,* 7 Haw. App. 496, 780 P.2d 581 (Ct. App. 1989), the court ruled that *Mansell*'s limitation on dividing Veteran's Administration (VA) benefits cannot be circumvented by awarding an offsetting interest in other property. It also held that *Mansell* applies to military disability retired pay as well as VA benefits.

Idaho

Divisible. *Ramsey v. Ramsey,* 96 Idaho 672, 535 P.2d 53 (1975) (reinstated by *Griggs v. Griggs,* 197 Idaho 123, 686 P.2d 68 (1984)). Courts cannot circumvent *Mansell*'s limitation on dividing VA benefits by using an offset against other property. *Bewley v. Bewley,* 116 Idaho 845, 780 P.2d 596 (Ct. App. 1989). *See Leatherman v. Leatherman,* 122 Idaho 247, 833 P.2d 105 (1992). A portion of a husband's civil service annuity attributable to years of military service during marriage was a divisible military service benefit, and thus subject to a statute relating to the modification of divorce decrees to include division of military retirement benefits. *Also see Balderson v. Balderson,* 127 Idaho 48, 896 P.2d 956 (Idaho Sup. Ct. May 22, 1995) (affirming lower court decision ordering service member to pay spouse her community share of military pension, even though he had decided to put off retirement); *Mosier v. Mosier,* 122 Idaho 37, 830 P.2d 1175 (1992); *Walborn v. Walborn,* 120 Idaho 494, 817 P.2d 160 (1991).

Illinois

Divisible. *In re Brown,* 225 Ill. App. 3d 733, 587 N.E.2d 648 (App. Ct. 1992); the court cited Congress's enactment of the Former Spouses'

Protection Act (Pub. L. No. 97-252, 96 Stat. 730-38 (1982)) as the basis to permit the courts to treat pay of military personnel in accordance with the law of the jurisdiction of the court (*In re Dooley,* 137 Ill. App. 3d 407, 484 N.E.2d 894 (App. Ct. 1985). The court in *Brown* held that a military pension may be treated as marital property under Illinois law and is subject to the division provisions of Section 5/503 of the Illinois Marriage and Dissolution of Marriage Act. *See In re Korper,* 131 Ill. App. 3d 753, 475 N.E.2d 1333 (App. Ct. 1985). *Korper* points out that under Illinois law, a pension is marital property even if it is not vested. In *Korper,* the member had not yet retired, and he objected to the spouse getting the cash-out value of her interest in retired pay. He argued that the USFSPA allowed division only of "disposable retired pay," and state courts therefore are preempted from awarding the spouse anything before retirement. The court rejected this argument, thus raising the (unaddressed) question whether a spouse could be awarded a share of "retired" pay at the time the member becomes *eligible* for retirement (even if he or she does not retire at that point). See *In re Luciano,* 104 Cal. App. 3d 956, 164 Cal. Rptr. 93 (Ct. App. 1980) for an application of such a rule. Note also Ill. Stat. Ann. ch. 40, para. 510.1 (Smith-Hurd Supp. 1988) (allows modification of agreements and judgments that became final between June 25, 1981, and February 1, 1983, unless party opposing modification shows that original disposition of military retired pay was appropriate).

Indiana

Divisible. Ind. Code § 31-1-11.5-2(d)(3) (1987) (amended in 1985 to provide that "property" for marital dissolution purposes includes "[t]he right to receive disposable retired pay, as defined in 10 U.S.C. § 1408(a), acquired during the marriage, that is or may be payable after the dissolution of the marriage"). The right to receive retired pay must be vested as of the date of the divorce petition for the spouse to be entitled to a share (*Kirkman v. Kirkman,* 555 N.E.2d 1293 (Ind. 1990)), but courts should consider the nonvested military retired benefits in adjudging a just and reasonable division of property (*In re Bickel,* 533 N.E.2d 593 (Ind. Ct. App. 1989)). *Also see Arthur v. Arthur,* 519 N.E.2d 230 (Ind. Ct. App. 1988) (second district ruled that § 31-1-11.5-2(d)(3) cannot be applied retroactively to allow division of military retired pay in case filed before law's effective date, which was September 1, 1985). *But see Sable v. Sable,* 506 N.E.2d 495 (Ind. Ct. App. 1987) (third district ruled that § 31-1-11.5-2(d)(3) can be applied retroactively).

Iowa

Divisible. Under authority of Iowa appellate court decisions, military retirement pay and benefits are divisible in divorce actions. See especially *In re Howell*, 434 N.W.2d 629 (Iowa 1989). The member had already retired in this case, but the decision may be broad enough to encompass nonvested retired pay as well. The court also ruled that disability payments from the VA, paid in lieu of a portion of military retired pay, are not marital property. Finally, it appears the court intended to award the spouse a percentage of *gross* military retired pay, but it actually "direct[ed] that 30.5% of [the husband's] *disposable retired pay,* except disability benefits, be assigned to [the wife] in accordance with section 1408 of Title 10 of the United States Code." (Emphasis added.) The *Mansell* case may have overruled state court decisions that the state court has authority to divide gross retired pay.

Note: A disabled veteran may be required to pay alimony and/or child support in divorce actions, even when his only income is veterans' disability and supplemental security income. *See In re Marriage of Anderson*, 522 N.W.2d 99 (Iowa Ct. App. 1994) (applying *Rose v. Rose*, 481 U.S. 619 (1987)). The Iowa Court of Appeals ruled, "It is clear veteran's benefits are not solely for the benefit of the veteran, but for his family as well."

Kansas

Divisible. KAN. STAT. ANN. § 23-201(b) (1987), effective July 1, 1987 (vested and nonvested military pensions are marital property); *In re Harrison*, 13 Kan. App. 2d 313, 769 P.2d 678 (Ct. App. 1989) (applies statute and held it overruled previous case law that prohibited division of military retired pay).

Kentucky

Divisible. *Jones v. Jones*, 680 S.W.2d 921 (Ky. 1984); *Poe v. Poe*, 711 S.W.2d 849 (Ky. Ct. App. 1986) (military retirement benefits are marital property even before they "vest"); KY. REV. STAT. ANN. § 403.190 (1994) (expressly defines marital property to include retirement benefits).

Louisiana

Divisible. *Swope v. Mitchell,* 324 So. 2d 461 (La. 1975); *Little v. Little,* 513 So. 2d 464 (La. Ct. App. 1987) (nonvested and unmatured military retired pay is marital property); *Warner v. Warner,* 651 So. 2d 1339 (La. 1995) (confirming that ten-year test found in 10 U.S.C. § 1408(d)(2) is prerequisite to direct payment, but not to award of share of retired pay to former spouse); *Gowins v. Gowins,* 466 So. 2d 32 (La. 1985) (soldier's participation in divorce proceedings constituted implied consent for court to exercise jurisdiction and divide soldier's military retired pay as marital property); *Jett v. Jett,* 449 So. 2d 557 (La. Ct. App. 1984); *Rohring v. Rohring,* 441 So. 2d 485 (La. Ct. App. 1983). *See also Campbell v. Campbell,* 474 So.2d 1339 (La. Ct. App. 1985) (court can award spouse share of disposable retired pay, not gross retired pay, and court cannot divide VA disability benefits paid in lieu of military retired pay).

Maine

Divisible. *Lunt v. Lunt,* 522 A.2d 1317 (Me. 1987). *See also* ME. REV. STAT. ANN. tit. 19, § 22-A(6) (1989) (provides parties become tenants-in-common of property that court fails to divide or set apart).

Maryland

Divisible. *Nisos v. Nisos,* 60 Md. App. 368, 483 A.2d 97 (Ct. Spec. App. 1984) (applies MD. CODE ANN. Fam. Law § 8-203(b), which provides that military pensions are to be treated the same as other pension benefits; such benefits are marital property under Maryland law; *see Deering v. Deering,* 292 Md. 115, 437 A.2d 883 (1981)). *See also Ohm v. Ohm,* 49 Md. App. 392, 431 A.2d 1371 (Ct. Spec. App. 1981) (nonvested pensions are divisible). "Window decrees" that are silent on division of retired pay cannot be reopened simply on the basis that Congress subsequently enacted the USFSPA. *Andresen v. Andresen,* 317 Md. 380, 564 A.2d 399 (1989).

Massachusetts

Divisible. *Andrews v. Andrews,* 27 Mass. App. Ct. 759, 543 N.E.2d 31 (App. Ct. 1989). Here, the spouse was awarded alimony from military retired pay; she appealed, seeking a property interest in the pension. The trial court's ruling was upheld, but the appellate court noted that "the judge could have assigned a portion of the pension to the wife [as property]."

Michigan

Divisible. *Keen v. Keen,* 160 Mich. App. 314, 407 N.W.2d 643 (Ct. App. 1987); *Giesen v. Giesen,* 140 Mich. App. 335, 364 N.W.2d 327 (Ct. App. 1985); *McGinn v. McGinn,* 126 Mich. App. 689, 337 N.W.2d 632 (Ct. App. 1983); *Chisnell v. Chisnell,* 82 Mich. App. 699, 267 N.W.2d 155 (Ct. App. 1978). Note also *Boyd v. Boyd,* 116 Mich. App. 774, 323 N.W.2d 553 (Ct. App. 1982) (only vested pensions are divisible).

Minnesota

Divisible. Military retired pay is not specifically addressed in a statute. Case law has treated it as any other marital asset, subject to equitable division. *Deliduka v. Deliduka,* 347 N.W.2d 52 (Minn. Ct. App. 1984). This case also holds that a court may award a spouse a share of gross retired pay, but was pre-*Mansell.* Note also *Janssen v. Janssen,* 331 N.W.2d 752 (Minn. 1983) (nonvested pensions are divisible).

Mississippi

Divisible. *Powers v. Powers,* 465 So. 2d 1036 (Miss. 1985). In July, 1994, a deeply divided Mississippi Supreme Court formally adopted the equitable distribution method of division of marital assets. *Ferguson v. Ferguson,* 639 So. 2d 921 (Miss. 1994); *Hemsley v. Hemsley* 639 So. 2d 909 (Miss. 1994). Marital property for the purpose of a divorce is defined as being "any and all property acquired or accumulated during the marriage." This includes military pensions that are viewed as personal property, and though USFSPA does not vest any rights in a spouse, a military pension is subject to being divided in a divorce. *Pierce v. Pierce,* 648 So. 2d 523 (Miss. 1995). In *Pierce,* the court expressly held that a claim for division of property can only be viewed as separate and distinct from a claim for alimony. Because property division is made regardless of fault or misconduct, military pensions may be divided even when the spouse has committed adultery, assuming the facts otherwise justify an equitable division of property.

Missouri

Divisible. Only disposable retired pay is divisible. *Moon v. Moon,* 795 S.W.2d 511 (Mo. Ct. App. 1990). *Fairchild v. Fairchild,* 747 S.W.2d 641 (Mo. Ct. App. 1988) (nonvested and nonmatured military retired pay are marital property); *Coates v. Coates,* 650 S.W.2d 307 (Mo. Ct. App. 1983).

Montana

Divisible. *In re Marriage of Kecskes,* 210 Mont. 479, 683 P.2d 478 (1984); *In re Miller,* 37 Mont. 556, 609 P.2d 1185 (1980), *vacated and remanded sub nom. Miller v. Miller,* 453 U.S. 918 (1981).

Nebraska

Divisible. *Ray v. Ray,* 222 Neb. 324, 383 N.W.2d 756 (1986); NEB. REV. STAT. § 42-366(8) (1993) (military pensions are part of marital estate whether vested or not, and may be divided as property or alimony).

Nevada

Divisible. All retirement benefits are divisible community property, whether vested or not, and whether matured or not. *Forrest v. Forrest,* 99 Nev. 602, 668 P.2d 275 (1983). The spouse has the right to elect to receive his or her share when the employee spouse becomes retirement eligible, whether or not retirement occurs at that point. *Gemma v. Gemma,* 105 Nev. 458, 778 P.2d 429 (1989); *Sertic v. Sertic,* 111 Nev. 1192, 901 P.2d 148 (1995). Partition of previously undivided benefits was considered doubtful, under a case that held a silent decree to be res judicata of *non*-division of the retirement benefits. *Tomlinson v. Tomlinson,* 102 Nev. 652, 729 P.2d 1363 (1986). However, without mentioning that opinion, the Nevada Supreme Court has since held that the parties to a divorce remain tenants-in-common of all assets omitted from the decree, whether by fraud or simple mistake. *Amie v. Amie,* 106 Nev. 541, 796 P.2d 233 (1990); *Williams v. Waldman,* 108 Nev. 466, 836 P.2d 614 (1992).

New Hampshire

Divisible. "Property shall include all tangible and intangible property and assets . . . belonging to either or both parties, whether title to the property is held in the name of either or both parties. Intangible property includes . . . employment benefits, [and] vested and non-vested pensions or other retirement plans. . . . [T]he court may order an equitable division of property between the parties. The court shall presume that an equal division is an equitable distribution. . . ." N.H. REV. STAT. ANN. § 458:16-a (1987) (effective Jan. 1, 1988). This provision was relied on by the New Hampshire Supreme Court in *Blanchard v. Blanchard,* 133 N.H. 427, 578 A.2d 339 (1990), when it overruled *Baker v. Baker,* 120 N.H. 645, 421 A.2d 998 (1980) (military retired pay not divisible as marital property, but may be considered "as a relevant factor in making equitable support orders and property distributions").

New Jersey

Divisible. *Castiglioni v. Castiglioni,* 192 N.J. Super. 594, 471 A.2d 809 (Super. Ct. Chancery Div. Family Part 1984); *Whitfield v. Whitfield,* 222 N.J. Super. 36, 535 A.2d 986 (Super. Ct. App. Div. 1987) (nonvested military retired pay is marital property); *Kruger v. Kruger,* 139 N.J. Super. 413, 354 A.2d 340 (Super. Ct. App. Div. 1976), *aff'd,* 73 N.J. 464, 375 A.2d 659 (1977). Postdivorce cost of living raises are divisible; *Moore v. Moore,* 114 N.J. 147, 553 A.2d 20 (1989) (police pension).

New Mexico

Divisible. *Walentowski v. Walentowski,* 100 N.M. 484, 672 P.2d 657 (1983) (USFSPA applied); *Stroshine v. Stroshine,* 98 N.M. 742, 652 P.2d 1193 (1982); *LeClert v. LeClert,* 80 N.M. 235, 453 P.2d 755 (1969). *See also White v. White,* 105 N.M. 800, 734 P.2d 1283 (Ct. App. 1987) (court can award share of gross retired pay, however, was pre-*Mansell*). In *Mattox v. Mattox,* 105 N.M. 479, 734 P.2d 259 (1987), the court cited (in dicta) the California *Gillmore* case with approval, suggesting that a court can order a member to begin paying the spouse his or her share when the member becomes eligible to retire—even if the member elects to remain on active duty.

New York

Divisible. Pensions in general are divisible. *Majauskas v. Majauskas,* 61 N.Y.2d 481, 463 N.E.2d 15, 474 N.Y.S.2d 699 (1984). Most lower courts hold that nonvested pensions are divisible. *See, e.g., Damiano v. Damiano,* 94 A.D.2d 132, 463 N.Y.S.2d 477 (App. Div. 1983). Case law seems to treat military retired pay as subject to division. *E.g., Lydick v. Lydick,* 130 A.D.2d 915, 516 N.Y.S.2d 326 (App. Div. 1987); *Gannon v. Gannon,* 116 A.D.2d 1030, 498 N.Y.S.2d 647 (App. Div. 1986). Disability payments are separate property as a matter of law, but a disability pension is marital property to the extent it reflects deferred compensation. *West v. West,* 101 A.D.2d 834, 475 N.Y.S.2d 493 (App. Div. 1984).

North Carolina

Divisible. N.C. GEN. STAT. § 50-20(b) (1988) expressly declares vested military pensions to be marital property; the pension must be vested as of the date the parties separate from each other. In *Milam v. Milam,* 92 N.C. App. 105, 373 S.E.2d 459 (Ct. App. 1988), the court ruled that a warrant officer's retired pay had "vested" when he reached the eighteen-year "lock-in" point. In *George v. George,* 115 N.C. App. 387, 444 S.E.2d 449 (Ct. App. 1994), the court held that an enlisted member's right to retirement benefits vests when he/she has completed twenty years of service. In *Lewis v. Lewis,* 83 N.C. App. 438, 350 S.E.2d 587 (Ct. App. 1986) the court held that a divorce court can award a spouse a share of *gross* retired pay, but, because of the wording (at that time) of the state statute, the amount cannot exceed 50 percent of the retiree's *disposable* retired pay, but was pre-*Mansell.* The parties are not, however, barred from a consensual division of military retired pay, even though it is "nonvested" separate property, and an agreement or court order by consent that divides such pension rights will be upheld. *Hoolapa v. Hoolapa,* 105 N.C. App. 230, 412 S.E.2d 112 (Ct. App. 1992). Lawyers considering valuation issues should also review *Bishop v. Bishop,* 113 N.C. App. 725, 440 S.E.2d 591 (Ct. App. 1994), which held that valuation must be determined as of the date of separation and must be based on a present value of pension payments that the retiree would be entitled to receive if he or she retired on the date of marital separation, or when first eligible to retire, if later. Subsequent pay increases attributable to length of service or promotions are not included.

North Dakota

Divisible. *Delorey v. Delorey,* 357 N.W.2d 488 (N.D. 1984). *See also Morales v. Morales,* 402 N.W.2d 322 (N.D. 1987) (equitable factors can be considered in dividing military retired pay, so 17.5 percent award to seventeen-year spouse is affirmed); *Bullock v. Bullock,* 354 N.W.2d 904 (N.D. 1984) (court can award spouse a share of gross retired pay, but was pre-*Mansell*).

Ohio

Divisible. *Anderson v. Anderson,* 13 Ohio App. 3d 194, 468 N.E.2d 784 (Ct. App. 1984). *See also Lemon v. Lemon,* 42 Ohio App. 3d 142, 537 N.E.2d 246 (Ct. App. 1988) (nonvested pensions are divisible as marital property).

Oklahoma

Divisible. *Stokes v. Stokes,* 738 P.2d 1346 (Okla. 1987) (based on statute that became effective June 1, 1987). The state attorney general had earlier opined that military retired pay was divisible, based on the prior law. Only a pension vested at the time of the divorce, however, is divisible. *Messinger v. Messinger,* 827 P.2d 865 (Okla. 1992). A former spouse is entitled to retroactive division of the retiree's military pension pursuant to their property settlement agreement that provided that the property settlement was subject to modification if the law in effect at the time of their divorce changed to allow such a division at a later date.

Oregon

Divisible. *In re Manners,* 68 Or. App. 896, 683 P.2d 134 (Ct. App. 1984); *In re Vinson,* 48 Or. App. 283, 616 P.2d 1180 (Ct. App. 1980). *See also In re Richardson,* 307 Or. 370, 769 P.2d 179 (1989) (nonvested pension plans are marital property). The date of separation is the date used for classification as marital property.

Pennsylvania

Divisible. *Major v. Major,* 359 Pa. Super. 344, 518 A.2d 1267 (Super. Ct. 1986) (nonvested military retired pay is marital property).

Puerto Rico

Not divisible as marital property. *Delucca v. Colon,* 119 P.R. Dec. 720 (1987) (citation to original Spanish version; English translation not published as of June, 1994). *Delucca* overruled *Torres v. Robles,* 115 P.R. Dec. 765 (1984), which had held that military retired pay is divisible. Pensions may be considered, however, in setting child support and alimony obligations.

Rhode Island

Divisible. R.I. GEN. LAWS § 15-5-16.1 (1988) gives courts very broad powers to effect equitable distribution of the parties' property. Implied consent by the soldier cannot be used, however, to satisfy the jurisdictional requirements of 10 U.S.C. § 1408(c)(4). *Flora v. Flora,* 603 A.2d 723 (R.I. 1992).

South Carolina

Divisible. *Tiffault v. Tiffault,* 303 S.C. 391, 401 S.E.2d 157 (1991) holds that vested military retirement benefits constitute an earned property right which, if accrued during the marriage, are subject to equitable distribution. Nonvested military retirement benefits are also subject to equitable division. *Ball v. Ball,* 312 S.C. 31, 430 S.E.2d 533 (Ct. App. 1993) (NCO acquired vested right to *participate* in military pension plan when he enlisted in army; this right, which is more than an expectancy, constitutes property subject to division). *But see Walker v. Walker,* 295 S.C. 286, 368 S.E.2d 89 (Ct. App. 1988) (wife lived with parents during entire period of husband's naval service; because she made no homemaker contributions, she was not entitled to any portion of military retired pay).

South Dakota

Divisible. *Gibson v. Gibson,* 437 N.W.2d 170 (S.D. 1989) (court states that military retired pay is divisible; in this case, it was reserve component retired pay—member served twenty years but had not yet reached age sixty); *Radigan v. Radigan,* 465 N.W.2d 483 (S.D. 1991) (husband must share with ex-wife any increase in his retirement benefits that results from his own, postdivorce efforts); *Hautala v. Hautala,* 417 N.W.2d 879 (S.D. 1987) (trial court awarded spouse 42 percent of nonvested military retired pay; award not challenged on appeal); *Moller v. Moller,* 356 N.W.2d 909 (S.D. 1984) (court commented approvingly on cases from other states that recognize divisibility but declined to divide retired pay here because 1977 divorce decree not appealed until 1983). *See generally Caughron v. Caughron,* 418 N.W.2d 791 (S.D. 1988) (present cash value of nonvested retirement benefit is marital property); *Hansen v. Hansen,* 273 N.W.2d 749 (S.D. 1979) (vested civilian pension is divisible); *Stubbe v. Stubbe,* 376 N.W.2d 807 (S.D. 1985) (civilian pension divisible; court observed that "this pension plan is vested in the sense that it cannot be unilaterally terminated by [the] employer, though actual receipt of benefits is contingent upon [the worker's] survival and no benefits will accrue to the estate prior to retirement").

Tennessee

Divisible. TENN. CODE ANN. § 36-4-121(b)(1) (1988) defines all vested pensions as marital property.

Texas

Divisible. *Cameron v. Cameron,* 641 S.W.2d 210 (Tex. 1982). *See also Grier v. Grier,* 731 S.W.2d 936 (Tex. 1987) (court can award spouse a share of gross retired pay, but postdivorce pay increases constitute separate property, but was pre-*Mansell*). Pensions need not be vested to be divisible. State law has been construed as a reservation of jurisdiction in every case, whether or not explicitly so stated in decree, so that pre-1981 omitted military retirement benefits remain susceptible to partition actions despite 1990 amendments to USFSPA. *See Lee v. Walton,* 888 S.W.2d 604 (Tex. Ct. App. 1994).

Utah

Divisible. *Greene v. Greene,* 751 P.2d 827 (Utah Ct. App. 1988). The case clarifies that nonvested pensions can be divided under Utah law, and in dicta it suggests that only disposable retired pay is divisible, not gross retired pay. *But see Maxwell v. Maxwell,* 796 P.2d 403 (Utah Ct. App. 1990) (because of stipulation between parties, court ordered military retiree to pay his ex-wife one-half the amount deducted from his retired pay for taxes).

Vermont

Probably divisible. VT. STAT. ANN. tit. 15, § 751 (1988) provides that, the "court shall settle the rights of the parties to their property by . . .

equit[able] divi[sion]. All property owned by either or both parties, however and whenever acquired, shall be subject to the jurisdiction of the court. Title to the property . . . shall be immaterial, except where equitable distribution can be made without disturbing separate property." *See also McDermott v. McDermott,* 150 Vt. 258, 552 A.2d 786 (1989).

Virginia

Divisible. VA. CODE ANN. § 20-107.3 (1988) defines marital property to include all pensions, whether or not vested. *See also Mitchell v. Mitchell,* 4 Va. App. 113, 355 S.E.2d 18 (Ct. App. 1987) and *Sawyer v. Sawyer,* 1 Va. App. 75, 335 S.E.2d 277 (Ct. App. 1985) (these cases hold that military retired pay is subject to equitable division); *Owen v. Owen,* 14 Va. App. 623, 419 S.E.2d 267 (Ct. App. 1992) (settlement agreement's guarantee/indemnification clause requires retiree to pay same amount of support to spouse despite retiree beginning to collect VA disability pay; held not to violate *Mansell*).

Washington

Divisible. *Konzen v. Konzen,* 103 Wash. 2d 470, 693 P.2d 97, *cert. denied,* 473 U.S. 906 (1985); *Wilder v. Wilder,* 85 Wash. 2d 364, 534 P.2d 1355 (1975) (nonvested pension held to be divisible); *Payne v. Payne,* 82 Wash. 2d 573, 512 P.2d 736 (1973); *In re Smith,* 98 Wash. 2d 772, 657 P.2d 1383 (1983).

West Virginia

Divisible. *Butcher v. Butcher,* 178 W. Va. 33, 357 S.E.2d 226 (1987) (vested and nonvested military retired pay is marital property subject to equitable distribution, and court can award spouse a share of gross retired pay, but was pre-*Mansell*).

Wisconsin

Divisible. *Thorpe v. Thorpe,* 123 Wis. 2d 424, 367 N.W.2d 233 (Ct. App. 1985); *Pfeil v. Pfeil,* 115 Wis. 2d 502, 341 N.W.2d 699 (Ct. App. 1983). *See also Leighton v. Leighton,* 81 Wis. 2d 620, 261 N.W.2d 457 (1978) (nonvested pension held to be divisible); *Rodak v. Rodak,* 150 Wis.

2d 624, 442 N.W.2d 489 (Ct. App. 1989) (portion of civilian pension that was earned *before* marriage is included in marital property and subject to division).

Wyoming

Divisible. *Parker v. Parker,* 750 P.2d 1313 (Wyo. 1988) (nonvested military retired pay is marital property).

Canal Zone

Divisible. *Bodenhorn v. Bodenhorn,* 567 F.2d 629 (5th Cir. 1978).

Appendix B

10 U.S.C. § 1408

Because the statute has changed so radically over time, it is critical for practitioners to note that the version of the statute that follows is by its own terms applicable to *current* divorces; it sets forth the language of the statute that was most current as of the time this book went to print. For cases involving "final orders" that became final *before* 1997, please refer to the sections of this book that discuss the statutory changes that have been made over time, as some very critical sections of the law have been inserted, deleted, or modified at various times over the years.

10 U.S.C. § 1408, as of 1997

§ 1408. Payment of retired or retainer pay in compliance with court orders.

(a) Definitions. In this section:

(1) The term "court" means—

(A) any court of competent jurisdiction of any State, the District of Columbia, the Commonwealth of Puerto Rico, Guam, American Samoa, the Virgin Islands, the Northern Mariana Islands, and the Trust Territory of the Pacific Islands;

(B) any court of the United States (as defined in section 451 of title 28) having competent jurisdiction;

(C) any court of competent jurisdiction of a foreign country with which the United States has an agreement requiring the United States to honor any court order of such country; and

(D) any administrative or judicial tribunal of a State competent to enter orders for support or maintenance (including a State agency administering a program under a State plan approved under part D of title IV of the Social Security Act [42 U.S.C.S. §§ 651 *et seq.*]), and, for purposes of this subparagraph, the term "State" includes the District of Columbia, the Commonwealth of Puerto Rico, the Virgin Islands, Guam, and American Samoa.

(2) The term "court order" means a final decree of divorce, dissolution, annulment, or legal separation issued by a court, or a court ordered, ratified, or approved property settlement incident to such a decree (including a final decree modifying the terms of a previously issued decree of divorce, dissolution, annulment, or legal separation, or a court ordered, ratified, or approved property settlement incident to such previously issued decree), or a support order, as defined in section 453(p) of the Social Security Act (42 U.S.C. 653(p)), which—

(A) is issued in accordance with the laws of the jurisdiction of that court;

(B) provides for—

(i) payment of child support (as defined in section 459(i)(2) of the Social Security Act (42 U.S.C. 659(i)(2));

(ii) payment of alimony (as defined in section 459(I)(3) of the Social Security Act (42 U.S.C. 659(i)(3)); or

(iii) division of property (including a division of community property); and

(C) in the case of a division of property, specifically provides for the payment of an amount, expressed in dollars or as a percentage of disposable retired pay, from the disposable retired pay of a member to the spouse or former spouse of that member.

(3) The term "final decree" means a decree from which no appeal may be taken or from which no appeal has been taken within the time allowed for taking such appeals under the laws applicable to such appeals, or a decree from which timely appeal has been taken and such appeal has been finally decided under the laws applicable to such appeals.

(4) The term "disposable retired pay" means the total monthly retired pay to which a member is entitled less amounts which—

(A) are owed by that member to the United States for previous overpayments of retired pay and for recoupments required by law resulting from entitlement to retired pay;

(B) are deducted from the retired pay of such member as a result of forfeitures of retired pay ordered by a court-martial or as a result of a waiver of retired pay required by law in order to receive compensation under title 5 or title 38;

(C) in the case of a member entitled to retired pay under chapter 61 of this title [10 U.S.C.S. §§ 1201 *et seq.*], are equal to the amount of retired pay of the member under that chapter computed using the percentage of the member's disability on the date when the member was retired (or the date on which the member's name was placed on the temporary disability retired list); or

(D) are deducted because of an election under chapter 73 of this title [10 U.S.C.S. §§ 1431 *et seq.*] to provide an annuity to a spouse or former spouse to whom payment of a portion of such member's retired pay is being made pursuant to a court order under this section.

(E), (F) [Redesignated]

(5) The term "member" includes a former member entitled to retired pay under section 12731 of this title.

(6) The term "spouse or former spouse" means the husband or wife, or former husband or wife, respectively, of a member who, on or before the date of a court order, was married to that member.

(7) The term "retired pay" includes retainer pay.

(b) Effective service of process. For the purposes of this section—

(1) service of a court order is effective if—

(A) an appropriate agent of the Secretary concerned designated for receipt of service court orders under regulations prescribed pursuant to subsection (i) or, if no agent has been so designated, the Secretary concerned, is personally served or is served by facsimile or electronic transmission or by mail;

(B) the court order is regular on its face;

(C) the court order or other documents served with the court order identify the member concerned and include, if possible, the social security number of such member; and

(D) the court order or other documents served with the court order certify that the rights of the member under the Soldiers' and Sailors' Civil Relief Act of 1940 (50 U.S.C. App. 501 *et seq.*) were observed; and

(2) a court order is regular on its face if the order—

(A) is issued by a court of competent jurisdiction;

(B) is legal in form; and

(C) includes nothing on its face that provides reasonable notice that it is issued without authority of law.

(c) Authority for court to treat retired pay as property of the member and spouse.

(1) Subject to the limitations of this section, a court may treat disposable retired pay payable to a member for pay periods beginning after June 25, 1981, either as property solely of the member or as property of the member and his spouse in accordance with the law of the jurisdiction

of such court. A court may not treat retired pay as property in any proceeding to divide or partition any amount of retired pay of a member as the property of the member and the member's spouse or former spouse if a final decree of divorce, dissolution, annulment, or legal separation (including a court ordered, ratified, or approved property settlement incident to such decree) affecting the member and the member's spouse or former spouse (A) was issued before June 25, 1981, and (B) did not treat (or reserve jurisdiction to treat) any amount of retired pay of the member as property of the member and the member's spouse or former spouse.

(2) Notwithstanding any other provision of law, this section does not create any right, title, or interest which can be sold, assigned, transferred, or otherwise disposed of (including by inheritance) by a spouse or former spouse. Payments by the Secretary concerned under subsection (d) to a spouse or former spouse with respect to a division of retired pay as the property of a member and the member's spouse under this subsection may not be treated as amounts received as retired pay for service in the uniformed services.

(3) This section does not authorize any court to order a member to apply for retirement or retire at a particular time in order to effectuate any payment under this section.

(4) A court may not treat the disposable retired pay of a member in the manner described in paragraph (1) unless the court has jurisdiction over the member by reason of (A) his residence, other than because of military assignment, in the territorial jurisdiction of the court, (B) his domicile in the territorial jurisdiction of the court, or (C) his consent to the jurisdiction of the court.

(d) Payments by Secretary concerned to (or for benefit of) spouse or former spouse.

(1) After effective service on the Secretary concerned of a court order providing for the payment of child support or alimony or, with respect to a division of property, specifically providing for the payment of an amount of the disposable retired pay from a member to the spouse or a former spouse of the member, the Secretary shall make payments (subject to the limitations of this section) from the disposable retired pay of the member to the spouse or former spouse (or for the benefit of such spouse or former spouse to a State disbursement unit established pursuant to section 454B of the Social Security Act [42 U.S.C.S. § 654b] or other public payee designated by a State, in accordance with part D of title IV of the Social

Security Act [42 U.S.C.S. §§ 651 *et seq.*], as directed by court order, or as otherwise directed in accordance with such part D) in an amount sufficient to satisfy the amount of child support and alimony set forth in the court order and, with respect to a division of property, in the amount of disposable retired pay specifically provided for in the court order. In the case of a spouse or former spouse who, pursuant to section 408(a)(3) of the Social Security Act (42 U.S.C. 608(a)[(3)](4)), assigns to a State the rights of the spouse or former spouse to receive support, the Secretary concerned may make the child support payments referred to in the preceding sentence to that State in amounts consistent with that assignment of rights. In the case of a member entitled to receive retired pay on the date of the effective service of the court order, such payments shall begin not later than 90 days after the date of effective service. In the case of a member not entitled to receive retired pay on the date of the effective service of the court order, such payments shall begin not later than 90 days after the date on which the member first becomes entitled to retired pay.

(2) If the spouse or former spouse to whom payments are to be made under this section was not married to the member for a period of 10 years or more during which the member performed at least 10 years of service creditable in determining the member's eligibility for retired pay, payments may not be made under this section to the extent that they include an amount resulting from the treatment by the court under subsection (c) of disposable retired pay of the member as property of the member or property of the member and his spouse.

(3) Payments under this section shall not be made more frequently than once each month, and the Secretary concerned shall not be required to vary normal pay and disbursement cycles for retired pay in order to comply with a court order.

(4) Payments from the disposable retired pay of a member pursuant to this section shall terminate in accordance with the terms of the applicable court order, but not later than the date of the death of the member or the date of the death of the spouse or former spouse to whom payments are being made, whichever occurs first.

(5) If a court order described in paragraph (1) provides for a division of property (including a division of community property) in addition to an amount of child support or alimony or the payment of an amount of disposable retired pay as the result of the court's treatment of such pay under subsection (c) as property of the member and his spouse, the Sec-

retary concerned shall pay (subject to the limitations of this section) from the disposable retired pay of the member to the spouse or former spouse of the member, any part of the amount payable to the spouse or former spouse under the division of property upon effective service of a final court order of garnishment of such amount from such retired pay.

(6)(A) The Secretary concerned may not accept service of a court order that is an out-of-State modification, or comply with the provisions of such a court order, unless the court issuing that order has jurisdiction in the manner specified in subsection (c)(4) over both the member and the spouse or former spouse involved.

(B) A court order shall be considered to be an out-of-State modification for purposes of this paragraph if the order—

(i) modifies a previous court order under this section upon which payments under this subsection are based; and

(ii) is issued by a court of a State other than the State of the court that issued the previous court order.

(e) Limitations.

(1) The total amount of the disposable retired pay of a member payable under all court orders pursuant to subsection (c) may not exceed 50 percent of such disposable retired pay.

(2) In the event of effective service of more than one court order which provides for payment to a spouse and one or more former spouses or to more than one former spouse the disposable retired pay of the member shall be used to satisfy (subject to the limitations of paragraph (1)) such court orders on a first-come, first-served basis. Such court orders shall be satisfied (subject to the limitations of paragraph (1)) out of that amount of disposable retired pay which remains after the satisfaction of all court orders which have been previously served.

(3)(A) In the event of effective service of conflicting court orders under this section which assert to direct that different amounts be paid during a month to the same spouse or former spouse of the same member, the Secretary concerned shall—

(i) pay to that spouse from the member's disposable retired pay the least amount directed to be paid during that month by any such conflicting court order, but not more than the amount of disposable retired pay which remains available for payment of such courts orders based on when such court orders were effectively served and the limitations of paragraph (1) and subparagraph (B) of paragraph (4);

(ii) retain an amount of disposable retired pay that is equal to the lesser of—

(I) the difference between the largest amount required by any conflicting court order to be paid to the spouse or former spouse and the amount payable to the spouse or former spouse under clause (i); and

(II) the amount of disposable retired pay which remains available for payment of any conflicting court order based on when such court order was effectively served and the limitations of paragraph (1) and subparagraph (B) of paragraph (4); and

(iii) pay to that member the amount which is equal to the amount of that member's disposable retired pay (less any amount paid during such month pursuant to legal process served under section 459 of the Social Security Act (42 U.S.C. 659) and any amount paid during such month pursuant to court orders effectively served under this section, other than such conflicting court orders) minus—

(I) the amount of disposable retired pay paid under clause (i); and

(II) the amount of disposable retired pay retained under clause (ii).

(B) The Secretary concerned shall hold the amount retained under clause (ii) of subparagraph (A) until such time as that Secretary is provided with a court order which has been certified by the member and the spouse or former spouse to be valid and applicable to the retained amount. Upon being provided with such an order, the Secretary shall pay the retained amount in accordance with the order.

(4)(A) In the event of effective service of a court order under this section and the service of legal process pursuant to section 459 of the Social Security Act (42 U.S.C. 659), both of which provide for payments during a month from the same member, satisfaction of such court orders and legal process from the retired pay of the member shall be on a first-come, first-served basis. Such court orders and legal process shall be satisfied out of moneys which are subject to such orders and legal process and which remain available in accordance with the limitations of paragraph (1) and subparagraph (B) of this paragraph during such month after the satisfaction of all court orders or legal process which have been previously served.

(B) Notwithstanding any other provision of law, the total amount of the disposable retired pay of a member payable by the Secretary concerned under all court orders pursuant to this section and all legal processes pursuant to section 459 of the Social Security Act (42 U.S.C. 659) with respect to a member may not exceed 65 percent of the amount of the retired pay payable to such member that is considered under section 462 of the Social Security Act (42 U.S.C. 662) to be remuneration for employment that is payable by the United States.

(5) A court order which itself or because of previously served court orders provides for the payment of an amount which exceeds the amount of disposable retired pay available for payment because of the limit set forth in paragraph (1), or which, because of previously served court orders or legal process previously served under section 459 of the Social Security Act (42 U.S.C. 659), provides for payment of an amount that exceeds the maximum amount permitted under paragraph (1) or subparagraph (B) of paragraph (4), shall not be considered to be irregular on its face solely for that reason. However, such order shall be considered to be fully satisfied for purposes of this section by the payment to the spouse or former spouse of the maximum amount of disposable retired pay permitted under paragraph (1) and subparagraph (B) of paragraph (4).

(6) Nothing in this section shall be construed to relieve a member of liability for the payment of alimony, child support, or other payments required by a court order on the grounds that payments made out of disposable retired pay under this section have been made in the maximum amount permitted under paragraph (1) or subparagraph (B) of paragraph (4). Any such unsatisfied obligation of a member may be enforced by any means available under law other than the means provided under this section in any case in which the maximum amount permitted under paragraph (1) has been paid and under section 459 of the Social Security Act (42 U.S.C. 659) in any case in which the maximum amount permitted under subparagraph (B) of paragraph (4) has been paid.

(f) Immunity of officers and employees of United States.

(1) The United States and any officer or employee of the United States shall not be liable with respect to any payment made from retired pay to any member, spouse, or former spouse pursuant to a court order that is regular on its face if such payment is made in accordance with this section and the regulations prescribed pursuant to subsection (i).

(2) An officer or employee of the United States who, under regulations prescribed pursuant to subsection (i), has the duty to respond to interrogatories shall not be subject under any law to any disciplinary action or civil or criminal liability or penalty for, or because of, any disclosure

of information made by him in carrying out any of his duties which directly or indirectly pertain to answering such interrogatories.

(g) Notice to member of service of court order on Secretary concerned.

A person receiving effective service of a court order under this section shall, as soon as possible, but not later than 30 days after the date on which effective service is made, send a written notice of such court order (together with a copy of such order) to the member affected by the court order at his last known address.

(h) Benefits for dependents who are victims of abuse by members losing right to retired pay.

(1) If, in the case of a member or former member of the armed forces referred to in paragraph (2)(A), a court order provides (in the manner applicable to a division of property) for the payment of an amount from the disposable retired pay of that member or former member (as certified under paragraph (4)) to an eligible spouse or former spouse of that member or former member, the Secretary concerned, beginning upon effective service of such court order, shall pay that amount in accordance with this subsection to such spouse or former spouse.

(2) A spouse or former spouse of a member or former member of the armed forces is eligible to receive payment under this subsection if—

(A) the member or former member, while a member of the armed forces and after becoming eligible to be retired from the armed forces on the basis of years of service, has eligibility to receive retired pay terminated as a result of misconduct while a member involving abuse of a spouse or dependent child (as defined in regulations prescribed by the Secretary of Defense or, for the Coast Guard when it is not operating as a service in the Navy, by the Secretary of Transportation); and

(B) the spouse or former spouse—

(i) was the victim of the abuse and was married to the member or former member at the time of that abuse; or

(ii) is a natural or adopted parent of a dependent child of the member or former member who was the victim of the abuse.

(3) The amount certified by the Secretary concerned under paragraph (4) with respect to a member or former member of the armed forces referred to in paragraph (2)(A) shall be deemed to be the disposable retired pay of that member or former member for the purposes of this subsection.

(4) Upon the request of a court or an eligible spouse or former spouse of a member or former member of the armed forces referred to in paragraph (2)(A) in connection with a civil action for the issuance of a court order in the case of that member or former member, the Secretary concerned shall determine and certify the amount of the monthly retired pay that the member or former member would have been entitled to receive as of the date of the certification—

(A) if the member or former member's eligibility for retired pay had not been terminated as described in paragraph (2)(A); and

(B) if, in the case of a member or former member not in receipt of retired pay immediately before that termination of eligibility for retired pay, the member or former member had retired on the effective date of that termination of eligibility.

(5) A court order under this subsection may provide that whenever retired pay is increased under section 1401a of this title (or any other provision of law), the amount payable under the court order to the spouse or former spouse of a member or former member described in paragraph (2)(A) shall be increased at the same time by the percent by which the retired pay of the member or former member would have been increased if the member or former member were receiving retired pay.

(6) Notwithstanding any other provision of law, a member or former member of the armed forces referred to in paragraph (2)(A) shall have no ownership interest in, or claim against, any amount payable under this section to a spouse or former spouse of the member or former member.

(7)(A) If a former spouse receiving payments under this subsection with respect to a member or former member referred to in paragraph (2)(A) marries again after such payments begin, the eligibility of the former spouse to receive further payments under this subsection shall terminate on the date of such marriage.

(B) A person's eligibility to receive payments under this subsection that is terminated under subparagraph (A) by reason of remarriage shall be resumed in the event of the termination of that marriage by the death of that person's spouse or by annulment or divorce. The resumption of payments shall begin as of the first day of the month in which that marriage is so terminated. The monthly amount of the payments shall be the amount that would have been paid if the continuity of the payments had not been interrupted by the marriage.

(8) Payments in accordance with this subsection shall be made out of funds in the Department of Defense Military Retirement Fund established

by section 1461 of this title or, in the case of the Coast Guard, out of funds appropriated to the Department of Transportation for payment of retired pay for the Coast Guard.

(9)(A) A spouse or former spouse of a member or former member of the armed forces referred to in paragraph (2)(A), while receiving payments in accordance with this subsection, shall be entitled to receive medical and dental care, to use commissary and exchange stores, and to receive any other benefit that a spouse or a former spouse of a retired member of the armed forces is entitled to receive on the basis of being a spouse or former spouse, as the case may be, of a retired member of the armed forces in the same manner as if the member or former member referred to in paragraph (2)(A) was entitled to retired pay.

(B) A dependent child of a member or former member referred to in paragraph (2)(A) who was a member of the household of the member or former member at the time of the misconduct described in paragraph (2)(A) shall be entitled to receive medical and dental care, to use commissary and exchange stores, and to have other benefits provided to dependents of retired members of the armed forces in the same manner as if the member or former member referred to in paragraph (2)(A) was entitled to retired pay.

(C) If a spouse or a dependent child eligible or entitled to receive a particular benefit under this paragraph is eligible or entitled to receive that benefit under another provision of law, the eligibility or entitlement of that spouse or former spouse or dependent child to such benefit shall be determined under such other provision of law instead of this paragraph.

(10)(A) For purposes of this subsection, in the case of a member of the armed forces who has been sentenced by a court-martial to receive a punishment that will terminate the eligibility of that member to receive retired pay if executed, the eligibility of that member to receive retired pay may, as determined by the Secretary concerned, be considered terminated effective upon the approval of that sentence by the person acting under section 860(c) of this title (article 60(c) of the Uniform Code of Military Justice).

(B) If each form of the punishment that would result in the termination of eligibility to receive retired pay is later remitted, set aside, or mitigated to a punishment that does not result in the termination of that eligibility, a payment of benefits to the eligible recipient under this subsection that is based on the punishment so vacated, set aside, or mitigated shall cease. The cessation of payments shall be effective as of the first day of the first month following the month in which the Secretary concerned notifies the recipient of such benefits in writing that payment of the benefits will cease. The recipient may not be required to repay the benefits received before that effective date (except to the extent necessary to recoup any amount that was erroneous when paid).

(11) In this subsection, the term "dependent child", with respect to a member or former member of the armed forces referred to in paragraph (2)(A), means an unmarried legitimate child, including an adopted child or a stepchild of the member or former member, who—

(A) is under 18 years of age;

(B) is incapable of self-support because of a mental or physical incapacity that existed before becoming 18 years of age and is dependent on the member or former member for over one-half of the child's support; or

(C) if enrolled in a full-time course of study in an institution of higher education recognized by the Secretary of Defense for the purposes of this subparagraph, is under 23 years of age and is dependent on the member or former member for over one-half of the child's support.

(i) Certification date.

It is not necessary that the date of a certification of the authenticity or completeness of a copy of a court order for child support received by the Secretary concerned for the purposes of this section be recent in relation to the date of receipt by the Secretary.

(j) Regulations.

The Secretaries concerned shall prescribe uniform regulations for the administration of this section.

(k) Relationship to other laws.

In any case involving an order providing for payment of child support (as defined in section 459(i)(2) of the Social Security Act [42 U.S.C.S. § 659(i)(2)]) by a member who has never been married to the other parent of the child, the provisions of this section shall not apply, and the case shall be subject to the provisions of section 459 of such Act [42 U.S.C.S. § 659].

HISTORY: (Added Sept. 8, 1982, P.L. 97-252, Title X, § 1002(a), 96 Stat. 730; Oct. 19, 1984, P.L. 98-525, Title VI, Part E, § 643(a)–(d), 98 Stat. 2547.) (As amended Nov. 14, 1986, P.L. 99-661, Div. A, Title VI, Part D, § 644(a), 100 Stat. 3887; April 21, 1987, P.L. 100-26, §§ 3(3) in part,

7(h)(1) in part, 101 Stat. 273, 282; Nov. 29, 1989, P.L. 101-189, Div. A, Title VI, Part F, § 653(a)(5), Title XVI, Part C, § 1622(e)(6), 103 Stat. 1462, 1605; Nov. 5, 1990, P.L. 101-510, Div. A, Title V, Part E, § 555(a)–(d), (f), (g), 104 Stat. 1569, 1570; Dec. 5, 1991, P.L. 102-190, Div. A, Title X, Part E, § 1061(a)(7), 105 Stat. 1472; Oct. 23, 1992, P.L. 102-484, Div. A, Title VI, Subtitle E, § 653(a), 106 Stat. 2426; Nov. 30, 1993, P.L. 103-160, Div. A, Title V, Subtitle E, § 555(a), (b), Title XI, Subtitle H, § 1182(a)(2), 107 Stat. 1666, 1771; Feb. 10, 1996, P.L. 104-106; Div. A, Title XV, § 1501(c)(16), 110 Stat. 499; Aug. 22, 1996, P.L. 104-193, Title III, Subtitle G, §§ 362(c), 363(c)(1)-(3), 110 Stat. 2246, 2249; Sept. 23, 1996, P.L. 104-201, Div. A, Title VI, Subtitle D, § 636, 110 Stat. 2579.)

Appendix C

32 C.F.R. §§ 63.1–63.6

Section 63.1 Purpose.

Under 10 U.S.C. 1408, this part establishes policy and authorizes direct payments to a former spouse of a member from retired pay in response to court-ordered alimony, child support, or division of property.

Section 63.2 Applicability and scope.

(a) This part applies to the Office of the Secretary of Defense, the Military Departments, the Coast Guard (under agreement with the Department of Transportation), the Public Health Service (PHS) (under agreement with the Department of Health and Human Services), and the National Oceanic and Atmospheric Administration (NOAA) (under agreement with the Department of Commerce). The term "Uniformed Services," as used herein, refers to the Army, Navy, Air Force, Marine Corps, Coast Guard, commissioned corps of the PHS, and the commissioned corps of the NOAA.

(b) This subpart covers members retired from the active and reserve components of the Uniformed Services who are subject to court orders awarding alimony, child support, or division of property.

Section 63.3 Definitions.

(a) Alimony. Periodic payments for the support and maintenance of a spouse or former spouse in accordance with State law under 42 U.S.C. 662(c). It includes, but is not limited to, spousal support, separate maintenance, and maintenance. Alimony does not include any payment for the division of property.

(b) Annuitant. A person receiving a monthly payment under a survivor benefit plan related to retired pay.

(c) Child support. Periodic payments for the support and maintenance of a child or children, subject to and in accordance with State law under 41 U.S.C. 662(b). It includes, but is not limited to, payments to provide for health care, education, recreation, and clothing or to meet other specific needs of such a child or children.

(d) Court. Any court of competent jurisdiction of any State, the District of Columbia, the Commonwealth of Puerto Rico, Guam, American Samoa, the Virgin Islands, the Northern Mariana Islands, and the Trust Territory of the Pacific Islands and any court of the United States as defined in 28 U.S.C. 451 having competent jurisdiction; or any court of competent jurisdiction of a foreign country with which the United States has an agreement requiring the United States to honor any court order of such country.

(e) Court order. As defined under 10 U.S.C. 1408(a)(2), a final decree of divorce, dissolution, annulment, or legal separation issued by a court, or a court ordered ratified, or approved property settlement incident to such a decree. It includes a final decree modifying the terms of a previously issued decree of divorce, dissolution, annulment, or legal separation, or a court ordered, ratified, or approved property settlement incident to such previously issued decree. The court order must provide for the payment to a member's former spouse of alimony, child support, or a division of property. In the case of a division of property, the court order must specify that the payment is to be made from the member's disposable retired pay.

(f) Creditable service. Service counted towards the establishment of any entitlement for retired pay. See paragraphs 10102 through 10108 of DOD 1340.12-M, 42 U.S.C. 212 for the PHS, and 33 U.S.C. 864 and 10 U.S.C. 6323 for NOAA.

(g) Designated agent. A representative of the Uniformed Service who will receive and process court orders under this part.

(h) Division of property. Any transfer of property or its value by an individual to his or her former spouse in compliance with any community property settlement, equitable distribution of property, or other distribution of property between spouses or former spouses.

(i) Entitlement. The legal right of a member to receive retired pay.

(j) Final decree. As defined under 10 U.S.C. 1408(a)(3), a decree from which no appeal may be taken or from which no appeal has been taken within the time allowed for taking such appeals under the laws applicable to such appeals or a decree from which timely appeal has been taken and such appeal has been finally decided under the laws applicable to such appeals.

(k) Former spouse. The former husband or former wife, or the husband or wife, or a member.

(l) Garnishment. The legal procedure through which payment is made from an individual's pay that is due or payable to another party in order to satisfy a legal obligation to provide child support, to make alimony payments, or both, under 5 C.F.R. Part 58 and 42 U.S.C. 659 or to enforce a division of property other than a division of retired pay as property under 10 U.S.C. 1408(d)(5).

(m) Member. A person originally appointed or enlisted in, or conscripted into, a Uniformed Service who has retired from the regular or reserve component of the Uniformed Service concerned.

(n) Renounced pay. Retired pay to which a member has an entitlement, but for which receipt of payment has been waived by the member.

(o) Retired pay. The gross entitlement due a member based on conditions of the retirement law, pay grade, years of service for basic pay, years of service for percentage multiplier, if applicable, and date of retirement (transfer to the Fleet Reserve or Fleet Marine Corps Reserve); also known as retainer pay.

Section 63.4 Policy.

It is the policy of the Uniformed Services to honor a former spouse's request for direct payment from a given member's retired pay in enforcement of a court order that provides for alimony, child support, or division of property, when the terms, conditions, and requirements in this part are satisfied.

Section 63.5 Responsibilities.

(a) The Assistant Secretary of Defense (Comptroller) shall establish policy and procedures, provide guidance, coordinate changes with the Uniformed Services, and monitor the implementation of this part within the Department of Defense.

(b) The Secretaries of the Military Departments and Heads of the other Uniformed Services shall implement this part.

Section 63.6 Procedures.

(a) Eligibility of former spouse.

(1) A former spouse of a member is eligible to receive direct payment from the retired pay of that member only pursuant to a court order that satisfies the requirements and conditions specified in this part. In the case of a division of property, the court order must specifically provide that payment is to be made from disposable retired pay.

(2) For establishing eligibility for direct payment under a court order that provides for a division of retired pay as property, a former

spouse must have been married to the member for 10 years or more, during which the member performed 10 years or more of creditable service. There is no 10-year marriage requirement for payment of child support, alimony, or both.

(b) Application by former spouse.

(1) A former spouse shall deliver to the designated agent of the member's Uniformed Service a signed DD Form 2293, Request for Former Spouse Payments from Retired Pay, or a signed statement that includes:

(i) Notice to make direct payment to the former spouse from the member's retired pay.

(ii) A copy of the court order and other accompanying documents certified by an official of the issuing court that provides for payment of child support, alimony, or division of property.

(iii) A statement that the court order has not been amended, superseded, or set aside.

(iv) Sufficient identifying information about the member to enable processing of the application. The identification should give the member's full name, social security number, and Uniformed Service.

(v) The full name, address, and social security number of the former spouse.

(vi) Before payment, the former spouse shall agree personally that any future overpayments are recoverable and subject to involuntary collection from the former spouse or his or her estate.

(vii) As a condition precedent to payment, the former spouse shall agree personally to notify the designated agent promptly if the operative court order upon which payment is based is vacated, modified, or set aside. This shall include notice of the former spouse's remarriage if all or part of the payment is for alimony or notice of a change in eligibility for child support payments under circumstances of the death, emancipation, adoption, or attainment of majority of a child whose support is provided through direct payment to a former spouse from retired pay.

(2) If the court order is for a division of retired pay as property and it does not state that the former spouse satisfied the eligibility criteria found in paragraph (a)(2) of this section, the former spouse shall furnish sufficient evidence for the designated agent to verify that the requirement was met.

(3) The notification of the designated agent shall be accompanied by certified or registered mail, return receipt requested, or by personal

service. Effective service is not accomplished until a complete application providing all information required by this part is received in the office of the designated agent, who shall note the date and time of receipt on the notification document.

(4) Not later than 90 days after effective service, the designated agent shall respond to the former spouse as follows: (I) If the court order will be honored, the former spouse shall be informed of the date that payments tentatively begin; the amount of each payment; the amount of gross retired pay, total deductions, and disposable retired pay (except in cases where full payment of a court-ordered fixed amount will be made); and other relevant information if applicable: or (ii) If the court order will not be honored, the designated agent shall explain in writing to the former spouse why the court order was not honored.

(5) The designated agent for each Uniformed Service is:

(i) Army: Commander, Army Finance and Accounting Center, Attention: FINCL-G, Indianapolis, IN 46249-0160, (317) 542-2155.

(ii) Navy: Director, Navy Family Allowance Activity, Anthony J. Celebrezze Federal Building, Cleveland, OH 44199-2087, (216) 522-5301.

(iii) Air Force: Commander, Air Force Accounting and Finance Center, Attention: JAL, Denver, CO 80279-5000, (303) 370-7524.

(iv) Marine Corps: Commanding Officer, Marine Corps Finance Center (Code AA), Kansas City, MO 64197-0001, (816) 926-7103.

(v) U.S. Coast Guard, Commanding Officer (L), Pay and Personnel Center, 444 Quincy Street, Topeka, Kansas 66683-3591; (139) 295-2516.

(vi) Office of General Counsel, Department of Health and Human Services, Room 5362, 330 Independence Avenue S.W., Washington, DC 20201, (202) 475-0153.

(vii) U.S. Coast Guard, Commanding Officer (L), Pay and Personnel Center, 444 Quincy Street, Topeka, Kansas 66683-3591, (913) 295-2516.

(6) U.S. Attorneys are not designated agents authorized to receive court orders or garnishments under this part.

(c) Review of Court Orders.

(1) The court order must be regular on its face, meaning that it is issued by a court of competent jurisdiction in accordance with the laws of the jurisdiction.

(2) The court order must be legal in form and must include nothing on its face that provides reasonable notice that it is issued without

authority of law. It is required that the court order be authenticated or certified within 90 days immediately preceding its service on the designated agent.

(3) The court order must be a final decree.

(4) If the court order was issued while the member was on active duty and the member was not represented in court, the court order or other court documents must certify that the rights of the member under the "Soldiers' and Sailors' Civil Relief Act of 1940" (50 U.S.C. Appendix 501-5910) were complied with.

(5) Sufficient information must be contained in the court order to identify the member.

(6) For court orders that provide for the division of retired pay as property, the following conditions apply:

(i) The court must have jurisdiction over the member by reason of (A) the member's residence, other than because of military assignment in the territorial jurisdiction of the court; (B) the member's domicile in the territorial jurisdiction of the court; or (C) the member's consent to the jurisdiction of the court.

(ii) The treatment of retired pay as property solely of the member or as property of the member and the former spouse of that member must be in accordance with the law of the jurisdiction of such court.

(iii) The court order or other accompanying documents served with the court order must show the former spouse was married to the member 10 years or more, during which the member performed at least 10 years of creditable service.

(7) Court orders awarding a division of retired pay as property that were issued before June 26, 1981, shall be honored if they otherwise satisfy the requirements and conditions specified in this part. A modification on or after June 26, 1981, of a court order that originally awarded a division of retired pay as property before June 26, 1981, may be honored for subsequent court-ordered changes made for clarification, such as the interpretation of a computation formula in the original court order. For court orders issued before June 26, 1981, subsequent amendments after that date to provide for a division of retired pay as property are unenforceable under this part. If the court order awarding a division of retired pay as property is issued on or after June 26, 1981, subsequent modifications of that court order shall be honored if they otherwise satisfy the requirements and conditions specified in this part.

(8) In the case of a division of property, the court must provide specifically for payment of a fixed amount expressed in U.S. dollars or

payment as a percentage or fraction of disposable retired pay. Court orders specifying a percentage or fraction of retired pay shall be construed as a percentage or fraction of disposable retired pay. A court order that provided for a division of retired pay by means of a formula wherein the elements of the formula are not specifically set forth or readily apparent on the face of the court order will not be honored unless clarified by the court.

(d) Garnishment Orders.

(1) If a court order provides for the division of property other than retired pay in addition to the amount of disposable retired pay to be paid to the member's former spouse, the former spouse may garnish that member's retired pay in order to enforce the division of property. The limitations of 15 U.S.C. 1673(a) and the limitations of Section 63.6(e) of this part apply in determining the amount payable to a former spouse.

(2) The designated agents authorized to receive service of process of garnishment orders under this party shall be those listed in Section 63.6(b)(5) of this part.

(3) Garnishment orders under this part for enforcement of a division of property other than retired pay shall be processed in accordance with 5 C.F.R. Part 581 to the extent that the procedures are consistent with this part.

(e) Limitation.

(1) Upon proper service, a member's retired pay may be paid directly to a former spouse in the amount necessary to comply with the court order, provided the total amount paid does not exceed:

(i) 50 percent of the disposable retired pay for all court orders and garnishment actions paid under this part.

(ii) 65 percent of the disposable retired pay for all court orders and garnishments paid under this part and garnishments under 42 U.S.C. 659.

(2) Disposable retired pay is the gross pay entitlement, including renounced pay, less authorized deductions. Disposable retired pay does not include annuitant payments under 10 U.S.C. Chapter 73. For court orders issued on or before November 14, 1986 (or amendments thereto), disposable retired does not include retired pay of a member retired for disability under 10 U.S.C. Chapter 61. The authorized deductions are:

(i) Amounts owed to the United States.

(ii) Fines and forfeitures ordered by a court-martial.

(iii) Amounts waived in order to receive compensation under title 5 or 38 of the U.S. Code.

(iv) Federal employment taxes and income taxes withheld to the extent that the amount deducted is consistent with the member's tax liability, including amounts for supplemental withholding under 26 U.S.C. 3402(I), when the member presents evidence to the satisfaction of the designated agent that supports such withholding. State employment taxes and income taxes when the member makes a voluntary request for such withholding from retired pay and the Uniformed Services have entered into an agreement with the State concerned for withholding from retired pay.

(v) Premiums paid as a result of an election under 10 U.S.C. Chapter 73 to provide an annuity to a spouse or former spouse to whom payment of a portion of such member's retired pay is being made pursuant to a court order under this part.

(vi) The amount of retired pay of the member under 10 U.S.C. Chapter 61 computed using the percentage of the member's disability on the date, when the member was retired (or the date on which the member's name was placed on the temporary disability retirement list), for court orders issued after November 14, 1986.

(vii) Other amounts required by law to be deducted.

(f) Notification of Member.

(1) As soon as possible, but not later than 30 calendar days after effective service of a court order or garnishment action under this part, the designated agent shall send written notice to the affected member at his or her last known address.

(2) This notice shall include:

(i) A copy of the court order and accompanying documentation.

(ii) An explanation of the limitations placed on the direct payment to a former spouse from a member's retired pay.

(iii) A request that the member submit notification to the designated agent if the court order has been amended, superseded, or set aside. The member is obligated to provide an authenticated or certified copy of the operative court documents when there are conflicting court orders.

(iv) The amount or percentage that will be deducted if the member fails to respond to the notification as prescribed by this part.

(v) The effective date that direct payments to the former spouse tentatively will begin.

(vi) Notice that the member's failure to respond within 30 days from the date that the notice is mailed may result in the payment of retired pay as provided in the notification.

(vii) That if the member submits information in response to this notification, the member thereby consents to the disclosure of such information to the former spouse or the former spouse's agent.

(3) If the member responds to the notification, the designated agent shall consider the response and will not honor the court order whenever it is shown that the court order is defective, or the court order is modified, superseded, or set aside.

(g) Designated agent liability.

(1) The United States and any officer or employee of the United States will not be liable with respect to any payment made from retired pay to any member or former spouse pursuant to a court order that is regular on its face if such payment is made in accordance with this Part.

(2) An officer or employee of the United States, who under this part has the duty to respond to interrogatories, will not be subject under any law to any disciplinary action or civil or criminal liability or penalty for, or because of, any disclosure or information made by him or her in carrying out any of the duties that directly or indirectly pertain to answering such interrogatories.

(3) If a court order on its face appears to conform to the laws of the jurisdiction from which it was issued, the designated agent will not be required to ascertain whether the court has obtained personal jurisdiction over the member.

(4) Whenever a designated agent is effectively served with interrogatories concerning implementation of this part, the designated agent shall respond to such interrogatories within 30 calendar days of receipt or within such longer period as may be prescribed by applicable State law.

(h) Payments.

(1) Subject to a member's eligibility for retired pay, effective service of a court order, and the limitations and requirements of this part, the Uniformed Service concerned shall begin payments to the former spouse not later than 90 days after the date of effective service.

(2) Payments shall conform with the normal pay and disbursement cycle for retired pay. Payments may be expressed as fixed in amount or as a percentage or fraction of disposable retired pay. With regard to payments based on a percentage or fraction of disposable retired pay, the amount will change in direct proportion and at the effective date of future cost-of-living adjustments that are authorized, unless the court order directs otherwise.

(3) Payments terminate on the date of the death of the member, death of the former spouse, or as stated in the applicable court order,

whichever occurs first. Payments shall be terminated or shall be reduced upon the occurrence of a condition that requires termination or reduction under applicable State law.

(4) When several court orders are served with regard to a member's retired pay, payment shall be satisfied on a first-come, first-served basis within the amount limitations prescribed in paragraph (e) of this section.

(5) If conflicting court orders are served on the designated agent that direct that different amounts be paid during a month to the same former spouse from a given member's retired pay, the designated agent shall authorize payment on the court order directing payment of the least amount. The difference in amounts on conflicting court orders shall be retained by the designated agent pending resolution by the court that has jurisdiction or by agreement of the parties. The amount retained shall be paid as provided in a subsequent court order or agreement. The total of all payments plus all moneys retained under this paragraph shall be within the limitation prescribed in paragraph (e) of this section.

(6) The designated agent shall comply with a stay of execution issued by a court of competent jurisdiction and shall suspend payment of disputed amounts pending resolution of the issue.

(7) When service is made and the identified member is found not to be currently entitled to payments the designated agent shall advise the former spouse that no payments are due from or payable by the Uniformed Service to the named individual. If the member is on active duty when service is accomplished, the designated agent shall retain the application until the member's retirement. In such case, payments to the former spouse, if otherwise proper, shall begin not later than 90 days from the date the member first becomes entitled to receive retired pay. If the member becomes entitled to receive retired pay more than 90 days after first being notified under paragraph (f) of this section, the notification procedures prescribed by that section shall be repeated by the designated agent.

(8) If moneys are only temporarily exhausted or otherwise unavailable, the former spouse shall be fully advised of the reason or reasons why and for how long the moneys will be unavailable. Service shall be retained by the designated agent and payments to the former spouse, if otherwise proper, shall begin not later than 90 days from the date the member becomes entitled to receive retired pay. If the member becomes entitled to receive retired pay more than 90 days after first being notified under paragraph (f) of this section, the notification procedures prescribed by that section shall be repeated by the designated agent.

(9) The order of precedence for disbursement of retired pay when the gross amount is not sufficient to permit all authorized deductions and collection shall follow Volume I, Part 3, Section 7040, "Order of Payment," in the Treasury Fiscal Requirements Manual for Guidance of Departments and Agencies. Court-ordered payments to a former spouse from retired pay shall be enforced over voluntary deductions and allotments.

(10) Payments made shall be prospective in terms of the amount stated in the court order. Arrearages will not be considered in determining the amount payable from retired pay.

(11) No right, title, or interest that can be sold, assigned, transferred, or otherwise disposed of, including by inheritance, is created under this part.

(12) At the request of the designated agent, the former spouse may be required to provide a certification of eligibility that attests in writing to the former spouse's continued eligibility and that includes a notice of change in status or circumstances that affect eligibility. After notice to the former spouse, payments to the former spouse may be suspended, or terminated, when the former spouse fails to comply, or refuses to comply, with the certification requirement.

(i) Reconsideration. A former spouse or member may request that the designated agent reconsider the designated agent's determination in response to service of an application for payments under this part or the member's answer to the designated agent with respect to notice of such service. For reconsideration, the request must express the issues the former spouse or the member believes are incorrectly resolved by the agent. The designated agent shall respond to the request for reconsideration, giving an explanation of the determination reached.

Appendix D

§ 63.6 Procedures

(a) Eligibility of former spouse.

(1) A former spouse of a member is eligible to receive direct payment from the retired pay of that member only pursuant to a court order that satisfies the requirements and conditions specified in this part. In the case of a division of property, the court order must specifically provide that payment is to be made from disposable retired pay.

(2) For establishing eligibility for direct payment under a court order that provides for a division of retired pay as property, a former spouse must have been married to the member for 10 years or more, during which the member performed 10 years or more of creditable service. There is no 10-year marriage requirement for payment of child support, alimony, or both.

(b) Application by former spouse.

(1) A former spouse shall deliver to the designated agent of the member's Uniformed Service a signed DD Form 2293, Request for Former Spouse Payments from Retired Pay, or a signed statement that includes:

(i) Notice to make direct payment to the former spouse from the member's retired pay.

(ii) A copy of the court order and other accompanying documents certified by an official of the issuing court that provides for payment of child support, alimony, or division of property.

(iii) A statement that the court order has not been amended, superseded, or set aside.

(iv) Sufficient identifying information about the member to enable processing of the application. The identification should give the member's full name, social security number, and Uniformed Service.

(v) The full name, address, and social security number of the former spouse.

(vi) Before payment, the former spouse shall agree personally that any future overpayments are recoverable and subject to involuntary collection from the former spouse or his or her estate.

(vii) As a condition precedent to payment, the former spouse shall agree personally to notify the designated agent promptly if the operative court order upon which payment is based is vacated, modified, or set aside. This shall include notice of the former spouse's remarriage if all or a part of the payment is for alimony or notice of a change in eligibility for child support payments under circumstances of the death, emancipation, adoption, or attainment of majority of a child whose support is provided through direct payment to a former spouse from retired pay.

(2) It the court order is for a division of retired pay as property and it does not state that the former spouse satisfied the eligibility criteria found in paragraph (a)(2) of this section, the former spouse shall furnish sufficient evidence for the designated agent to verify that the requirement was met.

(3) The notification of the designated agent shall be accomplished by certified or registered mail, return receipt requested, or by personal service. Effective service is not accomplished until a complete application providing all information required by this part is received in the office of the designated agent, who shall note the date and time of receipt on the notification document.

(4) Not later than 90 days after effective service, the designated agent shall respond to the former spouse as follows: (i) If the court order will be honored, the former spouse shall be informed of the date that payments tentatively begin; the amount of each payment; the amount of gross retired pay, total deductions, and disposable retired pay (except in cases where full payment of a court-ordered fixed amount will be made); and other relevant information if applicable: or (ii) If the court order will not be honored, the designated agent shall explain in writing to the former spouse why the court order was not honored.

(5) The designated agent for each Uniformed Service is:

(i) Army: Commander, Army Finance and Accounting Center, Attn: FINCL-G, Indianapolis, IN 46249-0160, (317) 542-2155.

(ii) Navy: Director, Navy Family Allowance Activity, Anthony J. Celebrezze Federal Building, Cleveland, OH 44199-2087, (216) 522-5301.

(iii) Air Force: Commander, Air Force Accounting and Finance Center, ATTN: JAL, Denver, CO 80279-5000, (303) 370-7524.

(iv) Marine Corps: Commanding Officer, Marine Corps Finance Center (Code AA), Kansas City, MO 64197-0001, (816) 926-7103.

(v) U.S. Coast Guard, Commanding Officer (L), Pay and Personnel Center, 444 Quincy Street, Topeka, Kansas 66683-3591; (913) 295-2516.

(vi) Office of General Counsel, Department of Health and Human Services, Room 5362, 330 Independence Avenue SW., Washington, DC 20201, (202) 475-0153.

(vii) U.S. Coast Guard, Commanding Officer (L), Pay and Personnel Center, 444 Quincy Street, Topeka, Kansas 66683-3591; (913) 295-2516.

(6) U.S. Attorneys are not designated agents authorized to receive court orders or garnishments under this part.

(c) Review of Court Orders.

(1) The court order must be regular on its face, meaning that it is issued by a court of competent jurisdiction in accordance with the laws of the jurisdiction.

(2) The court order must be legal in form and must include nothing on its face that provides reasonable notice that it is issued without authority of law. It is required that the court order be authenticated or certified within 90 days immediately preceding its service on the designated agent.

(3) The court order must be a final decree.

(4) If the court order was issued while the member was on active duty and the member was not represented in court, the court order or other court documents must certify that the rights of the member under the "Soldiers' and Sailors' Civil Relief Act of 1940" (50 U.S.C. Appendix 501-591) were complied with.

(5) Sufficient information must be contained in the court order to identify the member.

(6) For court orders that provide for the division of retired pay as property, the following conditions apply:

(i) The court must have jurisdiction over the member by reason of (A) the member's residence, other than because of military assignment in the territorial jurisdiction of the court; (B) the member's domicile in the territorial jurisdiction of the court; or (C) the member's consent to the jurisdiction of the court.

(ii) The treatment of retired pay as property solely of the member or as property of the member and the former spouse of that member must be in accordance with the law of the jurisdiction of such court.

(iii) The court order or other accompanying documents served with the court order must show the former spouse was married to the member 10 years or more, during which the member performed at least 10 years of creditable service.

(7) Court orders awarding a division of retired pay as property that were issued before June 26, 1981, shall be honored if they otherwise satisfy the requirements and conditions specified in this part. A modification on or after June 26, 1981, of a court order that originally awarded a division of retired pay as property before June 26, 1981, may be honored for subsequent court-ordered changes made for clarification, such as the interpretation of a computation formula in the original court order. For court orders issued before June 26, 1981, subsequent amendments after that date to provide for a division of retired pay as property are unenforceable under this part. If the court order awarding a division of retired pay as property is issued on or after June 26, 1981, subsequent modifications of that court order shall be honored if they otherwise satisfy the requirements and conditions specified in this part.

(8) In the case of a division of property, the court order must provide specifically for payment of a fixed amount expressed in U.S. dollars or payment as a percentage or fraction of disposable retired pay. Court orders specifying a percentage or fraction of retired pay shall be construed as a percentage or fraction of disposable retired pay. A court order that provides for a division of retired pay by means of a formula wherein the elements of the formula are not specifically set forth or readily apparent on the face of the court order will not be honored unless clarified by the court.

(d) Garnishment Orders.

(1) If a court order provides for the division of property other than retired pay in addition to an amount of disposable retired pay to be paid to the member's former spouse, the former spouse may garnish that member's retired pay in order to enforce the division of property. The limitations of 15 U.S.C. 1673(a) and the limitations of § 63.6(e) of this part apply in determining the amount payable to a former spouse.

(2) The designated agents authorized to receive service of process of garnishment orders under this part shall be those listed in § 63.6(b)(5) of this part.

(3) Garnishment orders under this part for enforcement of a division of property other than retired pay shall be processed in accordance with 5 CFR Part 581 to the extent that the procedures are consistent with this part.

(e) Limitations.

(1) Upon proper service, a member's retired pay may be paid directly to a former spouse in the amount necessary to comply with the court order, provided the total amount paid does not exceed:

(i) 50 percent of the disposable retired pay for all court orders and garnishment actions paid under this part.

(ii) 65 percent of the disposable retired pay for all court orders and garnishments paid under this part and garnishments under 42 U.S.C. 659.

(2) Disposable retired pay is the gross pay entitlement, including renounced pay, less authorized deductions. Disposable retired pay does not include annuitant payments under 10 U.S.C. Chapter 73. For court orders issued on or before November 14, 1986 (or amendments thereto), disposable retired does not include retired pay of a member retired for disability under 10 U.S.C. Chapter 61. The authorized deductions are:

(i) Amounts owed to the United States.

(ii) Fines and forfeitures ordered by a court-martial.

(iii) Amounts waived in order to receive compensation under title 5 or 38 of the U.S. Code.

(iv) Federal employment taxes and income taxes withheld to the extent that the amount deducted is consistent with the member's tax liability, including amounts for supplemental withholding under 26 U.S.C. 3402(i), when the member presents evidence to the satisfaction of the designated agent that supports such withholding. State employment taxes and income taxes when the member makes a voluntary request for such withholding from retired pay and the Uniformed Services have entered into an agreement with the State concerned for withholding from retired pay.

(v) Premiums paid as a result of a election under 10 U.S.C. Chapter 73 to provide an annuity to a spouse or former spouse to whom payment of a portion of such member's retired pay is being made pursuant to a court order under this part.

(vi) The amount of retired pay of the member under 10 U.S.C. Chapter 61 computed using the percentage of the member's disability on the date, when the member was retired (or the date on which the member's name was placed on the temporary disability retirement list), for court orders issued after November 14, 1986.

(vii) Other amounts required by law to be deducted.

(f) Notification of Member.

(1) As soon as possible, but not later than 30 calendar days after effective service of a court order or garnishment action under this part, the designated agent shall send written notice to the affected member at his or her last known address.

(2) This notice shall include:

(i) A copy of the court order and accompanying documentation.

(ii) An explanation of the limitations placed on the direct payment to a former spouse from a member's retired pay.

(iii) A request that the member submit notification to the designated agent if the court order has been amended, superseded, or set aside. The member is obligated to provide an authenticated or certified copy of the operative court documents when there are conflicting court orders.

(iv) The amount or percentage that will be deducted if the member fails to respond to the notification as prescribed by this part.

(v) The effective date that direct payments to the former spouse tentatively will begin.

(vi) Notice that the member's failure to respond within 30 days from the date that the notice is mailed may result in the payment of retired pay as provided in the notification.

(vii) That if the member submits information in response to this notification, the member thereby consents to the disclosure of such information to the former spouse or the former spouse's agent.

(3) If the member responds to the notification, the designated agent shall consider the response and will not honor the court order whenever it is shown that the court order is defective, or the court order is modified, superseded, or set aside.

(g) Designated agent liability.

(1) The United States and any officer or employee of the United States will not be liable with respect to any payment made from retired pay to any member or former spouse pursuant to a court order that is regular on its face if such payment is made in accordance with this Part.

(2) An officer or employee of the United States, who under this part has the duty to respond to interrogatories, will not be subject under any law to any disciplinary action or civil or criminal liability or penalty for, or because of, any disclosure of information made by him or her in carrying out any of the duties that directly or indirectly pertain to answering such interrogatories.

(3) If a court order on its face appears to conform to the laws of the jurisdiction from which it was issued, the designated agent will not

be required to ascertain whether the court has obtained personal jurisdiction over the member.

(4) Whenever a designated agent is effectively served with interrogatories concerning implementation of this part, the designated agent shall respond to such interrogatories within 30 calendar days of receipt or within such longer period as may be prescribed by applicable State law.

(h) Payments.

(1) Subject to a member's eligibility for retired pay, effective service of a court order, and the limitations and requirements of this part, the Uniformed Service concerned shall begin payments to the former spouse not later than 90 days after the date of effective service.

(2) Payments shall conform with the normal pay and disbursement cycle for retired pay. Payments may be expressed as fixed in amount or as a percentage or fraction of disposable retired pay. With regard to payments based on a percentage or fraction of disposable retired pay, the amount will change in direct proportion and at the effective date of future cost-of-living adjustments that are authorized, unless the court order directs otherwise.

(3) Payments terminate on the date of the death of the member, death of the former spouse, or as stated in the applicable court order, whichever occurs first. Payments shall be terminated or shall be reduced upon the occurrence of a condition that requires termination or reduction under applicable State law.

(4) When several court orders are served with regard to a member's retired pay, payment shall be satisfied on a first-come, first-served basis within the amount limitations prescribed in paragraph (e) of this section.

(5) If conflicting court orders are served on the designated agent that direct that different amounts be paid during a month to the same former spouse from a given member's retired pay, the designated agent shall authorize payment on the court order directing payment of the least amount. The difference in amounts on conflicting court orders shall be retained by the designated agent pending resolution by the court that has jurisdiction or by agreement of the parties. The amount retained shall be paid as provided in a subsequent court order or agreement. The total of all payments plus all moneys retained under this paragraph shall be within the limitation prescribed in paragraph (e) of this section.

(6) The designated agent shall comply with a stay of execution issued by a court of competent jurisdiction and shall suspend payment of disputed amounts pending resolution of the issue.

(7) When service is made and the identified member is found not to be currently entitled to payments the designated agent shall advise the former spouse that no payments are due from or payable by the Uniformed Service to the named individual. If the member is on active duty when service is accomplished, the designated agent shall retain the application until the member's retirement. In such case, payments to the former spouse, if otherwise proper, shall begin not later than 90 days from the date the member first becomes entitled to receive retired pay. If the member becomes entitled to receive retired pay more than 90 days after first being notified under paragraph (f) of this section, the notification procedures prescribed by that section shall be repeated by the designated agent.

(8) If moneys are only temporarily exhausted or otherwise unavailable, the former spouse shall be fully advised of the reason or reasons why and for how long the moneys will be unavailable. Service shall be retained by the designated agent and payments to the former spouse, if otherwise proper, shall begin not later than 90 days from the date the member becomes entitled to receive retired pay. If the member becomes entitled to receive retired pay more than 90 days after first being notified under paragraph (f) of this section, the notification procedures prescribed by that section shall be repeated by the designated agent.

(9) The order of precedence for disbursement of retired pay when the gross amount is not sufficient to permit all authorized deductions and collections shall follow Volume I, Part 3, Section 7040, "Order of Payment," in the Treasury Fiscal Requirements Manual for Guidance of Departments and Agencies. Court-ordered payments to a former spouse from retired pay shall be enforced over voluntary deductions and allotments.

(10) Payments made shall be prospective in terms of the amount stated in the court order. Arrearages will not be considered in determining the amount payable from retired pay.

(11) No right, title, or interest that can be sold, assigned, transferred, or otherwise disposed of, including by inheritance, is created under this part.

(12) At the request of the designated agent, the former spouse may be required to provide a certification of eligibility that attests in writing to the former spouse's continued eligibility and that includes a notice of change in status or circumstances that affect eligibility. After notice to the former spouse, payments to the former spouse may be suspended, or terminated, when the former spouse fails to comply, or refuses to comply, with the certification requirement.

(i) Reconsideration. A former spouse or member may request that the designated agent reconsider the designated agent's determination in response to service of an application for payments under this part or the member's answer to the designated agent with respect to notice of such service. For reconsideration, the request must express the issues the former spouse or the member believes were incorrectly resolved by the designated agent. The designated agent shall respond to the request for reconsideration, giving an explanation of the determination reached.

(Approved by the Office of Management and Budget under control numbers 0704-0160 and 0704-0182)

HISTORY:

[50 FR 2667, Jan. 18, 1985, as amended at 52 FR 25215, July 6, 1987]

Appendix E

The Military Retirement System: Statutory Provisions

10 U.S.C. § 1062

§ 1062. Certain former spouses

The Secretary of Defense shall prescribe such regulations as may be necessary to provide that an unremarried former spouse described in subparagraph (F)(i) of section 1072(2) of this title is entitled to commissary and exchange privileges to the same extent and on the same basis as the surviving spouse of a retired member of the uniformed services.
(Added Pub. L. 100-370, § 1(c)(1), July 19, 1988, 102 Stat. 841.)

10 U.S.C. § 1072

§ 1072. Definitions
In this chapter:

(1) The term "uniformed services" means the armed forces and the Commissioned Corps of the National Oceanic and Atmospheric Administration and of the Public Health Service.
(2) The term "dependent," with respect to a member or former member of a uniformed service, means—
 (A) the spouse;
 (B) the unremarried widow;
 (C) the unremarried widower;
 (D) an unmarried legitimate child, including an adopted child or a stepchild, who either—
  (i) has not passed his twenty-first birthday;
  (ii) is incapable of self-support because of a mental or physical incapacity that existed before that birthday and is, or was at the time of the member's or former member's death, in fact, dependent on him for over one-half of his support; or

(iii) has not passed his twenty-third birthday, is enrolled in a full-time course of study in an institution of higher learning approved by the administering Secretary and is, or was at the time of the member's or former member's death, in fact dependent on him for over one-half of his support;

(E) a parent or parent-in-law who is, or was at the time of the member's or former member's death, in fact dependent on him for over one-half of his support and residing in his household; and

(F) the unremarried former spouse of a member or former member who (i) on the date of the final decree of divorce, dissolution, or annulment, had been married to the member or former member for a period of at least 20 years during which period the member or former member performed at least 20 years of service which is creditable in determining that member's or former member's eligibility for retired or retainer pay, or equivalent pay, and (ii) does not have medical coverage under an employer-sponsored health plan;

(G) a person who (i) is the unremarried former spouse of a member or former member who performed at least 20 years of service which is creditable in determining the member or former member's eligibility for retired or retainer pay, or equivalent pay, and on the date of the final decree of divorce, dissolution, or annulment before April 1, 1985, had been married to the member or former member for a period of at least 20 years, at least 15 of which, but less than 20 of which, were during which period the member or former member performed at least 20 years of service which is creditable in determining the member's or former member's eligibility for retired or retainer pay, and (ii) does not have medical coverage under an employer-sponsored health plan; and

(H) a person who would qualify as a dependent under clause (G) but for the fact that the date of the final decree of divorce, dissolution, or annulment of the person is on or after April 1, 1985, except that the term does not include the person after the end of the one-year period beginning on the date of that final decree.

(3) The term "administering Secretaries" means the Secretaries of

executive departments specified in section 1073 of this title as
having responsibility for administering this chapter.
(4) The term "Civilian Health and Medical Program of the Uniformed
Services" means the program authorized under sections 1079 and
1086 of this title and includes contracts entered into under section
1091 or 1097 of this title and demonstration projects under section
1092 of this title.
(5) The term "covered beneficiary" means a beneficiary under this
chapter other than a beneficiary under section 1074(a) of this title.

(As amended Pub. L. 98-525, Title VI, § 645(a), Oct. 19, 1984, 98 Stat.
2548; Pub. L. 98-557, § 19(1), Oct. 30, 1984, 98 Stat. 2869; Pub. L. 99-
661, Div. A, Title VII, § 701(b), Nov. 14, 1986, 100 Stat. 3898; Pub. L.
101-189, Div. A, Title VII, § 731(a), Nov. 29, 1989, 103 Stat. 1481.).

10 U.S.C. § 1447

§ 1447. Definitions
In this subchapter [10 U.S.C.S. §§ 1447 *et seq.*]:

(1) "Plan" means the Survivor Benefit Plan established by this subchapter [10 U.S.C.S. §§ 1447 *et seq.*].
(2) "Base amount" means—
(A) in the case of a person who dies after becoming entitled to
retired or retainer pay, the amount of monthly retired or retainer pay to which the person—
(i) was entitled when he became eligible for that pay; or
(ii) later became entitled by being advanced on the retired
list, performing active duty, or being transferred from the
temporary disability retired list to the permanent disability retired list;
(B) in the case of a person who would have become eligible for
retired pay under chapter 67 of this title [10 U.S.C.S. §§ 1331
et seq.] but for the fact that he died before becoming 60 years
of age, the amount of monthly retired pay for which the person would have been eligible—
(i) if he had been 60 years of age on the date of his death,
for purposes of an annuity to become effective on the day
after his death in accordance with a designation made

under section 1448(e) of this title [10 U.S.C.S. § 1448(e)]:
or

(ii) upon becoming 60 years of age (if he had lived to that
age), for purposes of an annuity to become effective on
the 60th anniversary of his birth in accordance with a
designation made under section 1448(e) of this title [10
U.S.C.S. § 1448(e)]: or

(C) any amount which is less than the amount otherwise applicable under clause (A) or (B) with respect to an annuity provided under the Plan but which is not less than $300 and
which is designated by the person (with the concurrence of
the person's spouse, if required under section 1448(a)(3) of
this title) [10 U.S.C.S. § 1448(a)(3)]) providing the annuity
on or before (i) the first day for which he becomes eligible
for retired or retainer pay, in the case of a person providing a
standard annuity, or (ii) the end of the 90-day period beginning on the date on which he receives the notification required
by section 1331(d) of this title [10 U.S.C.S. § 1331(d)] that
he has completed the year of service required for eligibility
for retired pay under chapter 67 of this [10 U.S.C.S. §§ 1331
et seq.], in case of a person providing a reserve-component
annuity.

(3) "Widower" means the surviving wife of a person who, if not married to the person at the time he became eligible for retired or
retainer pay—

(A) was married to him for at least one year immediately before
his death; or

(B) is the mother of issue by that marriage.

(4) "Widower" means the surviving husband of a person who, if not
married to the person at the time she became eligible for retired
or retainer pay—

(A) was married to her for at least one year immediately before
her death; or

(B) is the father of issue by the marriage.

(5) "Dependent child" means a person who is—

(A) unmarried;

(B)(i) under 18 years of age; (ii) at least 18, but under 22, years
of age and pursuing a full-time course of study or training in
a high school, trade school, technical or vocational institute,

junior college, college, university, or comparable recognized educational institution; or (iii) incapable of supporting himself because of a mental or physical incapacity existing before his eighteenth birthday or incurred on or after that birthday, but before his twenty-second birthday, while pursuing such a full-time course of study or training; and

(C) the child of a person to whom the Plan applies, including (i) an adopted child, and (ii) a stepchild, foster child, or recognized natural child who lived with that person in a regular parent-child relationship.

For the purpose of this clause, a child whose twenty-second birthday occurs before July 1 or after August 31 of a calendar year, and while he is regularly pursuing such a course of study or training, is considered to have become 22 years of age on the first day of July after that birthday. A child who is a student is considered not to have ceased to be a student during an interim between school years if the interim is not more than 150 days and if he shows to the satisfaction of the Secretary of Defense that he has a bona fide intention of continuing to pursue a course of study or training in the same or a different school during the school semester (or other period unto which the school year is divided) immediately after the interim. Under this clause, a foster child, to qualify as the dependent child of a person to whom the Plan applies, must, at the time of the death of that person, also reside with, and receive over one-half of his support from, that person, and not be cared for under a social agency contract. The temporary absence of a foster child from the residence of that person, while he is a student as described in this clause, will not be considered to affect the residence of such a foster child.

(6) "Former spouse" means the surviving former husband or wife of a person who is eligible to participate in the Plan.

(7) "Court" has the meaning given that term by section 1408(a)(1) of this title [10 U.S.C.S. § 1408(a)(1)].

(8) "Court order" means a court's final decree of divorce, dissolution, or annulment or a court ordered, ratified, or approved property settlement incident to such a decree (including a final decree modifying the terms of a previously issued decree of divorce, dissolution, or annulment or of a court ordered, ratified, or approved property settlement agreement incident to such previously issued decree).

(9) "Final decree" means a decree from which no appeal may be taken or from which no appeal has been taken within the time allowed for the taking of such appeals under the laws applicable to such appeal has been finally decided under the laws applicable to such appeals.

(10) "Regular on its face," when used in connection with a court order, means a court order that meets the conditions prescribed in section 1408(b)(2) of this title [10 U.S.C.S. § 1408(b)(2)].

(11) "Retired pay" includes retainer pay.

(12) "Standard annuity" means an annuity provided by virtue of eligibility under section 1448(a)(1)(A).

(13) "Reserve-component" means an annuity provided by virtue of eligibility under section 1448(a)(1)(B) of this title [10 U.S.C.S. § 1448(a)(1)(B)].

(Added Sept. 21, 1972, Pub. L. 92-425, § 1(3), 86 Stat. 706; Oct. 14, 1976, Pub. L. 94-949, § 11, 90 Stat. 2375; Sept. 30, 1978, Pub. L. 95-3333397, Title II, § 201, 92 Stat. 843; Oct. 9, 1980, Pub. L. 96-402, § 2, 94 Stat. 1705; Sept. 8, 1982, Pub. L. 97-252, Title X, § 100(a), 96 Stat. 735; Sept. 24, 1983, Pub. L. 98-94, Title IX, Part D, § 941(c)(1), 97 Stat. 653; Nov. 8, 1985, Pub. L. 99-145, Title VII. Part A. § 719(1),(2), Part B, § 721(b), 99 Stat. 675, 676.)

10 U.S.C. § 1448

§ 1448. Application of plan

(a)(1) The program established by this subchapter [10 U.S.C.S. §§ 1447 *et seq.*] shall be known as the Survivor Benefit Plan. The following persons are eligible to participate in the Plan:
(A) Persons entitled to retired pay,
(B) Persons who would be eligible for retired pay under chapter 67 of this title [10 U.S.C.S. §§ 1331 *et seq.*] but for the fact that they are under 60 years of age.

(2) The Plan applies—
(A) to a person who is eligible to participate in the Plan under paragraph (1)(A) and who is married or has a dependent child when he becomes entitled to retired pay, unless he elects (with his spouse's concurrence, if required under paragraph (3)) not

to participate in the Plan before the first day for which he is eligible for that pay; and

(B) to a person who (i) is eligible to participate in the plan under paragraph (1)(B), (ii) is married or has a dependent child when he is notified under section 1331(d) of this title [10 U.S.C.S. § 1331(d)] that he has completed the years of service required for eligibility for retired pay under chapter 67 of this title [10 U.S.C.S. §§ 1331 *et seq.*] and (iii) elects to participate in the Plan (and makes a designation under subsection (e) before the end of the 90 day period beginning on the date he receives such notification.

A person described in subclauses (i) and (ii) of clause (B) who does not elect to participate in the Plan before the end of the 90 day period referred to in such clause shall remain eligible, upon reaching 60 years of age and otherwise becoming entitled to retired pay, to participate in the Plan in accordance with eligibility under paragraph (1)(A).

(3)(A) A married person who is eligible to provide a standard annuity may not without the concurrence of the person's spouse elect—

   (i)   not to participate in the Plan;

   (ii) to provide an annuity for the person's spouse at less than the maximum level; or

   (iii) to provide an annuity for a dependent child but not for the person's spouse.

(B) A married person who elects to provide a reserve-component annuity may not without the concurrence of the person's spouse elect—

   (i)   to provide an annuity for the person's spouse at less than the maximum level; or

   (ii) to provide an annuity for a dependent child but not for the person's spouse.

(C) A person may make an election described in subparagraph (A) or (B) without the concurrence of the person's spouse if the person establishes to the satisfaction of the Secretary concerned—

   (i)   that the spouse's whereabouts cannot be determined; or

   (ii) that, due to exceptional circumstances, requiring the person to seek the spouse's consent would otherwise be inappropriate.

(D) This paragraph does not affect any right or obligation to elect to provide an annuity for a former spouse (or for a former spouse and dependent child) under subsection (b)(2).

(E) If a married person who is eligible to provide a standard annuity elects to provide an annuity for a former spouse (or for a former spouse and dependent child) under subsection (b)(2), that person's spouse shall be notified of that election.

(4)(A) An election under paragraph (2)(A) not to participate in the Plan is irrevocable if not revoked before the date on which the person first becomes entitled to retired or retainer pay.

(B) An election under paragraph (2)(B) to participate in the Plan is irrevocable if not revoked before the end of the 90 day period referred to in such paragraph.

(5) Participation by person marrying after retirement, etc.—

(A) Election to participate in plan. - A person who is not married and has no dependent child upon becoming eligible to participate in the Plan but who later marries or acquires a dependent child may elect to participate in the Plan.

(B) Manner and time of election. - Such an election must be written, signed by the person making the election, and received by the Secretary concerned within one year after the date on which that person marries or acquires that dependent child.

(C) Limitation on revocation of election. - Such an election may not be revoked except in accordance with subsection (b)(3).

(D) Effective date of election. - The election is effective as of the first day of the first calendar month following the month in which the election is received by the Secretary concerned.

(E) Designation if rcsbp election. - In the case of a person providing a reserve-component annuity, such an election shall include a designation under subsection (e).

(6)(A) A person—

(i) who is a participant in the Plan and is providing coverage for a spouse or a spouse and child;

(ii) who does not have an eligible spouse beneficiary under the Plan; and

(iii) who remarries, may elect not to provide coverage under the person's spouse.

(B) If such an election is made, no reduction in the retired pay of such person under section 1452 of this title [10 U.S.C.S. § 1452] may be made. An election under this paragraph—

    (i)   is irrevocable;

    (ii) shall be made within one year after the person's remarriage; and

    (iii) shall be made in such form and manner as may be prescribed in regulations under section 1455 of this title [10 U.S.C.S. § 1455].

(C) If a person makes an election under this paragraph—

    (i)   not to participate in the Plan;

    (ii) to provide an annuity for the person's spouse at less than the maximum level; or

    (iii) to provide an annuity for a dependent child but not for the person's spouse, the person's spouse shall be notified of that election.

(D) This paragraph does not affect any right or obligation to elect to provide an annuity to a former spouse under subsection (b).

(b)(1) A person who is not married and does not have a dependent child when he becomes eligible to participate in the Plan may elect to provide an annuity to a natural person with an insurable interest in that person. In the case of a person providing a reserve-component annuity, such an election shall include a designation under subsection (e).

(2) A person who has a former spouse when he becomes eligible to participate in the Plan may elect to provide an annuity to that former spouse. In the case of a person with a spouse or a dependent child, such an election prevents payment of an annuity to that spouse or child (other than a child who is a beneficiary under an election under paragraph (4)), including payment under subsection (d). If there is more than one former spouse, the person shall designate which former spouse is to be provided the annuity. In the case of a person providing a reserve-component annuity, such an election shall include a designation under subsection (e).

(3)(A) A person—

    (i)   who is a participant in the Plan and is providing coverage for a spouse or a spouse and child (even though there is no beneficiary currently eligible for such coverage), and

    (ii) who has a former spouse who was not that person's former spouse when he become eligible to participate in the Plan, may (subject to subparagraph (B)) elect to provide an annuity to that former spouse. Any such election terminates any previous coverage under the Plan and must be written, signed by the person, and received by the Secretary concerned within one year after the date of the decree of divorce, dissolution, or annulment.

(B) A person may not make an election under subparagraph (A) to provide an annuity to a former spouse who that person married after becoming eligible for retired pay unless
  (i) the person was married to that former spouse for at least one year, or
  (ii) that former spouse is the parent of issue by that marriage.

(C) An election under this paragraph may not be revoked except in accordance with section 1450(f) of this title [10 U.S.C.S. § 1450(f)] and is effective as of the first day of the first calendar month following the month in which it is received by the Secretary concerned. This paragraph does not provide the authority to change a designation previously made under subsection (e).

(D) If a person who is married makes an election to provide an annuity to a former spouse under this paragraph, that person's spouse shall be notified of that election.

(4) A person who elects to provide an annuity for a former spouse under paragraph (2) or (3) may, at the time of the election, elect to provide coverage under that annuity for both the former spouse and a dependent child, if the child resulted from the person's marriage to that former spouse.

(5) A person who elects to provide an annuity to a former spouse under paragraph (2) or (3) shall, at the time of making the election, provide the Secretary concerned with a written statement (in a form to be prescribed by that Secretary and signed by such person and the former spouse) setting forth whether the election is being made pursuant to a written agreement previously entered into voluntarily by such person as a part of or incident to a proceeding of divorce, dissolution, or annulment and (if so) whether such voluntary written agreement has been incorporated in, or ratified or approved by, a court order.

(C) The application of the Plan to a person whose name is on the temporary disability retired list terminates when his name is removed from that list and he is no longer entitled to disability retired pay.

(d)(1) The Secretary concerned shall pay an annuity under this subchapter [10 U.S.C.S. §§ 1447 *et seq.*] to the surviving spouse of a member who dies on active duty after—

(A) becoming eligible to receive retired pay;

(B) qualifying for retired pay except that he has not applied for or been granted that pay; or

(C) completing 20 years of active service but before he is eligible to retire as a commissioned officer because he has not completed 10 years of active commissioned service.

(2) The Secretary concerned shall pay an annuity under this subchapter [10 U.S.C.S. §§ 1447 *et seq.*] to the dependent child of a member described in paragraph (1) if the member and the member's spouse die as a result of a common accident.

(3) If a member described in paragraph (1) is required under a court order or spousal agreement to provide an annuity to a former spouse, the Secretary—

(A) may not pay an annuity under paragraph (1) or (2); but

(B) shall pay an annuity to that former spouse as if the member had been a participant in the Plan and had made an election under subsection (b) to provide an annuity to the former spouse, or in accordance with that election, as the case may be, if the Secretary receives a written request from the former spouse concerned that the election be deemed to have been made in the same manner as provided in section 1450(f)(3) of this title [10 U.S.C.S. § 1450(f)(3)].

(4) An annuity that may be provided under this subsection shall be provided in preference to an annuity that may be provided under any other provision of this subchapter [10 U.S.C.S. §§ 1447 *et seq.*] on account of service of the same member.

(5) The amount of an annuity under this subsection is computed under section 1451(c) of this title [10 U.S.C.S. § 1451(c)].

(e) In any case in which a person electing to participate in the Plan is required to make a designation under this subsection, the person making such election shall designate whether, in the event he dies before becoming 60 years of age, the annuity provided shall become effective on the day after the date of his death or on the anniversary of his birth.

(f)(1) The Secretary concerned shall pay an annuity under this subchapter

[10 U.S.C.S. §§ 1447 *et seq.*] to the surviving spouse of a person who is eligible to provide a reserve-component annuity and who dies—

    (A) before being notified under section 1331(d) of this title [10 U.S.C.S. § 1331(d)] that he has completed the years of service required for eligibility for retired pay under chapter 67 of this title [10 U.S.C.S. §§ 1331 *et seq.*]; or

    (B) during the 90 day period beginning on the date he receives notification under section 1331(d) of this title [10 U.S.C.S. § 1331(d)] that he has completed the years of service required for eligibility for retired pay under chapter 67 of this title [10 U.S.C.S. §§ 1331 *et seq.*] if he has not made an election under subsection (a)(2)(B) to participate in the Plan.

(2) The Secretary concerned shall pay an annuity under this subchapter [10 U.S.C.S. §§ 1447 *et seq.*] to the dependent child of a person described in paragraph (1) if the person and the person's spouse die as a result of a common accident.

(3) If a person described in paragraph (1) is required under a court or spousal agreement to provide an annuity to a former spouse upon becoming eligible to be a participant in the Plan or has made an election under subsection (b) to provide an annuity to a former spouse, the Secretary—

    (A) may not pay an annuity under paragraph (1) or (2); but

    (B) shall pay an annuity to that former spouse as if the person had been a participant in the Plan and had made an election under subsection (b) to provide an annuity to the former spouse, or in accordance with that election, as the case may be, if the Secretary receives a written request from the former spouse concerned that the election be deemed to have been made in the same manner as provided in section 1450(f)(3) of this title [10 U.S.C.S. § 1450(f)(3)].

(4) The amount of an annuity under this subsection is computed under section 1451(c) of this title [10 U.S.C.S. § 1451(c)].

(g)(1) A person—

    (A) who is a participant in the Plan and is providing coverage under subsection (a) for a spouse or a spouse and child, but at less than the maximum level; and

    (B) who remarries, may elect, within one year of such remarriage, to increase the level of coverage provided under the Plan to a level not in excess of the current retired pay of that person.

(2) Such an election shall be contingent on the person paying to the United States the amount determined under paragraph (3) plus interest on such amount at a rate determined under regulations prescribed by the Secretary of Defense.

(3) The amount referred to in paragraph (2) is the amount equal to the difference between—

    (A) the amount that would have been withheld from such person's retired pay under section 1452 of this title [10 U.S.C.S. § 1452] if the higher level of coverage had been in effect from the time the person became a participant in the Plan; and

    (B) the amount of such person's retired pay actually withheld.

(4) An election under paragraph (1) shall be made in such manner as the Secretary shall prescribe and shall become effective upon receipt of the payment required by paragraph (2).

(5) A payment received under this subsection by the Secretary of Defense shall be deposited into the Department of Defense Military Retirement Fund. Any other payment received under this subsection shall be deposited in the Treasury as miscellaneous receipts.

(Added Sept. 21, 1972, P.L. 92-425, § 1(3), 86 Stat. 707; Oct. 14, 1976, P.L. 94-496, § 12, 90 Stat. 2375; Sept. 8, 1982, P.L. 97-252, Title X § 1003(b), 96 Stat. 735; Oct. 12, 1982, P.L. 97-295, § 1(18), 96 Stat. 1290; Sept. 24, 1983, P.L. 98-94, Title IX, Part D, § 941(a)(1), (2), (c)(2), 97 Stat. 652, 653; Nov. 8, 1985, P.L. 99-145, Title V, Part B, § 513(b), Title VII, Part A. §§ 712(a), 713(a), 715, 716(a), 719(3), (8)(A) in part, Part B, § 721(a), 99 Stat. 628, 670, 671, 673–676.)

10 U.S.C. § 1449

§ 1449. Mental incompetency of member

If a person to whom section 1448 of this title [10 U.S.C.S. § 1448] applies is determined to be mentally incompetent by medical officers of the armed force concerned or of the Department of Veterans Affairs, or by a court of competent jurisdiction, an election described in subsection (a)(2) or (b), of section 1448 of this title [10 U.S.C.S. § 1448(a)(2) or (b)] may be made on behalf of that person by the Secretary concerned. If a person for whom the Secretary has made an election is later determined to be mentally competent by an authority named in the first sentence, that person may, within 180 days after that determination, revoke that election. Any deductions made from retired or retainer pay by reason of such an election will not be refunded.

(Added Sept. 21, 1972, P.L. 92-425, § 1(3), 86 Stat. 708; Sept. 30, 1978, P.L. 95-397, Title II, § 207(a), 92 Stat. 848.)

10 U.S.C. § 1450

§ 1450. Payment of annuity: beneficiaries

(a) Effective as of the first day after the death of a person to whom section 1448 of this title [10 U.S.C.S. § 1448] applies (or such other day as that person may provide under subsection (j)), a monthly annuity under section 1451 of this title [10 U.S.C.S. § 1451] shall be paid to the person's beneficiaries under the Plan, as follows:

  (1) the eligible surviving spouse or the eligible former spouse;

  (2) the surviving dependent children in equal shares, if the eligible surviving spouse or the eligible former spouse is dead, dies, or otherwise becomes ineligible under this section;

  (3) the dependent children in equal shares if the person to whom section 1448 of this title [19 U.S.C.S. § 1448] applies (with the concurrence of the person's spouse, if required under section 1448(a)(3) of this title [10 U.S.C.S. § 1448(a)(3)]) elected to provide an annuity for dependent children but not for the spouse or former spouse; or

  (4) the natural person designated under section 1448(b) of this title [10 U.S.C.S. § 1448(b)], unless the election to provide an annuity to the natural person has been changed as provided in subsection (f).

(b) An annuity payable to the beneficiary terminates effective as of the first day of the month in which eligibility is lost. An annuity for a widow, widower, or former spouse shall be paid to the widow, widower, or former spouse while the widow, widower or former spouse is living or if the widow, widower, or former spouse remarries before reaching age 60, until the widow, widower, or former spouse remarries. If the widow, widower, or former spouse remarries before reaching age 60 and that marriage is terminated by death, annulment, or divorce, payment of the annuity will be resumed effective as of the day of the month in which the marriage is so terminated. However, if the widow, widower, or former spouse is also entitled to an annuity under the Plan based upon the marriage so terminated, the widow, widower, or former spouse may not receive both annuities but must elect which to receive.

(c) If, upon the death of a person to whom section 1448 of this title [10 U.S.C.S. § 1448] applies, the widow, widower, or former spouse of that person is also entitled to compensation under section 411(a) of title 38 [38 U.S.C.S. § 411(a)], the widow, widower, or former spouse may be paid an annuity under this section, but only in the amount that the annuity otherwise payable under this section would exceed that compensation. A reduction in an annuity under this section required by the preceding sentence shall be effective on the date of the commencement of the period of payment of such compensation under title 38 [38 U.S.C.S. §§ 101 *et seq.*].

(d) If, upon the death of a person to whom section 1448 of this title [10 U.S.C.S. § 1448] applies, that person had in effect a waiver of his retired pay for the purposes of subchapter III of chapter 83 of title 5 [5 U.S.C.S. §§ 8331 *et seq.*] an annuity under this section shall not be payable unless, in accordance with section 8339(j) of title 5 [5 U.S.C.S. § 8339(j)], he notified the Office of Personnel Management that he did not desire any spouse surviving him to receive an annuity under section 8341(b) of that title [5 U.S.C.S. § 8341(b)].

(e) If no annuity under this section is payable because of subsection (c), any amounts deducted from the retired pay of the deceased under section 1452 of this title [10 U.S.C.S. § 1452] shall be refunded to the widow, widower, or former spouse. If, because of subsection (c), the annuity payable is less than the amount established under section 1451 of this title [10 U.S.C.S. § 1451], the annuity payable shall be recalculated under that section. The amount of the reduction in the retired pay required to provide that recalculated annuity shall be computed under section 1452 of this title [10 U.S.C.S. § 1452], and the difference between the amount deducted prior to the computation of that recalculated annuity and the amount that would have been deducted on the basis of that recalculated annuity shall be refunded to the widow, widower, or former spouse.

(f)(1) A person who elects to provide an annuity to a person designated by him under section 1448(b) of this title [10 U.S.C.S. § 1448(b)] may, subject to paragraph (2), change that election and provide an annuity to his spouse or dependent child. The Secretary concerned shall notify the former spouse or other natural person previously designated under section 1448(b) of this title [10 U.S.C.S. § 1448(b)] of any change of election under the first sentence of this paragraph. Any such change of election is subject to the same rules with respect to execution, revocation, and effectiveness as are set forth in section 1448(a)(5) of this title [10 U.S.C.S. § 1448(a)(5)] (without regard to the eligibility of the person making the change of election to make an election under such section).

(2) A person who, incident to a proceeding of divorce, dissolution, or annulment, enters into a voluntary written agreement to elect under section 1448(b) of this title [10 U.S.C.S. § 1448(b)] to provide an annuity to a former spouse and who makes an election pursuant to such agreement may not change such election under paragraph (1) unless—

(A) in a case in which such agreement has been incorporated in or ratified or approved by a court order, the person—

(i) furnishes to the Secretary concerned a certified copy of a court order which is regular on its face and modifies the provisions of all previous court orders relating to the agreement to make such election so as to permit the person to change the election; and

(ii) certifies to the Secretary concerned that the court order is valid and in effect; or

(B) in a case in which such agreement has not been incorporated or ratified or approved by a court order, the person—

(i) furnishes to the Secretary concerned a statement, in such form as the Secretary concerned may prescribe, signed by the former spouse and evidencing the former spouse's agreement to a change in the election under paragraph (1); and

(ii) certifies to the Secretary concerned that the statement is current and in effect.

(3)(A) If a person described in paragraph (2) or (3) of section 1448(b) of this title [10 U.S.C.S. § 1448(b)(2) or (3)] enters, incident to a proceeding of divorce, dissolution or annulment, into a voluntary written agreement to elect under section 1448(b) of this title [10 U.S.C.S. § 1448(b)] to provide an annuity to a former spouse and such agreement has been incorporated in or ratified or approved by a court order or has been filed with the court of appropriate jurisdiction in accordance with applicable State law, and such person then fails or refuses to make such an election, such person shall be deemed to have made such an election if the Secretary concerned receives a written request, in such manner as the Secretary shall prescribe, from the former spouse concerned requesting that such an election be deemed to have been made and receives a copy of the court order, regular on its face, which incorporates, ratifies, or approves the voluntary written agreement of such person or receives a statement from the clerk of the court (or other appropriate official) that such agreement has been filed with the court in accordance with applicable State law.

(B) An election may not be deemed to have been made under subparagraph (A) in the case of any person unless the Secretary concerned receives a request from the former spouse of the person before October 1, 1985, or within one year of the date of the court order or filing involved, whichever is later.

(C) An election deemed to have been made under subparagraph (A) shall become effective on the first day of the first month which begins after the date of the court order or filing involved.

(4) Nothing in this chapter [10 U.S.C.S. §§ 1431 *et seq.*] authorizes any court to order any person to elect under section 1448(b) of this title [10 U.S.C.S. § 1448(b)] to provide an annuity to a former spouse unless such person has voluntarily agreed in writing to make such election.

(g) Except as provided in section 1449 of this title [10 U.S.C.S. § 1449] or in subsection (f) of this section, an election under this section may not be changed or revoked.

(h) Except as provided in section 1451 of this title [10 U.S.C.S. § 1451], an annuity under this section is in addition to any other payment to which a person is entitled under any other provision of law. Such annuity shall be considered as income under laws administered by the Veterans' Administration.

(i) Except as provided in subsection (1)(3)(B), an annuity under this section is not assignable or subject to execution, levy, attachment, garnishment, or other legal process.

(j) An annuity elected by a person providing a reserve-component annuity shall be effective in accordance with the designation made by such person under section 1448(e) of this title [10 U.S.C.S. § 1448(e)]. An annuity payable under section 1448(f) of this title [10 U.S.C.S. § 1448(f)] shall be effective on the day after the date of the death of the person upon whose service the right to the annuity is based.

(k)(1) If a widow, widower, or former spouse whose annuity has been adjusted under subsection (c) subsequently loses entitlement to compensation under section 1311(a) of title 38 [38 U.S.C.S. § 1311(a)] because of the remarriage of such widow, widower, or former spouse, and if at the time of such remarriage such widow, widower, or former spouse is 60 years of age or more, the amount of the annuity of such widow, widower, or former spouse shall be readjusted, effective on the effective date of such loss of compensation, to the amount of the annuity which would be in effect with respect to such widow, widower, or former spouse if the adjustment under subsection (c) had never been made.

(2) A widow, widower, or former spouse whose annuity is readjusted under paragraph (1) shall repay any amount refunded under subsection (e) by reason of the adjustment under subsection (c). If the repayment is not made in a lump sum, the widow, widower, or former spouse shall pay interest on the amount to be repaid commencing on the date on which the first such payment is due and applied over the period during which any part of the repayment remains to be paid. The manner in which such repayment shall be made, and the rate of any such interest, shall be prescribed in regulations under section 1455 of this title [10 U.S.C.S. § 1455]. An amount repaid under this paragraph (including any such interest) received by the Secretary of Defense shall be deposited into the Military Retirement Fund. Any other amount repaid under this paragraph shall be deposited into the Treasury as miscellaneous receipts.

(I)(1) Upon application of the beneficiary of a participant in the Plan whose retired pay has been suspended on the basis that the participant is missing (or of a participant in the Plan who would be eligible for retired pay under chapter 67 of this title [10 U.S.C.S. §§ 1331 *et seq.*] but for the fact that he is under 60 years of age and whose retired pay, if he were entitled to retired pay, would be suspended on the basis that he is missing), the Secretary concerned may determine for purposes of this subchapter [10 U.S.C.S. §§ 1447 *et seq.*] that a participant is presumed dead if he finds—

(A) that the participant has been missing for at least 30 days; and

(B) that the circumstances under which the participant is missing would lead a reasonably prudent person to conclude that the participant is dead.

(2) Upon a determination under paragraph (1) with respect to a participant in the Plan, an annuity otherwise payable under this subchapter [10

U.S.C.S. §§ 1447 *et seq.*] shall be paid as if the participant died on the date as of which the retired or retainer pay of the participant was suspended.

(3)(A) If, after a determination under paragraph (1), the Secretary concerned determines that the participant is alive, any annuity being paid under this subchapter [10 U.S.C.S. §§ 1447 *et seq.*] by reason of this subsection shall be terminated and the total amount of any annuity payments made by reason of this subsection shall constitute a debt to the United States which may be collected or offset—

    (i)   from any retired pay otherwise payable to the participant;

    (ii) if the participant is entitled to compensation under chapter 11 of title 38 [38 U.S.C.S. §§ 301 *et seq.*], from that compensation; or

    (iii) if the participant is entitled to any other payment from the United States, from that payment.

  (B) If the participant dies before the full recovery of the amount of annuity payments described in subparagraph (A) has been made by the United States, the remaining amount of such annuity payments may be collected from his beneficiary under the Plan if that beneficiary was the recipient of the annuity payments made by reason of this subsection.

(Added Sept. 21, 1972, P.L. 92-425, § 1(3), 86 Stat. 708; Oct. 14, 1976, P.L. 94-496, § 1(3), (4), 90 Stat. 2375; Sept. 30, 1978, P. L. 95-397, Title II, §§ 203, 207(b), (c), 92 Stat. 845, 848; July 10, 1981, P.L. 97-22, § 11(a)(3) in part, 95 Stat. 137; Sept. 8, 1982, P.L. 97-252, Title X § 1003(c), (d), 96 Stat. 736; Sept. 24, 1983, P.L. 98-94, Title IX, Part D § 941 (a)(3), 97 Stat. 653, 654; Oct. 19, 1984, P.L. 98-525, Title VI, Part E, §§ 642(b), 644, 98 Stat. 2546, 2548; Nov. 8, 1985, P.L. 99-145, Title VII, Part A, §§ 713(b), 717, 718, 719(4)–(6), (8)(A) in part, Part B, § 722, 723(a), (b), Title XIII, § 1303(a)(11), 99 Stat. 672, 674–677, 739.)

Appendix F

EXHIBITS

Exhibit 1.   Active Duty Pay Chart

The 1998 Air Force Times pay chart

This chart shows the monthly pay rates for 1998. Service members will get a 2.8 percent raise in their basic pay. Enlisted personnel who eat in military dining facilities get a new partial subsistence allowance. Basic allowance for quarters is being replaced by a new basic allowance for housing.

							Years of service								
	<2	2	3	4	6	8	10	12	14	16	18	20	22	24	26
Commissioned officers															
O-10	7566.30	7832.40	7832.40	7832.40	7832.40	8133.00	8133.00	8583.60	8583.60	9197.70	9197.70	9813.60	9813.60	9813.60	10424.70
O-9	6705.60	6881.40	7028.10	7028.10	7028.10	7206.60	7206.60	7506.60	7506.60	8133.00	8133.00	8583.60	8583.60	8583.60	9197.70
O-8	6073.50	6255.90	6404.10	6404.10	6404.10	6881.40	6881.40	7206.60	7206.60	7506.60	7832.40	8133.00	8333.70	8333.70	8333.70
O-7	5046.60	5389.80	5389.80	5389.80	5631.60	5631.60	5958.00	5958.00	6255.90	6881.40	7354.80	7354.80	7354.80	7354.80	7354.80
O-6	3740.40	4109.40	4379.10	4379.10	4379.10	4379.10	4379.10	4379.10	4527.90	5243.70	5511.30	5631.60	5958.00	6159.30	6461.70
O-5	2991.90	3512.70	3755.70	3755.70	3755.70	3755.70	3868.80	4077.60	4350.90	4676.70	4944.30	5094.60	5272.50	5272.50	5272.50
O-4	2521.50	3070.80	3275.40	3275.40	3336.30	3483.30	3721.20	3930.30	4109.40	4290.30	4407.90	4407.90	4407.90	4407.90	4407.90
O-3	2343.30	2619.90	2801.10	3099.00	3247.50	3363.60	3546.00	3721.20	3812.40	3812.40	3812.40	3812.40	3812.40	3812.40	3812.40
O-2	2043.60	2231.70	2681.70	2771.40	2828.70	2828.70	2828.70	2828.70	2828.70	2828.70	2828.70	2828.70	2828.70	2828.70	2828.70
O-1	1774.20	1846.50	2231.70	2231.70	2231.70	2231.70	2231.70	2231.70	2231.70	2231.70	2231.70	2231.70	2231.70	2231.70	2231.70
Officers with more than four years' active duty as enlisted or warrant officer															
O-3E	0.00	0.00	0.00	3099.00	3247.50	3363.60	3546.00	3721.20	3868.80	3868.80	3868.80	3868.80	3868.80	3868.80	3868.80
O-2E	0.00	0.00	0.00	2771.40	2828.70	2918.40	3070.80	3188.10	3275.40	3275.40	3275.40	3275.40	3275.40	3275.40	3275.40
O-1E	0.00	0.00	0.00	2231.70	2384.10	2471.70	2561.70	2650.50	2771.40	2771.40	2771.40	2771.40	2771.40	2771.40	2771.40
Warrant officers (for Army, Navy and Marine Corps)															
W-5	0.00	0.00	0.00	0.00	0.00	0.00	0.00	0.00	0.00	0.00	0.00	4074.60	4228.80	4351.20	4534.50
W-4	2387.40	2561.70	2561.70	2619.90	2739.30	2859.90	2979.90	3188.10	3336.30	3453.60	3546.00	3660.30	3782.70	3900.60	4077.60
W-3	2169.90	2353.80	2353.80	2384.10	2412.00	2588.40	2739.30	2828.70	2918.40	3005.70	3099.00	3219.90	3336.30	3336.30	3453.60
W-2	1900.50	2056.20	2056.20	2115.90	2231.70	2353.80	2443.20	2532.60	2619.90	2712.00	2801.10	2889.00	3005.70	3005.70	3005.70
W-1	1583.40	1815.30	1815.30	1967.10	2056.20	2144.40	2231.70	2323.50	2412.00	2501.70	2588.40	2681.10	2681.10	2681.10	2681.10
Enlisted members															
E-9	0.00	0.00	0.00	0.00	0.00	0.00	2777.40	2839.80	2904.00	2970.90	3037.50	3096.00	3258.60	3385.50	3576.00
E-8	0.00	0.00	0.00	0.00	0.00	2328.90	2396.40	2458.80	2522.70	2589.60	2648.40	2713.50	2873.10	3000.90	3193.50
E-7	1626.30	1755.60	1820.10	1884.30	1948.50	2010.60	2074.80	2139.60	2236.20	2299.80	2363.40	2394.30	2555.10	2682.30	2873.10
E-6	1398.90	1524.90	1588.20	1655.70	1718.10	1779.90	1845.30	1940.10	2001.30	2065.80	2097.00	2097.00	2097.00	2097.00	2097.00
E-5	1227.60	1336.20	1401.00	1462.20	1558.20	1621.80	1685.70	1748.10	1779.90	1779.90	1779.90	1779.90	1779.90	1779.90	1779.90
E-4	1144.80	1209.30	1280.40	1379.10	1433.70	1433.70	1433.70	1433.70	1433.70	1433.70	1433.70	1433.70	1433.70	1433.70	1433.70
E-3	1079.10	1137.90	1183.20	1230.30	1230.30	1230.30	1230.30	1230.30	1230.30	1230.30	1230.30	1230.30	1230.30	1230.30	1230.30
E-2	1038.30	1038.30	1038.30	1038.30	1038.30	1038.30	1038.30	1038.30	1038.30	1038.30	1038.30	1038.30	1038.30	1038.30	1038.30
E-1 >4	926.10	926.10	926.10	926.10	926.10	926.10	926.10	926.10	926.10	926.10	926.10	926.10	926.10	926.10	926.10
E-1 with less than 4 months—856.80															

Note: It is expected that basic pay will be limited to $9,225.00 per month. Figures for O-10 in the chart show what pay would be without the cap.

Exhibit 2. 1998 Nondisability Retired Pay Chart

Retired Pay Grade	Years of Service															
	15	16	17	18	19	20	21	22	23	24	25	26	27	28	29	30
Commissioned Officers																
C/S	3,286	3,542	3,803	4,068	4,338	4,612	4,843	5,073	5,304	5,535	5,765	5,996	6,226	6,457	6,688	6,918
O10	3,057	3,531	3,791	4,056	4,325	4,612	4,843	5,073	5,304	5,535	5,765	5,996	6,226	6,457	6,688	6,918
O-9	2,674	3,123	3,352	3,586	3,824	4,291	4,506	4,720	4,935	5,150	5,364	5,978	6,208	6,438	6,668	6,898
O-8	2,567	2,882	3,094	3,454	3,683	4,066	4,269	4,583	4,791	5,000	5,208	5,416	5,625	5,833	6,041	6,250
O-7	2,228	2,642	2,836	3,243	3,458	3,677	3,861	4,045	4,229	4,412	4,596	4,780	4,964	5,148	5,332	5,516
O-6	1,613	2,013	2,161	2,430	2,591	2,815	2,956	3,276	3,425	3,695	3,849	4,200	4,361	4,523	4,684	4,846
O-5	1,550	1,795	1,927	2,180	2,325	2,547	2,674	2,899	3,031	3,163	3,295	3,427	3,558	3,690	3,822	3,954
O-4	1,463	1,647	1,768	1,943	2,072	2,203	2,314	2,424	2,534	2,644	2,754	2,865	2,975	3,085	3,195	3,305
Commissioned Officers With Less Than 4 Years of Active Enlisted Service																
O-3	1,358	1,463	1,571	1,681	1,792	1,906	2,001	2,096	2,192	2,287	2,382	2,478	2,573	2,668	2,763	2,859
O-2	1,007	1,086	1,166	1,247	1,330	1,414	1,485	1,555	1,626	1,697	1,767	1,838	1,909	1,980	2,050	2,121
O-1	795	856	920	984	1,049	1,115	1,171	1,227	1,283	1,339	1,394	1,450	1,506	1,562	1,617	1,673
Commissioned Officers With More Than 4 Years of Active Enlisted Service																
O-3	1,378	1,485	1,594	1,706	1,819	1,934	2,031	2,127	2,224	2,321	2,418	2,514	2,611	2,708	2,804	2,901
O-2	1,166	1,257	1,350	1,444	1,540	1,637	1,719	1,801	1,883	1,965	2,047	2,129	2,210	2,292	2,374	2,456
O-1	987	1,064	1,142	1,222	1,303	1,385	1,454	1,524	1,593	1,662	1,732	1,801	1,870	1,939	2,009	2,078

(continued)

Exhibit 2.   Continued

Warrant Officers

Grade																
W-5	1,451	1,564	1,679	1,796	1,916	2,037	2,139	2,325	2,431	2,610	2,719	2,947	3,060	3,174	3,287	3,400
W-4	1,188	1,326	1,423	1,563	1,667	1,830	1,921	2,080	2,175	2,340	2,437	2,650	2,752	2,854	2,956	3,058
W-3	1,039	1,154	1,239	1,366	1,457	1,609	1,690	1,834	1,918	2,001	2,085	2,244	2,331	2,417	2,503	2,590
W-2	933	1,041	1,118	1,235	1,317	1,444	1,516	1,653	1,728	1,803	1,878	1,953	2,028	2,103	2,179	2,254
W-1	859	960	1,031	1,141	1,217	1,340	1,407	1,474	1,541	1,608	1,675	1,742	1,809	1,876	1,943	2,010

Enlisted Members

Grade																
SEM	1,548	1,669	1,791	1,916	2,043	2,173	2,281	2,390	2,499	2,607	2,716	2,825	2,933	3,042	3,151	3,259
E-9	1,034	1,140	1,224	1,339	1,428	1,548	1,625	1,792	1,873	2,031	2,115	2,324	2,413	2,503	2,592	2,682
E-8	898	994	1,067	1,167	1,245	1,356	1,424	1,580	1,652	1,800	1,875	2,075	2,155	2,235	2,315	2,395
E-7	796	883	948	1,042	1,111	1,197	1,257	1,405	1,469	1,609	1,676	1,867	1,939	2,011	2,083	2,154
E-6	712	793	851	924	986	1,048	1,100	1,153	1,205	1,258	1,310	1,363	1,415	1,467	1,520	1,572
E-5	634	683	733	784	837	889	934	978	1,023	1,067	1,112	1,156	1,201	1,245	1,290	1,334
E-4	510	550	591	632	674	716	752	788	824	860	896	931	967	1,003	1,039	1,075
E-3	438	472	507	542	578	615	645	676	707	738	768	799	830	861	891	922
E-2	369	398	428	457	488	519	545	571	597	622	648	674	700	726	752	778
E-1	329	355	381	408	435	463	486	509	532	555	578	601	625	648	671	694

Note: As a result of certain provisions for advancement on the retired list or under the "Tower Amendment" some individuals would receive amounts differing from those shown above.

Tables show figures for retirees under final pay, i.e. those entering the service prior to September 8, 1980.

Figures shown assume that active service and pay service are equal. Military retired pay reflects pay and pay cap increases prior to and including January 1, 1998.

Active duty basic pay cap of 9225.00 per month levels out retired pay in upper grades.

Public law 102-484 granted DoD Temporary Early Retirement Authority (TERA) for selected active duty members with as few as 15 years of service. Their retired pay is subject to reduction factors for service less than 20 years. The FY94 Defense Authorization Act extended TERA through September 30, 1999.

January 1, 1998   Department of Defense – Office of the Actuary

Exhibit 3. Deemed Election Request from Former Spouse to Pay Center

APPLICATION FOR FORMER SPOUSE PAYMENTS FROM RETIRED PAY *(Please read instructions on reverse before completing this form.)*	*Form Approved* *OMB No. 0704-0182* *Expires Jan 31, 1994*
Public reporting burden for this collection of information is estimated to average 1.2 hours per response, including the time for reviewing instructions, searching existing data sources, gathering and maintaining the data needed, and completing and reviewing the collection of information. Send comments regarding this burden estimate or any other aspect of this collection of information, including suggestions for reducing this burden, to Department of Defense, Washington Headquarters Services, Directorate for Information Operations and Reports, 1215 Jefferson Davis Highway, Suite 1204, Arlington, VA 22202-4302, and to the Office of Management and Budget, Paperwork Reduction Project (0704-0182), Washington, DC 20503. **PLEASE DO NOT RETURN YOUR FORM TO EITHER OF THESE ADDRESSES. SEND COMPLETED FORM TO THE APPROPRIATE SERVICE ADDRESS LISTED ON BACK.**	*FOR OFFICIAL USE*

PRIVACY ACT STATEMENT

AUTHORITY: Title 10 USC § 1408; EO 9397.

PRINCIPAL PURPOSE(S): To request direct payment through a Uniformed Service designated agent of court ordered child support, alimony, or division of property to a former spouse from the retired pay of a Uniformed Service member.

ROUTINE USE(S): Information provided will be disclosed to the retired member for verification and comment. Additionally, it may be disclosed to state social service agencies for human services benefit entitlement purposes; to the Internal Revenue Service, and state and local taxing authorities for income tax purposes.

DISCLOSURE: Voluntary; however, failure to provide requested information may delay or make impossible processing this direct payment request.

1. APPLICANT IDENTIFICATION	2. SERVICE MEMBER IDENTIFICATION
a. NAME *(As appears on court order)* *(Last, First, Middle Initial)*	a. NAME *(Last, First, Middle Initial)*
b. CURRENT NAME *(Last, First, Middle Initial)*	b. SOCIAL SECURITY NUMBER
c. SOCIAL SECURITY NUMBER	c. BRANCH OF SERVICE
d. ADDRESS *(Street, City, State, Zip Code)*	d. ADDRESS *(Street, City, State, Zip Code)* *(If known)*

3. REQUEST STATEMENT

I request direct payment from the retired pay of the above named Uniformed Service member based on the enclosed court order.

I request payment of:
- Child support in the amount of $_____ per month.
- Alimony, spousal support or maintenance in the amount of $_____, or _____ percent of disposable retired pay per month.
- A division of property in the amount of $_____, or _____ percent of disposable retired pay per month.

(continued)

Exhibit 3.   Continued

I certify that any request for current child and/or spousal support is not being collected under any other wage withholding or garnishment procedure authorized by statute. Furthermore, I certify that the court order has not been amended, superseded or set aide and is not subject to appeal. As a condition precedent to payment, I agree to refund all overpayments and that they are otherwise recoverable and subject to involuntary collection from me or my estate, and I will notify the Uniformed Service if the operative court order, upon which payment is based, is vacated, modified, or set aside. I also agree to notify the Uniformed Service of a change in eligibility for payments. This includes notice of my remarriage, if under the terms of the court order or the laws of the jurisdiction where it was issued, remarriage causes the payments to be reduced or terminated; or notice of a change in eligibility for child support payments by reason of the death, emancipation, adoption, or attainment of majority of a child whose support is provided through direct payments from retired pay. I hereby acknowledge that any payment to me cannot lawfully exceed 50 percent of the member's disposable retired pay which is gross retired pay minus deductions such as those authorized or required for income tax, Federal indebtedness, or disability reasons; that my payments may not exceed any lesser amount or percentage specified by court order; and that any court-ordered percentage must be construed as a percentage of disposable retired pay.

---

4. I HAVE ENCLOSED ALL PERTINENT DOCUMENTATION TO INCLUDE: *(X as applicable)*

	a. A certified, original copy made within 90 days preceding this application for payment of the operative court order and other certified accompanying documents that provide for payment of child support, alimony or a division of retired pay as property.
	b. Evidence of the date(s) of my marriage to the member if the application is for the direct payment of a division of the member's disposable retire pay as property. Give MARRIAGE DATE *(YYMMDD)* in this block unless stated in court order.

c. If payment request includes child support, give name(s) and birth date(s) of child(ren):

(1) Name of Child *(Last, First, Middle Initial)*	(2) Date of Birth *(YYMMDD)*

	d. Other information *(please identify)* or remarks.

5a. APPLICANT'S SIGNATURE	b. DATE SIGNED

INSTRUCTIONS FOR COMPLETION OF DD FORM 2293

GENERAL. These instructions govern an application for direct payment from retired pay of a Uniformed Service member in response to court ordered child support, alimony, or a division of property, under the authority of 10 USC § 1408.

SERVICE OF APPLICATION. You must serve the application by certified or registered mail with return receipt requested or by personal service delivered to the appropriate Uniformed Service designated agent. The Uniformed Services' designated agents are:

(continued)

Exhibit 3. Continued

(1) **ARMY:** Director, DFAS - Cleveland Center (Code L), PO Box 998002, Cleveland, OH 44199-8002;

(2) **NAVY:** Director, DFAS - Cleveland Center (Code L), PO Box 998002, Cleveland, OH 44199-8002;

(3) **AIR FORCE:** Director, DFAS - Cleveland Center (Code L), PO Box 998002, Cleveland, OH 44199-8002;

(4) **MARINE CORPS:** Director, DFAS - Cleveland Center (Code L), PO Box 998002, Cleveland, OH 44199-8002;

(5) **COAST GUARD:** Commanding Officer (LGL), United States Coast Guard, Pay and Personnel Center, 444 S.E. Quincy Street, Topeka, KS 66683-3591;

(6) **PUBLIC HEALTH SERVICE:** Office of General Counsel, Department of Health and Human Services, Room 722A, Humphrey Building, 200 Independence Avenue S.W., Washington, DC 20201;

(7) **NATIONAL OCEANIC AND ATMOSPHERIC ADMINISTRATION:** Same as U.S. Coast Guard.

IMPORTANT NOTE. Making a false statement or claim against the United States Government is punishable. The penalty for willfully making a false claim or false statement is a maximum fine of $10,000 or maximum imprisonment of 5 years or both *(18 USC § 287 and 1001)*.

ITEM 1. (a) Enter full name as it appears on court order;

(b) Enter current name if different than it appears on court order;

(c) Enter Social Security Number;

(d) Enter current address.

ITEM 2. (a) Enter former spouse's full name as it appears on the court order;

(b) Enter former spouse's Social Security Number;

(c) Enter former spouse's branch of service;

(d) Enter former spouse's current address, if known.

ITEM 3. Read the Request Statement carefully.

ITEM 4. A certified copy of a court order can be obtained from the court that issued the court order. Other documents include, but are not limited to, final divorce decree, property settlement order, and any appellate court orders. If the court order does not state that the former spouse was married to the member for ten years or more while the member performed ten years creditable service and the request is for payment of a division of property, the applicant must provide evidence to substantiate the ten years' marriage condition. Additional evidence must show that the ten years' requirement has been met, including: Uniformed Service orders, marriage certificate, and other documents that establish the period of marriage. Other information or documents included with the request should be clearly identified by the document's title and date. Remarks may be provided to clarify specific points.

ITEM 5. Self-explanatory.

Exhibit 4.   Letter Request for Retired Pay Information

[DATE]

Defense Finance and Accounting Service
Code: MLR
1240 E. 9th Street
Cleveland, Ohio 44137

Re: [MEMBER'S NAME], [SOCIAL SECURITY NUMBER]

To Whom It May Concern:

Enclosed is an Authorization for Release of Information executed by [MEMBER'S NAME]. Therefore, please provide the following information: [CHOOSE FROM THE FOLLOWING]:

1. The dates of the member's creditable service.
2. The dates of the member's eligibility for retirement and mandatory retirement.
3. The basis for computation of retired pay.
4. Whether the member has elected the Survivor's Benefit Plan and, if so, the designation of beneficiaries.
5. The amount of the gross retired pay and an itemization of all deductions from gross retired pay from _____ to _____.
6. The dates on which cost of living adjustments have been made.

Should you have any questions, feel free to contact me at your convenience. I appreciate your time and immediate attention to this matter.

Sincerely yours,

[NOTE: Apparently at random, certain clerks will decide that information that is supposed to be freely available is restricted by privacy limitations, and the practitioner may actually have to show the clerks their own regulations; when some information beyond gross pay is sought, the situation is less clear, and the practitioner may wish to avoid delay at the outset by accompanying a request for information with a subpoena signed by a judge (they usually ignore subpoenas issued by mere clerks, regardless of state law).]

Exhibit 5. Military-Specific Mortality Tables (Reprinted from Office of the Actuary, Department of Defense, FY 1996 DOD Statistical Report on the Military Retirement System 288–89 (1997).)

NONDISABILITY RETIRED LIFE EXPECTATIONS

AGE*	OFFICERS	ENLISTED	AGE*	OFFICERS	ENLISTED
30	49.98	46.06	70	14.03	12.30
31	49.00	45.11	71	13.34	11.71
32	48.03	44.15	72	12.67	11.14
33	47.05	43.20	73	12.01	10.59
34	46.07	42.24	74	11.37	10.06
35	45.09	41.28	75	10.75	9.55
36	44.12	40.33	76	10.15	9.06
37	43.14	39.37	77	9.57	8.59
38	42.16	38.42	78	9.01	8.15
39	41.19	37.47	79	8.47	7.72
40	40.21	36.52	80	7.95	7.32
41	39.24	35.57	81	7.45	6.94
42	38.27	34.62	82	6.98	6.57
43	37.30	33.68	83	6.53	6.22
44	36.34	32.74	84	6.10	5.88
45	35.38	31.81	85	5.70	5.56
46	34.43	30.88	86	5.32	5.26
47	33.48	29.96	87	4.97	4.97
48	32.54	29.04	88	4.64	4.69
49	31.61	28.14	89	4.33	4.43
50	30.68	27.25	90	4.04	4.18
51	29.76	26.36	91	3.78	3.94
52	28.85	25.49	92	3.54	3.72
53	27.94	24.64	93	3.31	3.50
54	27.04	23.79	94	3.10	3.30
55	26.15	22.96	95	2.91	3.11
56	25.27	22.14	96	2.74	2.94
57	24.40	21.34	97	2.58	2.78
58	23.53	20.55	98	2.44	2.63
59	22.67	19.77	99	2.32	2.51

(*continued*)

AGE*	OFFICERS	ENLISTED	AGE*	OFFICERS	ENLISTED
60	21.82	19.01	100	2.23	2.39
61	20.97	18.27	101	2.14	2.27
62	20.14	17.54	102	2.05	2.15
63	19.32	16.82	103	1.95	2.04
64	18.51	16.13	104	1.85	1.92
65	17.72	15.45	105	1.75	1.80
66	16.95	14.79	106	1.63	1.67
67	16.19	14.15	107	1.49	1.51
68	15.46	13.51	108	1.30	1.31
69	14.74	12.90	109	1.01	1.01
			110	0.50	0.50

*AGE NEAREST BIRTHDAY MALE

DISABILITY RETIRED LIFE EXPECTATIONS

AGE*	OFFICERS	ENLISTED	AGE*	OFFICERS	ENLISTED
16	52.06	49.90	63	16.22	13.74
17	51.26	49.08	64	15.59	13.21
18	50.45	48.26	65	14.95	12.71
19	49.66	47.45	66	14.32	12.23
20	48.86	46.64	67	13.70	11.76
21	48.07	45.83	68	13.08	11.28
22	47.28	45.02	69	12.47	10.81
23	46.50	44.22	70	11.86	10.33
24	45.71	43.41	71	11.27	9.86
25	44.91	42.60	72	10.70	9.40
26	44.12	41.79	73	10.14	8.97
27	43.31	40.97	74	9.60	8.56
28	42.50	40.14	75	9.08	8.18
29	41.69	39.33	76	8.58	7.81
30	40.87	38.52	77	8.11	7.46
31	40.05	37.72	78	7.65	7.13
32	39.23	36.91	79	7.22	6.80
33	28.40	36.09	80	6.81	6.48
34	37.57	35.27	81	6.43	6.16
35	36.74	34.43	82	6.07	5.84

(continued)

DISABILITY RETIRED LIFE EXPECTATIONS

AGE*	OFFICERS	ENLISTED	AGE*	OFFICERS	ENLISTED
36	35.91	33.59	83	5.73	5.52
37	35.08	32.75	84	5.40	5.20
38	34.25	31.91	85	5.10	4.88
39	33.43	31.07	86	4.82	4.56
40	32.60	30.24	87	4.56	4.24
41	31.77	29.41	88	4.31	3.92
42	30.95	28.59	89	4.08	3.61
43	30.13	27.76	90	3.86	3.33
44	39.32	26.94	91	3.65	3.06
45	38.53	26.12	92	3.46	2.84
46	27.74	25.31	93	3.28	2.66
47	26.97	24.51	94	3.11	2.56
48	26.22	23.72	95	2.95	2.46
49	25.48	22.95	96	2.80	2.37
50	24.76	22.20	97	2.65	2.28
51	24.05	21.56	98	2.52	2.19
52	23.35	20.75	99	2.39	2.11
53	22.67	20.05	100	2.26	2.03
54	22.00	29.37	101	2.14	1.95
55	21.34	18.71	102	2.02	1.87
56	20.69	18.05	103	1.91	1.78
57	20.04	19.39	104	1.79	1.70
58	19.40	16.74	105	1.68	1.61
59	18.76	16.10	106	1.56	1.51
60	18.12	15.48	107	1.42	1.39
61	17.49	14.87	108	1.24	1.23
62	16.85	14.29	109	0.98	0.97

*AGE NEAREST BIRTHDAY MALE

Exhibit 6. Nonmilitary-Specific Mortality Tables (Reprinted from *Vital Statistics of the United States, 1993,* vol. II, sec. 6 (life tables), U.S. Department of Health and Human Services, Public Health Service, Centers for Disease Control and Prevention, National Center for Health Statistics, 1997.)

Table 6-3. Expectation of Life at Single Years of Age, by Race and Sex: United States, 1993

Age	All races			White			All other					
							Total			Black		
	Both sexes	Male	Female	Both sexes	Male	Female	Both sexes	Male	Female	Both sexes	Male	Female
0	75.5	72.2	78.8	76.3	73.1	79.5	71.5	67.3	75.5	69.2	64.6	73.7
1	75.2	71.8	78.4	75.8	72.6	79.0	71.5	67.3	75.4	69.4	64.8	73.8
2	74.2	70.9	77.5	74.9	71.7	78.0	70.6	66.4	74.5	68.4	63.9	72.9
3	73.3	69.9	76.5	73.9	70.7	77.0	69.6	65.5	73.5	67.5	62.9	71.9
4	72.3	68.9	75.5	72.9	69.7	76.1	68.6	64.5	72.6	66.5	62.0	71.0
5	71.3	68.0	74.6	72.0	68.8	75.1	67.7	63.5	71.6	65.6	61.0	70.0
6	70.3	67.0	73.6	71.0	67.8	74.1	66.7	62.6	70.6	64.6	60.0	69.0
7	69.3	66.0	72.6	70.0	66.8	73.1	65.7	61.6	69.7	63.6	59.0	68.0
8	68.4	65.0	71.6	69.0	65.8	72.1	64.7	60.6	68.7	62.6	58.1	67.1
9	67.4	64.0	70.6	68.0	64.8	71.1	63.8	59.6	67.7	61.7	57.1	66.1
10	66.4	63.0	69.6	67.0	63.8	70.1	62.8	58.6	66.7	60.7	56.1	65.1
11	65.4	62.0	68.6	66.0	62.8	69.1	61.8	57.6	65.7	59.7	55.1	64.1
12	64.4	61.1	67.6	65.0	61.8	68.2	60.8	56.6	64.7	58.7	54.1	63.1
13	63.4	60.1	66.7	64.1	60.9	67.2	59.8	55.7	63.8	57.7	53.1	62.1
14	62.4	59.1	65.7	63.1	59.9	66.2	58.8	54.7	62.8	56.7	52.2	61.2
15	61.5	58.1	64.7	62.1	58.9	65.2	57.9	53.7	61.8	55.8	51.2	60.2
16	60.5	57.2	63.7	61.1	58.0	64.2	56.9	52.8	60.8	54.8	50.3	59.2
17	59.5	56.2	62.7	60.2	57.0	63.2	56.0	51.9	59.8	53.9	49.4	58.2
18	58.6	55.3	61.8	59.2	56.1	62.3	55.0	51.0	58.9	53.0	48.5	57.3
19	57.7	54.4	60.8	58.3	55.1	61.3	54.1	50.1	57.9	52.1	47.7	56.3
20	56.7	53.5	59.8	57.3	54.2	60.3	53.2	49.2	56.9	51.2	46.8	55.3
21	55.8	52.6	58.9	56.4	53.3	59.4	52.3	48.4	56.0	50.3	45.9	54.4
22	54.8	51.6	57.9	55.4	52.4	58.4	51.4	47.5	55.0	49.4	45.1	53.4
23	53.9	50.7	56.9	54.5	51.4	57.4	50.5	46.7	54.1	48.5	44.3	52.5
24	52.9	49.8	55.9	53.5	50.5	56.4	49.6	45.8	53.1	47.6	43.4	51.5
25	52.0	48.9	55.0	52.6	49.6	55.5	48.7	44.9	52.2	46.7	42.6	50.6
26	51.1	48.0	54.0	51.6	48.6	54.5	47.8	44.1	51.2	45.8	41.7	49.6
27	50.1	47.1	53.0	50.7	47.7	53.5	46.9	43.2	50.3	44.9	40.9	48.7
28	49.2	46.1	52.1	49.7	46.8	52.5	46.0	42.3	49.3	44.0	40.0	47.8
29	48.3	45.2	51.1	48.8	45.9	51.8	45.1	41.4	48.4	43.1	39.2	46.8
30	47.3	44.3	50.1	47.8	44.9	50.6	44.2	40.6	47.4	42.3	38.3	45.9
31	46.4	43.4	49.2	46.9	44.0	49.6	43.3	39.7	46.5	41.4	37.5	45.0
32	45.5	42.5	48.2	46.0	43.1	48.7	42.4	38.9	45.6	40.5	36.7	44.1
33	44.5	41.6	47.3	45.0	42.2	47.7	41.5	38.0	44.6	39.6	35.8	43.2
34	43.6	40.7	46.3	44.1	41.3	46.7	40.6	37.2	43.7	38.8	35.0	42.2
35	42.7	39.8	45.4	43.2	40.4	45.8	39.7	36.3	42.8	37.9	34.2	41.3
36	41.8	38.9	44.4	42.2	39.5	44.8	38.8	35.5	41.9	37.1	33.4	40.4
37	40.8	38.0	43.5	41.3	38.6	43.9	38.0	34.6	41.0	36.2	32.6	39.5
38	39.9	37.1	42.5	40.4	37.7	42.9	37.1	33.8	40.1	35.4	31.8	38.6
39	39.0	36.2	41.6	39.4	36.8	41.9	36.2	33.0	39.1	34.5	31.0	37.8
40	38.1	35.4	40.6	38.5	35.9	41.0	35.4	32.2	38.2	33.7	30.2	36.9
41	37.2	34.5	39.7	37.6	35.0	40.0	34.5	31.4	37.3	32.9	29.5	36.0
42	36.3	33.6	38.7	36.7	34.1	39.1	33.7	30.6	36.4	32.1	28.7	35.1
43	35.4	32.7	37.8	35.8	33.2	38.1	32.8	29.8	35.6	31.3	27.9	34.2
44	34.5	31.8	36.9	34.8	32.3	37.2	32.0	29.0	34.7	30.4	27.2	33.4
45	33.6	31.0	35.9	33.9	31.4	36.3	31.2	28.2	33.8	29.6	26.4	32.5
46	32.7	30.1	35.0	33.0	30.5	35.3	30.3	27.4	32.9	28.8	25.7	31.7
47	31.8	29.2	34.1	32.1	29.6	34.4	29.5	26.6	32.0	28.1	24.9	30.8
48	30.9	28.4	33.2	31.2	28.7	33.5	28.7	25.8	31.2	27.3	24.2	30.0
49	30.0	27.5	32.3	30.3	27.9	32.6	27.9	25.1	30.3	26.5	23.5	29.1

(continued)

Exhibit 6. Continued

Age	All races			White			All other					
							Total			Black		
	Both sexes	Male	Female	Both sexes	Male	Female	Both sexes	Male	Female	Both sexes	Male	Female
50	29.2	26.7	31.4	29.5	27.0	31.7	27.1	24.3	29.5	25.7	22.8	28.3
51	28.3	25.8	30.5	28.6	26.2	30.7	26.3	23.6	28.6	25.0	22.0	27.5
52	27.4	25.0	29.6	27.7	25.3	29.9	25.5	22.8	27.8	24.2	21.4	26.7
53	26.6	24.2	28.7	26.8	24.5	29.0	24.7	22.1	26.9	23.5	20.7	25.9
54	25.7	23.4	27.8	26.0	23.6	28.1	23.9	21.4	26.1	22.7	20.0	25.1
55	24.9	22.6	27.0	25.2	22.8	27.2	23.2	20.6	25.3	22.0	19.3	24.3
56	24.1	21.8	26.1	24.3	22.0	26.3	22.4	20.0	24.5	21.3	18.7	23.5
57	23.3	21.0	25.3	23.5	21.2	25.5	21.7	19.3	23.7	20.6	18.0	22.8
58	22.5	20.2	24.4	22.7	20.5	24.6	21.0	18.6	23.0	19.9	17.4	22.0
59	21.7	19.5	23.6	21.9	19.7	23.8	20.3	17.9	22.2	19.3	16.8	21.3
60	20.9	18.8	22.8	21.1	18.9	23.0	19.6	17.3	21.4	18.6	16.2	20.6
61	20.2	18.0	22.0	20.4	18.2	22.2	18.9	16.7	20.7	18.0	15.6	19.8
62	19.5	17.3	21.2	19.6	17.5	21.4	18.2	16.0	20.0	17.3	15.1	19.1
63	18.7	16.6	20.4	18.9	16.8	20.6	17.6	15.4	19.2	16.7	14.5	18.4
64	18.0	16.0	19.7	18.1	16.1	19.8	16.9	14.8	18.5	16.1	13.9	17.8
65	17.3	15.3	18.9	17.4	15.4	19.0	16.3	14.3	17.8	15.5	13.4	17.1
66	16.6	14.7	18.2	16.7	14.8	18.3	15.6	13.7	17.1	14.9	12.9	16.4
67	15.9	14.0	17.4	16.0	14.1	17.5	15.0	13.1	16.4	14.3	12.3	15.8
68	15.3	13.4	16.7	15.4	13.5	16.8	14.4	12.6	15.8	13.7	11.8	15.2
69	14.6	12.8	16.0	14.7	12.9	16.1	13.8	12.0	15.1	13.2	11.3	14.5
70	14.0	12.2	15.3	14.0	12.3	15.3	13.2	11.5	14.5	12.6	10.8	13.9
71	13.3	11.6	14.6	13.4	11.7	14.6	12.7	11.0	13.8	12.1	10.4	13.3
72	12.7	11.1	13.9	12.8	11.1	14.0	12.1	10.5	13.2	11.6	9.9	12.8
73	12.1	10.5	13.2	12.2	10.6	13.3	11.6	10.0	12.6	11.1	9.5	12.2
74	11.5	10.0	12.6	11.6	10.0	12.6	11.0	9.6	12.0	10.6	9.1	11.6
75	10.9	9.5	11.9	11.0	9.5	12.0	10.5	9.1	11.5	10.2	8.7	11.1
76	10.4	9.0	11.3	10.4	9.0	11.3	10.0	8.7	10.9	9.7	8.3	10.6
77	9.8	8.5	10.7	9.9	8.5	10.7	9.5	8.2	10.3	9.2	7.9	10.0
78	9.3	8.0	10.1	9.3	8.0	10.1	9.0	7.8	9.8	8.7	7.5	9.5
79	8.8	7.5	9.5	8.8	7.5	9.5	8.5	7.3	9.2	8.3	7.1	9.0
80	8.3	7.1	8.9	8.3	7.1	8.9	8.0	6.9	8.7	7.8	6.7	8.5
81	7.8	6.7	8.4	7.8	6.7	8.4	7.6	6.5	8.2	7.4	6.3	8.0
82	7.3	6.2	7.8	7.3	6.2	7.8	7.1	6.1	7.7	7.0	5.9	7.5
83	6.8	5.9	7.3	6.8	5.9	7.3	6.7	5.8	7.2	6.6	5.6	7.1
84	6.4	5.5	6.8	6.4	5.5	6.8	6.3	5.4	6.8	6.2	5.3	6.7
85	6.0	5.2	6.4	6.0	5.2	6.4	5.9	5.1	6.3	5.9	5.0	6.3

Exhibit 7. Total Military Lifetime Retired Pay Lump-Sum Equivalency Table (Reprinted from Office of the Actuary, Department of Defense, FY 1996 DOD Statistical Report on the Military Retirement System 286–87 (1997).)

LUMP-SUM-EQUIVALENT* VALUE OF MILITARY NON-DISABILITY RETIRED PAY IN DOLLARS AT THE TIME OF RETIREMENT AS OF JANUARY 1, 1997

RET PAY GRD	YEARS OF SERVICE															
	15	16	17	18	19	20	21	22	23	24	25	26	27	28	29	30
COMMISSIONED OFFICERS																
C/S	942,725	1,003,113	1,062,639	1,120,893	1,178,021	1,233,625	1,275,288	1,314,395	1,351,397	1,385,999	1,417,889	1,447,517	1,474,360	1,498,845	1,520,677	1,539,591
O10	877,027	999,989	1,059,286	1,117,587	1,174,491	1,233,625	1,275,288	1,314,395	1,351,397	1,385,999	1,417,889	1,447,517	1,474,360	1,498,845	1,520,677	1,539,591
O-9	767,148	884,450	936,620	988,083	1,038,440	1,147,763	1,186,547	1,222,934	1,257,380	1,289,592	1,319,264	1,443,171	1,470,098	1,494,435	1,516,130	1,535,140
O-8	736,450	816,197	864,529	951,712	1,000,150	1,087,580	1,124,139	1,187,438	1,220,691	1,252,031	1,280,896	1,307,497	1,332,039	1,353,998	1,373,566	1,390,929
O-7	639,194	748,228	792,438	893,573	939,050	983,530	1,016,702	1,048,044	1,077,500	1,104,792	1,130,376	1,153,958	1,175,510	1,194,991	1,212,358	1,227,578
O-6	462,756	570,092	603,829	669,560	703,608	752,961	778,392	848,799	872,650	925,251	946,653	1,013,938	1,032,715	1,049,911	1,065,020	1,078,470
O-5	444,682	508,353	538,445	600,675	631,374	681,276	704,134	751,120	772,263	792,035	810,398	827,325	842,559	856,549	869,023	879,957
O-4	419,722	466,439	494,017	535,373	562,669	589,262	609,336	628,049	645,634	662,074	677,340	691,650	704,501	716,112	726,460	735,523
COMMISSIONED OFFICERS WITH LESS THAN 4 YEARS OF ACTIVE ENLISTED SERVICE																
O-3	389,599	414,329	438,971	463,181	486,633	509,820	526,915	543,066	558,496	572,679	585,848	598,223	609,304	619,315	628,234	636,266
O-2	288,900	307,561	325,805	343,597	361,173	378,219	391,039	402,895	414,286	424,939	434,590	443,718	452,065	459,612	466,117	472,026
O-1	228,079	242,424	257,067	271,130	284,865	298,242	308,355	317,911	326,893	335,294	342,851	350,050	356,631	362,583	367,664	372,324
COMMISSIONED OFFICERS WITH MORE THAN 4 YEARS OF ACTIVE ENLISTED SERVICE																
O-3	395,336	420,560	445,397	470,070	493,965	517,309	534,815	551,098	566,649	581,193	594,702	606,914	618,303	628,600	637,557	645,613
O-2	334,515	355,989	377,219	397,878	418,200	437,867	452,657	466,632	479,766	492,048	503,455	513,970	523,343	532,036	539,786	546,579
O-1	283,162	301,330	319,099	336,709	353,841	370,462	382,876	394,863	405,878	416,175	425,982	432,786	442,829	450,095	456,794	462,456
WARRANT OFFICERS																
W-5	416,280	442,933	469,148	494,868	520,306	544,860	563,254	602,399	619,390	653,560	668,732	711,446	724,629	736,772	747,378	756,665
W-4	340,827	375,530	397,616	430,668	452,688	489,491	505,849	538,920	554,165	585,951	599,375	639,746	651,693	662,491	672,117	680,554
W-3	298,080	326,819	346,203	376,386	395,661	430,378	445,021	475,183	488,684	501,063	512,801	541,732	551,997	561,051	569,117	576,401
W-2	267,670	294,817	312,393	340,291	357,643	386,243	399,202	428,286	440,274	451,482	461,890	471,481	480,245	488,163	495,448	501,625
W-1	246,440	271,877	288,083	314,390	330,487	358,425	370,500	381,908	392,629	402,653	411,963	420,543	428,384	435,471	441,788	447,323

(continued)

Exhibit 7. Continued

LUMP-SUM-EQUIVALENT* VALUE OF MILITARY NON-DISABILITY RETIRED PAY IN DOLLARS AT THE TIME OF RETIREMENT AS OF JANUARY 1, 1997

RET PAY GRD	YEARS OF SERVICE															
	15	16	17	18	19	20	21	22	23	24	25	26	27	28	29	30
ENLISTED MEMBERS																
SEM	436,914	464,922	492,139	519,062	545,350	571,208	590,068	608,034	624,829	640,186	654,593	667,779	679,508	690,243	699,759	707,845
E-9	291,841	317,562	336,337	362,747	381,184	406,917	420,369	455,898	468,309	498,741	509,744	549,351	559,036	567,941	575,619	582,522
E-8	253,455	276,892	293,195	316,151	332,335	356,446	368,372	401,964	413,052	442,016	451,900	490,492	499,263	507,131	514,104	520,187
E-7	224,666	245,971	260,496	282,287	296,566	314,651	325,171	357,442	367,296	395,113	403,939	441,325	449,221	456,305	462,582	467,842
E-6	200,958	220,900	233,842	250,320	263,199	275,484	284,557	293,332	301,288	308,920	315,728	322,188	327,823	332,869	337,554	341,434
E-5	178,943	190,258	201,417	212,393	223,425	233,688	241,615	248,811	255,782	262,017	268,007	273,257	278,244	282,496	286,477	289,741
E-4	143,945	153,210	162,398	171,215	179,915	188,212	194,534	200,473	206,026	211,185	215,948	220,071	224,031	227,585	230,736	233,487
E-3	123,623	131,482	139,316	146,833	154,289	161,663	166,854	171,979	176,772	181,226	185,098	188,869	192,292	195,365	197,869	200,256
E-2	104,148	110,868	117,608	123,805	130,265	136,427	140,985	145,267	149,269	152,741	156,177	159,321	162,174	164,733	167,000	168,979
E-1	92,858	98,890	104,693	110,531	116,117	121,707	125,723	129,493	133,017	136,288	139,306	142,065	144,798	147,034	149,012	150,735

NOTE: AS A RESULT OF CERTAIN PROVISIONS FOR ADVANCEMENT ON THE RETIRED LIST OR UNDER THE 'TOWER AMENDMENT' SOME INDIVIDUALS WOULD RECEIVE AMOUNTS DIFFERING FROM THOSE SHOWN ABOVE.

TABLES SHOW FIGURES FOR RETIREES UNDER FINAL PAY. I.E. THOSE ENTERING THE SERVICE PRIOR TO SEPTEMBER 8, 1980.

FIGURES SHOWN ASSUME THAT ACTIVE SERVICE AND PAY SERVICE ARE EQUAL.

MILITARY RETIRED PAY REFLECTS PAY AND PAY CAP INCREASES PRIOR TO AND INCLUDING JANUARY 1, 1997.

ACTIVE DUTY PAY CAP OF 9016.80 PER MONTH LEVELS OUT RETIRED PAY IN UPPER GRADES.

PUBLIC LAW 102-484 GRANTED DOD TEMPORARY EARLY RETIREMENT AUTHORITY (TERA) FOR SELECTED ACTIVE DUTY MEMBERS WITH AS FEW AS 15 YEARS OF SERVICE. THEIR RETIRED PAY IS SUBJECT TO REDUCTION FACTORS FOR SERVICE LESS THAN 20 YEARS. THE FY94 DEFENSE AUTHORIZATION ACT EXTENDED TERA THROUGH SEPTEMBER 30, 1999.

*THE LUMP-SUM-EQUIVALENT IS THE AMOUNT OF MONEY REQUIRED TO BE ON HAND AT THE TIME OF RETIREMENT TO PAY A LIFETIME ANNUITY THAT INCREASES WITH INFLATION AT 3.50% ANNUALLY. THE INTEREST RATE USED IN DISCOUNTING TO THE PRESENT VALUE IS 6.50% RESULTING IN WHAT IS COMMONLY REFERRED TO AS A REAL INTEREST RATE OF 3.00%. LONGEVITY IS BASED ON MILITARY SPECIFIC TABLES THAT ASSUME AN ENTRY AGE OF 23 FOR COMMISSIONED OFFICERS AND WARRANT OFFICERS AND 20 FOR ENLISTED.

WARNING: THESE FIGURES SHOULD NOT BE USED IN PROPERTY SETTLEMENTS FOR THE FOLLOWING REASONS:

  (1) THEY ASSUME FULL FUTURE COST-OF-LIVING ADJUSTMENTS (WHICH HAVE BEEN DETERMINED IN SOME COURTS NOT TO BE PROPERTY).
  (2) THE INVESTMENT RETURN IS LOW (PRODUCING LARGE LUMP-SUMS) BECAUSE OF THE CONSERVATIVE PORTFOLIO OF GOVERNMENT TRUST FUNDS.
  (3) ONLY THE MORTALITY OF THE RETIREE IS CONSIDERED (SOME COURTS REQUIRE THE USE OF THE SPOUSE'S MORTALITY).

Exhibit 7. Continued

MILITARY RETIRED PAY, LUMP-SUM-EQUIVALENT* AT RETIREMENT, AND ANNUAL DEPOSIT# NECESSARY
TO ACCUMULATE THE LUMP-SUM-EQUIVALENT* FOR NONDISABILITY RETIREMENTS AS OF JANUARY 1, 1997

RETIRED PAY GRADE	TITLE ARMY/NAVY	RETIREMENT AFTER 20 YEARS				RETIREMENT AFTER 30 YEARS			
		MONTHLY RET PAY	LUMP-SUM EQUIVALENT*	MONTHLY DEPOSIT#	ANNUAL DEPOSIT#	MONTHLY RET PAY	LUMP-SUM EQUIVALENT*	MONTHLY DEPOSIT#	ANNUAL DEPOSIT#
COMMISSIONED OFFICERS									
C/S	CHIEF OF STAFF	4,612	1,233,625	2,565	30,774	6,918	1,539,591	1,439	17,263
O10	GENERAL/ADMIRAL	4,612	1,233,625	2,565	30,774	6,918	1,539,591	1,439	17,263
O-9	LIEUTENANT GENERAL/VICE ADMIRAL	4,291	1,147,763	2,386	28,632	6,898	1,535,140	1,435	17,214
O-8	MAJOR GENERAL/REAR ADMIRAL (UH)	4,066	1,087,580	2,261	27,130	6,250	1,390,929	1,300	15,597
O-7	BRIGADIER GENERAL/REAR ADMIRAL (LH)	3,677	983,530	2,045	24,535	5,516	1,227,578	1,147	13,765
O-6	COLONEL/CAPTAIN	2,815	752,961	1,565	18,783	4,846	1,078,470	1,008	12,093
O-5	LIEUTENANT COLONEL/COMMANDER	2,547	681,276	1,416	16,995	3,954	879,957	822	9,867
O-4	MAJOR/LIEUTENANT COMMANDER	2,203	589,262	1,225	14,700	3,305	735,523	687	8,247
COMMISSIONED OFFICERS WITH LESS THAN 4 YEARS OF ACTIVE ENLISTED SERVICE									
O-3	CAPTAIN/LIEUTENANT	1,906	509,820	1,060	12,718	2,859	636,266	595	7,134
O-2	1ST LIEUTENANT/LIEUTENANT (JG)	1,414	378,219	786	9,435	2,121	472,026	441	5,293
O-1	2ND LIEUTENANT/ENSIGN	1,115	298,242	620	7,440	1,673	372,324	348	4,175
COMMISSIONED OFFICERS WITH MORE THAN 4 YEARS OF ACTIVE ENLISTED SERVICE									
O-3	CAPTAIN/LIEUTENANT	1,934	517,309	1,075	12,905	2,901	645,613	603	7,239
O-2	1ST LIEUTENANT/LIEUTENANT (JG)	1,637	437,867	910	10,923	2,456	546,579	511	6,129
O-1	2ND LIEUTENANT/ENSIGN	1,385	370,462	770	9,241	2,078	462,456	432	5,186
WARRANT OFFICERS									
W-5	CHIEF WARRANT OFFICER	2,037	544,860	1,133	13,592	3,400	756,665	707	8,484
W-4	CHIEF WARRANT OFFICER	1,830	489,491	1,018	12,211	3,058	680,554	636	7,631
W-3	CHIEF WARRANT OFFICER	1,609	430,378	895	10,736	2,590	576,401	539	6,463
W-2	CHIEF WARRANT OFFICER	1,444	386,243	803	9,635	2,254	501,625	469	5,625
W-1	WARRANT OFFICER	1,340	358,425	745	8,941	2,010	447,323	418	5,016

Exhibit 7. Continued

MILITARY RETIRED PAY, LUMP-SUM-EQUIVALENT* AT RETIREMENT, AND ANNUAL DEPOSIT# NECESSARY
TO ACCUMULATE THE LUMP-SUM-EQUIVALENT* FOR NONDISABILITY RETIREMENTS AS OF JANUARY 1, 1997

RETIRED PAY GRADE	TITLE ARMY/NAVY	RETIREMENT AFTER 20 YEARS				RETIREMENT AFTER 30 YEARS			
		MONTHLY RET PAY	LUMP-SUM EQUIVALENT*	MONTHLY DEPOSIT#	ANNUAL DEPOSIT#	MONTHLY RET PAY	LUMP-SUM EQUIVALENT*	MONTHLY DEPOSIT#	ANNUAL DEPOSIT#
ENLISTED MEMBERS									
SEM	SENIOR ENLISTED MEMBER	2,173	571,208	1,187	14,249	3,259	707,845	661	7,937
E-9	SGT MAJOR/MASTER CHIEF PETTY OFFICER	1,548	406,917	846	10,151	2,682	582,522	544	6,532
E-8	MASTER SGT/SENIOR CHIEF PETTY OFFICER	1,356	356,446	741	8,892	2,395	520,187	486	5,833
E-7	SGT FIRST CLASS/CHIEF PETTY OFFICER	1,197	314,651	654	7,849	2,154	467,842	437	5,246
E-6	STAFF SGT/PETTY OFFICER FIRST CLASS	1,048	275,484	573	6,872	1,572	341,434	319	3,829
E-5	SERGEANT/PETTY OFFICER SECOND CLASS	889	233,688	486	5,830	1,334	289,741	271	3,249
E-4	CORPORAL/PETTY OFFICER THIRD CLASS	716	188,212	391	4,695	1,075	233,487	218	2,618
E-3	PRIVATE FIRST CLASS/SEAMAN	615	161,663	336	4,033	922	200,256	187	2,245
E-2	PRIVATE/SEAMAN APPRENTICE	519	136,427	284	3,403	778	168,979	158	1,895
E-1	RECRUIT/SEAMAN RECRUIT	463	121,707	253	3,036	694	150,735	141	1,690

NOTE: AS A RESULT OF CERTAIN PROVISIONS FOR ADVANCEMENT ON THE RETIRED LIST OR UNDER THE 'TOWER AMENDMENT' SOME INDIVIDUALS WOULD RECEIVE AMOUNTS DIFFERING FROM THOSE SHOWN ABOVE.

TABLES SHOW FIGURES FOR RETIREES UNDER FINAL PAY. I.E. THOSE ENTERING THE SERVICE PRIOR TO SEPTEMBER 8, 1980.

FIGURES SHOWN ASSUME THAT ACTIVE SERVICE AND PAY SERVICE ARE EQUAL.

MILITARY RETIRED PAY REFLECTS CPI AND PAY CAP INCREASES PRIOR TO AND INCLUDING JANUARY 1, 1997.

ACTIVE DUTY PAY CAP OF 9016.80 PER MONTH LEVELS OUT RETIRED PAY IN UPPER GRADES.

#DEPOSIT IS THE AMOUNT NECESSARY TO ACCUMULATE AT 6.50% INTEREST TO THE LUMP-SUM-EQUIVALENT.

*THE LUMP-SUM-EQUIVALENT IS THE AMOUNT OF MONEY REQUIRED TO BE ON HAND AT THE TIME OF RETIREMENT TO PAY A LIFETIME ANNUITY THAT INCREASES WITH INFLATION AT 3.50% ANNUALLY. THE INTEREST RATE USED IN DISCOUNTING TO THE PRESENT VALUE IS 6.50% RESULTING IN WHAT IS COMMONLY REFERRED TO AS A REAL INTEREST RATE OF 3.00%. LONGEVITY IS BASED ON MILITARY SPECIFIC TABLES THAT ASSUME AN ENTRY AGE OF 23 FOR COMMISSIONED OFFICERS AND WARRANT OFFICERS AND 20 FOR ENLISTED MEMBERS.

WARNING: THESE FIGURES SHOULD NOT BE USED IN PROPERTY SETTLEMENTS FOR THE FOLLOWING REASONS:

(1) THEY ASSUME FULL FUTURE COST-OF-LIVING ADJUSTMENTS (WHICH HAVE BEEN DETERMINED IN SOME COURTS NOT TO BE PROPERTY).
(2) THE INVESTMENT RETURN IS LOW (PRODUCING LARGE LUMP-SUMS) BECAUSE OF THE CONSERVATIVE PORTFOLIO OF GOVERNMENT TRUST FUNDS.
(3) ONLY THE MORTALITY OF THE RETIREE IS CONSIDERED (SOME COURTS REQUIRE THE USE OF THE SPOUSE'S MORTALITY).

Exhibit 8.   1997 BAQ Table

Basic allowance for quarters

| | Dependents | | |
| | Without | | With |
	Full	**Partial**	
0–10	824.70	50.70	1015.20
0–9	824.70	50.70	1015.20
0–8	824.70	50.70	1015.20
0–7	824.70	50.70	1015.20
0–6	756.60	39.60	914.10
0–5	728.70	33.00	881.10
0–4	675.30	26.70	776.70
0–3	541.20	22.20	642.60
0–2	429.30	17.70	518.70
0–1	361.50	13.20	490.50
0–3E	584.40	22.20	690.60
0–2E	496.80	17.70	623.10
0–1E	427.20	13.20	575.70
W–5	686.10	25.20	749.70
W–4	609.30	25.20	607.30
W–3	512.10	20.70	629.70
W–2	454.80	15.90	579.30
W–1	380.70	13.80	501.00
E–9	500.40	18.60	659.70
E–8	459.30	15.30	608.10
E–7	392.40	12.99	564.60
E–6	355.20	9.90	521.70
E–5	327.60	8.70	469.20
E–4	285.00	8.10	408.00
E–3	279.60	7.80	379.80
E–2	227.10	7.20	361.50
E–1	202.50	6.90	361.50

Exhibit 9. 1998 BAS Table

Basic allowance for subsistence

Officers
(including commissioned officers, warrants and aviation cadets).

$155.70 a month

Enlisted (daily)

Rations in kind not available

<4 mos.	$7.73
Others	$8.38

On leave or authorized to mess separately

<4 mos.	$6.86
Others	$7.43

Emergency conditions where no government messing is available

<4 mos.	$10.26
Others	$11.10

Receiving rations in kind—partial

$0.31

Exhibit 10.   1997 and 1998 Basic Military Compensation Tables

ASSUME ALL CASH BMC PAY GRADE AVERAGES

YEARS OF SERVICE

PAY GRADE	UNDER 2	2	3	4	6	8	10	12	14	16	18	20	22	24	26
COMMISSIONED OFFICERS															
C/S	0.00	0.00	0.00	0.00	0.00	0.00	0.00	0.00	0.00	0.00	0.00	0.00	0.00	0.00	128312.71
O-10	0.00	0.00	0.00	0.00	0.00	0.00	0.00	0.00	0.00	0.00	0.00	0.00	0.00	0.00	128286.49
O-9	0.00	0.00	0.00	0.00	0.00	0.00	0.00	0.00	0.00	0.00	0.00	0.00	0.00	0.00	127340.38
O-8	0.00	0.00	0.00	0.00	0.00	0.00	0.00	0.00	0.00	0.00	0.00	0.00	116752.68	116869.34	116795.48
O-7	0.00	0.00	0.00	0.00	0.00	0.00	0.00	0.00	0.00	0.00	105269.62	0.00	105247.30	105342.14	105277.25
O-6	49539.04	55619.44	58697.28	68029.94	67611.30	67618.77	67605.60	67573.59	69650.11	78857.34	82017.33	83426.86	87239.09	89589.83	93117.44
O-5	42618.32	49085.70	51470.86	58860.26	58655.15	58652.51	60112.72	62868.94	66555.52	70963.66	74490.77	76395.41	78569.97	0.00	0.00
O-4	38485.91	41884.04	44046.21	51474.23	52182.38	53910.72	56780.24	59383.41	61719.80	64126.99	65706.98	0.00	0.00	0.00	0.00
O-3	32965.74	35368.43	41105.19	47523.75	49255.36	50612.56	52740.15	54846.56	55963.03	0.00	0.00	0.00	0.00	0.00	0.00
O-2	28575.64	29404.84	34135.80	42170.16	42839.77	0.00	0.00	0.00	0.00	0.00	0.00	0.00	0.00	0.00	0.00
O-1	0.00	0.00	0.00	0.00	0.00	0.00	0.00	0.00	0.00	0.00	0.00	0.00	0.00	0.00	0.00
O-3E	0.00	0.00	0.00	48102.43	49929.86	51308.74	53430.33	55569.40	57408.07	0.00	0.00	0.00	0.00	0.00	0.00
O-2E	0.00	0.00	0.00	43243.94	43928.36	44976.38	46754.92	48126.01	49145.04	0.00	0.00	0.00	0.00	0.00	0.00
O-1E	0.00	0.00	0.00	35274.77	37266.32	38415.34	39593.76	40758.57	42232.93	0.00	0.00	0.00	0.00	0.00	0.00
ALLO3	38485.91	41884.04	44046.21	47523.79	49255.77	50618.17	52771.26	55092.43	57144.88	0.00	0.00	0.00	0.00	0.00	0.00
ALLO2	32965.74	35368.43	41105.19	42171.99	42913.99	44976.38	46754.92	48126.01	49145.04	0.00	0.00	0.00	0.00	0.00	0.00
ALLO1	28575.64	29404.84	34135.80	35274.77	37266.32	38415.34	39593.76	40758.57	42232.93	0.00	0.00	0.00	0.00	0.00	0.00
ALL CO	29784.39	34590.84	39648.49	45890.36	48421.41	50296.47	52862.45	57124.74	58800.94	67224.77	70055.39	77009.07	80963.32	89660.51	96015.59

Exhibit 10. Continued

ASSUME ALL CASH BMC PAY GRADE AVERAGES

								YEARS OF SERVICE							
PAY GRADE	UNDER 2	2	3	4	6	8	10	12	14	16	18	20	22	24	26
WARRANT OFFICER															
W-5	0.00	0.00	0.00	0.00	0.00	0.00	0.00	0.00	0.00	0.00	0.00	60984.52	63041.41	64665.99	67153.51
W-4	0.00	0.00	0.00	0.00	0.00	0.00	0.00	0.00	50851.49	52234.48	53316.90	54686.28	56152.98	57617.17	59868.27
W-3	0.00	0.00	0.00	0.00	39221.86	41268.49	43043.80	44087.75	45135.30	46154.20	47244.98	48656.14	50013.34	50013.24	51381.28
W-2	0.00	34173.62	34168.61	34877.68	36259.80	37718.58	38784.46	39851.90	40892.61	41988.10	43028.60	44054.97	45415.07	0.00	0.00
W-1	27570.82	30166.46	30220.50	31941.95	32989.50	34045.26	35098.15	36198.92	37258.03	38338.16	39384.50	40496.05	0.00	0.00	0.00
ALL WO	27570.82	32024.33	32309.33	34015.12	35208.97	36562.90	37707.07	39016.24	41402.73	43516.23	46113.07	48686.47	51590.51	55320.52	60111.01
ALLOFF	29769.22	34562.29	39552.45	45679.80	48118.19	49677.66	51910.60	55531.96	57790.47	64378.84	67289.33	71482.95	77853.13	83555.98	88587.24
ENLISTED MEMBERS															
M/S	0.00	0.00	0.00	0.00	0.00	0.00	0.00	0.00	0.00	0.00	0.00	0.00	0.00	0.00	0.00
E-9	0.00	0.00	0.00	0.00	0.00	0.00	0.00	45622.68	46371.48	47128.99	47907.59	48591.48	50488.79	51972.09	54215.87
E-8	0.00	0.00	0.00	0.00	0.00	38932.62	39713.82	40390.86	41145.26	41935.60	42631.56	43397.60	45258.81	46752.82	48999.19
E-7	0.00	0.00	32378.50	0.00	33718.31	34406.91	35170.97	35938.38	37082.31	37835.09	38587.88	38956.94	40860.85	42366.35	44596.81
E-6	26561.33	28184.84	28902.66	29647.10	30309.83	31004.39	31775.67	32896.32	33612.64	34380.90	34755.82	0.00	0.00	0.00	0.00
E-5	23534.09	24923.10	25706.26	26443.99	27603.51	28365.30	29085.14	29765.32	30108.12	0.00	0.00	0.00	0.00	0.00	0.00
E-4	21350.04	22145.93	23022.60	24203.91	24851.52	0.00	0.00	0.00	0.00	0.00	0.00	0.00	0.00	0.00	0.00
E-3	20053.15	20757.04	21299.25	21860.02	0.00	0.00	0.00	0.00	0.00	0.00	0.00	0.00	0.00	0.00	0.00
E-2	18785.94	0.00	0.00	0.00	0.00	0.00	0.00	0.00	0.00	0.00	0.00	0.00	0.00	0.00	0.00
E-1>4	17076.03	0.00	0.00	0.00	0.00	0.00	0.00	0.00	0.00	0.00	0.00	0.00	0.00	0.00	0.00
E-1<4	16001.63	0.00	0.00	0.00	0.00	0.00	0.00	0.00	0.00	0.00	0.00	0.00	0.00	0.00	0.00
All ENL	18554.87	21321.25	22718.39	24495.72	26179.90	28933.00	30115.07	31926.76	33152.50	36326.74	37478.41	40907.13	44083.21	47701.97	53097.79
ALL DOD	19167.71	22435.11	24581.81	27385.12	29942.24	33575.58	34227.28	36519.10	38820.32	41937.49	44350.26	48278.54	59009.17	62351.41	73608.24

Exhibit 10. Continued

BASIC MILITARY COMPENSATION*

Average Annual Basic Military Compensation (BMC) (Amounts rounded to nearest dollar)

Pay Grade	Under 2	Over 2	Over 3	Over 4	Over 6	Over 8	Over 10	Over 12	Over 14	Over 16	Over 18	Over 20	Over 22	Over 24	Over 26/30
							YEARS OF SERVICE								
O-10	0	0	0	0	0	0	0	0	0	0	0	0	0	0	136,820
O-9	0	0	0	0	0	0	0	0	0	0	0	0	0	0	136,374
O-8	0	0	0	0	0	0	0	0	0	0	0	0	125,527	125,649	125,545
O-7	0	0	0	0	0	0	0	0	0	0	113,491	0	113,457	113,554	113,481
O-6	0	0	0	74,648	74,169	74,210	74,210	74,215	76,294	85,759	89,007	90,461	94,377	96,793	100,422
O-5	0	60,914	64,195	64,335	64,380	64,386	65,947	68,848	72,676	77,212	80,832	82,785	85,016	0	0
O-4	47,060	53,711	56,196	56,198	56,954	58,796	61,880	64,706	67,170	69,685	71,324	0	0	0	0
O-3	42,184	45,672	47,890	51,465	53,247	54,640	56,914	59,154	60,335	0	0	0	0	0	0
O-2	36,037	38,497	44,377	45,472	46,160	0	0	0	0	0	0	0	0	0	0
O-1	31,143	32,011	37,054	0	0	0	0	0	0	0	0	0	0	0	0
COMMISSIONED OFFICERS WITH OVER 4 YEARS OF ACTIVE SERVICE AS AN ENLISTED MEMBER OR WARRANT OFFICER															
O-3E	0	0	0	52,658	54,287	55,739	58,037	60,303	62,257	0	0	0	0	0	0
O-2E	0	0	0	47,057	47,739	48,815	50,644	52,052	53,099	0	0	0	0	0	0
O-1E	0	0	0	38,478	40,523	41,699	42,912	44,102	45,609	0	0	0	0	0	0
WARRANT OFFICERS															
W-5	0	0	0	0	0	0	0	0	55,168	56,641	57,777	66,592	68,594	70,380	72,928
W-4	0	0	0	0	0	0	46,928	48,001	49,077	50,125	51,245	59,235	60,818	62,409	64,837
W-3	0	0	37,575	42,659	42,994	45,102	42,327	43,423	44,493	45,617	46,686	52,695	54,092	54,092	55,514
W-2	0	37,595	37,575	38,318	39,735	41,232	38,348	39,482	40,561	41,678	42,756	47,741	49,143	0	0
W-1	30,514	33,226	33,256	35,089	36,184	37,257	0	0	0	0	0	43,918	0	0	0

*Basic Military Compensation (BMC) combines basic pay, basic allowance for housing and basic allowance for subsistence and the federal tax advantage on the tax free allowances. The BMC is at best, a guide to income for any member in a given grade and year of service. (As of January 1, 1998 based on 2.8% increase in Basic Pay)

(continued)

Exhibit 10. Continued

ARMED FORCES ENLISTED PAY Basic Pay Pay Rates, Effective January 1, 1998

Pay Grade	Under 2	Over 2	Over 3	Over 4	Over 6	Over 8	Over 10	Over 12	Over 14	Over 16	Over 18	Over 20	Over 22	Over 24	Over 26
										YEARS OF SERVICE					
E-9							2777.40	2839.80	2904.00	2970.90	3037.50	3096.00	3258.60	3385.50	3576.00
E-8						2328.90	2396.10	2458.80	2522.70	2589.60	2648.40	2713.50	2873.10	3000.90	3193.50
E-7	1626.30	1755.60	1820.10	1884.30	1948.50	2010.60	2074.80	2139.60	2236.20	2299.80	2363.40	2394.30	2555.10	2682.30	2873.10
E-6	1398.90	1524.90	1588.20	1655.70	1718.10	1779.90	1845.30	1940.10	2001.30	2065.80	2097.00	2097.00	2097.00	2097.00	2097.00
E-5	1227.60	1336.20	1401.00	1462.20	1558.20	1621.80	1685.70	1748.10	1779.90	1779.90	1779.90	1779.90	1779.90	1779.90	1779.90
E-4	1144.80	1209.30	1280.40	1379.10	1433.70	1433.70	1433.70	1433.70	1433.70	1433.70	1433.70	1433.70	1433.70	1433.70	1433.70
E-3	1079.10	1137.90	1183.20	1230.30	1230.30	1230.30	1230.30	1230.30	1230.30	1230.30	1230.30	1230.30	1230.30	1230.30	1230.30
E-2	1038.30	1038.30	1038.30	1038.30	1038.30	1038.30	1038.30	1038.30	1038.30	1038.30	1038.30	1038.30	1038.30	1038.30	1038.30
E-1	926.10	926.10	926.10	926.10	926.10	926.10	926.10	926.10	926.10	926.10	926.10	926.10	926.10	926.10	926.10

Note: While serving as the senior enlisted member of the Service, basic pay is $4,346.40 regardless of years of service.

ENLISTED PERSONNEL* Average Annual Basic Military Compensation (BMC) (Amounts rounded to nearest dollar)

Pay Grade	Under 2	Over 2	Over 3	Over 4	Over 6	Over 8	Over 10	Over 12	Over 14	Over 16	Over 18	Over 20	Over 22	Over 24	Over 26
										YEARS OF SERVICE					
E-9	0	0	0	0	0	0	0	49,615	0	51,168	51,958	52,660	54,611	56,171	58,558
E-8	0	0	0	0	0	0	43,297	43,980	44,766	45,580	46,295	47,084	48,999	50,532	52,843
E-7	33,264	34,815	35,589	36,360	36,932	37,654	38,431	39,221	40,399	41,174	41,950	42,327	44,287	45,838	48,132
E-6	29,438	30,873	31,570	32,417	33,195	33,944	34,737	35,910	36,660	37,450	37,833	0	0	0	0
E-5	26,023	27,387	28,213	29,002	30,129	30,848	31,592	32,351	32,734	0	0	0	0	0	0
E-4	23,513	24,332	25,226	26,407	27,060	0	0	0	0	0	0	0	0	0	0
E-3	22,183	22,907	23,465	24,045	0	0	0	0	0	0	0	0	0	0	0
E-2	21,492	0	0	0	0	0	0	0	0	0	0	0	0	0	0
E-1>4	19,834	0	0	0	0	0	0	0	0	0	0	0	0	0	0

*Basic Military Compensation (BMC) combines basic pay, basic allowance for housing and basic allowance for subsistence and the federal tax advantage on the tax free allowances. The BMC is at best, a guide to income for any member in a given grade and year of service. (As of January 1, 1998 based on 2.8% increase in Basic Pay)

Exhibit 11. 1997 Regular Military Compensation Table

ASSUME ALL CASH RMC PAY GRADE AVERAGES

PAY GRADE	UNDER 2	2	3	4	6	YEARS OF SERVICE 8	10	12	14	16	18	20	22	24	26
COMMISSIONED OFFICERS															
C/S	0.00	0.00	0.00	0.00	0.00	0.00	0.00	0.00	0.00	0.00	0.00	0.00	0.00	0.00	134240.??
O-10	0.00	0.00	0.00	0.00	0.00	0.00	0.00	0.00	0.00	0.00	0.00	0.00	0.00	0.00	134214.??
O-9	0.00	0.00	0.00	0.00	0.00	0.00	0.00	0.00	0.00	0.00	0.00	0.00	0.00	0.00	133258.??
O-8	0.00	0.00	0.00	0.00	0.00	0.00	0.00	0.00	0.00	0.00	0.00	0.00	122609.23	122797.34	122667.??
O-7	0.00	0.00	0.00	0.00	0.00	0.00	0.00	0.00	0.00	0.00	110925.21	0.00	110895.08	111023.14	110935.??
O-6	0.00	0.00	0.00	72921.94	72441.70	72482.53	72465.33	72421.40	74507.63	83712.71	86869.68	88279.85	92092.54	94443.26	97970.??
O-5	53312.54	59575.12	62922.03	62868.21	62881.61	62871.00	64391.96	67226.90	70949.74	75362.24	78889.35	80793.98	82968.55	0.00	0.00
O-4	46001.23	52469.49	54892.15	54895.22	55623.12	57422.72	60434.98	63189.48	65587.88	68029.83	69626.81	0.00	0.00	0.00	0.00
O-3	41232.06	44630.18	46792.34	50269.88	52001.50	53358.69	55581.71	57767.39	58916.99	0.00	0.00	0.00	0.00	0.00	0.00
O-2	35216.27	37619.24	43355.96	44420.96	45090.59	0.00	0.00	0.00	0.00	0.00	0.00	0.00	0.00	0.00	0.00
O-1	30322.22	31167.07	36094.85	0.00	0.00	0.00	0.00	0.00	0.00	0.00	0.00	0.00	0.00	0.00	0.00
O-3E	0.00	0.00	0.00	51113.72	52940.03	54356.74	56589.41	58795.32	60701.43	0.00	0.00	0.00	0.00	0.00	0.00
O-2E	0.00	0.00	0.00	45878.68	46582.46	47631.04	49409.75	50780.17	51799.50	0.00	0.00	0.00	0.00	0.00	0.00
O-1E	0.00	0.00	0.00	37542.10	39531.52	40680.54	41859.32	43024.07	44498.60	0.00	0.00	0.00	0.00	0.00	0.00
ALLO3	41232.06	44630.18	46792.34	50269.94	52002.06	53366.75	55627.14	58117.03	60376.43	0.00	0.00	0.00	0.00	0.00	0.00
ALLO2	35216.27	37619.24	43355.96	44423.45	45192.30	47631.04	49409.75	50780.17	51799.50	0.00	0.00	0.00	0.00	0.00	0.00
ALLO1	30322.22	31167.07	36094.85	37542.10	39531.52	40680.54	41859.32	43024.07	44498.60	0.00	0.00	0.00	0.00	0.00	0.00
ALL CO	31655.94	36772.01	41892.17	48498.96	51148.99	53089.12	55840.31	60619.02	62325.78	71351.35	74212.08	81447.30	85485.83	94517.55	101000.??

(continued)

Exhibit 11. Continued

ASSUME ALL CASH RMC PAY GRADE AVERAGES

YEARS OF SERVICE

PAY GRADE	UNDER 2	2	3	4	6	8	10	12	14	16	18	20	22	24	26
WARRANT OFFICER															
W-5	0.00	0.00	0.00	0.00	0.00	0.00	0.00	0.00	0.00	0.00	0.00	64759.29	66811.82	68466.06	70966.1?
W-4	0.00	0.00	0.00	0.00	0.00	0.00	0.00	0.00	0.00	0.00	0.00	57808.53	59351.75	60903.19	63267.4?
W-3	0.00	0.00	0.00	0.00	41962.10	44001.21	45777.26	46821.35	53841.70	55265.71	56383.14	51389.77	52746.96	52747.15	54131.3?
W-2	0.00	36669.26	36663.65	37372.13	38754.55	40213.65	41279.32	42346.90	47869.04	48887.64	49978.48	46550.26	47909.72	0.00	0.0?
W-1	29600.78	32224.48	32294.83	34051.46	35126.19	36181.55	37235.31	38335.74	39394.14	40475.05	41523.99	42635.54	0.00	0.00	0.0?
ALL WO	29600.78	34285.24	34606.24	36396.47	37588.40	38939.97	40079.10	41409.93	43896.90	46086.19	48779.64	51436.74	54462.54	58439.94	63497.0?
ALLOFF	31641.85	36744.35	41796.83	48284.37	50837.78	52451.58	54850.41	58929.43	61255.46	68318.57	71273.87	75591.84	82200.87	88104.13	93241.5?
ENLISTED MEMBERS															
M/S	0.00	0.00	0.00	0.00	0.00	0.00	0.00	0.00	0.00	0.00	0.00	0.00	0.00	0.00	0.0?
E-9	0.00	0.00	0.00	0.00	0.00	0.00	0.00	48569.60	49318.40	50057.81	50837.18	51521.00	53420.01	54944.66	67740.9?
E-8	0.00	0.00	0.00	0.00	0.00	41608.47	42389.67	43047.24	43801.72	44591.92	45287.88	46053.93	47915.14	49409.16	57271.4?
E-7	0.00	0.00	34861.09	0.00	36172.18	36852.21	37616.34	38383.74	39527.70	40280.47	41033.26	41402.31	43306.21	44811.64	51655.5?
E-6	28801.73	30266.15	30924.06	31751.83	32505.07	33235.34	34006.60	35147.67	35877.17	36645.42	37020.34	0.00	0.00	0.00	47042.1?
E-5	25498.45	26831.98	27642.06	28402.62	29493.10	30190.00	30928.61	31666.93	32039.64	0.00	0.00	0.00	0.00	0.00	0.0?
E-4	23053.06	23849.52	24718.67	25862.56	26500.62	0.00	0.00	0.00	0.00	0.00	0.00	0.00	0.00	0.00	0.0?
E-3	21685.40	22389.92	22932.13	23492.99	0.00	0.00	0.00	0.00	0.00	0.00	0.00	0.00	0.00	0.00	0.0?
E-2	21089.56	0.00	0.00	0.00	0.00	0.00	0.00	0.00	0.00	0.00	0.00	0.00	0.00	0.00	0.0?
E-1>4	19549.21	0.00	0.00	0.00	0.00	0.00	0.00	0.00	0.00	0.00	0.00	0.00	0.00	0.00	0.0?
E-1<4	18472.76	0.00	0.00	0.00	0.00	0.00	0.00	0.00	0.00	0.00	0.00	0.00	0.00	0.00	0.0?
ALLENL	20643.59	22983.41	24407.61	26221.09	27948.17	30843.54	32096.74	34051.44	35339.75	38692.96	39874.11	43446.57	46686.90	50428.62	56072.??
ALLDOD	21244.62	24141.00	26332.49	29230.41	31873.66	35679.34	36389.73	38891.39	41301.50	44618.42	47112.21	51196.36	62383.72	65822.30	77553.4?

Appendix G

DESIGNATED AGENTS AND SERVICE CONTACTS FOR SURVIVOR'S BENEFIT PLANS

The present designated agents for each of the uniformed services are identified below with addresses and telephone numbers.[1] Note that U.S. Attorneys are *not* designated agents to receive court orders for military members.

Practitioners are cautioned that the services shuffle their acronyms and department designations with some frequency, and will be involved in a process of consolidation of services for some years to come. It is probably worth the price of a confirming call to ensure that the address to which you are sending important documents is current.

Army, Air Force, Navy, and Marine Corps:
Defense Finance and Accounting Service
Cleveland Center
Retired Pay Department (Code RO)
P.O. Box 99191
Cleveland, OH 44199-1126
800/321-1080
216/522-5955 (collect)

Coast Guard, National Oceanic and Atmospheric Administration:
Commanding Officer (RPD)
U.S. Coast Guard Pay and Personnel Center
Defense Finance and Accounting Service
444 S.E. Quincy Street
Topeka, KS 66683-3591
800/772-8724
913/295-2520

---

1. These are the addresses as made available by the pay centers when this book was completed. Mailing addresses, along with other pertinent information, are published in the Federal Register when changes are made.

Public Health Service:
USPHS, Compensation Branch
Parklawn Building
5600 Fishers Lane, Room 4-50
Rockville, MD 20857
800/638-8744
301/443-2475

Army Reserves:
Army Reserve Personnel Center (ARPERCEN)
Attn: DARP-PAR-SCP
9700 Page Boulevard
St. Louis, MO 63132-5200

Navy Reserves:
Naval Reserve Personnel Center
440 Dauphine, Code 05 (Admin. and Personnel)
New Orleans, LA 70149
800/535-2699

Air Force Reserves:
Air Reserve Personnel Center (ARPC-DPAAR)
Denver, CO 80205

Marine Corps Reserves:
Commanding Officer
USMC Finance Center, Retired Pay Branch
Kansas City, MO 64197

Coast Guard Reserves:
U.S. Coast Guard Military Pay Center
Retired Pay Branch
Room 301, Federal Building
444 S.E. Quincy Street
Topeka, KS 66683

Appendix H

CONTACT SOURCES FOR FURTHER INFORMATION AND PUBLICATIONS

Former Spouses Organizations

Committee for Justice and Equality for the Military Wife
Doris Mozley, Chair
812 Botetourt Gardens
Norfolk, VA 23507
757/622-4258

Ex-POSE
Ex-Partners of Servicemen/women for Equality
P.O. Box 11191
Alexandria, VA 22312
703/941-5844

National Action for Former Military Spouses
(believed not to be in formal existence)
1700 Legion Drive
Winter Park, FL 32789

National Organization for Women
1208 Main Street, N.W.
Washington, D.C. 20005
202/737-1133

Members and Former Members Organizations

Air Force Association (AFA)
1501 Lee Hwy.
Arlington, VA 22209
703/247-5800

Air Force Sergeants Association (AFSA)
P.O. Box 50
Temple Hills, MD 20757
301/899-3500

American Military Retirees Association (AMRA)
Admin. Office-426 U.S. Oval, Suite 1200
Plattsburg, NY 12903-3334

American Retirees Association
7564 Trade Street
San Diego, CA 92121
619/239-9000

American Retirees Association
2009 N. 14th St., Suite 300
Arlington, VA 22201
703/527-3065

Army and Air Force Mutual Aid Association
Fort Myer
Arlington, VA 22211-5002
800/336-4538
703/522-3060

Coast Guard Chief Petty Officer Association
5520G Hempstead Way
Springfield, VA 22151
703/941-0395

Coast Guard Enlisted Association
5520G Hempstead Way
Springfield, VA 22151
703/941-0395

Enlisted Association of the National Guard
National Guard
1219 Prince Street
Alexandria, VA 22314

Marine Corps Association
P.O. Box 1775 MCCDC
Quantico, VA 22134
703/640-6161

Marine Corps League
P.O. Box 3070
Merrifield, VA 22116-3070
800/1MCL-1775
703/548-7607

Marine Corps Reserve Officers' Association (MCROA)
110 N. Royal St., Suite 406
Alexandria, VA 22314
703/548-7607

Military Retirees Spouses
4701 Appaloosa Trail
Santa Maria, CA 93455
(believed to be formally disbanded)

National Association for Uniformed Services (NAUS)
5535 Hempstead Way
Springfield, VA 22151
703/750-1342

Navy Mutual Aid Association
Henderson Hall
29 Carpenter Rd.
Arlington, VA 22212
800/628-6011

Noncommissioned Officers Association (NCOA)
225 N. Washington St.
Alexandria, VA 22314
703/549-0311

Reserve Officers Association (ROA)
1 Constitution Ave., N.E.
Washington, D.C. 20002
202/479-2200

The Retired Enlisted Association (TREA)
1111 S. Abilene Court
Aurora, CO 80012
800/338-9337

The Retired Officers Association (TROA)
201 N. Washington Street
Alexandria, VA 22314-2539
703/549-2311

WISE
Women in Search of Equity for Military in Divorce
P.O. Box 4383
Annapolis, MD 21403
e-mail: JOINWISE@aol.com
www.americanretirees.com/wise.htm

Reference Works and Other Resources

Uniformed Services Almanac, Inc. publishes a series of annual "Almanacs"—*The Retired Military Almanac, Uniformed Services Almanac, Reserve Forces Almanac,* and *National Guard, Almanac.* For $7.50 a copy, they are an excellent source of up-to-date copies of charts, references, addresses, and layperson-level discussions of many of the esoteric terms, expressions, programs, and acronyms involved in military retirement matters. Uniformed Services Almanac, Inc., P.O. Box 4144, Falls Church, VA 22044-0144; 888/872-9698 (toll free) or 703/532-1631; fax 703/532-1635; e-mail: MILITARYALMANAC@MSN.COM.

The Pension Rights Center is the publisher of *Your Pension Rights at Divorce, What Women Need to Know*
Pension Rights Center
918 16th Street, N.W., Suite 704
Washington, D.C. 20006
202/296-3776

Divorce Taxation Education, Inc. has previously published several texts relating to military and other federal and private retirement plans.
DTE, Inc.
1710 Rhode Island Ave., N.W.
Washington, D.C. 20036
202/466-8204

The Bureau of National Affairs, Inc. publishes, among other things, a weekly summary of cases from around the country in its *Family Law Reporter.* Cases are well summarized, and all citations are indexed regularly by topic.
Bureau of National Affairs, Inc.
1231 25th Street, N.W.
Washington, D.C. 20037
202/452-4995

The Congressional Research Service is a federal government agency, reporting directly to Congress, which conducts research, analyzes legislation, and provides reports to members of Congress and congressional staffers. The service has performed several studies relating to the military retirement benefits area.
Congressional Research Service, Library of Congress,
101 Independence Avenue, S.E.
Washington, D.C. 20540
202/707-5700

GLOSSARY

GLOSSARY OF TERMS, ABBREVIATIONS, AND ACRONYMS

20/10

A shorthand description for a former spouse (or, sometimes, the marriage itself) when the member has received credit for twenty years or longer military service, the parties have been married for at least ten years, and the time of the marriage and time of the service have overlapped for at least ten years. This is essentially the requirement for direct payments of a portion of military retired pay as property to a former spouse by the military pay center.

20/20/20

A shorthand description for a former spouse (or, sometimes, the marriage itself) when the member has received credit for twenty years or longer military service, the parties have been married for at least twenty years, and the time of the marriage and time of the service have overlapped for at least twenty years. This is essentially the requirement for spousal entitlement for permanent postdivorce medical and other privileges.

Active Duty

Full-time duty in the active military service of a uniformed service, including full-time training duty, annual training duty, and attendance while in the active service, at a school designated as a service school by law or by the secretary concerned.

Active Duty for Training

Full-time duty in the active military service of the United States for training purposes.

Active-Duty List

A single list for the army, navy, air force, or marines, which contains the names of all officers of that armed force, other than officers described in 10 U.S.C. § 641 who are serving on active duty.

Active Service

Service on active duty.

Advance Leave

Leave authorized in advance of that accrued.

Advance Payment

Payment of pay (pay and allowances in certain cases) before it is earned.

Allotment

A definite portion of the pay and allowances of a person in the military service, which is authorized to be paid to a qualified allottee.

Allottee

The person or institution to whom the allotment is made payable.

Allotter

The person from whose pay the allotment is made.

Allowance

A monetary amount paid to an individual in lieu of furnished quarters, subsistence, or the like.

Appropriation

An amount of money specifically authorized by Congress, against which obligations may be incurred and from which payments may be made.

Armed Forces of the United States

Includes the army, navy, air force, marines, and Coast Guard, and all components thereof.

Basic Allowance for Quarters (BAQ)

An amount of money prescribed and limited by law, which an officer or enlisted member receives to pay for quarters not provided by the government.

Basic Allowance for Subsistence (BAS)

A cash allowance, by law payable to officers at all times, to help reimburse them for the expense of subsisting themselves. For enlisted personnel, a cash allowance payable (1) when rations in kind are not available, (2) when permitted to ration separately, or (3) when assigned to duty under emergency conditions where no messing facilities of the United States are available.

Basic Pay

The pay of an officer or enlisted member according to rank and longevity, before additional amounts are added for quarters, subsistence, flying status, overseas duty, and so on.

Beneficiary

The recipient of certain benefits due as a result of relationship to, or designation by, a member.

Commissioned Officer

Unless otherwise qualified, a member of the uniformed services having the rank or grade of second lieutenant, ensign or above, either permanent or temporary, in any of the uniformed services.

Commuted Rations

The monetary allowance given in lieu of subsistence to entitled personnel on leave or otherwise authorized to mess separately.

Dependent

In relation to a member of a uniformed service, dependent means:

(1) Spouse;
(2) Unmarried child (including any of the following categories of children if such child is in fact dependent on the member: a stepchild, an adopted child, or an illegitimate child whose alleged member father has been judicially decreed to be the father of the child or judicially ordered to contribute to the child's support, or whose parentage has been admitted in writing by the member) who either:
  (a) is under twenty-one years of age, or
  (b) is incapable of self-support because of a mental or physical incapacity, and in fact relies on the member for over one-half of the dependent's support;
(3) A parent (including a stepparent or parent by adoption, and any person, including a former stepparent, who has stood in loco parentis to the member at any time for a continuous period of at least five years before reaching twenty-one years of age) who in fact relies on the member for over one-half of the dependent's support; however, the dependency of such a parent is determined on the basis of an affidavit submitted by the parent and any other evidence required under regulations prescribed by the secretary concerned, and the parent is not considered a dependent of the member claiming the dependence unless:
  (a) the member has provided over one-half of the support for the period prescribed by the secretary concerned, or
  (b) due to changed circumstances arising after the member enters on active duty, and in fact relies on the member for over one-half of the dependent's support.

The relationship between a stepparent and stepchild is terminated by the stepparent's divorce from the parent by blood.

Disbursing Officer

An officer responsible and accountable for the disbursement and collection of public funds, especially military pay and allowances.

Disposable Pay

That portion of gross military retired pay considered by the military pay center to be subject to court orders for division as property or subject to garnishment through legal process in enforcement of a court order.

Dual Status

Enlisted members of the Naval or Marine Corps Reserve on duty as temporary officers under 10 U.S.C. § 5596.

Duty Station

The place at which the member is assigned for regular duty; also, the place at which the member performs an assigned duty.

Enforced Separation

Involuntary separation of the member from dependents as a result of official orders.

Enlisted Member

A person enlisted, enrolled, or conscripted into the military service.

Enlistee

A person who has voluntarily enlisted for military service.

Enlistment

(1) A voluntary entrance into military service under enlisted status, as distinguished from induction through selective service; (2) A period of

time, contractual or prescribed by law, which enlisted members serve between enrollment and discharge.

Entitlement

To have the legal right to receive items of pay and/or allowances.

Erroneous Payment

A payment of pay and/or allowances to a member to which he or she is not entitled.

Exigencies of the Service

Urgent demands of the military service.

Expiration of Term of the Service

The end of a required or contracted period of service.

Extension of Enlistment

Contracted agreement that extends an enlisted member's current enlistment for a stated period beyond normal expiration of that enlistment.

Fleet Reserve or Fleet Marine Corps Reserve

A component of the regular service to which members may be transferred and released from active duty after obtaining twenty or more years of active federal service.

FUSFSPA

The Uniformed Services Former Spouses Protection Act (USFSPA); some courts have appended the word "federal" to the act's title, and amended the acronym accordingly.

Government Quarters or Housing Facilities

Includes the following: (1) any sleeping accommodations or family-type housing owned or leased by the U.S. government, (2) lodgings or other quarters obtained by U.S. government contract, (3) dormitories or similar facilities operated by cost-plus-a-fixed-fee contractors, (4) any sleeping or housing facilities furnished by a foreign government, (5) transient facilities such as guest houses, hostess houses, and hotel-type accommodations (accommodations built and operated by nonappropriated fund activities are considered to be rental quarters for the purpose of BAQ eligibility); payment of service charges for laundering of linens, janitorial services, and so on, has no effect on whether the facilities are considered government quarters or housing facilities, (6) quarters in a state-owned National Guard camp.

Home

The place recorded as home when the member was ordered to active duty.

Induction

To take a person into any of the armed services of the United States without voluntary action on his or her part.

Legal Process

The term legal process means any writ, order, summons, or other similar process in the nature of garnishment, which

(1) is issued by
  (a) a court of competent jurisdiction in any state, territory, or possession of the United States,
  (b) a court of competent jurisdiction in any foreign country with which the United States has entered into an agreement that requires the United States to honor such process, or
  (c) an authorized official pursuant to an order of such a court of competent jurisdiction or pursuant to state or local law, and
(2) is directed to, and the purpose of which is to compel, a governmental

entity—which holds moneys that are otherwise payable to an individual—to make a payment from such moneys to another party to satisfy a legal obligation of such individual to provide child support or make alimony payments.

Lost Time

That period of time not included in determining cumulative years of service for all military purposes.

Member

A person appointed or enlisted in, or conscripted into, a uniformed service (usually used to also include former members).

Member (ROTC)

A student who is enrolled in the Senior Reserve Officers' Training Corps of an armed force, under 10 U.S.C. § 2104.

Net

Sometimes used by lawyers, or courts, as a term meant to indicate "disposable retired pay." Note that this meaning has shifted over the years, and the term has been used so loosely that it is difficult to say if it was ever deliberately used to refer to pretax retirement benefits or posttax retirement benefits, or was intended to have some other meaning.

Officer

A commissioned or warrant officer.

Overpayment

An amount paid to a member that is in excess of that to which he or she is entitled.

Parent

The natural father or mother, and father or mother through adoption. It also includes persons who have stood in loco parentis to a member. Also see definition for "dependent".

Permanent Change of Station

The assignment, detail, or transfer of a member or unit to a different duty station under competent orders that neither specify the duty as temporary, nor provide for further assignment to a new station or direct return to the old station.

Permanent Station

In general, the post of duty or official station to which the member is assigned for permanent duty.

Punitive Discharge

A dishonorable or bad-conduct discharge ordered as punishment under the Uniform Code of Military Justice.

Rations in Kind

Meals furnished rather than money in lieu thereof.

Reenlistment Bonus

Special pay to an enlisted member who reenlists under the provisions of 37 U.S.C. § 308.

Reserve Components

The U.S. Army National Guard, U.S. Army Reserve, U.S. Naval Reserve, Marine Corps Reserve, Air National Guard of the United States, U.S. Air Force Reserve, Coast Guard Reserve, and the Reserve Corps of the Public Health Service.

Retired List

Any one of several lists of military members retired from the regular or reserve components of the armed forces.

Saved Pay

Special pay provisions that allow military members, under certain circumstances, to retain entitlement to amounts of pay and/or allowances authorized under prior laws or for a lower grade from which promoted.

SBP

Survivor's Benefit Plan or, sometimes, payments made under that plan.

Separation

Discharge, release from active duty, retirement, death, or, in the case of enlisted members, the date when the enlisted member begins to serve on a voluntary extension of enlistment for any period of time.

SSB

Special Separation Benefit. One of the three primary "early-out" programs developed by the military to ease the post–cold war drawdown in military forces. This program calculated a single lump-sum cash payment to the military member, depending on rank and years of service.

Statutory Limitation

The legal limits or restrictions as provided by law.

Total Forfeiture

Forfeiture of all pay and allowances as punishment under the Uniform Code of Military Justice.

Uniformed Services

The U.S. Army, U.S. Navy, Marine Corps, U.S. Air Force, Coast Guard, Public Health Service, and the commissioned corps of the Environmental Science Services Administration, now known as the National Oceanic and Atmospheric Administration.

United States

The forty-eight contiguous states, the District of Columbia, and the states of Alaska and Hawaii.

Variable Reenlistment Bonus

Special pay to an enlisted member with a critical skill, in addition to a regular reenlistment bonus, under the provisions of 37 U.S.C. § 308g.

VSI

Variable Separation Incentive. One of the three primary "early-out" programs developed by the military to ease the post–cold war drawdown in military forces. This program calculated a series of annual payments to the military member, depending on rank and years of service.

Warrant Officer

A person who holds a commission or warrant in a warrant officer grade.

TABLE OF CASES

INDEX

state court limitations regarding
   division of, 25–26
state rulings on, 29–30
Disposable retired pay, 5, 25, 179
Divorce
   default, 59, 194–96
   extended medical benefits by separation
      versus, 137–38
   military-related cases involving courts
      of more than one country, 200–204
   military service after, 167–71
   no-fault, 138
   omission of military retirement benefits
      from settlements, 7
   one-party, 138
Divorce courts, treatment of military
   retirement benefits in, 31–32, 57–
   58
Divorce judgment, availability of default,
   59
Dollar plus percentage award, 56
Dollars plus future percentage awards,
   enforceability of, 111–14
Domicile, jurisdiction by, 60–61
Dual compensation rules, 173, 175
Dual status, 334
Duty station, 334

E

Early-out payments, 94–99
   fifteen-year retirement, 96–97
   Special Separation Benefit as, 96, 97,
      98
   treatment of, in divorce and postdivorce
      cases, 97–99
   in valuation of military retirement
      benefits, 52
   Voluntary Separation Incentive as, 95,
      97, 98
Early retirement, 171
Employee Retirement Income Security
   Act (1974), 8
Employment compensation, importance of
   pension benefits as, 8
Enforced separation, 334
Enlisted member, 334

Enlistee, 334
Enlistment, 334–35
Entitlement, 335
Erroneous payment, 335
Exchange store use, 52, 162–63
Exigencies of the service, 335
Expiration of term of the service, 335
EX-POSE (Ex-Partners of Servicemen/
   women for Equality), 11*n*
Extension of enlistment, 335

F

Fallback clause, 117–18
Federal Employees Retirement System
   (FERS) retirements, 22
Federal Uniformed Services Former
   Spouses Protection Act, 335. *See
   also* Uniformed Services Former
   Spouses Protection Act
Fifteen-year retirement, 96–97
First come, first served requirement, 109
Fleet Maine Corps Reserve, 335
Fleet reserve, 335
Former spouses, 1
   definition of, 11*n*
   eligibility of
      for medical benefits, 133–40
      for nondisability benefits, 5
   limitations on payments to, 110–11
   remarriage by, 171–73
   restrictions on medical rights of, 137
   right to portion of retired pay, 13
   transitional health care coverage for,
      139
Formula orders, 45–46
Forum shopping, efforts to prevent, 57,
   63–64

G

Garnishment
   of attorneys' fees, 81–82
   and first come, first served requirement,
      109
   under Social Security Act, 130–32
   submission to military pay center, 132